Natural Computing Series

The Natural Computing book series covers theory, experiment, and implementations at the intersection of computation and natural systems. This includes:

- **Computation inspired by Nature**: Paradigms, algorithms, and theories inspired by natural phenomena. Examples include cellular automata, simulated annealing, neural computation, evolutionary computation, swarm intelligence, and membrane computing.
- **Computing using Nature-inspired novel substrates**: Examples include biomolecular (DNA) computing, quantum computing, chemical computing, synthetic biology, soft robotics, and artificial life.
- **Computational analysis of Nature**: Understanding nature through a computational lens. Examples include systems biology, computational neuroscience, quantum information processing.

Hitoshi Iba • João E. Batista • Jinglue Xu

Large Language Models and Evolutionary Computation

Generative AI for Meta-heuristics

Springer

Hitoshi Iba
Department of Information and Communication Engineering, Graduate School of Information Science and Technology
The University of Tokyo
Bunkyo-ku, Tokyo, Japan

João E. Batista
RIKEN Center for Computational Science
Kobe, Hyogo, Japan

Jinglue Xu
Sakana AI
Tokyo, Japan

ISSN 1619-7127 ISSN 2627-6461 (electronic)
Natural Computing Series
ISBN 978-981-95-8596-0 ISBN 978-981-95-8597-7 (eBook)
https://doi.org/10.1007/978-981-95-8597-7

This Springer imprint is published by the registered company Springer Nature Singapore Pte Ltd.
The registered company address is: 152 Beach Road, #21-01/04 Gateway East, Singapore 189721, Singapore

Preface

This book provides theoretical and practical knowledge of an LLM (Large Language Model)-based approach to metaheuristics. In this book, the basic theory and the latest techniques are explained in an easy-to-understand manner, with concrete examples. Another emphasis is its real-world applicability. We give empirical examples from practical data and show that the proposed approaches are successful when addressing tasks from the recent research areas such as (1) LLMs for EC (Evolutionary computation), (2) training LLMs for EC, (3) automated machine learning, and (4) program synthesis, etc., details of which will be provided in the appendix for the sake of readers' study. These materials will include a description of available resources for readers interested in gaining hands-on experience with the subject. The fundamental themes of this book, therefore, include recent research on the promising combination of Generative AI, LLMs, evolutionary computation, and metaheuristics. The ultimate goal of this book is to enable readers to apply these ideas to artificial intelligence on their own.

This book is intended for beginners interested in artificial intelligence and artificial life (from undergraduate to graduate students), researchers in related fields, and engineers considering their applications. Therefore, most topics in this book begin with accessible subjects that require no specialized knowledge, though some connect to unsolved problems and cutting-edge research themes. More precisely, Chap. 1 explains the fundamental concepts, Chap. 2 introduces practical examples as an accessible introduction, and Chap. 3 and beyond delve into more specialized topics and theoretical underpinnings. After that, we will outline several challenges in integrating LLMs and metaheuristics. These include scalability, robustness, and open-ended optimization problems, which are critical to the effective application of metaheuristics to LLMs. If you find these topics intriguing, it would be worthwhile to investigate the related literature and the latest trends. As you will see by reading through to the conclusion, AI research has undergone various transformations. This book clearly explains research integrating evolutionary computation and LLMs. This is because the true purpose of AI research lies in approaching the essence of intelligence.

We hope you will thoroughly enjoy the fascination of this field through this book.

Acknowledgments The first author, Hitoshi Iba, takes this opportunity to express his deepest gratitude to his professors, seniors, juniors, and the staff of the Iba Laboratory, Department of Electronic Information Engineering, Graduate School of Information Science and Technology, The University of Tokyo. The philosophical and enjoyable discussions about AI that he had with colleagues in his laboratory and at ETL (Electro-technical laboratory, where he was previously employed) undoubtedly form the core of this book. Furthermore, he sincerely thanks his wife, Yumiko, and his children (Kohki, Hirono, and Hiroto), who have always supported his research life behind the scenes.

Seeing his name on the cover of this book, the second author, Jinglue Xu, reflects on those who have shaped his academic journey. It was under the mentorship of Hitoshi Iba during his PhD that he discovered the fascinating world of evolutionary computation, a field that continues to inspire his research today—and it is a privilege to now contribute to this book alongside him. He is also profoundly grateful to Sakana AI for opening a new chapter in his professional life. To Yujin Tang, Takuya Akiba, and David Ha: thank you for welcoming him into such an innovative team. The opportunity to contribute alongside them has been both an honor and a privilege.

As this is the first book to bear his name on the cover, the third author, João E. Batista, would like to thank everyone who has supported his academic journey thus far. Without their encouragement, he would undoubtedly have chosen a different path in life. He wants to offer special thanks to Sara Silva, his MSc and PhD advisor for supporting his research from day one; to Marco Nobile for establishing the connection between Nobile's research group in Lisbon and Iba Laboratory at the University of Tokyo, which allowed the author to meet and undertake an internship under Hitoshi Iba; and finally to Mohamed Wahib, for welcoming the author into Wahib's team and enabling the return to Japan as a postdoctoral researcher.

Tokyo, Japan
March 2026

Hitoshi Iba
Jinglue Xu
João E. Batista

Contents

Chapter 1
Introduction

Chapter 1 briefly introduces the background on LLMs (large language models) and evolutionary computation (EC). More precisely, we provide essential knowledge of metaheuristics, including genetic algorithms (GAs), genetic programming (GP), multi-objective optimization, etc. Next, we explain the basic frameworks of EDAs (estimation of distribution algorithms) and how they are similar to the probabilistic mechanisms of LLMs. Thereafter, we discuss how research on LLMs and metaheuristics relates to each other. Especially, the research on "LLMs as metaheuristics" is the main subject of this book and will be discussed in detail in future chapters.

1.1 Large Language Models (LLMs) and Generative AI

Generative AI is a technology that uses deep learning and machine learning methods to automatically generate human-like text, images, music, video, and other digital content. Large language models (LLMs) are a type of generative AI that specializes in natural language processing, learning from vast amounts of text data to achieve a higher level of language understanding.

LLMs have increasingly shown behaviors resembling human language capabilities, demonstrating significant progress in the field of artificial intelligence. These models have been successfully applied in diverse tasks such as translation, coding, and question answering. A wide array of variants marks the current landscape of LLMs, each tailored to specific applications, languages, and purposes. These models vary not only in size, ranging from very large to comparatively tiny models, but also in their intended use cases, such as question-answering chatbots, coding assistants, legal analysis, and more. In addition to these variations, there have been significant augmentations to LLMs, enhancing their capabilities. These enhancements include code generation and compilation, which enable models to generate and compile code, and multimodality, which allows models to process and create both text and images. Other notable advancements include the ability for

H. Iba et al., *Large Language Models and Evolutionary Computation*,
Natural Computing Series, https://doi.org/10.1007/978-981-95-8597-7_1

models to utilize external tools, perform document retrieval, and more, broadening the scope of tasks LLMs can handle. Despite these advancements, there remains a challenge in effectively utilizing these generally pretrained LLMs in interactive environments that require advanced skills such as reasoning, planning, or decision-making. Reinforcement learning is a viable solution to such problems, but it requires substantial data and lacks interpretability. This gap calls for novel approaches to leverage LLMs' potential beyond their current applications.

One of the blind spots of LLMs is their lack of proficiency in arithmetic and elementary mathematics. LLMs are "probabilistic parrots" and only output a probabilistic mixture of what they have been told (data stored on the Internet web) [4]. Therefore, LLMs can give correct answers to questions for which data is on the Web. Still, they also make mistakes or give hallucinating answers to simultaneous equations and even simple algebraic calculations. In addition, LLMs are not good at logical thinking and are incapable of mathematical reasoning such as syllogisms, proof by contradiction, and inductive reasoning.

On the other hand, humans are good at mathematics and abstract thinking. Does this really stem from accumulated experience? If not, then the expectation of mathematical achievement in LLMs may be misplaced.

In addition, the following shortcomings and questions have also been raised about LLMs:

- Correctness cannot be guaranteed. Since it is a statistical method, it does not always give the best answer.
- Development cost is high. For a network with billions to trillions of parameters, the language structure and context are learned using hundreds of TB of text data.
- Prompt engineering is required. This requires artisanal trial and error and empirical knowledge. Prompt engineering is complex to study from a scientific or algorithmic perspective.
- There are biases in the data. Therefore, LLMs' answers may also be biased. The answers may be tainted by severe slander and hate.
- It is difficult to exchange information among different LLMs. It is not easy to integrate multiple LLMs. For example, in the past, Google Search Engine did not disclose information. This can hamper research and development.
- The ways LLMs answer differ from human thinking. In particular, there are differences in cognitive bias.

1.2 Evolutionary Computation

1.2.1 What Is Evolutionary Computation?

The objective of the evolutionary method is to exploit this concept to establish an effective computing system (an evolutionary system). Evolutionary computation (EC) attempts to "borrow" Nature's methods of problem solving and has been widely applied to find solutions to optimization problems, to synthesize programs automatically, and to accomplish other AI (artificial intelligence) tasks for the sake of effective learning and formation of hypotheses. EC imitates the evolutionary mechanisms of living organisms to create, combine, and select data structures. This method takes the mechanisms of reproduction and selection as a model and is widely applied in engineering fields. This is called the "evolutionary approach."

The data handled by EC has a two-layer structure, phenotype (PTYPE), and genotype (GTYPE, or "genetic code", corresponding to the chromosomes in a cell). The GTYPE is the analogue of the gene; it is a set of low-level, local rules that are the object of the action of genetic operators (see Fig. 1.1). The

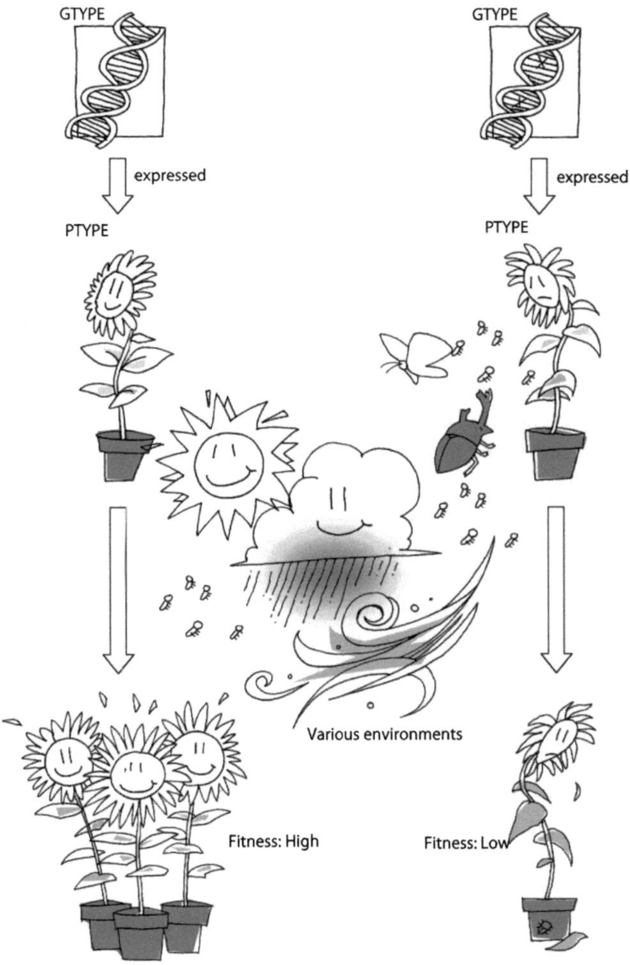

Fig. 1.1 GTYPE and PTYPE

Table 1.1 Analogy with biological organisms

	GTYPE Genotype	PTYPE Phenotype	Fitness value
Biology	Genes	Proteins produced, expressed functionalities	Ease of survival, number of offspring
GP	Tree structure	Programs, conceptual structures	Performance measures
GA	Character strings, numerical values, Automata	Functional values, generated strings	Closeness to optimal solution

PTYPE represents the phenotype and expresses the global behaviors and structures accompanying the expression of the GTYPE in the environment. The fitness value is uniquely determined by the PTYPE within the context of the environment; therefore, fitness selection is dependent on PTYPE. Table 1.1 shows the analogues in EC for biological functions.

In EC, a population consists of multiple individuals. Each individual has its own GTYPE (i.e., genetic code), and its fitness value is determined with respect to the expressed PTYPE. These individuals reproduce or recombine to create a succeeding generation. This process is controlled to increase the number of likely offspring of individuals in keeping with the high quality of their fitness and to suppress reproduction by individuals with low fitness (the biological term for this is "selection", i.e., the survival of the fittest). Genetic operators are applied to cause crossover, mutation, and other patterns of transmission of GTYPE during reproduction, to create the GTYPE of the succeeding generation. These various operators in EC recombine genes in ways that mimic mutation and other biological processes. The frequency of application of these operators and the locations in GTYPE at which they are applied is generally determined by a random process. It is intended that each succeeding generation contains individuals whose expressions differ slightly from those of the previous generation, so that their fitness values are higher, thereby raising the overall fitness of the population. In the same way, each succeeding generation gives birth to the next. As this process is repeated, the basic theory of EC holds that the overall population's fitness increases over generations. Figure 1.2 shows the illustrative image of EC, in which the fitness value of each individual is represented within the ellipse. The larger the value, the better the figure's fitness.

Thus, we can summarize the basic flow of EC as follows. A group of individuals is designated as a set $M(t) = \{g_t(m)\}$ of genotype GTYPE at the t-th generation. The fitness value $u_t(m)$ of the phenotype PTYPE $p_t(m)$ for each $g_t(m)$ is then determined in the environment. The genetic operators are generally applied to the GTYPE with good (high) fitness values; as a result, these replace the GTYPE with bad (low) fitness values. This selection is based on the fitness value, and the set of the next generation of GTYPEs, $M(t+1) = \{g_{t+1}(m)\}$, is produced. This process is then repeated.

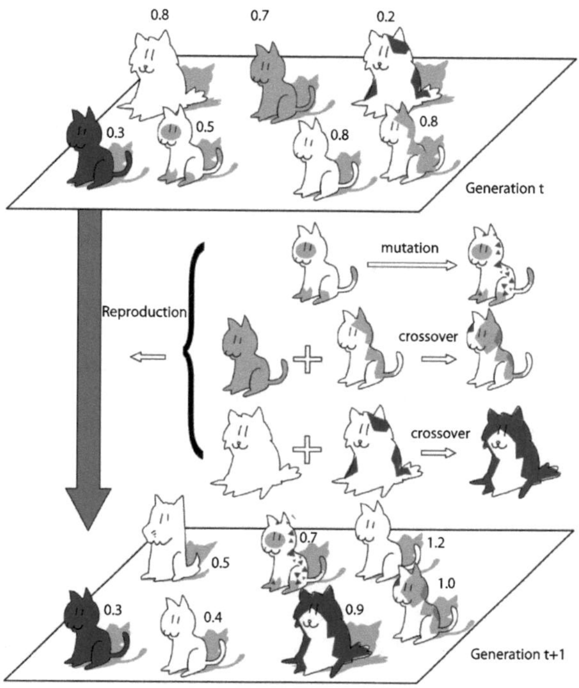

Fig. 1.2 Evolutionary computation

1.2.2 Basic Principles of Genetic Algorithms

The objective of GA is to search for the solution to a problem. Several approaches to this have been proposed, in addition to GA. In this chapter, we will first examine what it means to search, and then consider the kinds of situations that constitute problems.

The origins of a genetic algorithm (GA) can be traced back to earlier research by John Holland and his colleagues. In the chapter "The Optimal Allocation of Trials" in his book [13], he ascribed the success of GA on the balance of "exploitation," through search of known regions, with "exploration," through search, at finite risks, of unknown regions.

Information handled using GA comprises a two-layer structure consisting of GTYPE and PTYPE. The PTYPE results from the expression of the GTYPE. The operators of genetic algorithms (GA operators) act on the GTYPE, and the fitness value is determined from the PTYPE, based on the environment. For the time being, we assume that the larger the fitness value, the better.

For the time being, we will think of a one-dimensional bit string (a string of 0s and 1s) as the GTYPE of GA and take the result of the binary conversion of this string as the PTYPE (this conversion will be explained in the next section). The location of the gene on the chromosome is called the "locus" in biology. With GA, as well, we use the word "locus" to specify the location of the GTYPE. For example, for GTYPE 010, the genes would be as follows:

- Gene of the first locus $\rightarrow 0$
- Gene of the second locus $\rightarrow 1$
- Gene of the third locus $\rightarrow 0$

Before going any further, let us take a brief look at the selection process. With GA, selection takes place in such a way that the larger the fitness value of an organism, the higher the probability for it to reproduce. On the other hand, the organisms with smaller fitness values are more likely to die out. The simplest way of achieving this is to create a roulette wheel of all individuals. Each individual gets a surface area in the roulette proportional to its fitness value; hence, it is called a "weighted roulette". Selection is performed by rotating this roulette wheel and choosing the individual in the place where the roulette wheel stops. This is called "fitness-proportionate strategy".

When reproduction occurs, the operators shown in Fig. 1.3 are applied to the selected GTYPE to generate a new GTYPE for the subsequent generation. These operators are called GA operators. To keep the explanation simple, we express the GTYPE as a one-dimensional array here. Each operator is analogous to the recombination or mutation of a gene in a biological organism. Generally, the frequency and sites at which these operators are applied are determined randomly.

The basic flow of GA can be summarized as follows (Fig. 1.4). Suppose that the GTYPE $\{g_t(i)\}$ is a group of individuals at generation t. For the phenotype $p_t(i)$ of each $g_t(i)$, a fitness value $f_t(i)$ is calculated in the environment. The GA operators are generally applied to GTYPEs with a larger (better) fitness value, and the newly bred GTYPE is substituted for a GTYPE with a smaller fitness value. Based on the

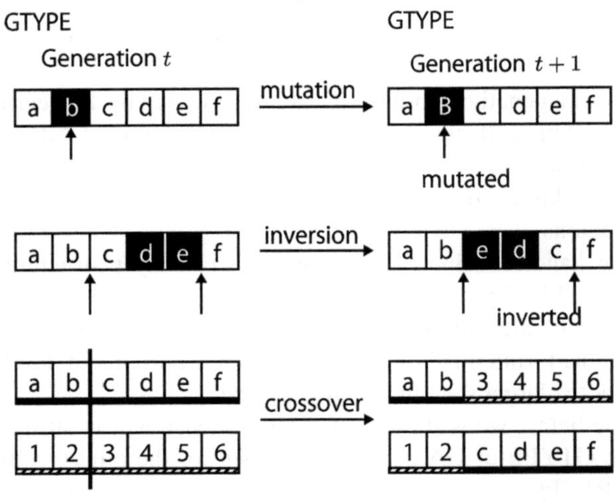

Fig. 1.3 GA operators

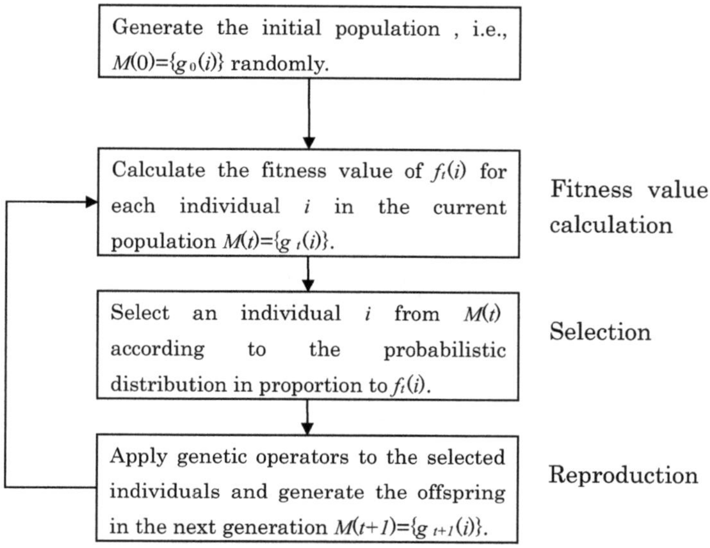

Fig. 1.4 Flowchart of GA

above, selection is carried out based on fitness values, and the group $\{g_{t+1}(i)\}$ for the next generation $(t + 1)$ is generated. The process described above is repeated every generation.

The alteration of generations with GA will be as shown in Fig. 1.5. In this figure, G represents the elite ratio (i.e., the percentage of individuals with the highest scores that will be copied and carried over to the next generation).

1.2.3 Real-Valued GA

When optimizing an objective function defined in a real-valued space, real-valued GAs have been proposed, which use a real-valued vector as a gene. We will explain a representative technique for this approach.

Differential evolution (DE [33]) is one category of evolutionary computation that derives an approximate solution to real-valued optimization problems. DE is known to be effective at providing algorithms for various problems, such as nonlinear, non-differentiable, and multimodal problems.

Individuals in DE are real-valued vectors (points in the search space). The flow of this method is outlined below (see Figs. 1.6 and 1.7):

Step1 Input random numbers in each individual (vector) to generate the initial population. Here, the number of elements in the population is N, and each individual is denoted as $\vec{x_i}$ $(i = 0, 1, \cdots, N - 1)$.

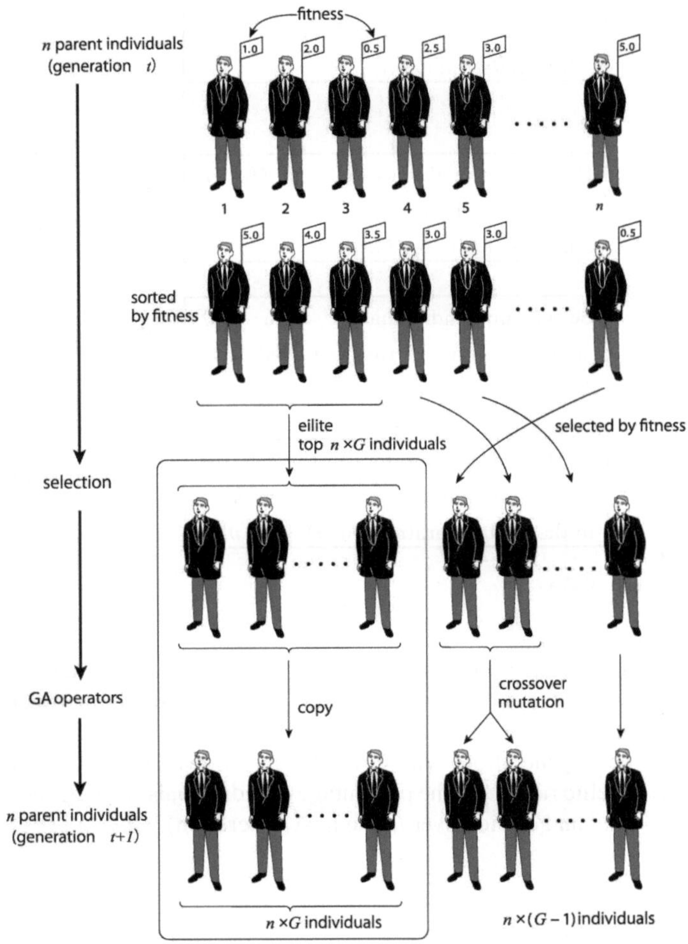

Fig. 1.5 Selection and reproduction of GA

Step2 Three individuals are randomly chosen from the solution set and are labeled as $\vec{x_{r1}}, \vec{x_{r2}}, \vec{x_{r3}}$ $(r1, r2, r3 \in \{0, 1, \cdots, N - 1\})$. The individual after mutation, $\vec{v_i}$, is generated as

$$\vec{v_i} = \vec{x_{r1}} + F \times (\vec{x_{r2}} - \vec{x_{r3}}) \qquad (F \text{ is a constant}). \tag{1.1}$$

This is repeated N times to generate N individuals $\vec{v_0}, \cdots, \vec{v_{N-1}}$.

Step3 Generate a child population $\vec{u_i}$ from the parent population $\vec{x_i}$. The elements in $\vec{u_i}$ are selected from elements in $\vec{x_i}$ and $\vec{v_i}$ based on the crossover rate CR.

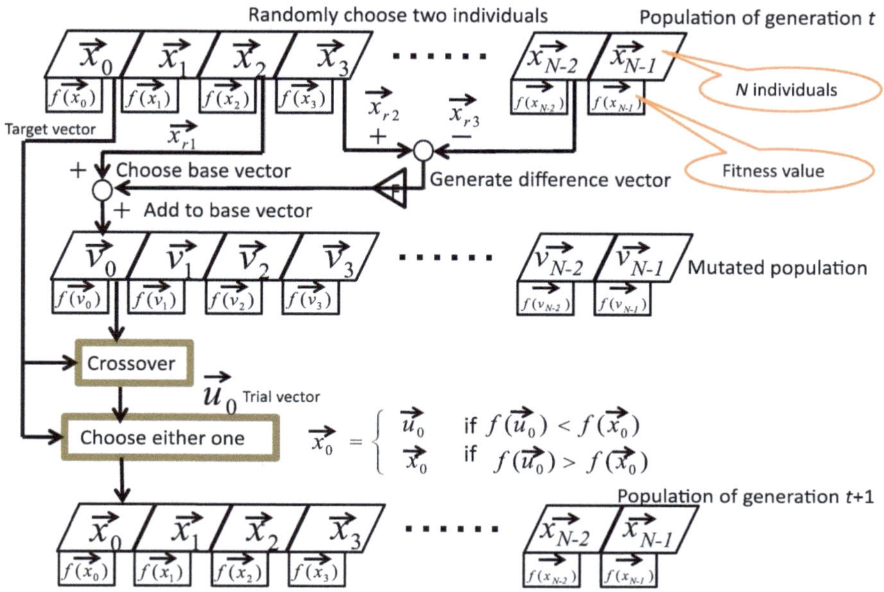

Fig. 1.6 Generation alternation in DE [28]

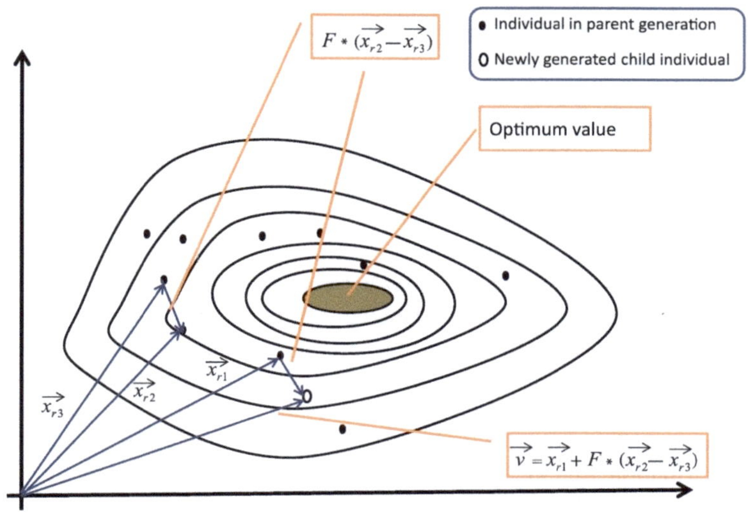

Fig. 1.7 Crossover and mutation in DE [33]

$$u_{i,j} = \begin{cases} x_{i,j} & \text{if } rand \geq CR, \\ v_{i,j} & \text{if } rand < CR. \end{cases} \tag{1.2}$$

Here, $u_{i,j}, x_{i,j}, v_{i,j}$ are the j-th element of the i-th individual (vector) $\vec{u_i}, \vec{x_i}, \vec{v_i}$, and $rand$ is a random number within the interval [0,1]. As a result, the elements in $\vec{u_i}$ contain the elements of both $\vec{x_i}$ and $\vec{v_i}$.

Step4 Evaluate the child population $\vec{u_i}$ generated in **S**tep3 and the parent population $\vec{x_i}$, and decide which solution to adopt.

$$\vec{x_i} = \begin{cases} \vec{x_i} & \text{if } fit(\vec{x_i}) > fit(\vec{u_i}), \\ \vec{u_i} & \text{if } fit(\vec{x_i}) < fit(\vec{u_i}). \end{cases} \tag{1.3}$$

Here, $fit()$ is the evaluation function and $fit(x)$ is the evaluated value of x (i.e., the larger, the better).

Step5 Repeat *S*tep2 ~**S**tep4 for a fixed number of generations, and output the most valuable individual from the final set of solutions as the optimum solution.

Conventional GAs crossover vectors of two individuals and children obtained by crossover are included in the next generation regardless of the fitness value. Mutation occurs at a fixed parameter value (mutation rate); hence, the amount of mutation does not differ between early generations and later generations near convergence.

In contrast, DE crossovers [one individual + difference vector of two individuals] and one individual. A crossover that uses a difference vector instead of just the position vectors of individuals increases the likelihood of producing children in regions of high fitness. Faster population convergence can be achieved because a generated child individual does not remain as is; it remains only if it is better than the parent generation. Moreover, mutation in DE is based on the difference vector between individuals; the mutation rate varies with the population. As a result, the mutation rate is high in early generations and decreases toward convergence. In other words, evolution progresses effectively, and setting mutation parameters is unnecessary because the mutation rate is automatically adjusted.

CMA-ES (covariance matrix adaptation evolution strategy) [8] is another method for real-valued optimization, in which several candidate solutions are selected from a normal distribution $N(\boldsymbol{m}, \sigma^2\boldsymbol{C})$. It repeatedly updates the mean $\boldsymbol{m}$ and the variance-covariance matrix $\boldsymbol{C}$ based on the evaluation results of each candidate, thereby finding the optimal solution. By learning the covariance matrix of the normal distribution used to generate candidate solutions, optimization functions can be efficiently explored with high noise. CMA-ES is utilized in many practical fields, and recent reports describe its integration with deep learning and reinforcement learning.

1.2.4 Basic Principles of Genetic Programming

The aim of genetic programming (GP) is to extend genetic forms from GA to the expression of trees and graphs and to apply them to the synthesis of programs and the formation of hypotheses or concepts. Researchers are using GP to improve their software for designing control systems and robot structures.

Various discussions exist regarding the origins of genetic programming (GP), and GP-like concepts were proposed from the dawn of AI research. However, it was John Koza who vigorously advanced GP research from the early days of evolutionary computation studies through the 1990s.

GP is one of the fields of evolutionary computation. When the concepts of GP are applied in AI (artificial intelligence), the processes of learning, hypothesis formation, and problem solving are called "evolutionary learning" or genetic-based machine learning (GBML). This learning method is based on fitness and involves transforming knowledge by eliminating unfit solutions through selection, thereby preserving appropriate solutions in the subsequent generation.

The procedures of GA are extended in GP to handle graph structures[1] (in particular, tree structures). Tree structures are generally well described by S-expressions in LISP. Thus, it is pretty standard to handle LISP programs as "genes" in GP.[2]

A tree is a graph with a structure as follows, incorporating no cycles:

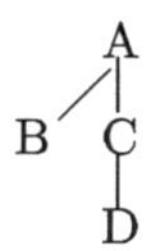

More precisely, a tree is an acyclical connected graph, with one node defined as the root of the tree. A tree structure can be expressed as an expression with parentheses. The above tree would be written as follows:

```
(A (B)
   (C (D)))
```

In addition, the above can be simplified to the following expression:

```
(A B
  (C D))
```

[1] In addition to tree or graph structures, linear representations and grammatical representations are also used as expressions for GP. However, for simplicity, we will standardize on tree structures.

[2] As long as the reader understands that the program is expressed in a tree format, there should be no need to read a LISP program. The following explanations are intended to be easily understood by a reader who does not know LISP.

This notation is called an "S-expression" in LISP. Hereinafter, a tree structure will be identified with its corresponding S-expression. The following terms will be used for the tree structure:

- Node: Symbolized with A, B, C, D, etc.
- Root: A.
- Terminal node: B, D (also called a "terminal symbol" or "leaf node").
- Nonterminal node: A, C (also called a "non-terminal symbol" and an "argument of the S-expression").
- Child: From the viewpoint of A, nodes B and C are children (also, "arguments of function A").
- Parent: The parent of C is A.

Other common phrases will also be used as convenient, including "number of children," "number of arguments," "grandchild," "descendant," and "ancestor." These are not explained here, as their meanings should be apparent from the context.

The following genetic operators acting on the tree structure will be incorporated:

1. **Gmutation** Alteration of the node label
2. **Ginversion** Reordering of siblings
3. **Gcrossover** Exchange of a subtree

These are natural extensions of existing GA operators and act on sequences of bits. These operators are shown below in examples where they have been applied in LISP expression trees (S-expressions) (Fig. 1.8). The underlined portion of the statement is the expression that is acted upon:

Gmutation

Parent:(+ x $\underline{y}$)

⇓

Child:(+ x $\underline{z}$)

Ginversion Parent:(progn $\underline{\text{(incf } x\text{) (setq } x \text{ 2)}}$ (print x))

⇓

Child:(progn $\underline{\text{(setq } x \text{ 2) (incf } x\text{)}}$ (print x))

Gcrossover Parent_1:(progn (incf x) $\underline{\text{(setq } x \text{ 2)}}$ (setq y x))

Parent_2:(progn (decf x) (setq x (∗ $\underline{\text{(sqrt } x\text{)}}$ x)) (print x))

⇓

Child_1:(progn (incf x) $\underline{\text{(sqrt } x\text{)}}$ (setq y x))

Child_2:(progn (decf x) (setq x (∗ $\underline{\text{(setq } x \text{ 2)}}$ x)) (print x))

Table 1.2 provides a summary of how the program was changed as a result of these operators. "progn" is a function acting on the arguments in the order of their presentation and returns the value of the final argument. The function "setq" sets the value of the first argument to the evaluated value of the second argument. It is apparent from this table that mutation has caused a slight change in the program's behavior, and that crossover has replaced actions in parts of the programs of all parents. The actions of the genetic operators have produced programs that are individual children but inherit the characteristics of their parent programs.

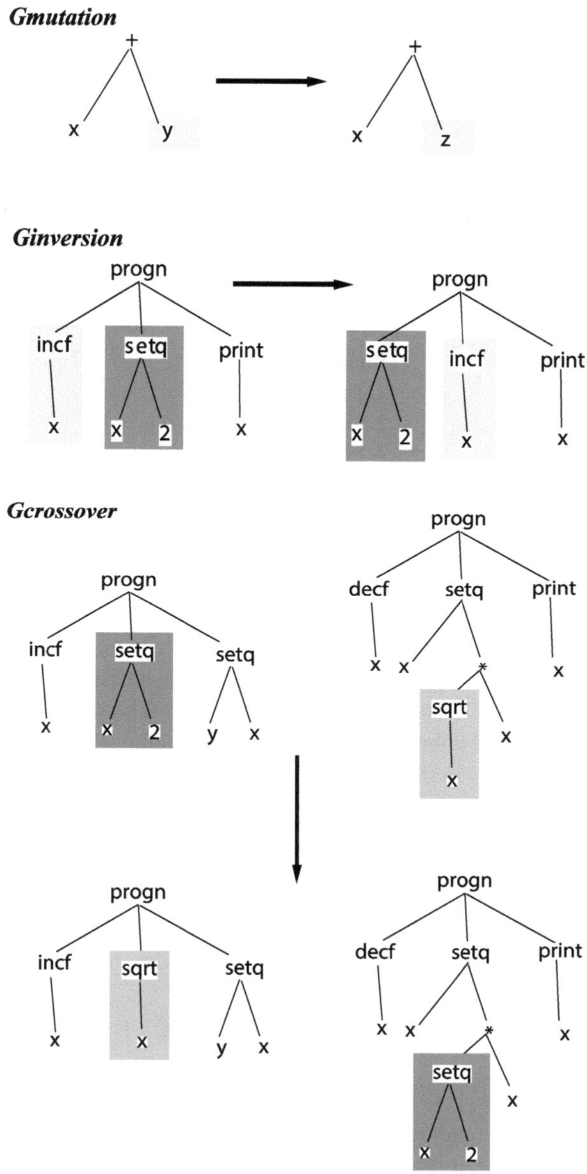

Fig. 1.8 Genetic operators in GP

Except for the aspect that the genetic operator acts on the structural representation, the GP employs a standard GA process (see Fig. 1.5). The original program (the structural representation) changes a little at a time under the action of the genetic operators illustrated in Table 1.2. The GP searches for the desired program using the same selection operations.

Table 1.2 Program changes due to GP operators

Operator	Program before operation	Program after operation
Mutation	Add x and y.	Add x and z.
Inversion	1. Add 1 to x. 2. Set $x = 2$ 3. Print x(=2) and return 2.	1. Set $x = 2$. 2. Add 1 to x. 3. Print x(=3) and return 3.
Crossover	Parent$_1$: 1. Add 1 to x. 2. Set $x = 2$. 3. Set $y = x(= 2)$ and return 2.	Child$_1$: 1. Add 1 to x. 2. Take the square root of x. 3. Set $y = x$ and return the value.
	Parent$_2$: 1. Subtract 1 from x. 2. Set $x = \sqrt{x} \times x$. 3. Print x and return the value.	Child$_2$: 1. Subtract 1 from x. 2. Set $x = 2$ and its value (=2) is multiplied by x(=2). The result value (=4) is set to x again. 3. Print x(=4) and return 4.

1.2.5 Evolution Strategy

In Europe (particularly Germany), a research group with a similar approach to GAs had been active since the 1960s. This school is called evolutionary strategy (hereafter abbreviated as ES), whose founder is Ingo Rechenberg. Early ES differed from GAs in the following two points [20]:

1. Primarily uses mutation as an operator.
2. Handles real-valued representations.

Each individual in the ES is represented as a pair of real vectors, $(\vec{x}, \vec{\sigma})$. Here, $\vec{x}$ is a position vector in the search space, and $\vec{\sigma}$ is a standard deviation vector. Then, mutation is expressed as follows:

$$\vec{x}^{t+1} = \vec{x}^{t} + N(\vec{0}, \vec{\sigma}), \tag{1.4}$$

where $N(\vec{0}, \vec{\sigma})$ is a random variable following a Gaussian distribution with mean $\vec{0}$ and standard deviation $\vec{\sigma}$.

In the initial conception of the ES algorithm, exploration is performed on a population consisting of a single individual. In this case, an offspring generated by mutation (denoted as $\vec{x}^{t+1}$ in the above equation) is only adopted as a member of the new population (i.e., as a parent for the next generation) when its fitness is better than that of the parent (i.e., $\vec{x}^{t}$).

Unlike GAs, ES does not involve crossover, enabling quantitative analysis. The impact of mutation rates, for instance, has been mathematically analyzed [29, 32]. In addition, a theorem regarding convergence has been proven [1].

Interestingly, the "$\frac{1}{5}$ rule" was proposed to optimize convergence rates. Here, the "$\frac{1}{5}$ rule" states: "Set the proportion of successful mutations to $\frac{1}{5}$. If this ratio is greater (less) than $\frac{1}{5}$, increase (decrease) $\vec{\sigma}$." In practice, the ratio of successful mutations over the past k generations, $\varphi(k)$, is observed, and mutations are controlled using the following formula:

$$\vec{\sigma}^{t+1} = \begin{cases} c_d \times \vec{\sigma}^t & if \;\; \varphi(k) < 1/5, \\ c_i \times \vec{\sigma}^t & if \;\; \varphi(k) > 1/5, \\ \vec{\sigma}^t & if \;\; \varphi(k) = 1/5. \end{cases} \tag{1.5}$$

In particular, the literature [32] recommends $c_d = 0.82$ and $c_i = 1/0.82$. The intuitive meaning of this rule is: "If you succeed, continue searching with larger step sizes. Otherwise, reduce the step size."

Eventually, ES was expanded into a search method involving multiple individuals. In this case, in addition to the mutation operator described above, crossover and averaging operators (the one that averages two parent vectors) were introduced. Furthermore, unlike GAs, ES employs the following two types of selection methods:

1. $(\mu + \lambda)$–ES
   A parent population consisting of μ individuals produces λ offspring. From the total population of $(\mu + \lambda)$ individuals, μ individuals are selected to become the parents of the next generation.
2. (μ, λ)–ES
   A parent population consisting of μ individuals produces λ offspring (where $\mu < \lambda$). From the population of λ individuals, μ individuals are selected to become the parents of the next generation.

Generally, the (μ, λ)-ES is considered to perform better in time-varying environments or noisy conditions.

ES has been applied to various optimization problems [18] and later extended to combinatorial (i.e., non-real-valued) problems [12]. Unfortunately, since Rechenberg had not published much in English, this research apparently received little attention outside Germany until the early 1990s. For literature on ES and comparisons with GAs, see [1, 20].

In Sects. 3.4.3 and 3.6.2, we will discuss research on optimizing ES hyperparameters using LLMs.

1.3 Multi-objective Optimization

1.3.1 Risk or Return?

In life, we often wish to pursue two or more mutually conflicting goals. In finance, return and risk are generally conflicting objectives (see Fig. 1.9). In asset

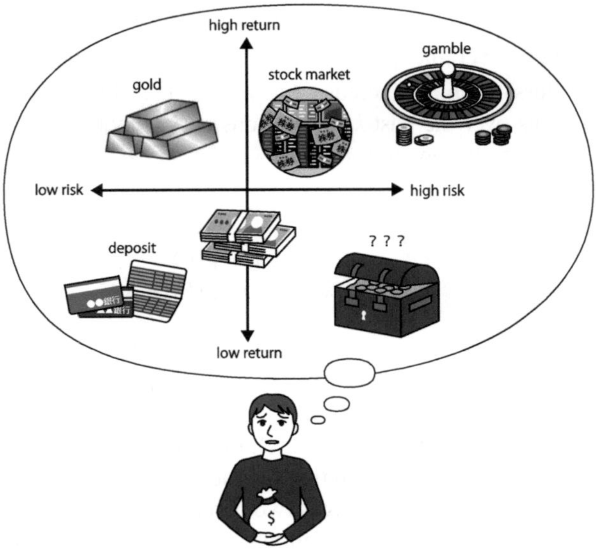

Fig. 1.9 Risk vs. returns

management and investment, return is the profit gained through management, and risk is the uncertainty and magnitude of fluctuations, all involving present assets and the possibility of a specific future gain on those assets. Risk can be gauged from price volatility (the coefficient of variation). High volatility means large price fluctuations. Ordinary volatility is generally expressed in terms of standard deviation.

In general, risk and return are in a "trade-off" relationship. High-return, low-risk financial products would be ideal, but they are not that easy to find. Usually, the choice is one of the following two:

- Low risk, low return: The possibility of loss of the principal is low, but management returns will be small.
- High risk, high return: Losses may occur, but any returns might be large.

In considering the optimization problem, we have so far limited the discussion to maximization of a single objective (the fitness function). As in risk versus return, however, it is often necessary to consider optimization when there are multiple objectives, that is, "multi-objective optimization."

Pareto optimality may be defined more formally as follows. Let two points $x = (x_1, \cdots, x_n)$ and $y = (y_1, \cdots, y_n)$ exist in an n-dimensional search space, with each dimension representing an objective (an evaluation) function, and with the objective being a minimization of each to the degree possible. The domination of y by x (written as $x <_p y$) may be therefore defined as

$$x <_p y \iff (\forall i)(x_i \leq y_i) \land (\exists i)(x_i < y_i). \tag{1.6}$$

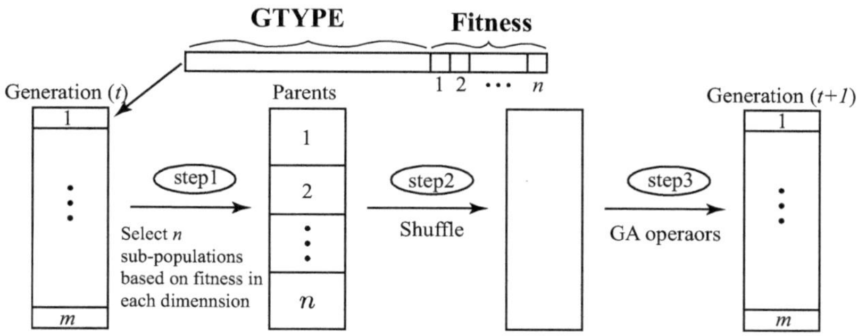

Fig. 1.10 VEGAs (vector-evaluated genetic algorithms)

In the following, we will refer to n (the number of different evaluation functions) as the "dimension number." Any point that is not inferior to any other point will be called "non-dominated" or "non-inferior," and the curve (or curved surface) formed by the set of Pareto-optimal solutions will be called the "Pareto front."

On this basis, it is possible to apply GA to multi-objective optimization. In the following example, we use the VEGA (vector-evaluated genetic algorithms) system proposed by Schaffer et al. [30, 31]. Selection with VEGA is performed as follows (see Fig. 1.10), where n is the evaluation dimension number (the number of different evaluation functions) and m is the population size:

1. Let the n subsets be $Sub_i (i = 1, \cdots, n)$.
2. In Sub_i, retain the individual selected only by evaluation function i.
3. Mix $Sub_1, Sub_2, \cdots, Sub_n$ and shuffle.
4. Produce the next-generation offspring, using the genetic operator on these sets.

Note that the selection is based upon every evaluation function (i.e., the function value in every dimension). In contrast, reproduction is performed not for each subset but rather for the complete set. In other words, crossover is performed for the individuals in Sub_i and $Sub_j (i \neq j)$. In this way, we preserve the superior individuals in each dimension and, at the same time, select those superior to the average in one or more dimensions.

Let us now consider the VEGA operation, as applied to optimization of the binary function:

$$F_{21}(t) = t^2, \tag{1.7}$$

$$F_{22}(t) = (t - 2)^2, \tag{1.8}$$

where t is the only independent variable. The graphical appearance of this function is shown in Fig. 1.11 (called "Pareto map"). The VEGA objective is to select non-dominated points, such as those shown in the figure.

Figure 1.12 shows the results for generations 0 and 3. The population size is set to 30 individuals in each dimension, and a crossover ratio of 0.95 and a mutation ratio

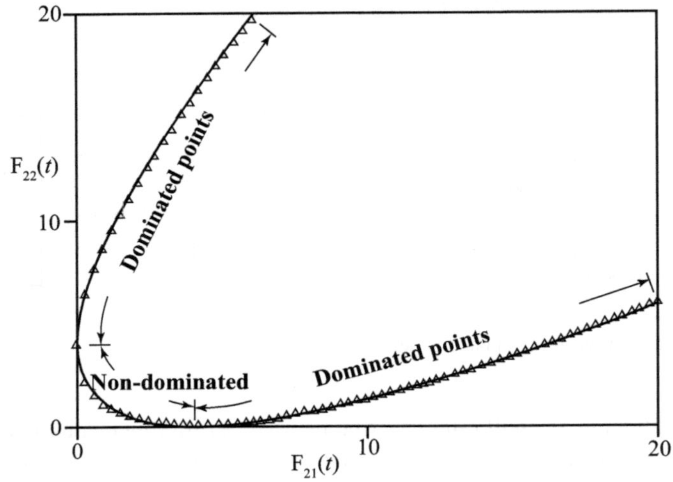

Fig. 1.11 Pareto maps

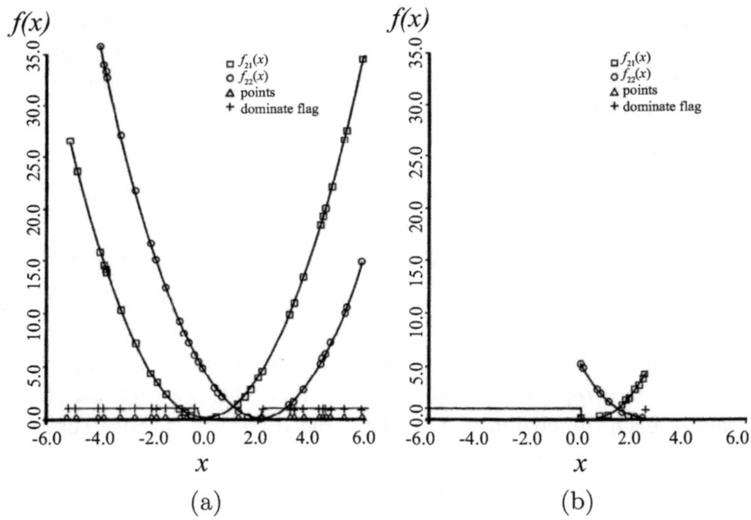

Fig. 1.12 Results of multi-objective optimization. (**a**) Generation 0. (**b**) Generation 3

of 0.01 are applied. As shown, the VEGA can effectively find a front (a Pareto front) containing no dominated points. However, it has lost several intermediate points. VEGA selection, as shown in this example, involves a problem that can be described as follows. The selection pressure (in biological terms, the degree of selectivity applied to the survival and proliferation of the organism's population) on the optimum values in at least one dimension (evaluation function) works as desired. In

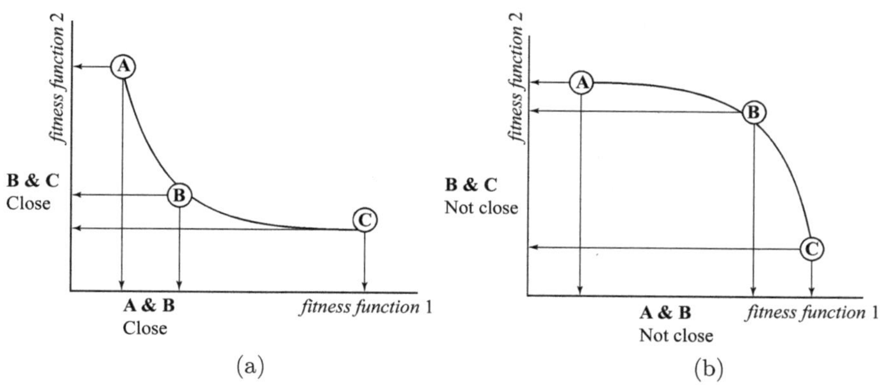

Fig. 1.13 Pareto fronts. (**a**) Concave. (**b**) Convex

the unlikely event that a utopian individual (an individual superior in all dimensions) exists, it may be possible to find it through genetic operation on the superior parents in only one dimension. In most cases, however, no utopian individual exists. It is then necessary to obtain the Pareto-optimal points, some of which are intermediate in all dimensions. In an ideal GA, it is desirable to have the same selection pressure apply to all of these. With VEGA selection, however, an intermediate point cannot survive. In effect, species differentiation occurs within the population, with each species exhibiting superiority in its own dimension. The danger of this is greater when the Pareto-optimal region is convex rather than concave (see Fig. 1.13). Two modifications have been proposed to resolve this difficulty. One is to apply an excess of heuristic selection pressure on the non-dominated individuals in each generation. The other is to increase interspecies crossbreeding. Although ordinary GA selection is random, this is effective because utopian individuals are more readily produced by interspecies than intraspecies crossover.

1.4 EDA: Estimation of Distribution Algorithm

This section explains EDA in detail. As will be explained in Sect. 1.5.1, readers will come to understand the relationship between probabilistic models and LLMs. Therefore, we describe the learning of probabilistic models using EDA, an extension of evolutionary computation. Especially, how the structure of probabilistic models reflects the difficulty of learning.

1.4.1 Evolution Without Crossover

Based upon evolutionary theory, GA combines high-quality substructures (promising sub-solutions) to generate new candidate solutions. The high-quality sub-solutions generated are called "building blocks."

Optimization by GA depends upon the following items:

1. Maintaining diversity with a population of building blocks
2. Selection
3. Replacement of genes by crossover and mutation

However, the interaction between variables (loci) is not well considered. Generated building blocks can be destroyed, so even simple problems cannot be solved.

Therefore, efforts are underway to improve optimization algorithms without relying on the evolutionary (genetic) model. The key to this is the third feature mentioned above (i.e., genetic manipulation). In extreme cases, it is an attempt to construct more efficient GAs by eliminating crossovers and mutations.

One method to prevent the collapse of building blocks is the estimation of distribution algorithm (EDA [24]). This method extracts probabilistic information from selected partial solutions (individuals) and uses it to generate new solutions (child genes). Another method considers genetic linkage based on solution representation and breeding operations (linkage learning genetic algorithm: LLGA [9]).

In the following sections, we present an approach that integrates evolutionary computation methods and probabilistic learning.

1.4.2 What If We Eliminate Crossovers and Mutations from GA?

Problem-specific interaction between variables (loci) can be explicitly represented by a simultaneous probability distribution. It is computed from the data of selected individuals. New offspring genes are generated based on this probability distribution (this is called "sampling"). Selection and generation of new offspring are identical to those in a standard GA. Figure 1.14 shows the flowchart of the EDA.

The basic idea of EDA is that individuals selected from the surviving population contain useful partial solutions (building blocks). Important steps in EDA are as follows:

Step 1 Obtain information about the relationships (simultaneous probability distributions) between the loci represented by the partial solutions.

Step 2 Generate children based on the obtained distribution (sampling).

Step 3 Repeat the above *Step 1* and *Step 2* so that more useful partial solutions are gradually synthesized.

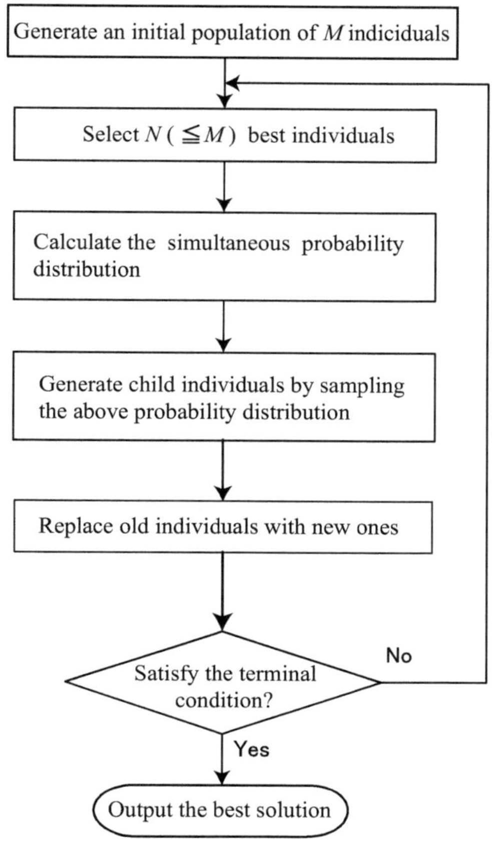

Fig. 1.14 EDA flowchart

Note that no crossover or mutation appears in the above steps. In conventional GA, there is no *Step 1*. Children are generated mainly by crossover or mutation rather than by sampling (i.e., no *Step 2*). In other words, it is implicitly assumed that useful sub-solutions are synthesized by crossover or mutation. In contrast, EDA actively exploits relationships among loci and aims to achieve a more efficient synthesis of partial solutions.

An essential part of EDA is computing simultaneous probability distributions. There are several different approaches to this. We explain representative examples below.

The simplest way to compute the probability distribution is to consider all variables (loci) as univariate (i.e., independent). In the following, suppose that the gene $\mathbf{x}$ is composed of n loci $X_1, \cdots, X_n$.[3] Then, the simultaneous probability distribution $p_l(\mathbf{x})$ of gene $\mathbf{x}$ is obtained by multiplying n marginal probabilities $p(X_i = x_i)$, i.e.,

$$p_l(\mathbf{x}) = \prod_{i=1}^{n} p_l(X_i = x_i), \tag{1.9}$$

where l is the number of generations.

Representative examples of this approach include the univariate marginal distribution algorithm (UMDA) [21], population-based incremental learning (PBIL [2]), and compact genetic algorithm (CGA [11]). These algorithms perform well if there is no strong interaction between the variables [26].

1.4.2.1 Univariate Marginal Distribution Algorithm (UMDA)

In UMDA, simultaneous probability distributions are decomposed as the product of independent univariate marginal distributions, each of which is inferred from the marginal frequencies, i.e.,

$$p_l(X_i = x_i) = \frac{\sum_{j=1}^{N} \delta_j(X_i = x_i)}{N}, \tag{1.10}$$

where N is the number of selected individuals. In this case, if the value X_i of the i-th locus of an individual j is x_i, then

$$\delta_j(X_i = x_i) = 1; \tag{1.11}$$

otherwise,

$$\delta_j(X_i = x_i) = 0. \tag{1.12}$$

UMDA has been theoretically proven to approximate the behavior of the standard genetic algorithm, which performs uniform crossover [23].

As an example of UMDA, consider the OneMax problem in four variables. The objective function for the OneMax problem is defined by

$$f_{\mathrm{OneMax}}(\mathbf{x}) = \sum_{i=1}^{n} x_i, \tag{1.13}$$

[3] In this section, loci are represented by upper case letters (e.g., X_i), and the actual values taken at the loci are represented by lower case letters (e.g., x_i). In the case of binary gene expression, X_i is either 0 or 1.

Table 1.3 Initial population in OneMax problem

X_1	X_2	X_3	X_4	Fitness value
1	0	1	0	2
0	0	1	1	2
1	1	0	1	3
1	0	1	1	3
1	1	1	0	3
0	1	0	1	2

Table 1.4 Probability distributions in OneMax problem

	X_1	X_2	X_3	X_4
	1	1	0	1
	1	0	1	1
Selected individuals	1	1	1	0
Frequency	3	2	2	2
Probability$p(X_i = 1)$	1.0	0.67	0.67	0.67

Table 1.5 Generation of child individuals by sampling

X_1	X_2	X_3	X_4	Fitness value
1	1	1	1	4
1	0	1	1	3
1	1	1	1	4
1	1	0	1	3
1	0	1	0	2
1	1	0	1	3

where the optimal solution is $\{1, 1, \cdots, 1\}$ (i.e., all individuals with one locus).

First, a population of individuals is randomly initialized to solve the problem. Then, individuals with high-fitness values are selected from the population.

For example, suppose that an initial population (the number of populations: 6) is generated as shown in Table 1.3 and that three individuals with the fitness value of three are selected.

Next, the probabilities and marginal frequencies for each variable are calculated from the selected individuals. In Table 1.4, the probabilities and marginal frequencies are calculated with $X_i = 1$.

This probability distribution is sampled to generate a new child's genes (see Table 1.5). In other words, the child individuals for the population size (i.e., six individuals) are generated by setting $X_1 = 1$ with probability 1.0, $X_2 = 1$ with probability 0.67, and so on. At this stage, the UMDA algorithm stops because the solution $\{1, 1, 1, 1, 1\}$ can be obtained.

When all $p_l(\mathbf{x})$ are positive, UMDA will converge, albeit conditionally, to a population containing the globally optimal solution if an elite strategy is used [7].

However, the probability of the simultaneous probability distribution can be zero by UMDA. Consider the OneMax problem again. For another initial population (Table 1.6), the marginal frequencies and probabilities in the population obtained by

Table 1.6 Another initial population in the OneMax problem

X_1	X_2	X_3	X_4	Fitness value
1	0	1	1	3
1	0	0	0	1
0	1	0	0	1
0	0	1	1	2
1	0	1	1	3
0	0	1	1	2

Table 1.7 Selected individuals and their probability distribution

	X_1	X_2	X_3	X_4
	1	0	1	1
	0	0	1	1
Selected individuals	1	0	1	1
Frequency	2	0	3	3
Probability $p(X_i = 1)$	0.67	0.0	1.0	1.0

selecting half of the best ones (called truncated selection[4]) are given in Table 1.7. As shown in the table, individuals with fitness values of 3 and 2 were selected.

In this case, the simultaneous probability distribution of the correct answer 1111 is as follows:

$$p_l(\mathbf{x} = 1111) = \prod_{i=1}^{4} p_l(X_i = 1), \tag{1.14}$$

$$= 0.67 \times 0.0 \times 1.0 \times 1.0 = 0.0. \tag{1.15}$$

As a result, X_2 becomes zero for all child genes, and the algorithm cannot find the optimal solution.

One solution to this problem is the Laplace correction [5]. This correction method is given as follows:

$$p_l(X_i = x_i) = \frac{\sum_{j=1}^{N} \delta_j(X_i = x_i) + 1}{N + r_i}, \tag{1.16}$$

where r_i is the number of different values that the variableX_i can take. In this way, each of the probabilities $p_l(X_i = x_i)$ will be positive, and the optimal solution is guaranteed to be obtained.

[4] Parents are randomly selected from the top T individuals, where T is the truncation size.

1.4.2.2 Population-Based Incremental Learning: PBIL

In PBIL, a population is represented by the following vector of probabilities:

$$(p_l(\mathbf{x}) = (p_l(X_1 = x_1), \cdots, p_l(X_i = x_i), \cdots, p_l(X_n = x_n)), \tag{1.17}$$

where $p_l(X_i = x_i)$ expresses the probability that the value of the i-th element (locus) X_i is x_i at the l-th generation. By sampling $p_l(\mathbf{x})$ every generation, M individuals are generated, of which N best individuals are selected (M is the population size). The selected individuals are used to rewrite the probability vector using the Hebbian rule below:

$$p_{l+1}(X_i = x_i) = (1 - \alpha) \cdot p_l(X_i = x_i) + \alpha \cdot \frac{1}{N} \cdot \sum_{k=1}^{N} x^l_{i,k:M}, \tag{1.18}$$

where $\alpha \in (0, 1]$ and $x^l_{i,k:M}$ represents the value of the i-th locus X_i of the k-th selected individual. Thus, the information about the generated building blocks is used to update the probability vector via the Hebbian rule.

As an example of PBIL, consider the subset sum problem for four integers $\{1, 2, 3, 4\}$. This is the problem of finding a subset whose sum equals a given number. If the target value is 6, then the correct solutions are $\{1, 2, 3\}$ and $\{2, 4\}$. If the solution is expressed in binary numbers, then the optimal solution is $\{X_1, X_2, X_3, X_4\} = \{1, 1, 1, 0\}$ or $\{0, 1, 0, 1\}$. Suppose that the initial probability vector is $p_0(x) = \{0.6, 0.5, 0.8, 0.3\}$ and that the individuals shown in Table 1.8 are selected. In this case, if $\alpha = 0.8$, the probability will be updated as shown in the table. For instance, the following update is given:

$$p_1(X_1 = 1) = (1 - 0.8) \times 0.6 + 0.8 \times 0.67, \tag{1.19}$$

$$= 0.656. \tag{1.20}$$

New child individuals are then generated by the sampling function $p_{l+1}(X_i = x_i)$.

Table 1.8 Selected individuals and probability distribution in the subset sum problem

	X_1	X_2	X_3	X_4
	1	0	1	1
	1	1	0	0
Selected individuals	0	1	1	0
Frequency	2	2	2	1
Probability $p_0(X_i = 1)$	0.67	0.67	0.67	0.33
Probability $p_1(X_i = 1)$	0.656	0.636	0.696	0.324

1.4.2.3 Compact GA: CGA

In CGA, each element of the probability vector is initialized to be 0.5, i.e., $p_0(\mathbf{x}) = (0.5, 0.5, \cdots, 0.5)$. Thereafter, two individuals **a** and **b** are randomly selected from the population, and the probability vectors are updated according to the rules described below. Suppose that **a** is better than **b**. For any locus i whose values differ between **a** and **b** (i.e., the variable index i for $a_i \neq b_i$), the following updates are used:

$$p_{l+1}(X_i = a_i) = p_l(X_i = a_i) + \frac{1}{K}, \tag{1.21}$$

$$p_{l+1}(X_i \neq a_i) = p_l(X_i \neq a_i) - \frac{1}{K}, \tag{1.22}$$

where K is a parameter for updating. This process is performed until the probability vector converges.

1.4.3 EDAs for Multivariate Dependency

Mutual information maximizing input clustering (MIMIC) algorithm [6], combining optimizers with mutual information trees (COMIT) [3], and bivariate marginal distribution algorithm (BMDA) [26] are methods for solving problems in which the interaction between variables is given in pairs. For problems with dependencies of up to two variables, these methods can accurately estimate simultaneous probability distributions.

Factorized distribution algorithm (FDA [22]), extended compact genetic algorithm (ECGA [10]), Bayesian optimization algorithm (BOA [27]), and estimation of Bayesian networks algorithm (EBNA [17]) allow some estimation of multivariate dependencies.

In the following, we will describe the FDA. FDA assumes decomposability of the objective function. Decomposability means that the function can be decomposed. For example, the decomposition of four variables is given in the following equation:

$$f(x1, x2, x3, x4) = f(x1) + f(x1, x2) + f(x1, x2, x3) + f(x2, x3, x4). \tag{1.23}$$

In general, an additively decomposed function (ADF) is defined as follows:

$$f(x) = \sum_{i=1}^{m} f_i(x_{s_i}), \tag{1.24}$$

where $S_i \in \{1, 2, \cdots, n\}$ is a set of subscripts. In addition, f_i is a function that depends on the variable X_j when $j \in S_i$.

In the FDA, the dependency of variables is described as a conditional distribution of the following form:

$$p_\beta(x) = \prod_{i=1}^{m} p(x_{b_i} | x_{c_i}). \tag{1.25}$$

For example, we obtain the following equation for Eq. (1.23):

$$p_\beta(x) = p(x_1) \cdot p(x_2|x_1) \cdot p(x_3|x_1, x_2) \cdot p(x_4|x_2, x_3). \tag{1.26}$$

Furthermore, we assume the Boltzmann distribution, i.e.,

$$p(x) = \frac{e^{\beta f(x)}}{Z_\beta}, \tag{1.27}$$

where Z_β is called the partition function, and the following equation holds:

$$Z_\beta = \sum_y e^{\beta f(y)}. \tag{1.28}$$

β is a user-defined constant that determines Boltzmann selection schedule (see [22] for more details).

1.5 Example of Solution by UMDA

Let us apply UMDA to the following three problems: subset sum, OneMax, and n-queens. The subset sum and OneMax problems are linear, and the variables used are not strongly related. On the other hand, the variables used in the n-queen problem are position dependent. To solve the subset sum and OneMax problems, we encode the solution as a binary string. For the n-queen problem, we represent the queens' positions as permutations.

The fitness value for the OneMax problem is defined as the sum (i.e., the number of ones) of each individual. For example, the value of the individual $\{1, 1, 0, 0, 1, 0\}$ is 3. The algorithm terminates when the optimal value is obtained. For comparison, standard GA is applied to the same problem. Single-point crossover and mutation are used for this GA. The parameters used in the experiments are as follows: number of runs = 10, population size = 10×size of problem, crossover rate = 0.7, mutation rate = 0.1, elite ratio = 10%. Truncated selection is used in UMDA. The experimental results are given in Fig. 1.15. The figure shows the average number of successful generations (i.e., when the correct answers are obtained) as a function

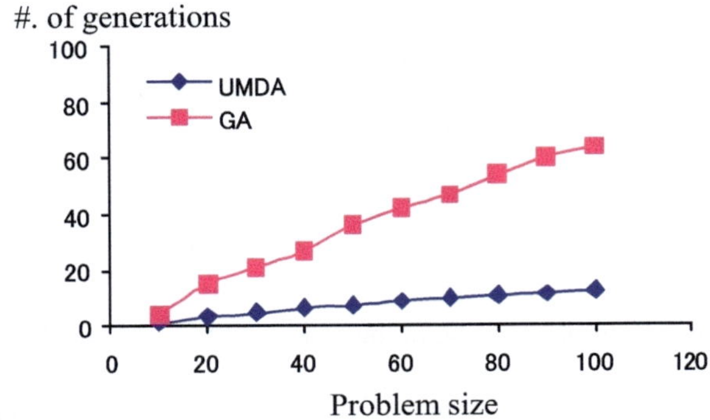

Fig. 1.15 Average of successful generations in the OneMax problem

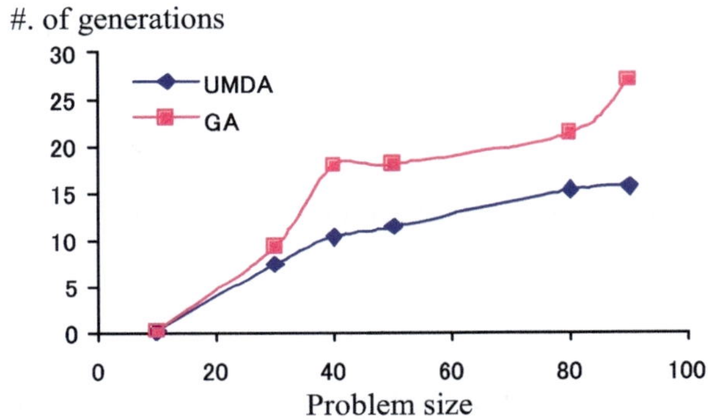

Fig. 1.16 Average of successful generations in the subset sum problem

of problem size. As shown in the figure, the increase in the number of required generations is significantly smaller for UMDA.

In the subset sum problem, the difference between the sum of the chosen variables and the optimal value is used as the fitness. For example, let the optimal value be 6 for the set of integers $\{1, 2, 3, 4\}$. In this case, the fitness value of the individual $\{1, 0, 0, 1\}$ is 1. The algorithm terminates when the fitness value is 0. Comparative experiments were performed for GA with one-point crossover and mutation. The parameters are as follows: number of runs = 50, population size = 1000, crossover rate = 0.7, mutation rate = 0.1, elite ratio = 10%. The results of the experiment are shown in Fig. 1.16. The results are not as striking as for OneMax, but show the superiority of UMDA for large problem sizes.

The goal of the n-queen problem is to place n queens on a chessboard of $n \times n$ so that they do not attack each other (see Fig. 1.17). The solution candidate $\{x_1, x_2, \cdots, x_n\}$ is represented by a permutation of n elements, where x_i is the row number of a queen placed in column i. The fitness value is the number of queens that do not attack each other. To improve the performance in UMDA, we employed

Fig. 1.17 Eight queens on a 8 × 8 chessboard

Fig. 1.18 Average computation time for n-queen problems

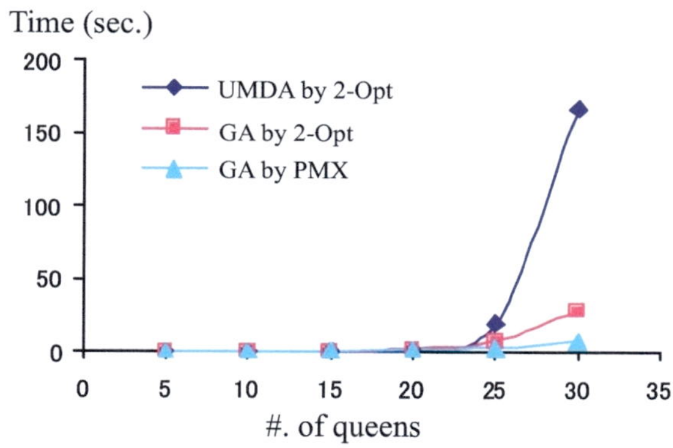

the 2-opt algorithm[5] as a local heuristic search. For comparison, a GA with 2-opt and swap mutation and a GA with PMX and swap mutation were applied to the same problem.[6] The parameters were as follows: number of runs = 50, population size = 10×variable size, crossover rate = 0.7, mutation rate = 0.1, elite ratio = 10%. The results of the experiment are shown in Fig. 1.18. In this problem, the effect of UMDA was not observed when the number of queens was smaller. This is because the problem's variables (placement locations) are not independent. For this type of problem, a multivariate-dependent method as described in Sect. 1.4.3 would be more suitable.

The most essential part of EDA is estimating probability distributions. Representative methods and their characteristics are given in Table 1.9. As shown in the table, each approach has its advantages and disadvantages. A more efficient method, RECEDA (real-coded estimation of distribution), which integrates reinforcement

---

[5] Two edges are randomly selected and they are exchanged. If the distance is shortened, the exchanged path is adopted.

[6] See [14, sec.1.8.2] for details of PMX and swap mutation.

Table 1.9 Overview of different EDA algorithms

Method	Features	Applications	Lit.
UMDA	Works well for linear problems with independent variables, but needs extensions and heuristics for combinatorial problems	Classification problem, feature extraction	[21]
PBIL	Suitable for problems with independent variables in binary representation. Uses probability vectors instead of population	Neural net weight learning, genetic programming, path optimization problems, etc.	[2]
CGA	Processes each variable independently, consumes less memory than standard GA	Recurrent neural network learning in continuous time	[11]
MIMIC	Searches for the best permutation of variables and estimates the probability distribution using Kullback-Leibler divergence	Applicable to problems with at most two variable dependencies	[6]
COMIT	Learns the structure of a Bayesian network and estimates the simultaneous probability distribution based on the maximum weight spanning tree (MWST) algorithm		[3]
BMDA	Constructs a graph representing the dependent relationship. The graph does not have a cycle and is not necessarily connected		[26]
FDA	Integrates evolutionary computation and simulated annealing (SA). Assumes decomposition of simultaneous probability distributions	Additively decomposable function	[22]
BOA	Uses Bayesian networks to estimate simultaneous probability distributions. Capable of incorporating prior knowledge about the problem	Decomposable problem with a certain restriction	[27]
ECGA	Decomposes a simultaneous probability distribution into a product of marginal distributions	Silicon cluster problem	[10]
EBNA	Uses Bayesian networks to decompose simultaneous probability distributions. Employs BIC scores, penalized K2 algorithm, and PC algorithm, etc., for estimating the model	Feature extraction problems, job shop scheduling problems, k-nearest neighbor weighting problems, and traveling salesman problems	[17]

learning and EDA, has also been proposed [25]. In addition, EDA has been extended as EDP (estimation of distribution programming [15]), which is applicable to a GP framework for the sake of automatic program synthesis.

1.5.1 LLMs ≈EDAs?

LLMs learn patterns and combinations of words by training based on large amounts of text data. By doing so, it builds models that predict which words will follow a given word. More specifically, it uses a technique called "attention" in Transformer to learn how each word in a sentence is related to other words. This allows LLMs to estimate conditional probabilities based on context.

This LLM mechanism is similar to model estimation with EDA. EDA also performs sampling, from which a probabilistic model is estimated. Note that the sampling depends on the fitness value. Therefore, it corresponds to the EDA context. In this sense, both EDAs and LLMs can be viewed as probability estimation mechanisms that function in the same way.

Following the above idea, Meyerson et al. [19] devised a crossover through LLM called LLM crossover (LMX). LMX, like EDA, builds a probabilistic model of the parents and generates children according to the model. The advantage of LMX is that a generic language representation can be used as a gene for evolutionary computation. In ordinary evolutionary computation, the GTYPE design determines the search efficiency. In LMX, PTYPE itself can be used as a GTYPE. Experimental results have shown the effectiveness of LMX for binary strings, style transformation of plain-text sentences, symbolic regression, image generation via text-to-image prompting, and Python code generation.

It has been proven that LMX theoretically approximates EDA [19]. More precisely, the following equation holds:

$$\mathrm{LMX}(x_1, \cdots, x_k) \approx D^*_{EDA}, \tag{1.29}$$

where the left-hand side is the probabilistic model generated by LMX for the parents $x_1, \cdots, x_k$. The right-hand side is the most probable model that an ideal EDA would generate based on the parents $x_1, \cdots, x_k$. For example, it will be given as follows:

$$D^*_{EDA} = \underset{D \in \mathcal{D}_{LM}}{\mathrm{argmax}} \; p(D) \prod_{i=1}^{k} p(x_i \mid D), \tag{1.30}$$

where $p(D)$ is the prior probability of D. $\mathcal{D}_{LM}$ is the distribution space of all possible datasets for which the LLM is trained.

1.6 LLMs and Metaheuristics

Search methods based on biological or physical phenomena are called "metaheuristics." GA, GP, simulated annealing (SA), neural network, and reinforcement learning are also metaheuristics in a broad sense, because they are based on evolutionary theory, physical phenomena, brain plasticity, behaviorism, etc.

Metaheuristics are broadly classified as follows (see Fig. 1.19):

- Evolutionary computation
- Swarm intelligence
- Human and society-inspired methods
- Physics-based methods

These metaheuristic methods are frequently applied to various areas.

There are two possible directions for research on LLMs and metaheuristics:

- Metaheuristics for LLMs; LLMs via metaheuristics
- LLMs for metaheuristics; Metaheuristics via LLMs

In the first direction, we use metaheuristics to improve LLM performance. For example, Genetic prompt search (GPS [35]) aims to generate effective prompts for LLMs through evolutionary computation. GPS has been proposed to improve few-shot learning with high-performing prompts. Tianrungroj and Iba [34] integrated learning classifier systems (LCS) and LLMs to construct ROIL (rule optimization

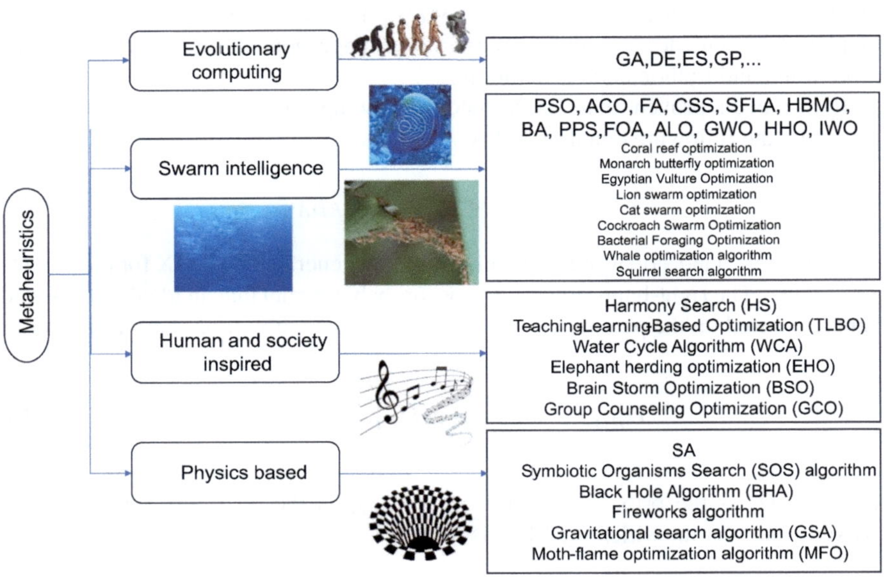

Fig. 1.19 Overview of metaheuristics

method using LLMs for imitation learning) in the natural language domain. LCS is a kind of GBML, which searches for classier rules by means of evolutionary computation. ROIL has been successfully applied to a text-based e-commerce website navigation problem in the WebShop environment. Kobayashi et al. [16] proposed an image generation support system that combines a diffusion model with interactive evolutionary computation (IEC). This system allowed users to intuitively control the generation process by evolving the genes of generated images.

The second direction is the main subject of this book. This is the use of LLMs to replace some functionality of evolutionary computation and metaheuristics, making them applicable to a broader range of domains, such as natural language processing, programming code, and images. This idea leads to the approach described in Sect. 1.5.1, which considers LLMs as EDAs. The following chapters discuss LLM-based metaheuristics in more detail.

References

1. Bäck, T., Hoffmeister, F., Schwefel, H.-P.: A survey of evolution strategies. In: Proceedings of 4th International Conference on Genetic Algorithms (ICGA91). Morgan Kaufmann (1991)
2. Baluja, S.: Population Based Incremental Learning: A Method for Integrating Genetic Search Based Function Optimization and Competitive Learning. Technical Report No.CMU-CS-94-163, Carnegie Mellon University (1994)
3. Baluja, S., Davies, S.: Using Optimal Dependency Trees for Combina torial Optimization: Learning the Structure of Search Space. Technical Report CMU-CS-97-107 (1997)
4. Bender, E., et al.: On the dangers of stochastic parrots: can language models be too big? In: Proceedings of the 2021 ACM Conference on Fairness, Accountability, and Transparency (FAccT'21), pp. 610–623 (2021)
5. Cestnik, B.: Estimating probabilities: a crucial task in machine learning. In: Proceedings of the European Conference in Artificial Intelligence, pp. 147–149 (1990)
6. DeBonet, J., Isbell, C., Viola, P.: MIMIC: finding optima by estimating probability densities. In: Advances in Neural Information Processing Systems, vol. 9. Bradford Books, London (1997)
7. González, C., Lozano, J., Larrañaga, P.: Mathematical modeling of discrete estimation of distribution algorithms. In: Larrañaga, P., Lozano, J. (eds.) Estimation of Distribution Algorithms: A New Tool for Evolutionary Optimization. Kluwer Academic Publishers, Boston (2001)
8. Hansen, N., Ostermeier, A.: Adapting arbitrary normal mutation distributions in evolution strategies: the covariance matrix adaptation. In: Proceedings of IEEE International Conference on Evolutionary Computation (CEC), pp. 312–317 (1996)
9. Harik, G.: Learning Gene Linkage to Efficiently Solve Problems of Bounded Difficulty using Genetic Algorithms. Ph.D. thesis, Department of Computer Science, University of Michigan (1997)
10. Harik, G.: Linkage Learning via Probabilistic Modeling in the ECGA. Technical report, Illigal Report No. 99010, Illinois Genetic Algorithm Laboratory, University of Illinois (1999)
11. Harik, F. Lobo, G.R., Goldberg, D.: The compact genetic algorithm. In: Proceedings of the IEEE Conference on Evolutionary Computation, pp. 523–528 (1998)
12. Herdy, M.: Application of the evolution strategy to discrete optimization problems. In: Schwefel, H.-P., Männer, R. (eds.) Parallel Problem Solving from Nature (PPSN). Springer, Berlin/Heidelberg (1990)
13. Holland, J.H.: Adaptation in Natural and Artificial Systems. MIT Press, Cambridge (1975)

14. Iba, H., Noman, N.: New Frontier in Evolutionary Algorithms: Theory and Applications. Imperial College Press, London (2011)
15. Iba, T. Paul, H., Hasegawa, Y.: Applied Genetic Programming and Machine Learning. CRC Press International Series on Computational Intelligence. CRC Press, Boca Raton (2019)
16. Kobayashi, H., et al.: Image generation with diffusion model by interactive evolutionary computation. In: Proceedings of the 2023 IEEE Conference on Systems, Man, and Cybernetics (SMC 2023), pp. 2984–2990 (2023)
17. Larrañaga, P., et al.: Combinatorial optimization by learning and simulation of Bayesian networks. In: Proceedings of the Sixteenth Conference on Uncertainty in Artificial Intelligence, pp. 343–352 (2000)
18. Lohmann, R.: Structure evolution and incomplete induction. In: Proceedings of 2nd Parallel Problem Solving from Nature. North-Holland (1992)
19. Meyerson, E., et al.: Language model crossover: variation through FewShot prompting. ACM Trans. Evol. Learn. **4**, 1–40 (2024)
20. Michalewics, Z.: Genetic Algorithms + Data Structures = Evolution Programs. MIT Press, Cambridge (1992)
21. Mühlenbein, H.: The equation for response to selection and its use for prediction. Evol. Comput. **5**(3), 303–346 (1998)
22. Mühlenbein, H., Mahnig, T.: The factorized distribution algorithm for additively decomposed functions. In: Proceedings of the 1999 Congress on Evolutionary Computation, pp. 752–759. IEEE Press (1999)
23. Mühlenbein, H., Mahnig, T.: Evolutionary algorithms: from recombination to search distributions. In: Kallel, L., Naudits, B., Rogers, A. (eds.) Theoretical Aspects of Evolutionary Computing. Springer, Berlin/Heidelberg (2001)
24. Mühlenbein, H., Paas, G.: From recombination of genes to the estimation of distributions I: binary parameters. In: Lecture Notes in Computer Science 1411: Parallel Problem Solving from Nature-PPSN IV, pp. 178–187 (1996)
25. Paul, T., Iba, H.: Reinforcement learning estimation of distribution algorithm. In: Proceedings of Genetic and Evolutionary Computation (GECCO2003), pp. 1259–1270 (2003)
26. Pelikan, M., Mühlenbein, H.: The bivariate marginal distribution algorithm. In: Advances in Soft Computing-Engineering Design and Manufacturing, pp. 521–535. Springer, London (1999)
27. Pelikan, M., Goldberg, D., Cantu-Paz, E.: Linkage problem, distribution estimation and Bayesian networks. Evol. Comput. **8**(3), 311–340 (2000)
28. Price, K., Storn, R., Lampinen, J.: Differential Evolution: A Practical Approach to Global Optimization. Springer, Berlin/Heidelberg (2005)
29. Rechenberg, I.: Evolution strategy and human decision making. In: Willumeit, H.P. (ed.) Human Decision Making and Manual Control, pp. 349–359. North Holland, Amsterdam (1986)
30. Schaffer, J.: Multiple objective optimization with vector evaluated genetic algorithms. In: Proceedings of an International Conference on Genetic Algorithms and Their Applications, pp. 93–100 (1985)
31. Schaffer, J., Grefenstette, J.: Multi-objective learning via genetic algorithms. In: Proceedings of the 9th International Joint Conference on Artificial Intelligence,pp. 593–595 (1985)
32. Schwefel, H.: Numerical Optimization of Computer Models. Wiley, New York (1981)
33. Storn, R., Price, K.: Differential evolution–a simple and efficient heuristic for global optimization over continuous spaces. J. Glob. Optim. **11**(4), 341–359 (1997)
34. Tianrungroj, Y., Iba, H.: ROIL: Rule optimization via large language model for imitation learning. In: Proceedings of 2024 IEEE Congress on Evolutionary Computation (CEC 2024), pp. 1–8 (2024)
35. Xu, H., et al.: GPS: genetic prompt search for efficient few-shot learning. In: Proceedings of the 2023 IEEE Conference on Systems, Man, and Cybernetics (SMC 2023), pp. 8162–8171 (2022)

Chapter 2
Examples of Using LLMs as Metaheuristics

Chapter 2 explains examples of using LLMs as metaheuristics. We will examine specific examples of how to prompt LLMs to perform genetic operations in evolutionary computation. We will also attempt to synthesize heuristics for combinatorial optimization. Furthermore, we will explore how LLMs can efficiently perform evolutionary exploration of symbol regression problems within GP. The effectiveness and scalability of LLMs, as revealed through these examples, will be discussed in detail in later chapters.

2.1 Large Language Models as Genetic Algorithm Optimizers

2.1.1 LLMs for Combinatorial Optimization

Combinatorial optimization is a subfield of mathematical optimization that involves searching for an optimal combination under given constraints to maximize or minimize a specific objective. Such problems frequently arise in practical applications, including the traveling salesman problem (TSP[1]), knapsack problem, job shop scheduling problem (JSSP) [35], set covering problem (SCP) [1], and facility location problem (FLP) [37]. These problems are generally classified as NP-hard,, making the design of efficient solution methods a significant challenge. The goal is to examine whether LMEA is an effective approach for combinatorial optimization problems.

[1] Each city's location is given, and the goal is to determine a route that visits every city exactly once with minimal total distance.

H. Iba et al., *Large Language Models and Evolutionary Computation*,
Natural Computing Series, https://doi.org/10.1007/978-981-95-8597-7_2

Various approaches such as genetic algorithms (GAs) [15], Tabu Search [25], branch and bound, and greedy algorithms have been proposed. However, these methods often suffer from the drawback of becoming trapped in local optima,, and as the problem scale and complexity increase, reaching the global optimum becomes increasingly difficult. Against this backdrop, the development of efficient algorithms remains a critical area of research.

In recent years, studies integrating evolutionary computation with large language models (LLMs) have attracted attention. For example, Pier Luca Lanzi and Daniele Loiacono successfully combined interactive evolutionary computation (IEC) with LLMs to generate novel game designs [18]. Additionally, Erik Hemberg et al. proposed a method for evolving code by combining LLMs with genetic programming (GP) [11].

In this section, two LLM-based optimization methods, i.e., optimization by PROmpting (OPRO) and LLM-driven EA (LMEA), are applied to three distinct problems: the open shop problem, the knapsack problem, and the facility location problem. Search performance is compared with that of the traditional GA optimizer. Liu, S. et al. demonstrated that LMEA converges in fewer generations than OPRO when applied to the TSP [41]. However, several limitations remain in the prior work:

- Performance comparisons were conducted for only a single optimization problem.
- The target problem was relatively simple for LLMs to interpret.
- The effects of different individual representations remain unclear.
- A direct comparison between LMEA and GA has not been conducted.

To address these limitations, we investigate whether similar performance differences occur in more complex problem settings or with other individual representations [16]. By applying LMEA to the open shop problem, it becomes possible to assess its effectiveness in more complex problem settings than TSP, where fitness evaluation from individual representations is nontrivial. Furthermore, applying LMEA to the knapsack problem and the facility location problem enables evaluation of its effectiveness on problems that use different individual representations than those in the TSP.

2.1.2 LLM-Based Optimization

2.1.2.1 Optimization by Prompting (OPRO)

OPRO is a method that uses large language models (LLMs) to optimize by describing problems in natural language [41]. In this approach, the LLM generates new individuals using a meta-prompt that includes parent individuals. After evaluating the generated individuals, the results are incorporated into the following prompt. Unlike parent individuals, newly generated individuals are guided toward the optimal solution. OPRO has been applied to mathematical optimization problems, such as linear regression and the TSP, with performance comparisons against the nearest neighbor and farthest insertion methods on TSP instances of 10, 15, 20, and 50 cities. OPRO demonstrated superior performance for 10- and 15-city instances, while farthest insertion outperformed OPRO in 20- and 50-city instances. Additionally, a comparison across multiple LLMs revealed that GPT-4 reached the global optimum approximately 4 times faster than GPT-3.5-turbo and Text-Bison.

2.1.2.2 LLM-Driven EA (LMEA)

An overview of LMEA is presented in Fig. 2.1. In usual GAs, crossover and mutation are performed based on predefined algorithms, requiring the design of problem-specific genetic operators, which is a notable limitation. In contrast, the proposed LMEA performs crossover and mutation using large language models (LLMs), eliminating the need for expert knowledge or manual design of operators tailored to specific problem characteristics [19]. While LMEA and OPRO are both optimization methods utilizing large language models (LLMs), they differ significantly in the structure of their prompts. LMEA generates new individuals by providing explicit instructions for crossover and mutation within the prompt, whereas OPRO directly generates individuals based on the current population.

Fig. 2.1 LMEA

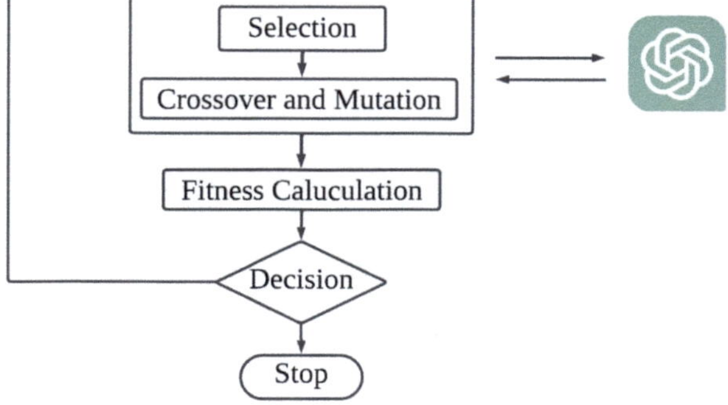

In previous studies, LMEA was applied to the TSP using the same city configurations and heuristics as those used in prior research on OPRO, allowing for direct comparison [19]. The results showed that LMEA achieved the best performance for 10- and 15-city instances but was outperformed by heuristic methods for 20- and 25-city instances. While LMEA demonstrates a higher likelihood of reaching the global optimum compared to OPRO, it has the drawback of increased generation time per individual due to longer prompts and outputs.

The following explains the detailed implementation of LMEA and OPRO:

- **Prompts**
  The prompts used in LMEA are constructed based on the study by Liu et al. [19]. The prompts can be broadly divided into three components. As an example, the prompts used for the knapsack problem (see 41 page for detailed definition) are described.
- **Description of problem and objective function**
  First, the problem setting is provided to the LLM as follows. In the case of the knapsack problem, this includes the weight constraint and the weight and value of each item. Subsequently, the objective function is specified.

Description of the problem and the objective function

You are given the weight capacity and the value and weight of each item:
W
$[(w_1, v_1), (w_2, v_2), \ldots, (w_n, v_n)]$
Your task is to find a way to put items in that will meet the weight capacity limit and maximize value.

- **Population and fitness**
  Next, the representation of individuals and the population, including each individual's fitness, is provided to the LLM.

Population generation

Give me a new array that is different from all arrays above, and has a value higher than any of the above. The array should start with <res> and end with </res>. You have to generate N new arrays.

- **Crossover and mutation**
  Finally, instructions for selection, crossover, and mutation are given using the prompt shown below.

Crossover and mutation

Please follow the instructions step-by-step to generate new traces:
1. Select two arrays from the above arrays.
2. Crossover the two arrays chosen in Step 1 and generate a new array
3. Mutate the array generated in Step 2 and generate a new array
4. Keep the array generated in Step 3, repeat Steps 1, 2, 3, until you have N generated arrays.

Directly give me all the chosen arrays at step 1, bracket them with <selection>, and </selection>, and all the generated arrays at step 3, bracketed them with <res> and </res>

- **Population generation**
  The prompts used in OPRO are based on the study by Yang et al. [41]. As only the individual generation process differs from that of LMEA, the corresponding prompt segment is presented below.

Population generation

Give me a new array that is different from all arrays above, and has a value higher than any of the above. The array should start with <res> and end with </res>. You have to generate N new arrays.

2.1.3 Experiments

The three methods, i.e., LMEA, OPRO, and GA, were applied to the open shop problem, the knapsack problem, and the facility location problem. The open shop problem was selected for the following reasons:

- Unlike the TSP, which involves the relatively simple task of finding the shortest path to visit all cities, the open shop problem requires determining a schedule that minimizes the total completion time of all jobs, under complex constraints involving multiple machines and jobs, each with specified processing times.
- Although both problems use permutation-based individual representations, fitness evaluation in the TSP involves merely summing the distances between coordinates. In contrast, fitness calculation in the Open Shop Problem is significantly more complex.

The knapsack and facility location problems were selected for the following reasons:

- They employ individual representations that differ from those of TSP.
- They utilize different crossover and mutation operations than those used in TSP.
- Unlike TSP, which provides only city coordinates, the knapsack problem involves values and weights for each item, along with a maximum weight constraint, and the facility location problem includes factors such as installation and transportation costs, making both problems more complex.

For each optimization problem, three distinct problem instances were prepared. Experiments were conducted 20 times for the open shop problem and 10 times each for the knapsack and facility location problems for each method. The methods were compared from the three perspectives:

- The mean and standard deviation across generations, visualized in graphs
- The optimality gap in the final generation, calculated as in the following equation:

$$\frac{|\text{optimal fitness} - \text{final generation fitness}|}{\text{optimal fitness}} \tag{2.1}$$

- The average number of generations required to reach the optimal solution

In all experiments, an elitism strategy was adopted, with the GA elite rate set to 50%. For the LLM-based methods, the elite rate was set to 100%, assuming that even low-fitness individuals would help the LLM learn trends in the solution space. Additionally, to assess the effectiveness of delivering problem settings to the LLM, a comparative experiment was conducted on the open shop problem with and without such settings. Unlike prior studies, which adjusted the LLM's temperature when no improvements were observed over several generations, this study made no such adjustments. The LLM model used was GPT-4o-2024-08-06.

The details of the three problems are explained below.

2.1.3.1 Open Shop Problem

The open shop problem is a type of scheduling problem. A closely related problem is the job shop scheduling problem (JSSP), which is defined as follows [35]. Given n jobs $J_1, J_2, ..., J_n$ and m machines $M_1, M_2, ..., M_m$, each operation O_{ij} corresponds to the processing of job J_i on machine M_j. Each machine can perform only one operation at a time, and once started, an operation cannot be interrupted. Each operation O_{ij} is processed for a specific duration p_{ij}, during which it exclusively occupies machine M_j. While the JSSP imposes precedence constraints on the order of operations within each job, the open shop problem removes these constraints. The objective is to construct a Gantt chart that minimizes the makespan—the total time required to complete all jobs—while satisfying all operational constraints.

Table 2.1 Parameters of open shop problem

Method	Setting	Population size	Generations
LMEA/OPRO	3×3	10	30
	4×4	10	50
	5×5	10	50
GA	3×3	50	30
	4×4	50	50
	5×5	50	50

Experiments were conducted for each method using three problem settings: three machines–three jobs, four machines–four jobs, and five machines–five jobs. In the three machines–three jobs instance, processing times were randomly generated, while the four machines–four jobs and five machines–five jobs instances utilized benchmark problems from the OR-Library [5]. Each method was tested 20 times per problem setting. The parameters for each experiment are summarized in Table 2.1. For methods using large language models (LLMs), the number of individuals was limited to 10 to reduce computational cost and prevent degradation in inference quality, unlike the larger population sizes typically used in GAs. The population size and number of generations of GA are set to 30 or 50 for all three combinatorial problems. These values were selected as they are commonly used in combinatorial optimization problems with relatively small search spaces.

2.1.3.2 Knapsack Problem

The knapsack problem involves maximizing value under constraints such as capacity or weight. This study focuses on the 0–1 knapsack problem. Given n items, each item is assigned a value v_i and weight w_i. A maximum knapsack capacity W is also provided. The objective is to maximize the total value of selected items without exceeding the capacity W. The 0–1 knapsack problem can be formulated as follows:

$$
\begin{aligned}
\text{Max} \quad & \sum_{i=1}^{n} v_i x_i \\
\text{s.t.} \quad & \sum_{i=1}^{n} w_i x_i \leq W, \\
& x_i \in \{0, 1\}, \\
& \forall i = 1, 2, \ldots, n,
\end{aligned}
$$

where $x_i = 1$ (0) indicates that item i is (not) selected. Two-point crossover is used in GA. The problem settings consisted of 10-item, 15-item, and 20-item instances. The 10- and 15-item instances were drawn from the dataset available at http://artemisa.unicauca.edu.co/~johnyortega/instances_01_KP/, while the 20-item

Table 2.2 Parameters of knapsack problem

Method	Setting	Population size	Generations
LMEA/OPRO	10 items	10	30
	15 items	10	30
	20 items	10	50
GA	10 items	50	30
	15 items	50	30
	25 items	50	50

instance was generated randomly. For each problem setting, experiments were conducted 10 times for each method. The parameters used in each experiment are summarized in Table 2.2.

2.1.3.3 Facility Location Problem

The facility location problem seeks to identify a facility placement strategy that minimizes total cost. While various formulations exist depending on how the objective function is defined, this experimental study focuses on the uncapacitated facility location problem (UFLP), the simplest form without capacity constraints. The problem is defined as follows [37]. Let $A = \{a_1, a_2, \ldots, a_m\}$ be the set of m facilities, and $B = \{b_1, b_2, ..., b_n\}$ the set of n customers. Each facility a_i incurs a fixed installation cost c_i, and each customer-facility pair (a_i, b_j) is associated with a transportation cost d_{ij}. Every customer must be served by exactly one facility, and since there are no capacity constraints, each facility has unlimited supply. The objective is to determine the facility configuration that minimizes the sum of installation and transportation costs. In the formulation, $x_i = 1$ indicates that facility a_i is installed, while $x_i = 0$ indicates otherwise. Similarly, $y_{ij} = 1$ denotes that customer b_j is assigned to facility a_i, $y_{ij} = 0$ otherwise. The formal definition of the problem is as follows:

$$
\begin{aligned}
\min \quad & \sum_{i=1}^{m} c_i x_i + \sum_{i=1}^{m} \sum_{j=1}^{n} d_{ij} y_{ij} \\
\text{s.t.} \quad & \sum_{i=1}^{m} y_{ij} = 1 \\
& y_{ij} \leq x_i \\
& x_i \in \{0, 1\} \\
& y_{ij} \in \{0, 1\} \\
& \forall i = 1, 2, \ldots, m \quad j = 1, 2, \ldots, n.
\end{aligned}
$$

Table 2.3 Parameters of facility location problem

Method	Setting	Population size	Generations
LMEA / OPRO	15×15	10	50
	20×20	10	50
	25×25	10	50
GA	15×15	30	50
	20×20	30	50
	25×25	30	50

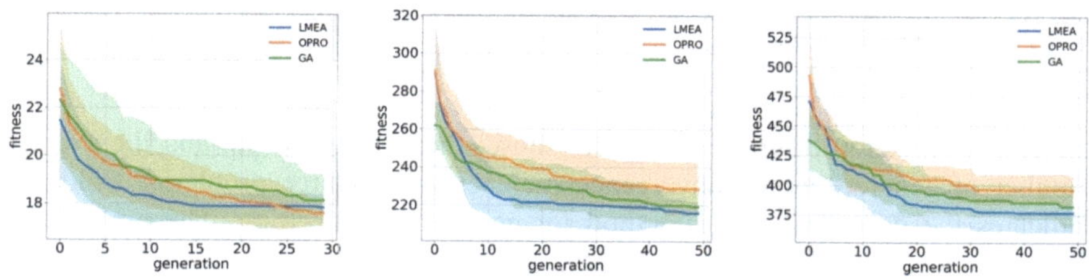

(a) 3 machines - 3 jobs (b) 4 machines - 4 jobs (c) 5 machines - 5 jobs

Fig. 2.2 Open shop problem. (**a**) Three machines–three jobs. (**b**) Four machines–four jobs. (**c**) Five machines–five jobs

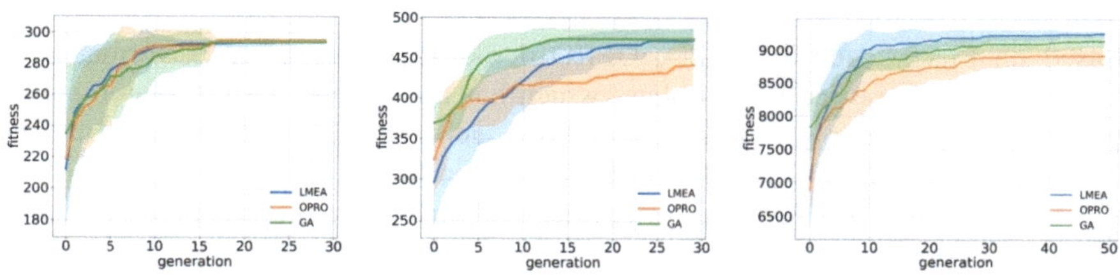

(a) 10 items (b) 15 items (c) 20 items

Fig. 2.3 Knapsack problem. (**a**) 10 items. (**b**) 15 items. (**c**) 20 items

The problem settings were conducted for facility and customer counts of (15, 15), (20, 20), and (25, 25). Each problem was generated by randomly assigning facility installation costs in the range $[10, 400]$ and transportation costs in the range $[1, 200]$. A two-point crossover was used in the GA. For each problem setting, experiments were conducted 10 times for each method. The parameters for each experiment are shown in Table 2.3.

2.1.4 Results

Figures 2.2, 2.3, and 2.4 show a graph plotting the average fitness of each generation. The blue, orange, and green lines represent LMEA, OPRO, and GA, respectively. These figures correspond to the open shop problem, the knapsack problem, and

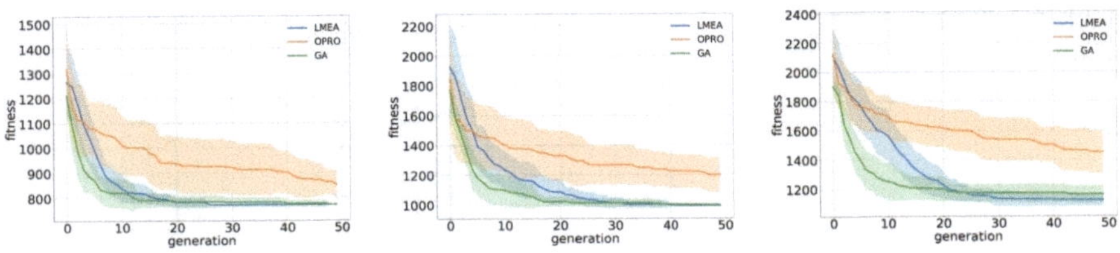

(a) 15 facilities - 15 customers (b) 20 facilities - 20 customers (c) 25 facilities - 25 customers

Fig. 2.4 Facility location problem. (**a**) 15 facilities–15 customers. (**b**) 20 facilities–20 customers. (**c**) 25 facilities–25 customers

the facility location problem. Table 2.4 shows the optimality gap and the average number of generations to convergence for each of the three problems. Bold text indicates the best-performing method for each problem setting. The numbers in parentheses next to the required generations indicate how many times the optimal solution was reached.

2.1.4.1 Open Shop Problem

Based on Fig. 2.2 and Table 2.4, OPRO demonstrated superior performance in the three-machine three-job problem, which has a relatively narrow search space. However, in broader search spaces, LMEA achieved the highest performance. Furthermore, in all problem settings, LMEA outperformed GA.

The reason for LMEA's superiority across all problem settings is possibly due to its ability to perform more efficient crossover operations compared to conventional sequence-based methods such as partially mapped crossover (PMX) [13, sec.1.8.2], cyclic crossover (CX) [22], and order crossover (OX) [8], by leveraging the LLM's understanding of the problem-specific solution space. On the other hand, OPRO tends to generate offspring that differ from their parents due to the nature of the prompts, thereby enhancing population diversity and leading to favorable results in problems with a narrow search space.

2.1.4.2 Knapsack Problem

Figure 2.3 shows that all three methods reached the convergence phase at approximately the same number of generations for the 10-item problem. In the 15-item problem, GA slightly outperformed LMEA in fitness at generation 50, although the difference was marginal. However, LMEA exhibited slower convergence compared to other problem settings. For the 20-item problem, LMEA achieved the best performance. Additionally, OPRO showed a tendency for decreased performance as the search space expanded.

Table 2.4 Optimality gap and the number of generations

	Optimality gap (%)			# Generations (# Successes)		
Problem	LMEA	OPRO	GA	LMEA	OPRO	GA
Open Shop(3 × 3)	5.00 ± 3.35	**3.53 ± 2.88**	6.76 ± 6.47	9.40 ± 10.52 (5)	15.5 ± 7.43 (8)	10.00 ± 7.74 (4)
Open Shop(4 × 4)	**11.90 ± 3.23**	18.47 ± 7.20	13.63 ± 5.00	N/A (0)	N/A (0)	N/A (0)
Open Shop(5 × 5)	**25.60 ± 5.47**	32.00 ± 4.00	27.40 ± 5.87	N/A (0)	N/A (0)	N/A (0)
Knapsack(10 items)	0.24 ± 0.71	**0.00 ± 0.00**	0.31 ± 0.31	15.44 ± 8.20 (9)	27.00 ± 8.27 (10)	21.40 ± 7.44 (5)
Knapsack(15 items)	1.77 ± 3.27	8.13 ± 5.60	**1.48 ± 2.70**	19.17 ± 6.11 (6)	39.00 ± 0.00 (1)	9.14 ± 3.24 (7)
Knapsack(20 items)	**0.28 ± 0.43**	3.94 ± 1.71	4.23 ± 1.10	27.00 ± 8.27 (7)	N/A (0)	24.00 ± 0.00 (1)
FLP(15 × 15)	**0.00 ± 0.00**	10.34 ± 7.47	**0.00 ± 0.00**	17.80 ± 6.76 (10)	50.00 ± 0.00 (1)	16.90 ± 15.69 (10)
FLP(20 × 20)	**0.00 ±0.00**	17.14 ± 12.06	0.48 ± 1.07	27.20 ± 7.84 (10)	N/A (0)	25.88 ± 15.54 (8)
FLP(25 × 25)	**4.41 ± 3.96**	34.84 ± 14.07	8.21 ± 5.78	26.33 ± 6.35 (3)	N/A (0)	36.00 ± 0.00 (1)

The reason LMEA performed well in the 10- and 20-item problems is likely similar to the observation in the open shop problem: The LLM may have accomplished more efficient crossover operations than two-point crossover by leveraging an understanding of the problem-specific solution space. As for the slower convergence of LMEA in the 15-item problem, this may be attributed to the use of decimal weights and profits, rather than the integer values used in the other settings. Since LLMs are known to have limited mathematical reasoning capabilities, they may struggle to outperform GA on problems involving decimal values.

2.1.4.3 Facility Location Problem

Figure 2.4 shows that LMEA achieved the highest fitness in the final generation in all problem settings. However, for problems with narrower search spaces, such as the 15 facilities–15 customers and 20 facilities–20 customers instances, the performance differences among the methods were minimal. Similar to the knapsack problem, OPRO exhibited a decline in performance as the search space expanded.

The consistent superior performance of LMEA across all problem settings is due, as previously discussed, to the LLM's ability to comprehend the problem-specific solution space and perform more effective crossover operations accordingly.

2.1.5 How LLMs Improve GA Search

The experimental results in this section demonstrated that, compared to the conventional GA, the proposed LMEA achieves superior performance across various optimization problems. In the case of the open shop problem, despite its complexity and fitness evaluation more complex than that of the TSP addressed in previous studies, LMEA outperformed GA. This suggests that large language models (LLMs) may be able to identify common characteristics and patterns among high-fitness individuals from sequence data. Additionally, LMEA consistently performed strongly on both the knapsack problem and the facility location problem, regardless of differences in individual representation. These results suggest that LMEA is an effective optimization method irrespective of the type of solution representation.

To verify the hypothesis that the LLM may comprehend problem-specific solution spaces, a comparative experiment was conducted using the four-machine four-job setting of the open shop problem, with and without the problem description in the prompt. Figure 2.5 shows the result of this experiment. The blue curve shows the case described in the problem, while the orange curve shows the case without it. Table 2.4 compares the optimality gaps between the two conditions. Although no significant differences in fitness were observed at the 50th generation, the performance was better when the problem description was included in the prompt. In addition, convergence was reached more rapidly when the problem setting was provided.

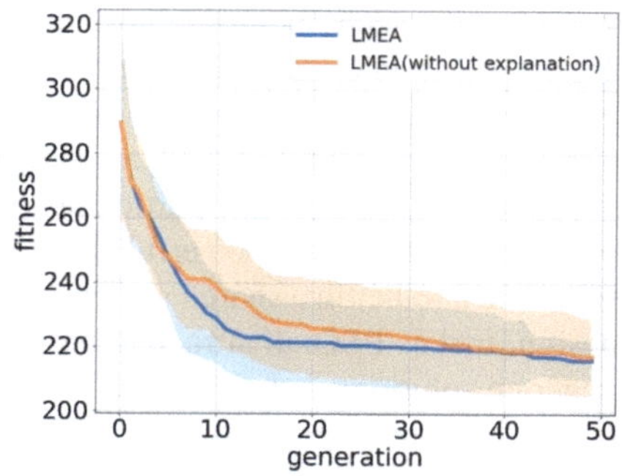

Fig. 2.5 Differences in graph based on the presence or absence of problem formulation

Table 2.5 Performance comparison for four machines–four jobs

GA	LMEA	LMEA (without explanation)
13.63 ± 5.00	11.90 ± 3.23	**12.49 ± 6.33**

Furthermore, it can be stated that LMEA does not solve the combinatorial optimization problems simply because the LLM possesses prior knowledge of them. Table 2.5 compares the performance of LMEA without problem description and GA on a four-machine four-job open shop problem. The table shows that LMEA outperforms GA in terms of optimality gap. This result provides evidence that the LLM's effectiveness is not merely due to prior familiarity with the problem, but rather its ability to generalize across problem structures.

The superior performance of LMEA compared to OPRO can be attributed to fundamental differences in their prompt design. While OPRO does not use any characteristics of parent individuals during offspring generation, LMEA inherits features from them. Given that LLMs possess strong reasoning capabilities to identify common patterns among high-fitness individuals, leveraging this information in LMEA is likely to improve its performance.

2.2 LLMs as Particle Swarm Optimization

2.2.1 Metaheuristics via LLMs

Large language models (LLMs) have recently gathered attention for their capacity to directly address optimization tasks by formulating problems in natural language and utilizing the LLM's reasoning abilities to generate candidate solutions [19, 20, 41, 42]. Compared with traditional techniques that require hand-engineered operators or domain-specific expertise, LLM-based approaches can flexibly encode search strategies, constraints, and heuristics via prompts, thereby offering a more generalizable mechanism for controlling the optimization process.

Although such methods have demonstrated promise, prior work often integrates LLMs into existing frameworks without explicitly leveraging *swarm intelligence* algorithms. The swarm intelligence methods naturally lend themselves to multi-agent coordination and can benefit from LLM-enhanced communication or decision-making [40]. In particular, particle swarm optimization (PSO) [14, 31] provides a simple yet powerful framework in which particles cooperate and learn from one another in a shared search space. This simplicity, alongside its agent-based design, makes PSO an attractive basis for investigating how LLMs might guide or generate solutions in a collective, multi-agent setting.

In this section, we introduce *language model particle swarm optimization (LMPSO)*, a novel approach that explicitly incorporates an LLM into PSO by treating each particle's update step as a prompt-driven process [33]. Rather than employing problem-specific update formulas, LMPSO constructs structured prompts, which encode velocity, position, and other contextual information, and feeds them to an LLM to obtain new candidate solutions. This design extends PSO into a hyper-heuristic framework, in which an LLM can dynamically generate or refine heuristics without requiring extensive handcrafted operators [6, 9].

One key advantage of LLM-based optimization is its capacity to handle solution representations that may be cumbersome or infeasible in standard PSO pipelines. For instance, while PSO was initially designed for continuous optimization problems, applying it to combinatorial problems like the traveling salesman problem (TSP) has traditionally required developing velocities, directions between particles' positions, and tailored update rules [39]. LMPSO simplifies this process by using natural language prompts, eliminating the need for manually crafted operators and encoding schemes.

Additionally, LMPSO functions as a hyper-heuristics, enabling the improvement of existing heuristics through a prompt-driven search, as demonstrated in prior research on evolving heuristic strategies [7, 30]. Also, LLMs' ability to understand the context of a given problem can be used to generate effective solutions, particularly for problems with rich data, such as symbolic regression.

The goal here is not to compare solution diversity with existing LLM-based optimizers, but to highlight how explicitly incorporating an LLM into a multi-agent, swarm intelligence framework can expand the range of solvable problems and the forms of final solutions. Through experiments across both combinatorial and natural language tasks, we demonstrate LMPSO's effectiveness in addressing problems that require flexible or context-rich representations.

2.2.2 Language Model Particle Swarm Optimization (LMPSO)

In this section, we introduce *language model particle swarm optimization (LMPSO)*, which leverages an interactive LLM to update each particle's position in the particle swarm optimization algorithm.

Algorithm 2.1 Language model particle swarm optimization

1: **Input:** Optimization Problem T, Objective function f, number of particles N, maximum generations G
2: **Output:** The best solution g_{best}
3: Initialize the positions x_i^t of N particles randomly within the search space
4: Initialize the velocities v_i^t of N particles with a prompt like "Generate a position randomly"
5: **for** $t = 1$ to G **do**
6:     **for** each particle i in the swarm **do**
7:         **if** $f(x_i^t)$ is better than $f(pbest_i)$ **then**
8:             Update $pbest_i \leftarrow x_i^t$
9:         **end if**
10:         **if** $f(pbest_i)$ is better than $f(gbest)$ **then**
11:             Update $gbest \leftarrow pbest_i$
12:         **end if**
13:         $v_i^{t+1} \leftarrow$ Construct with T, $pbest_i$ and $gbest$
14:         *prompt* $\leftarrow$ Construct with T, v_i^t, x_i^t, and v_i^{t+1}
15:         Query the LLM with prompt to generate a new position x_i'
16:         **if** x_i' satisfies constraints **then**
17:             Update $x_i^{t+1} \leftarrow x_i'$
18:         **else**
19:             Retry up to a fixed number of times or reinitialize x_i^{t+1} randomly if retries exceed the limit
20:         **end if**
21:     **end for**
22: **end for**
23: **return** $gbest$

LMPSO, as shown in Algorithm 2.1, extends standard PSO by using the LLM to update solutions through prompts that define each particle's velocity. The optimization process begins with the initialization of particle positions, generated either randomly or by the LLM, and velocities represented as prompts such as "Generate a position randomly" (see lines 3–4). The main loop iterates for up to G generations (line 5), where each particle's objective value $f(x_i^t)$ is evaluated to update the personal best $pbest_i$ and global best $gbest$ (lines 7–12).

At each generation, a new velocity v_i^{t+1} is constructed based on the problem T, $pbest_i$, and $gbest$ (line 13), and a meta-prompt incorporating T, v_i^t, x_i^t, and v_i^{t+1} guides the LLM to generate a candidate solution $x\prime_i$ (lines 14–15). If $x\prime_i$ satisfies constraints, it becomes the new position; otherwise, retries or random reinitialization maintains diversity (lines 16–19). This process continues until the maximum generations G, after which the global best $gbest$ is returned as the optimal solution (line 23).

The core difference between LMPSO and standard PSO only lies in the generation of the following position x_i^{t+1} in line 15. Still, it fundamentally shifts how solutions are updated within PSO, making the method more flexible and adaptable to a broader range of problems.

The algorithm complexity of LMPSO can be represented as $O(N \cdot G \cdot C)$, where N is the number of particles, G is the maximum number of generations, and C is the complexity of the LLM inference process for generating a new solution.

An interactive LLM is a large language model designed to facilitate natural, multi-turn conversations [23, 36]. In this setup, the system defines the overall interaction policy and response style, the user provides instructions or queries, and the assistant (LLM) generates relevant responses. In LMPSO, each particle acts as the "assistant," receiving optimization instructions and producing a corresponding solution. To enable this process, we construct a structured prompt called a *meta-prompt*. The original concept of the meta-prompt was introduced by Yang et al. [41], where it serves as a guiding template for the LLM to generate solutions. In LMPSO, the meta-prompt is designed to follow the PSO paradigm, incorporating the following components:

1. **Description of the Optimization Problem**
   A brief description is provided to the system that indicates the nature of the optimization task and the expected direction of solution generation.
2. **Inertia Term** v_i^t.
   By indicating how the current position was generated (i.e., its velocity), we capture the concept of inertia. This is specified in the user's instructions.
3. **Current Position** x_i^t.
   The current position serves as a reference for producing the next position. This is conveyed in the assistant's response.
4. **Direction for Generating the Next Position** v_i^{t+1}
   The velocity here incorporates information about the personal best and global best, thereby guiding the generation of the next position. This directive is included in the user's instructions.

As solutions are updated, the meta-prompt is also revised, thereby adjusting the guidance each particle receives in its search for the optimal solution.

Figure 2.6 illustrates an example of the meta-prompt for the traveling salesman problem (TSP).

In this example, the coordinates of the cities are provided as system content, as shown in the blue box in Fig. 2.6. The user's instruction is represented as the green chat bubble, and the assistant's response is shown in the gray chat bubble. The LLM generates the following position based on the interaction between the user and the assistant, as represented by the orange chat bubble.

2.2.3 Experiments

We used `meta-llama/Llama-3.1-8B-Instruct` as the large language model (LLM) for solution generation in this study. Llama is an open-source LLM developed by Meta, and Llama-3.1-8B-Instruct is its instruct-tuned variant [38]. To maintain output diversity, we set the LLM's temperature parameter to 0.9 throughout

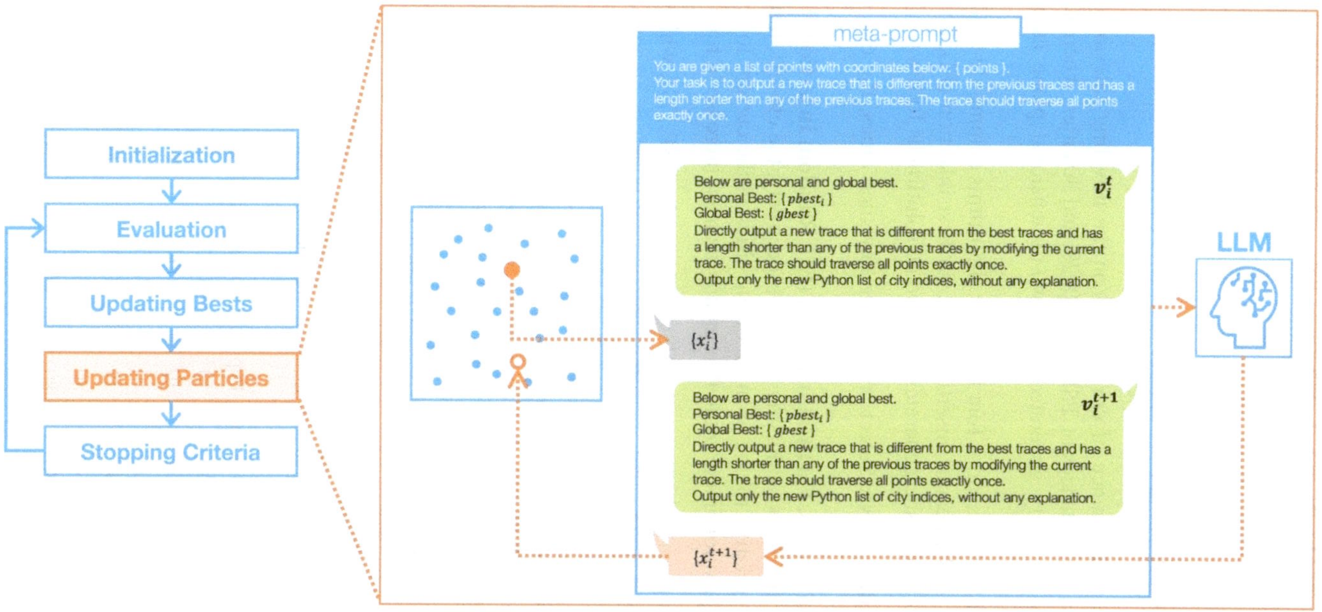

Fig. 2.6 An overview of LMPSO. The meta-prompt shown in the figure is an example of the traveling salesman problem. The components in { } represent the dynamic parts of the prompt that are updated based on the algorithm's current state

the experiments. Because LMPSO's runtime can grow significantly due to the LLM's inference speed, we chose suitable values for the maximum number of generations and the swarm size for each problem to avoid excessively long execution times.

2.2.3.1 Combinatorial Optimization

We evaluated the performance of our method on the traveling salesman problem (TSP). We tested three instances of TSP with 10, 20, and 30 cities, where each city's coordinates were randomly generated in a two-dimensional plane using integer values in the range 0–100.

We compared LMPSO against four heuristic algorithms commonly used for TSP: nearest neighbor (NN), nearest insertion (NI), farthest insertion (FI), and random insertion (RI). Each heuristic generates a candidate solution as follows:

- **Nearest Neighbor (NN):** Select, among the unvisited cities, the one closest to the current city.
- **Nearest Insertion (NI), Farthest Insertion (FI), Random Insertion (RI):** From the unvisited cities, choose the city that is, respectively, the closest, farthest, or a random choice relative to one or more of the cities in the current tour, and then insert it at the position in the route that incurs the least increase in total distance.

In addition, we compared LMPSO to a PSO tailored for TSP [39], which encodes particle velocity as a set of swap operations and updates positions by applying these operations.

Because generating a single solution via the LLM is computationally expensive, we set the maximum number of generations to 100 and used 10 particles for LMPSO as shown in Table 2.6. For the sake of fair comparison (i.e., matching the total number of objective function evaluations), the designed PSO also employed 10 particles and 100 generations. We conducted experiments using five different random city layouts for each problem size (10, 20, and 30 cities).

Table 2.6 Experimental settings and time costs for solving each problem using LMPSO. Time cost is reported as the mean and standard deviation over multiple runs, with the number of runs shown in parentheses

Problem	Max gen.	Pop. size	# of Evals.	Max Tokens	Time cost (s)
TSP (10 cities)	100	10	1000	50	681.0 ± 7.0 (5)
TSP (20 cities)	100	10	1000	100	1411 ± 26 (5)
TSP (30 cities)	100	10	1000	150	3340 ± 150 (5)
Heuristic improvement	40	25	1000	1000	34,900 ± 0 (1)
Symbolic regression (dim-2)	50	80	4000	200	5810 ± 970 (5)
Symbolic regression (dim-5)	50	80	4000	200	5830 ± 540 (5)
Symbolic regression (dim-10)	50	80	4000	200	5760 ± 680 (5)

Table 2.7 Results on TSP instances

Method	Optimality gap (%)		
	10 cities	20 cities	30 cities
NN	0.11 ± 0.09	0.14 ± 0.05	0.20 ± 0.07
NI	0.06 ± 0.04	0.14 ± 0.06	0.16 ± 0.06
FI	$\mathbf{0.00 \pm 0.00}$	$\mathbf{0.01 \pm 0.01}$	$\mathbf{0.05 \pm 0.03}$
RI	0.85 ± 0.08	1.74 ± 0.17	2.25 ± 0.36
PSO	0.08 ± 0.08	0.90 ± 0.07	1.39 ± 0.07
LMPSO	0.02 ± 0.02	0.42 ± 0.12	0.73 ± 0.05

2.2.3.2 Results

Table 2.7 summarizes the results for TSP with 10, 20, and 30 cities. Each algorithm's performance was evaluated using five different random city layouts, and we report the mean and standard deviation of the optimality gap relative to the global optimum (computed by the Concorde TSP solver [2]).

As shown in Table 2.7, LMPSO achieves competitive performance on the 10-city instance, ranking second only to FI. Notably, it outperforms the TSP-specific PSO across all problem sizes, suggesting that LMPSO is effective even for combinatorial optimization. However, for 20-city and 30-city instances, LMPSO's performance is lower than that of heuristics such as NN, NI, and FI.

The time taken for each problem is shown in Table 2.6. The time required for the problem increases with the number of cities, i.e., with the 30-city instance taking the most time.

2.2.4 Heuristics Improvement

One advantage of using an LLM is the ability to treat natural language as the search space. In fact, many studies have attempted to generate better programs using LLMs [7, 30]. In this experiment, we investigated whether LMPSO could improve existing TSP heuristic algorithms.

2.2.4.1 Experimental Setup

We treated the Python implementations of NN, NI, FI, and RI as strings representing the heuristics. We randomly chose one of these four as the initial solution for each particle and then ran LMPSO to improve the heuristic. We tested five different 100-city TSP instances and used the total distance obtained from each heuristic as the objective function value. After exploring several combinations of maximum generations and swarm sizes, we found that 40 generations and 25 particles (i.e., 1000 total solutions) were sufficient to achieve good performance while meeting time constraints. We chose 1000 total solutions to ensure a wide variety of heuristics could be generated without excessively long runtimes.

2.2.4.2 Heuristic Generated by LMPSO

By running LMPSO on the Python implementations of NN, NI, FI, and RI (treated as string-based heuristics), we obtained a hybrid heuristic that combines several decision criteria and random operations. The resulting algorithm operates as follows:

1. Create `tour`, initially containing only city 0, and place the remaining cities into `remaining`.
2. Repeatedly insert unvisited cities into the tour, using the following decision patterns:
   - **Pattern A**: If the x coordinate of the last city in the tour is greater than the global minimum x value:
     - `farthest` = the city among unvisited ones whose distance to any city in the tour is maximal.
     - `farthest_from_center` = in practice, the city closest to the tour center (`tour_center`).
     - Determine which city to insert based on angles and distance to the center.
   - **Pattern B**: Otherwise (i.e., if the last city's x coordinate is not larger than the global minimum x value):
     - `nearest_to_median` = the city closest to the center.
     - `farthest_from_median` = in practice, the city whose distance from the last city is maximal.
     - Decide which city to insert by comparing distances to the center.
3. Insert the chosen city at the position in the tour that minimizes additional travel distance.
4. Perform random partial reversals (`tour[::-1]`) or partial rotations (moving some leading or trailing cities) with a certain probability to avoid local optima.
5. Repeat these steps until all cities have been inserted into the tour.

Starting from the existing heuristics (NN, NI, FI, RI), LMPSO produced a new heuristic that mixes prior elements with new elements such as angles, center-based calculations, random reversals, and partial rotations. While this resulted in a unique approach, the generated code sometimes exhibited inconsistencies between variable names and their behavior, as well as potentially redundant or random operations whose direct impact on overall performance remained unclear.

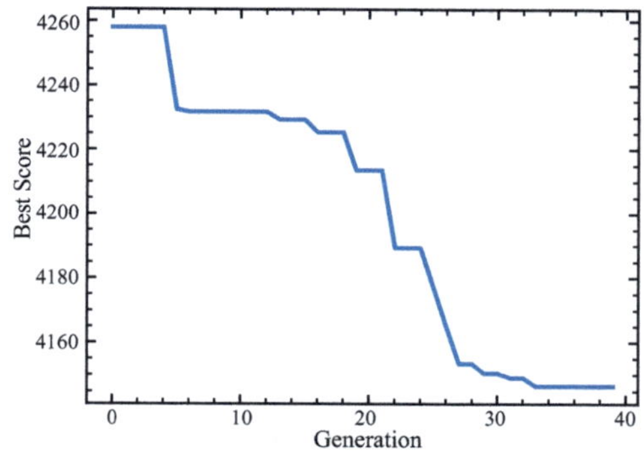

Fig. 2.7 Search process of LMPSO for heuristic improvement on the TSP. The vertical axis represents the total travel distance obtained by applying the current best heuristic to five distinct 100-city TSP instances

2.2.4.3 Search Process

Figure 2.7 illustrates how LMPSO explores and refines heuristics over multiple iterations. Solutions generated early in the search often featured intricate branching conditions, insertion strategies, or elements such as a "center" or "density." However, except for the significant improvement in generation 5, these initial approaches failed to gradually improve the heuristic, as shown in Fig. 2.7.

During the mid-phase of the search, LMPSO continued to refine branching conditions and methods for determining insertion locations. Notably, angle-based criteria began appearing in some solutions around generation 21. By approximately generation 25, techniques such as partial reversals, tour rotations, and angle-based strategies emerged in the best-performing solutions. These techniques persisted into the final stages of the search, which involved further refinement of branching criteria, insertion methods, and parameter tuning.

Ultimately, LMPSO identified its best solution at generation 33. The improvements leading to this point included detailed angle-based logic and route-modification operations, which had gradually evolved from the foundational strategies of earlier generations.

2.2.4.4 Comparison with Other Methods

Table 2.8 shows the results of applying the heuristics generated by LMPSO and other baseline heuristics to five 100-city TSP instances. The optimality gap values represent the mean and standard deviation across these five test instances. As shown in Table 2.8, the LMPSO-generated heuristic achieved the best performance among all compared methods.

Table 2.8 Results of improving heuristics

Method	Optimality gap (%) 100 cities
NN	0.28 ± 0.09
NI	0.21 ± 0.04
FI	0.07 ± 0.01
RI	5.69 ± 0.37
PSO	4.60 ± 0.23
LMPSO	$\mathbf{0.06 \pm 0.02}$

2.2.5 Symbolic Regression

2.2.5.1 Experimental Setups

Symbolic regression aims to discover an optimal mathematical expression that fits a given set of data points. In the experiment of the combinatorial optimization problem, the solutions generated by the LLM are a sequence of numbers that hold little inherent meaning on their own. However, in symbolic regression, the solutions are mathematical expressions that have a clear structure and meaning. By testing LMPSO on symbolic regression tasks, we sought to assess its effectiveness in solving problems with structured solutions.

For LMPSO, the meta-prompt included a description of the symbolic regression task, a random subset of 20 data points, instructions to produce diverse expressions, and a note that shorter expressions were preferable. The random subset of 20 data points was included in the prompt to guide the LLM in generating expressions that fit the data. The initial solutions were expressions generated by prompting the LLM with the same problem description and data points.

Genetic programming (GP) is widely used for solving this task [4], as it represents expressions as trees that evolve. We compared LMPSO with the `gplearn` GP library on symbolic regression tasks from the Penn machine learning benchmarks (PMLB) [29], focusing on black-box functions with 2 to 10 dimensions. Because the proper functional form is unknown, we measured performance using the mean absolute error (MAE).

After testing various combinations of maximum generations and swarm sizes (to achieve 4000 total evaluations), we found that 50 generations and 80 particles provided a reasonable balance between solution diversity and convergence. For a fair comparison, we also set GP's maximum generations to 50 and its population size to 80, resulting in the same total number of evaluations as LMPSO. We adopted the typical GP objective function (MAE) and included the following operators: addition, subtraction, multiplication, division, log, sqrt, abs, neg, inv, max, and min. In the meta-prompt for LMPSO, we also included instructions to use these operators, if necessary, to fit the data. Finally, we set the `gplearn` parameters to a crossover probability of 0.7 and a mutation probability of 0.1. We ran five trials for each problem instance to evaluate each method's performance.

Table 2.9 Results for symbolic regression tasks

Dataset name	Dim	R^2	
		LMPSO	GP
vineyard	2	**0.68 ± 0.05**	0.42 ± 0.11
analcatdata_apnea2	3	−0.07 ± 0.00	− 0.07 ± 0.00
ESL	4	**0.78 ± 0.02**	0.70 ± 0.02
cloud	5	**0.85 ± 0.02**	0.71 ± 0.03
machine_cpu	6	**0.87 ± 0.06**	0.61 ± 0.17
pm10	7	**0.16 ± 0.03**	− 0.13 ± 0.14
house_8L	8	**0.03 ± 0.16**	− 1.33 ± 0.69
BNG_lowbwt	9	**0.06 ± 0.50**	− 0.62 ± 0.61
SWD	10	**0.26 ± 0.05**	− 0.17 ± 0.21

2.2.5.2 Comparison of Results

We compared LMPSO and GP on symbolic regression tasks from PMLB (2D–10D). Both methods were run five times, and we report the mean and standard deviation of the coefficient of determination (R^2) for the final solutions in Table 2.9. A value of R^2 close to 1 indicates high predictive accuracy. From Table 2.9, LMPSO produced expressions with higher R^2 values than those from GP, indicating superior modeling ability on most test problems.

2.2.5.3 Search Process

We analyzed the results for the 9D dataset `1193_BNG_lowbwt`, focusing on the best MAE and expression length during the optimization process. Figure 2.8 compares

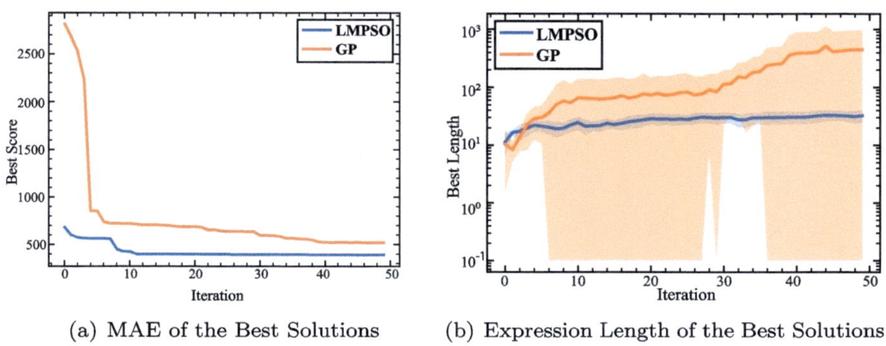

Fig. 2.8 Comparison of LMPSO and GP over five runs for `1193_BNG_lowbwt` (9D). "Best Score" represents the mean absolute error of the cumulative best solution, while "Best Length" indicates the length of the best solution at each generation. The shaded area represents the standard deviation, with a minimum of 0.1 set to accommodate logarithmic scaling in (**b**). (**a**) MAE of the best solutions. (**b**) Expression length of the best solutions

the performances of LMPSO and GP throughout the optimization. Since a lower MAE indicates a better solution, LMPSO consistently outperformed GP from the initial generation and maintained a lower MAE throughout the search, as shown in Fig. 2.8a. Shorter expressions are generally associated with better generalization in symbolic regression. The best solutions generated by GP were significantly longer than those produced by LMPSO, highlighting LMPSO's advantages in this regard (Fig. 2.8b). Furthermore, Fig. 2.8b shows that the length of the best solutions generated by LMPSO remained relatively stable across generations and different runs, demonstrating LMPSO's ability to produce concise solutions with shorter expression lengths consistently.

2.2.5.4 Generated Solutions

Table 2.10 presents the solutions generated by LMPSO for the 2D dataset `vineyard`. As shown in Table 2.10, generation 1 produces a very simple expression that employs $|x_1 - 10|$. Subsequently, from generations 5 to 10, the model begins incorporating squared terms, such as $(x_1 - 11)^2$, further to adjust the error with respect to the data (for instance, $\frac{(x_1-11)^2}{5}$ appears at generation 10). Between generations 15 and 30, additional terms related to x_0, such as $(x_0 - 3)$ and $(x_0 - 4)^2$,

Table 2.10 Best solutions for the generation of LMPSO on the 2D dataset `vineyard`

Generation	Best solution
1	$20 - 2 \cdot \lvert x_1 - 10\rvert$
5	$20 + (x_0 - 3) - (\lvert x_1 - 10\rvert + 0.5)$
10	$20 + (x_0 - 3) - \left(\frac{(x_1-11)^2}{5} + 0.1\right)$
15	$20 + (x_0 - 3) - 0.4 \cdot \left(\frac{(x_1-11)^2}{5} + (x_0 - 4)^2\right)$
20	$20 + (x_0 - 3) - 0.46 \cdot \left(\frac{(x_1-11)^2}{5} + (x_0 - 4)^2\right) + \frac{x_1-10}{100}$
25	$20 + (x_0 - 3) - 0.457 \cdot \left(\frac{(x_1-11)^2}{5} + (x_0 - 4)^2\right) + 0.025 \cdot (x_1 - 10)$
30	$20 + (x_0 - 3) - 0.455 \cdot \left(\frac{(x_1-11)^2}{5} + (x_0 - 4)^2\right) + 0.05 \cdot (x_1 - 10)$
35	$20 + (x_0 - 3) - 0.45 \cdot \left(\frac{(x_1-11)^2}{5} + (x_0 - 4)^2\right) + 0.05 \cdot (x_1 - 10 + \sin(x_1 - 10))$
40	$20 + (x_0 - 3) - 0.45 \cdot \left(\frac{(x_1-11)^2}{5} + (x_0 - 4)^2\right) + 0.525 \cdot \sin(x_1 - 11)$
45	$20 + (x_0 - 3) - 0.45 \cdot \left(\frac{(x_1-11)^2}{5} + (x_0 - 4)^2\right) + 0.55 \cdot (\sin(x_1 - 10.5) + 0.1 \cdot \sin(x_1 - 10.55))$
50	$20 + (x_0 - 3) - 0.446 \cdot \left(\frac{(x_1-11)^2}{5} + (x_0 - 4)^2\right) + 0.576 \cdot \sin(x_1 - 10.51) + 0.084 \cdot \sin(x_1 - 10.54)$

are introduced, reflecting interactions among multiple variables and indicating further parameter fine-tuning. Moreover, starting from generation 35, sin terms are introduced to account for periodic variations and capture subtle changes in the data. By generation 50, the algorithm yields a more advanced expression that combines multiple sin terms (e.g., $\sin(x_1 - 10.51)$, $\sin(x_1 - 10.54)$), demonstrating that LMPSO thoroughly explores the solution space while increasing the model's complexity. The tendency to generate simple expressions at the beginning and gradually increase complexity is consistent with the behavior observed in the search process for symbolic regression tasks.

2.2.6 How LMPSO Integrates PSO and LLMs

In this section, we introduced *LMPSO*, an optimization method that directly employs an interactive large language model (LLM) to generate solutions within the particle swarm optimization (PSO) framework. We applied LMPSO to three types of problems: the traveling salesman problem (TSP), heuristic-improvement tasks (where solutions are treated as strings in a natural language search space), and symbolic regression.

Based on our experimental results, we highlight several key observations regarding LMPSO:

- **An Extension of PSO Using LLMs.** While traditional PSO often requires problem-specific designs (e.g., tailoring velocity updates and solution representations), LMPSO preserves the PSO framework while leveraging prompt engineering to adapt to diverse tasks. In other words, *simply changing the prompt* allows LMPSO to tackle different optimization problems, including those involving natural language solution representations, which would be impractical in standard PSO.
- **Challenges for Large-Scale Problems.** As in prior research, using an LLM to optimize large-scale solution representations directly proved difficult. However, our experiments suggest that converting combinatorial tasks into heuristic-improvement problems enables LMPSO to effectively generate solutions without directly manipulating extensive solution representations.
- **Effectiveness as a Hyper-Heuristic.** When applied to TSP heuristics, LMPSO demonstrated its effectiveness as a hyper-heuristic by generating high-performing hybrid heuristics. By combining elements from multiple existing heuristics with novel components (e.g., center- or angle-based operations) absent in traditional methods, LMPSO demonstrated its ability to extend beyond @human-designed approaches and create innovative solutions.
- **Performance in Symbolic Regression.** In symbolic regression experiments, LMPSO achieved higher coefficients of determination than a standard genetic programming (GP) library. By including prompts that encourage shorter expressions, LMPSO generated concise yet accurate solutions.

2.3 Large Language Models for AutoML

2.3.1 AutoML-Zero

In recent years, machine learning techniques, including deep learning, have achieved remarkable results across diverse fields such as image recognition, natural language processing, and speech recognition. The performance of these methods heavily depends on the network architecture, learning algorithm, and hyperparameter settings. Traditionally, designing these factors required specialized knowledge and extensive trial and error. Automated machine learning (AutoML [12]) has attracted attention as a potential solution to this problem. AutoML is a framework that automatically explores optimal models and learning methods, with representative subfields including neural architecture search (NAS) and hyperparameter optimization. Indeed, in domains such as image classification [27, 43] and object detection [43], models automatically generated by AutoML have outperformed human-designed ones.

AutoML-Zero [26] is an automated machine learning framework that minimizes artificial constraints without the assumption of existing learning algorithms or model structures, which conventional AutoML methods have taken for granted. This method aims to evolve model structures and learning procedures from scratch by combining primitive operators such as arithmetic operations, matrix manipulations, and probabilistic processing (Fig. 2.9). This approach enables the exploration of any machine learning algorithm expressible as an operator combination, while minimizing human design bias.

Each individual in AutoML-Zero corresponds to a single machine learning model and is represented as a program composed of predefined operators. The program is divided into three functional components: *Setup*, *Predict*, and *Learn* (see Fig. 2.10). *Setup* is executed only once before training and corresponds to hyperparameter tuning in conventional machine learning. *Predict* is executed when

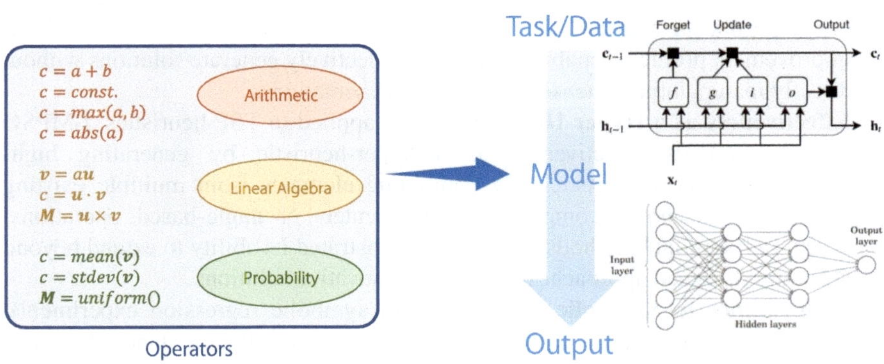

Fig. 2.9 AutoML-Zero

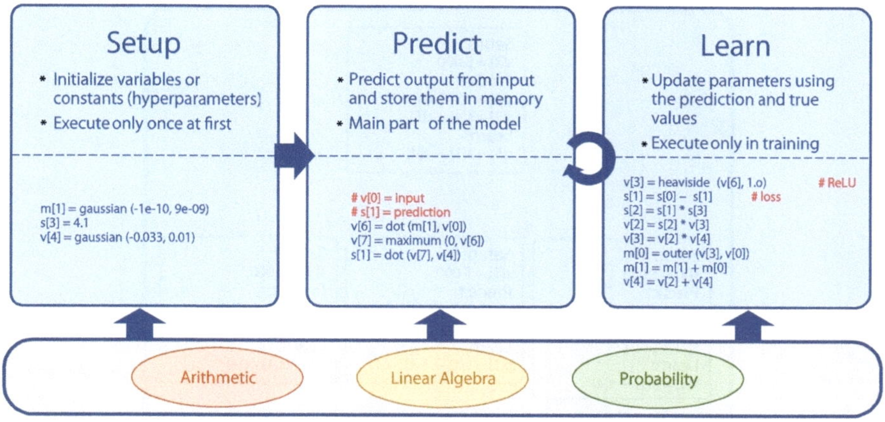

Fig. 2.10 Three functions of AutoML-Zero

generating output from input and plays a central role as the model structure. *Learn* is executed only during training, following *Predict*. It is designed to update the values of variables used in *Predict* according to the output from *Predict* and the true values. The operators constituting these three components perform computations by acting on scalars, vectors, and matrices stored in shared memory. This design enables diverse representations, not limited to neural networks, including algorithms such as linear regression and gradient descent methods.

AutoML-Zero employs exploration by means of evolutionary algorithms called "Regularized Evolution [27]." Initial individuals start from empty code containing no operators. During evolution, the oldest individual is removed first. Subsequently, based on tournament selection [10], the best-performing individual is selected, and mutations are applied to that individual. Three types of mutations exist (see Fig. 2.11): (1) insertion or deletion of operators at random positions, (2) random replacement within an entire function, and (3) modification of memory addresses or constant values. However, crossover, commonly used in evolutionary methods, is not employed.

When applying AutoML-Zero to image classification tasks, it was confirmed that algorithms equivalent to backpropagation and gradient descent methods are automatically evolved from an initial population of empty codes. However, challenges have been identified, including the high computational cost of exploration and the difficulty of representing more complex models. This is because traditional operators do not include loop processing or high-dimensional tensor operations.

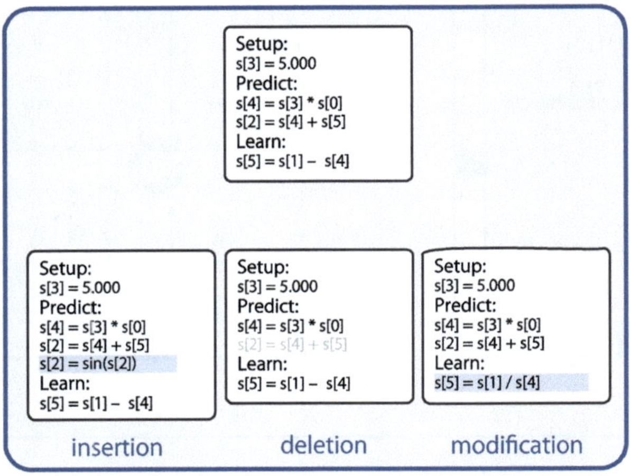

Fig. 2.11 Random mutation for AutoML-Zero

2.3.2 LLM-Based Evolutionary Search

In AutoML-Zero, challenges included low search efficiency across vast search spaces and insufficient model expressiveness due to a lack of high-functionality operators. Particularly, random evolution via mutation yields a low probability of generating high-quality individuals, and even with refined evolutionary techniques, avoiding large-scale searches is expected to remain difficult. Therefore, interpreting individuals' computational processes and suppressing functionally meaningless evolution are required. For example, consider mutations that insert an operator that assigns a value to a specific memory location. If the insertion is performed immediately before an operator that assigns a related value to that memory, it will result in ineffective evolution that merely increases code redundancy. Thus, such evolution should be eliminated without compromising diversity.

To address this difficulty, this section discusses the application of LLMs to AutoML-Zero. Specifically, we feed an individual code as a prompt into the LLM and aim to generate a refined code that would be difficult to generate with conventional random exploration.

In the following experiments, we combine random mutation with LLM-driven evolution (Fig. 2.12). This approach achieves exploration that is not overly dependent on the LLM's learning bias and leverages its efficient search capabilities. Furthermore, regarding the mutation method, we have made some modifications rather than directly adopting the approach used in the original AutoML-Zero.

The pseudocode for using an LLM is shown in Algorithm 2.2. The number of generations G and the population size P are user-defined parameters for each experiment.

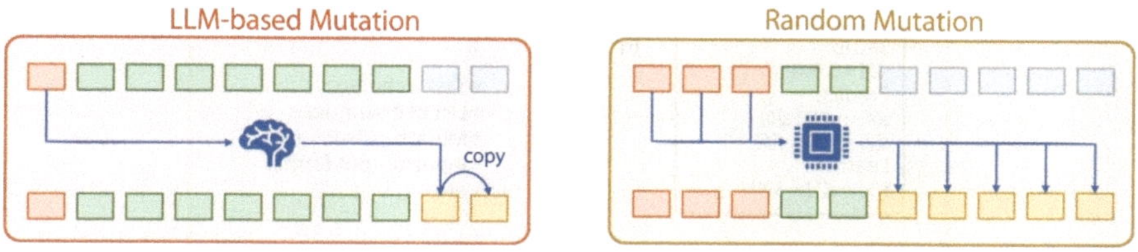

Fig. 2.12 Mutation and selection for AutoML-Zero

Algorithm 2.2 LLM-based evolutionary search

```
G ← 2000                                              ▷ Number of generations
P ← 50                                                ▷ Population size
initialize population with empty code
for g = 1 to G do
    for each individual p in population do
        reset memory value
        train p using D_train
        evaluate p on D_test to get loss
        if g mod 1000 > 750 then then
            add length penalty to loss
        end if
    end for
    Sort population by loss
    if mutate by LLM then                             ▷ LLM-based mutation
        copy top 80% of population into new_population
        while size of new_population < P do
            select a model randomly from the top 50%
            apply mutation by LLM and add to new_population
        end while
    else                                              ▷ Normal mutation
        copy top 80% of population into new_population
        while size of new_population < P do
            select a model randomly from the top 50%
            apply mutation and add to new_population
        end while
    end if
    population ← new_population
end for
```

The operations performed in each generation are broadly categorized into "performance evaluation" and "evolution." For the former, memory is first reset, and then *Setup* is executed. Subsequently, *Predict* and *Learn* are sequentially executed for each data point in the training dataset D_{train} to advance learning. Finally, only *Predict* is executed for each data point in the test dataset D_{test}. The mean squared error (MSE) between the obtained output and the actual value is calculated as the loss, which is considered the fitness of the individual during evolution. To simplify redundant code without compromising performance, a penalty proportional to code

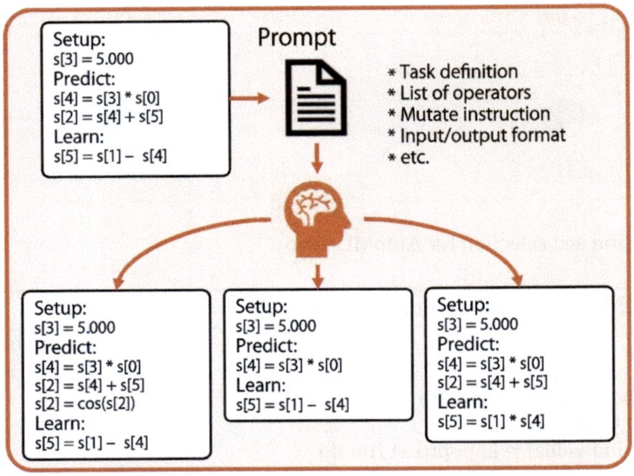

Fig. 2.13 LLM-based mutation

length is added to the loss in some generations. Inputs, outputs, and actual values are stored and referenced via pre-specified memory.

During the evolutionary process, two types of mutation are applied: conventional random mutation (Fig. 2.11) and LLM-based mutation (Fig. 2.13). Specifically, not all mutations are performed by LLM; instead, LLM-based mutation is used only in specific generations, while random mutation is used in the remaining generations. The whole evolutionary strategy remains consistent: Individuals in the top 80% of performance are copied as they are, while the remaining 20% are newly generated. The top 50% of individuals are subject to mutation.

For random mutations, one of the following operations is applied to an individual: (1) insertion of an operator, (2) deletion of an operator, or (3) modification of an operator. When using an LLM, the target code and the prompt shown in Listing 2.1 are input to the LLM to generate individuals through evolution. The LLM is executed multiple times as needed, repeating until the remaining 20% of individuals are generated.

The prompt includes an overview of the problem, available operators, detailed rules, datasets, task content, codes subject to mutation, and output format instructions. Through these, the LLM generates new entities. Note that we instruct the prompt to perform a clean-up task. This corresponds to the edit operator often used in GP to suppress bloat. The LLM model used is Gemini-2.5-Flash.

Listing 2.1 Prompt for LLM

```
# Problem Description
You are working with a simplified programming language designed for
    machine learning tasks. A program in this language is divided into
    three sections:
Setup - initializes memory values.
```

```
Predict - computes the model's prediction.
Learn - updates memory values based on the prediction error.

# Available Operators
All operations act on a shared memory array s[]. Each operator writes
    its result into s[k].
- scalar_add(i, j, k) -> s[k] = s[i] + s[j]
- scalar_sub(i, j, k) -> s[k] = s[i] - s[j]
- scalar_mul(i, j, k) -> s[k] = s[i] * s[j]
- scalar_const(c, k) -> s[k] = c (allowed only in Setup)
- scalar_sin(i, k) -> s[k] = sin(s[i])
- scalar_cos(i, k) -> s[k] = cos(s[i])
- scalar_exp(i, k) -> s[k] = exp(s[i])

# Memory Rules and Constraints
- The input value (Input) is stored in s[0].
- The ground-truth label (Answer) is stored in s[1].
- Your predicted output must be stored in s[2].
- You may use indices up to {max_memory_size}.
- Instruction limits per section:
   - Setup: max {max_setup_instructions} instructions
  - Predict: max {max_predict_instructions} instructions
  - Learn: max {max_learn_instructions} instructions
- All temporary memory values use consecutive indices beginning with
    s[3], ''based on their order of appearance'' in the code.

# Dataset and Tasks
Each dataset represents a mathematical function that can be constructed
    using the available operators.
You have three tasks:
1. Clean up the code
Remove unnecessary instructions from the code and renumber temporary
    memory locations so they are consecutive.
2. Mutate and Improve the Model
Make a small change to alter the model's function.

# Input
You will be given a code snippet in the following format:
{input_code}

# Output
Produce 10 mutated versions of the given code.
Separate each version with a line containing only: '--------'.
    """
```

In the following experiments, we adopted the function identification task (i.e., symbolic regression in GP), where both the input and the output are scalars. Therefore, the operators used are limited to scalar operators as shown in Table 2.11.

For a symbol regression problem, we set $y = 5\sin(3x)\cos(x)$ as the objective function. The experimental conditions are as follows: The number of generations G is set to 2000, the population size P to 50, the number of training data points D_{train} to 100, and the number of test data points D_{test} to 100.

Table 2.11 List of operators used in the experiments

Name	Input	Output	Process
`scalar_add(i, j, k)`	Scalar	Scalar	$s[k] = s[i] + s[j]$
`scalar_sub(i, j, k)`	Scalar	Scalar	$s[k] = s[i] - s[j]$
`scalar_mul(i, j, k)`	Scalar	Scalar	$s[k] = s[i] \times s[j]$
`scalar_const(c, k)`	Constant	Scalar	$s[k] = c$
`scalar_sin(i, k)`	Scalar	Scalar	$s[k] = \sin(s[i])$
`scalar_cos(i, k)`	Scalar	Scalar	$s[k] = \cos(s[i])$
`scalar_exp(i, k)`	Scalar	Scalar	$s[k] = \exp(s[i])$

Table 2.12 Fitness of the best individuals

	Fitness(= loss)		Generations in which LLM-
Trial	random only	random+LLM	based mutations survived
1	**2.46518**	3.04189	–
2	2.66107	0.89696	350
3	2.90056	3.48665	150, 350, 650, 1350
4	2.79248	2.20733	50
5	3.57588	**0.06940**	50, 150, 350, 450, 550, 750, 1050

For the sake of comparison, we conducted five experiments for each of the following methods: (1) a method applying random mutations in all generations and (2) a method introducing mutations via LLM once every 100 generations in addition to random mutations.

The fitness of the best individual in the final generation and the generations in which those individuals survived after LLM-based mutation are given in Table 2.12. More precisely, the generations shown here refer to those in which the individuals achieving the best fitness survived mutation via LLM and were not eliminated during the evolutionary process. The best fitness among the five trials is highlighted in bold. Furthermore, the corresponding evolved codes[2] are shown in Fig. 2.14a and b. Additionally, the fitness transition is shown in Fig. 2.16. The solid line in the figure represents the average of the five trials, while the shaded areas indicate the range of standard deviation. Figure 2.15 plots the behavior of the evolved expressions (Fig. 2.14a and b) against the target function (i.e., $y = 5\sin(3x)\cos(x)$). As shown in the figure, although the expression generated by LLM-based mutation differs from the target function, it exhibits nearly identical behavior.

Comparing the performance of random mutation with that of LLM-based mutation in Fig. 2.16, we can confirm that using LLM generally results in the generation of superior individuals on average. Furthermore, as shown in Table 2.12, the best fitness attained with solely random mutation was 2.46518, whereas the LLM-based method achieved a significantly improved value of 0.06940, demonstrating that

[2] These codes are identical to the following equations: (a) $y = 4\cos^{16}(9.947037 - x)$ and (b) $y = 4\sin(3x) \cdot (2\cos(x) - \sin(\cos(x) - \sin(9.492605)) - \sin(9.492605))$.

```
Setup:
Predict:
s[2] = 9.947037;
s[2] = s[2] − s[0];
s[2] = cos(s[2]);
s[2] = s[2] ∗ s[2];
s[2] = s[2] ∗ s[2];
s[2] = s[2] ∗ s[2];
s[2] = s[2] ∗ s[2];
s[2] = s[2] + s[2];
s[2] = s[2] + s[2];
Learn:
```

(a) Random mutation only

```
Setup:
Predict:
s[3] = cos(s[0]);
s[4] = 9.492605;
s[5] = sin(s[4]);
s[5] = s[3] − s[5];
s[3] = s[3] + s[5];
s[4] = sin(s[5]);
s[2] = s[0] + s[0];
s[3] = s[3] − s[4];
s[4] = s[0] + s[2];
s[5] = sin(s[4]);
s[5] = s[5] + s[5];
s[5] = s[5] + s[5];
s[2] = s[5] ∗ s[3];
Learn:
```

(b) Random and LLM-based mutation

Fig. 2.14 Evolved codes of the best individuals

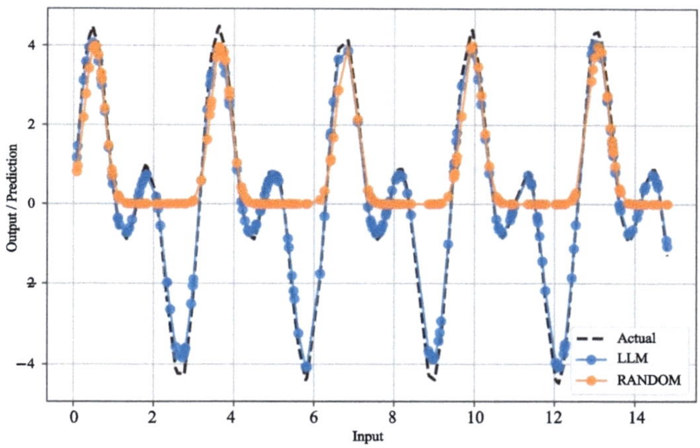

Fig. 2.15 Comparison of evolved expressions

LLM substantially enhances exploration performance. Figure 2.17 shows how LLM works for AutoML-zero. LLM enables the simplification of redundant code while achieving code mutations that are impossible with conventional random mutations.

In the previous experiment, the LLM was configured to be used once every 100 generations. In the following experiment, we compared the timing of LLM-based mutations across multiple conditions to assess the LLM's effectiveness. The task targeted the objective function $y = 0.6xe^{0.2x} + 2\cos(2x)$. Experimental conditions were set as follows: generation count $G = 2000$, population size $P = 70$, training data size $D_{train} = 100$, and test data size $D_{test} = 100$.

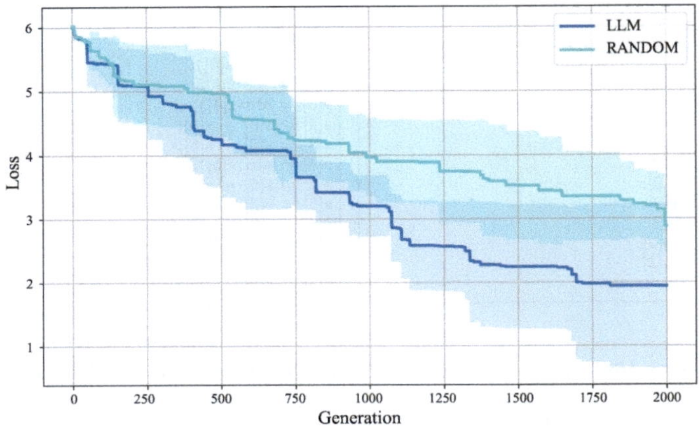

Fig. 2.16 Performance comparison of two types of mutations

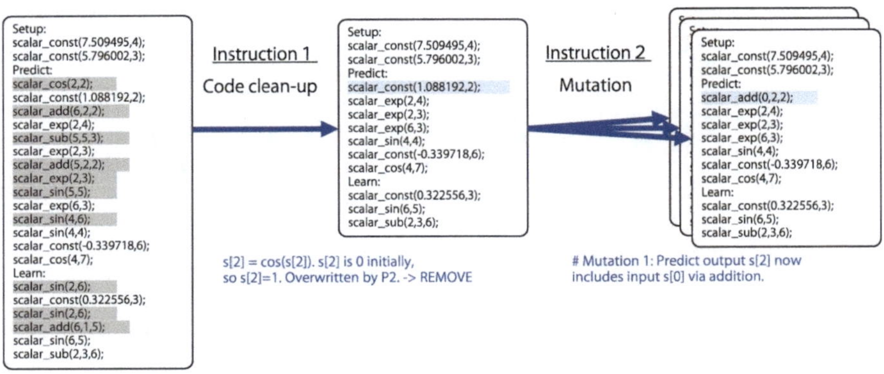

Fig. 2.17 How LLM works

The experiment will be conducted under the following four conditions, and the results will be compared:

1. No LLM usage
2. LLM usage every 100 generations
3. LLM usage every 25 generations, only for the first 500 generations
4. LLM usage when fitness fails to improve for 100 consecutive generations

The fitness values of the final generation for each condition, along with the generations in which the best individuals survived after mutation via LLM, are shown in Table 2.13. The fitness transition under each condition is shown in Fig. 2.18.

Table 2.13 Comparison of different LLM usages

LLM usage	Fitness values	Generations in which LLM-based mutations survived
No LLM	5.39021	–
Every 100 gen.	2.95680	150, 250, 1450
Every 25 gen. early	2.31804	95, 120, 195, 220, 270, 370, 445, 470, 495
LLM when stuck	3.09847	1217

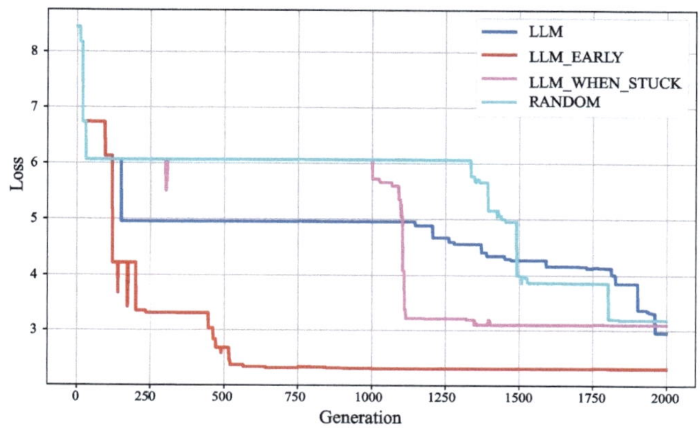

Fig. 2.18 Fitness transition for different LLM usages

From the figure, we observe that fitness improves when using the LLM every 100 or 25 generations, but only during the initial 500 generations. Table 2.13 shows that, mainly when the LLM is used early on, the mutations generated by the LLM do not directly affect fitness. Instead, fitness improvement occurs through subsequent random mutations. On the other hand, some LLM-based mutations generated individuals that random mutations could also produce. For example, as seen in the LLM output in Listing 2.2, a mutation has occurred where a single exponential operator has been inserted into *Predict*. This mutation could also arise from a random mutation. Therefore, the LLM is not enabling exploration that random mutation cannot achieve; instead, it is thought to contribute to exploration by generating promising individuals with a higher probability.

Listing 2.2 LLM output examples (partial)

```
### Mutated Version 6: Insert a scalar_exp instruction before P4
(The temporary variable 's[3]' remains at index 3, as no new temporary
    write targets are introduced beyond 's[3]')
'''
Setup:
Predict:
scalar_add(0,0,2);
scalar_const(2.000000,3);
scalar_mul(2,3,2);
```

```
scalar_exp(2,2); // New instruction
scalar_sin(2,2);
Learn:
scalar_cos(1,3);
--------
'''
```

Furthermore, as shown in Fig. 2.14, many evolved individuals do not contain operators in either *Setup* or *Learn*. This may be because *Setup* and *Learn* are not essential for the chosen task. Originally, *Setup* was designed for setting constants and hyperparameters, and *Learn* for adjusting variables. However, in the case of a scalar function, directly specifying constants in *Predict* is equivalent, and if appropriate coefficients are given, adjustments in *Learn* are also unnecessary. Therefore, this result does not indicate an inherent inadequacy in the structure of individuals expressed by the three functional components (i.e., *Setup*, *Predict*, and *Learn*). Instead, it is likely attributable to the task's simplicity. Conversely, suppose tasks involving vectors or matrices as operators—such as affine transformations or image classification—are chosen. In that case, it becomes challenging to describe appropriate variables via random mutations directly in probabilistic terms. This would necessitate the use of *Setup* and *Learn*.

Based on the above, it can be concluded that LLMs effectively enhance the search efficiency of AutoML-Zero for function identification (i.e., symbolic regression). However, further analysis is likely needed regarding the specific contributions of LLMs.

2.4 LLM-Driven Evolutionary Program Synthesis at Scale

This section examines recent advances in large-scale program evolution guided by large language models. Building upon the foundations established in earlier sections, we explore how industrial and open-source systems have extended LLM-based evolutionary computation to tackle complex algorithmic discovery, mathematical optimization, and infrastructure design problems.

2.4.1 LLM-Guided Program Evolution

The methods discussed in Sects. 2.1–2.3 demonstrate that large language models can serve as effective variation operators within evolutionary computation frameworks. However, these approaches operate at relatively modest scales, typically evolving short solution representations or compact code snippets. Recent work has dramatically expanded this paradigm, developing industrial-strength systems capable of evolving entire codebases, discovering novel mathematical constructions, and optimizing production infrastructure. Three notable systems exemplify this trend: AlphaEvolve from Google DeepMind [21], ShinkaEvolve [17], and CodeEvolve [3]. Despite their independent development and differing emphases, these systems share a common architectural foundation that can be understood through a unified mathematical framework.

2.4.1.1 The Program Evolution Problem

At the highest level, LLM-guided program evolution addresses the following optimization problem. Let $\mathcal{P}$ denote the space of all syntactically valid programs expressible in a given language (or a set of languages), and let h map each program from $\mathcal{P}$ to $\mathbb{R}^d$ be an evaluation function that maps each program to a vector of d performance metrics. The goal is to find a program $P^* \in \mathcal{P}$ that optimizes these metrics:

$$P^* = \arg\max_{P \in \mathcal{P}} f(h(P)), \tag{2.2}$$

where f maps from $\mathbb{R}^d$ to $\mathbb{R}$ and aggregates the multiple objectives into a scalar fitness value. In the simplest case where $d = 1$, the function f is the identity, but multi-objective formulations prove essential for complex discovery tasks.

This formulation differs fundamentally from traditional genetic programming (GP) in a crucial respect. Whereas GP typically represents programs as syntax trees with predefined node types and applies structural mutations (subtree crossover, point mutation), LLM-guided evolution operates directly on program text. The LLM serves as a learned variation operator that leverages its pretrained knowledge of programming patterns, mathematical structures, and domain-specific conventions to propose semantically meaningful modifications.

2.4.1.2 Core Architectural Components

All three systems organize their evolutionary search around four principal components: a program database, a prompt construction mechanism, an LLM ensemble, and an evaluation pipeline. Understanding how these components interact reveals the essential structure of LLM-guided program evolution (see Fig. 2.19).

The program database $\mathcal{D}_t$ at generation t maintains a collection of evaluated programs along with their fitness scores, auxiliary metrics, and lineage information. Unlike the simple population structures employed in LMEA (Sect. 2.1) or LMPSO (Sect. 2.2), these databases employ sophisticated mechanisms to maintain diversity. AlphaEvolve draws inspiration from MAP-Elites and island models to balance exploitation of high-performing programs against exploration of the search space. ShinkaEvolve and CodeEvolve similarly employ island-based architectures where multiple subpopulations evolve semi-independently, with periodic migration of elite individuals between islands. Formally, the database can be represented as a

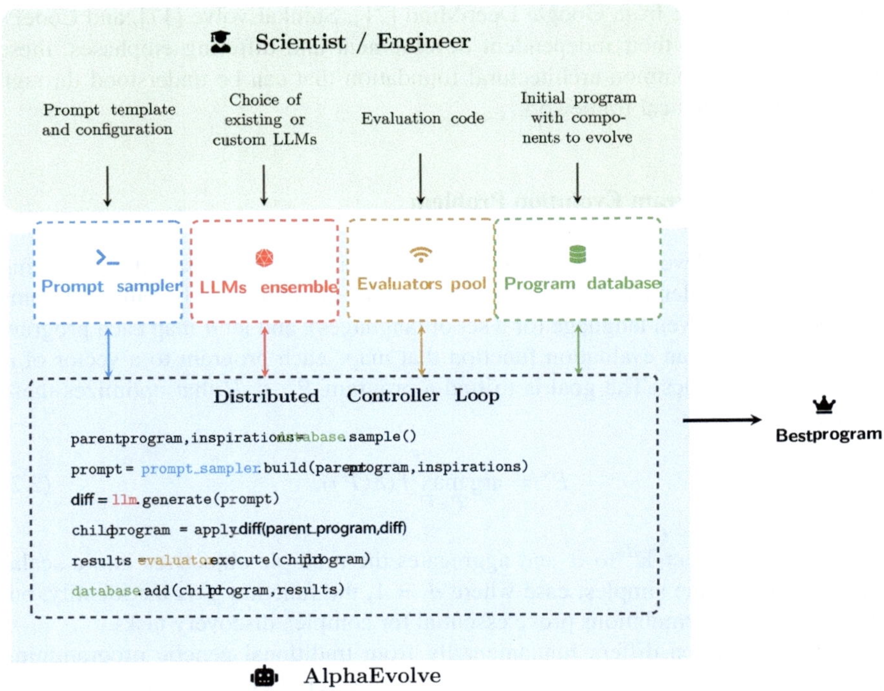

Fig. 2.19 Overview of the AlphaEvolve discovery process. The user provides an initial program, with evolvable components identified, along with evaluation code and optional configuration settings. AlphaEvolve then enters an evolutionary loop. A prompt sampler draws from the program database to construct rich prompts, which are passed to language models to generate code modifications. These modifications are applied to produce new candidate programs, which are subsequently evaluated. High-performing solutions are added back into the program database, enabling the iterative discovery of increasingly effective programs [21]

partitioned structure:

$$\mathcal{D}_t = \bigcup_{i=1}^{K} \mathcal{D}_t^{(i)}, \tag{2.3}$$

where K denotes the number of islands and $\mathcal{D}_t^{(i)}$ contains the programs currently residing on island i. Each island maintains its own elite set, and migration policies govern the transfer of promising programs across the partition boundaries.

The prompt construction mechanism transforms the current evolutionary state into a structured input for the LLM. This represents perhaps the most significant departure from classical evolutionary computation, where variation operators are defined algorithmically. In LLM-guided evolution, the "operator" is implicitly encoded in the prompt, which typically includes the following elements: a description of the optimization task, the program to be modified (the parent), contextual information such as high-performing programs from the database (inspirations), evaluation feedback from previous generations, and instructions specifying the desired form of modification. The prompt sampler in AlphaEvolve, for instance, constructs elaborate contexts that may include mathematical definitions, equations, or even PDF documents describing the problem domain. ShinkaEvolve and CodeEvolve adopt similar strategies, providing the LLM with both the immediate parent program and additional "inspiration" programs sampled from the population to facilitate semantic crossover.

The LLM ensemble component addresses a practical observation that different language models exhibit varying strengths across problem types and evolutionary stages. AlphaEvolve employs Gemini 2.0 Flash for high-throughput candidate generation alongside Gemini 2.0 Pro for occasional deeper reasoning. ShinkaEvolve formalizes this intuition through a bandit-based selection mechanism that adaptively allocates queries among available models (GPT, Gemini, Claude, DeepSeek) based on their historical contribution to fitness improvements. CodeEvolve similarly uses a weighted ensemble, sampling Gemini Flash with 80% probability and Gemini Pro with 20% probability. This ensemble approach reflects a broader principle that the variation operator in LLM-guided evolution is not fixed but can be dynamically tuned to the problem structure.

Finally, the evaluation pipeline executes candidate programs and computes their fitness. A critical insight shared across all three systems is that evaluation can be structured as a cascade where inexpensive preliminary tests filter out obviously poor candidates before committing to expensive assessment. AlphaEvolve explicitly implements such cascades, beginning with quick sanity checks and progressing to computationally intensive assessments only for promising candidates. This hierarchical evaluation strategy proves essential for maintaining reasonable computational budgets when each LLM query and program execution carries a nontrivial cost.

2.4.1.3 The Evolutionary Loop

Given these components, the evolutionary loop proceeds according to Algorithm 2.3, which abstracts the standard structure underlying AlphaEvolve, ShinkaEvolve, and CodeEvolve.

Several aspects of this loop merit emphasis. First, the parallelism inherent in the island model enables efficient utilization of computational resources, with LLM queries and program evaluations proceeding concurrently across islands. AlphaEvolve implements this through Python's `asyncio`, achieving high throughput despite the latency of individual LLM calls. Second, the novelty filter (line 11) prevents the population from collapsing to a narrow region of program space. ShinkaEvolve implements this through embedding-based similarity checking, where candidate programs whose code embeddings exhibit high cosine similarity to existing population members are rejected or subjected to additional LLM-based novelty assessment. Third, the archive policy (line 13) determines

Algorithm 2.3 Unified LLM-Guided program evolution

Input: Task description T, evaluation function h, budget B
Output: Best program P^*
Initialize program database $\mathcal{D}_0$ with seed programs
$t \leftarrow 0$
while computational budget not exhausted **do**
  for each island i in parallel **do**
    Sample parent P from $\mathcal{D}_t^{(i)}$ according to selection policy
    Sample inspirations $I \subseteq \mathcal{D}_t^{(i)} \setminus \{P\}$
    Construct prompt from T, P, I, and historical feedback
    Select LLM ℓ from ensemble according to allocation policy
    Generate candidate P' by querying ℓ with prompt
    if P' passes syntactic validation and novelty filter **then**
      Evaluate P' through cascade and compute $\mathbf{m} \leftarrow h(P')$
      Update $\mathcal{D}_t^{(i)}$ with $(P', \mathbf{m})$ according to archive policy
    end if
  end for
  Perform inter-island migration according to topology
  Update LLM allocation weights based on recent performance
  $t \leftarrow t + 1$
end while
return $P^* = \arg\max_{P \in \mathcal{D}_t} f(h(P))$

which programs survive across generations. All three systems employ some form of elitism,, preserving high-performing individuals while making room for novel candidates that may lead to future improvements.

2.4.1.4 Contrast with Earlier Approaches

The unified framework reveals how these large-scale systems extend the simpler LLM-based evolutionary methods discussed earlier in this chapter. LMEA (Sect. 2.1) can be viewed as a special case where the program database reduces to a single flat population, the prompt construction includes explicit crossover and mutation instructions, and no ensemble or cascade mechanisms are employed. Similarly, LMPSO (Sect. 2.2) instantiates the framework with PSO-inspired selection and velocity-based prompt construction, but again without the sophisticated diversity maintenance or adaptive model selection that characterize the newer systems.

The progression from LMEA to AlphaEvolve, ShinkaEvolve, and CodeEvolve mirrors a familiar pattern in evolutionary computation where initial demonstrations of feasibility give way to engineered systems that address scalability, robustness, and efficiency concerns. What distinguishes the LLM-guided paradigm is that many of these engineering choices (parent selection, variation strategy, diversity maintenance) can be partially delegated to the LLM itself through careful prompt design. AlphaEvolve takes this principle to its fullest with its meta-prompt evolution, in which a secondary evolutionary loop optimizes the prompt templates used to guide the primary search. This recursive structure hints at the deeper potential of LLM-guided evolution, where systems not only discover better programs but also discover better ways of discovering programs.

The mathematical framework presented here also clarifies the relationship between LLM-guided program evolution and the AutoML-Zero approach discussed in Sect. 2.3. AutoML-Zero operates within a constrained program space defined by a fixed set of primitive operators, with random mutations providing the mechanism for variation. The LLM-guided systems generalize this by expanding the program space to include arbitrary code expressible in standard programming languages and by replacing random mutation with learned variation operators. This generalization comes at the cost of requiring pretrained language models, but yields dramatic improvements in sample efficiency; whereas AutoML-Zero may require millions of evaluations to discover simple learning algorithms, CodeEvolve achieves state-of-the-art results on mathematical optimization benchmarks with approximately 150 program evaluations.

The unified framework thus provides a conceptual foundation for understanding both the commonalities and the design choices that differentiate these systems. In the following subsections, we examine specific aspects of this framework in greater depth, beginning with the strategies employed to maintain population diversity and select promising parents for variation.

2.4.2 Population Diversity and Parent Selection Strategies

The effectiveness of any evolutionary algorithm depends critically on its ability to balance exploration of the search space against exploitation of promising regions. This tension manifests acutely in LLM-guided program evolution, where the vast space of possible programs demands mechanisms that prevent premature convergence while still directing computational resources toward fruitful areas. The three systems under consideration have each developed sophisticated approaches to this challenge, drawing on ideas from quality-diversity optimization, island-based parallel evolution, and adaptive selection schemes.

2.4.2.1 Island Models for Structured Diversity

All three frameworks adopt island models as their primary mechanism for maintaining population diversity. In this architecture, the total population is partitioned into semi-isolated subpopulations that evolve largely independently, with occasional migration of individuals between islands. This structure offers several advantages for LLM-guided evolution. Different islands can explore distinct regions of the program space without interference, effectively conducting parallel searches that may converge to qualitatively different solutions. The migration mechanism then allows successful innovations discovered on one island to propagate throughout the population, combining the benefits of independent exploration with information sharing.

CodeEvolve implements a straightforward island topology using a ring graph C_K connecting K islands, where each island periodically sends its top-performing programs to its neighbors. The migration policy is elitist, transferring only the best 10% of programs at fixed intervals (every 40 epochs in their experiments). Importantly, a program may migrate from its origin island only once, preventing cycles where the same individual circulates indefinitely. Upon arrival at a new island, migrated programs are treated as roots of fresh evolutionary trees, losing their ancestry information but retaining their code and fitness values.

ShinkaEvolve adopts a similar island structure but introduces additional mechanisms to protect diversity within each island. The best program on each island is explicitly protected from migrating out, ensuring that each subpopulation retains its champion even as other high performers spread to neighboring islands. This asymmetric migration policy prevents the scenario where a single dominant solution colonizes all islands and eliminates diversity. The framework also maintains a fixed-size archive with an elite size constraint, automatically removing the worst individuals when the population exceeds capacity while guaranteeing that top performers survive.

AlphaEvolve draws inspiration from MAP-Elites (see Sect. 3.2.2),, a quality-diversity algorithm that maintains a grid of solutions spanning multiple behavioral dimensions. While the precise implementation details remain proprietary, the published description emphasizes that the program database balances exploitation of high-scoring programs against exploration through diversity preservation. The combination of MAP-Elites-style behavioral characterization with island-based parallel search enables AlphaEvolve to maintain a rich repertoire of qualitatively distinct programs even as evolution progresses toward higher fitness values.

2.4.2.2 Parent Selection Mechanisms

Given a diverse population, the next design choice concerns which programs should serve as parents for generating new candidates. This selection step profoundly influences the evolutionary dynamics, determining whether the search intensifies around current optima or ventures into unexplored territory. The three systems employ notably different selection strategies, each reflecting distinct assumptions about how to navigate the exploration-exploitation trade-off.

CodeEvolve uses rank-based selection, where programs are sorted by fitness and selection probability depends on rank rather than raw fitness values. Specifically, if program P has rank $r(P)$ in the sorted population (with rank one denoting the best), its selection probability is

$$\Pr(P) = \frac{r(P)^{-1}}{\sum_{P' \in \mathcal{D}} r(P')^{-1}}. \tag{2.4}$$

This formulation ensures that higher-ranked programs receive more attention while still allowing lower-ranked individuals a chance to serve as parents. The use of ranks rather than raw fitness values provides robustness against fitness landscapes with extreme value ranges, a common occurrence in program optimization where some candidates may fail catastrophically, while others achieve near-optimal performance.

ShinkaEvolve introduces two alternative selection strategies that make the exploration-exploitation trade-off more explicit. The first, power-law sampling, generalizes rank-based selection by introducing a temperature parameter α that controls selection pressure. Programs are again ranked by fitness, but the selection probability follows

$$p_i \propto r_i^{-\alpha}, \tag{2.5}$$

where r_i is the rank of the i-th program. Setting $\alpha = 0$ yields uniform random selection (pure exploration), while $\alpha \to \infty$ concentrates all probability mass on the top-ranked program (pure exploitation). Intermediate values allow practitioners to tune the balance according to problem characteristics.

The second strategy in ShinkaEvolve, termed weighted performance-novelty sampling, explicitly incorporates both fitness and exploration potential into the selection criterion. For each program P_i, the framework tracks not only its fitness $F(P_i)$ but also the number of offspring $N(P_i)$ it has previously generated. The selection weight combines a performance component

$$s_i = \sigma(\lambda(F(P_i) - \alpha_0)), \tag{2.6}$$

where σ denotes the logistic function, λ controls sensitivity to fitness differences, and α_0 is the median population fitness, with a novelty component

$$h_i = \frac{1}{1 + N(P_i)}, \tag{2.7}$$

that favors programs with fewer prior offspring. The final selection probability is proportional to $w_i = s_i \cdot h_i$, ensuring that both high-performing and under-explored programs receive evolutionary attention. This multiplicative combination means that a program must score reasonably well on both criteria to have substantial selection probability, preventing the algorithm from wasting resources on either poor performers or exhaustively exploited solutions.

AlphaEvolve's selection mechanism operates through its prompt sampler, which chooses parents and "inspiration" programs from the database according to policies designed to balance quality and diversity. While specific algorithmic details are not fully disclosed, the framework explicitly supports sampling from both top performers and randomly selected archive members, mirroring the dual emphasis on exploitation and exploration evident in the other systems.

2.4.2.3 Novelty Filtering and Stepping Stones

Beyond parent selection, maintaining diversity requires mechanisms to prevent the population from collapsing to a narrow set of similar programs. This concern motivates the novelty filtering approaches adopted by ShinkaEvolve and, implicitly, by the other systems.

ShinkaEvolve implements a two-stage novelty rejection process. When a candidate program is generated, the framework first extracts its mutable code regions and computes their embedding using a pretrained code encoder. If the maximum cosine similarity between this embedding and those of existing population members exceeds a threshold (typically 0.95), the candidate is flagged as potentially redundant. A secondary check then, optionally, invokes an LLM to assess whether the flagged program is "meaningfully different" from its nearest neighbors in the embedding space. Only candidates passing both filters are admitted to the population. This embedding-based approach provides a computationally efficient proxy for semantic similarity, filtering out trivial variations while allowing substantively novel programs to enter the population.

The concept of stepping stones provides a complementary perspective on diversity maintenance. In complex optimization landscapes, the path to a global optimum may pass through intermediate solutions that appear suboptimal when evaluated in isolation but serve as essential building blocks for subsequent improvements. Traditional fitness-based selection tends to eliminate such stepping stones before their potential can be realized. The quality-diversity principles underlying these frameworks address this limitation by explicitly valuing behavioral diversity alongside fitness, preserving a portfolio of qualitatively distinct programs that may prove helpful as evolution continues.

CodeEvolve operationalizes stepping stones through its inspiration-based crossover mechanism (discussed in detail in the following subsection), which samples high-performing programs to serve as semantic templates for generating new candidates. By maintaining a diverse archive of successful programs, the framework ensures that valuable design patterns discovered early in evolution remain available for recombination with later innovations. The deliberate delay of inspiration-based crossover until after the first migration wave further supports this goal, allowing initial diversity to develop before recombination mechanisms that might otherwise cause premature convergence.

2.4.2.4 Connection to Classical Evolutionary Computation

The diversity maintenance and selection strategies employed by these systems represent natural extensions of ideas long studied in evolutionary computation. Island models date to the earliest days of parallel genetic algorithms, where they were introduced to exploit distributed computing resources while incidentally providing diversity benefits. Quality-diversity algorithms emerged more recently from the observation that maintaining behavioral diversity can improve both final solution quality and robustness to deceptive fitness landscapes. The contribution of LLM-guided evolution frameworks lies not in these individual components but in their integration with language-model-based variation operators.

This integration creates new opportunities and challenges. On one hand, the semantic understanding embedded in pretrained language models may enable more intelligent diversity maintenance than purely syntactic approaches. An LLM-based novelty filter can potentially recognize when two syntactically different programs implement equivalent functionality, or when a superficially small edit produces a substantial behavioral change. On the other hand, the stochastic nature of LLM generation introduces additional variance into the evolutionary process, potentially requiring larger populations or more conservative selection pressure to achieve reliable progress.

The empirical results reported by all three systems suggest that the current balance of techniques proves effective across a range of problem domains. CodeEvolve achieves state-of-the-art results on mathematical optimization benchmarks with populations of approximately 40 individuals per island. ShinkaEvolve demonstrates that careful attention to sample efficiency enables meaningful progress with as few as 150 program evaluations on circle packing problems. AlphaEvolve operates at a larger scale but achieves correspondingly more ambitious goals, including improvements to Google's production infrastructure and novel mathematical discoveries. These results validate the diversity maintenance strategies described here while leaving room for future refinements as the field matures (see Fig. 2.20).

2.4.3 LLM as Variation Operator: From Mutation to Meta-Prompting

In classical evolutionary computation, variation operators such as mutation and crossover are defined algorithmically, typically through domain-specific rules that manipulate solution representations according to fixed procedures. As shown in Sect. 1.2.4, genetic programming, for instance, mainly employs subtree crossover, which exchanges randomly selected branches between parent trees, and point mutation, which replaces individual nodes with alternatives of compatible type. These operators encode human intuitions about what constitutes a reasonable modification, but their fixed nature limits adaptability to problem structure and evolutionary context. The LLM-guided evolution paradigm fundamentally reconceptualizes variation by delegating modification generation to a language model, whose pretrained knowledge enables contextually appropriate changes that would be difficult to specify algorithmically.

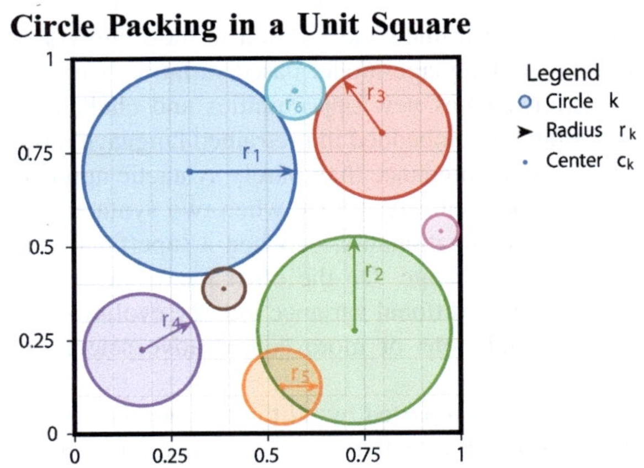

$$\max \sum_{k=1}^{n} r_k$$

$$\text{subject to: } \|c_k - c_j\|_2 \geq r_k + r_j \quad \forall k \neq j, \quad r_k \leq x_k \leq 1 - r_k, \quad r_k \leq y_k \leq 1 - r_k$$

Fig. 2.20 The circle packing problem. Given a unit square, the goal is to place n nonoverlapping circles such that the sum of their radii is maximized. This combinatorial-continuous optimization problem features numerous local optima, making it a challenging benchmark for LLM-guided program evolution systems such as AlphaEvolve, ShinkaEvolve, and CodeEvolve

2.4.3.1 Diff-Based Code Editing

A striking convergence across AlphaEvolve, ShinkaEvolve, and CodeEvolve is their shared adoption of diff-based editing as the primary mechanism for program modification. Rather than asking the LLM to generate complete programs from scratch, these systems prompt the model to produce targeted changes expressed as explicit patches. The canonical format uses SEARCH/REPLACE blocks that specify both the code to be modified and its replacement.

This design choice reflects several practical considerations. First, diff-based editing constrains the LLM's output space, reducing the likelihood of syntactically invalid or semantically incoherent generations. When the model must identify a specific code region before proposing changes, it must carefully attend to the existing program structure rather than hallucinate arbitrary modifications. Second, targeted edits preserve the accumulated evolutionary progress embodied in the parent program. A complete rewrite risks discarding beneficial code patterns that required many generations to discover, while a surgical modification can refine specific aspects while retaining proven components. Third, diff-based outputs are more amenable to validation and debugging, as human reviewers can quickly assess whether a proposed change is reasonable without parsing an entire program.

The LMEA approach discussed in Sect. 2.1 does not employ diff-based editing; instead, it prompts the LLM to generate complete offspring individuals. This more straightforward approach suffices for the short solution representations typical of combinatorial optimization problems, where individuals might be permutations of a few dozen elements. However, as program complexity increases, the advantages of diff-based editing become pronounced. AlphaEvolve evolves entire codebases spanning multiple functions and files, making complete regeneration both computationally expensive and prone to introducing inconsistencies. The diff-based paradigm scales naturally to such settings, with the LLM proposing localized changes, while the surrounding code remains stable.

All three systems implement safeguards to ensure that diff-based edits produce valid programs. The SEARCH block must match existing code exactly; if no match is found, the edit is rejected, and the LLM may be queried again with feedback on the failure. ShinkaEvolve and CodeEvolve additionally support marking certain code regions as immutable, preventing the LLM from modifying scaffolding or evaluation harnesses that must remain fixed. When an LLM proposes changes to protected areas, the systems can invoke a reflexion-style [32] correction loop that informs the model of its error and requests a revised proposal.

2.4.3.2 Inspiration-Based Crossover

Traditional crossover operators in genetic programming combine genetic material from two parents by exchanging subtrees or code segments. While effective in some domains, this approach faces fundamental difficulties when applied to general program text. Arbitrary splicing of code fragments typically produces syntactically invalid or semantically nonsensical results because variable bindings, type constraints, and control-flow dependencies are disrupted. Previous attempts to apply crossover to program evolution have required careful engineering of representation schemes that maintain validity under recombination, limiting the expressiveness of evolvable programs.

CodeEvolve introduces inspiration-based crossover as an alternative that sidesteps these difficulties by leveraging the LLM's semantic understanding. Rather than mechanically splicing code, the system samples a set of high-performing programs from the archive and provides them to the LLM as "inspirations" alongside the primary parent. The prompt instructs the model to generate a new program that draws on design patterns and successful strategies from the inspiration set while building upon the parent's foundation. This formulation treats crossover as a creative synthesis task that the LLM can perform using its knowledge of programming patterns and problem-solving strategies.

The inspiration mechanism appears in different forms across the three systems. AlphaEvolve's prompt sampler includes both parent programs and additional archive members as context, enabling the LLM to recognize and recombine successful patterns even without explicit crossover instructions. ShinkaEvolve similarly provides inspiration programs sampled according to either rank-based or uniform selection, depending on whether the current operation emphasizes exploitation or exploration. The key insight shared across these implementations is that semantic crossover can be achieved by presenting multiple successful programs to an LLM and requesting synthesis, rather than by defining explicit recombination rules.

CodeEvolve introduces a noteworthy refinement to prevent inspiration-based crossover from causing premature convergence. The mechanism is activated only after the first migration wave, ensuring that initial population diversity has developed before recombination begins. In the early generations, evolution proceeds through mutation alone, allowing each island to explore distinct regions of the program space. Once migration introduces successful programs from other islands, inspiration-based crossover can combine innovations discovered independently, accelerating progress without sacrificing the diversity that parallel island evolution provides.

2.4.3.3 Meta-Prompting and Prompt Evolution

The prompt that guides LLM-based variation encodes implicit assumptions about which modifications are desirable. A prompt emphasizing "small, targeted improvements" will elicit different proposals than one requesting "creative alternatives" or "radical simplifications." Recognizing this sensitivity, CodeEvolve and AlphaEvolve have developed mechanisms to evolve or adapt the prompts themselves, adding a meta-level to the evolutionary process.

CodeEvolve implements meta-prompting exploration as one of two variation modes, selected stochastically at each generation. In exploitation mode, the system uses depth-based refinement that preserves the current prompt and asks the LLM to incrementally improve the parent program. In exploration mode, a separate MetaPromptingLLM generates an entirely new prompt by analyzing the current parent program and its evaluation results. This new prompt may emphasize different aspects of the problem, suggest alternative solution strategies, or reframe the optimization goal. The program generated using this evolved prompt becomes the root of a fresh evolutionary lineage, potentially escaping local optima that constrained earlier generations.

The exploration probability parameter p_{explr} controls the balance between these modes. CodeEvolve's experiments use $p_{\text{explr}} = 0.3$, meaning that 30% of variation events involve meta-prompting, while 70% proceed through standard exploitation. This ratio reflects a general principle in evolutionary computation that most variation should refine existing solutions, while a minority explores more radical alternatives. The meta-prompting mechanism operationalizes this principle at the level of search strategy rather than solution representation.

AlphaEvolve takes prompt evolution further through its meta-prompt evolution mechanism, which explicitly optimizes the prompt templates stored in a dedicated database via a secondary evolutionary loop. The prompts themselves become individuals subject to selection and variation, with fitness determined by the quality of programs they help generate. This recursive structure creates a coevolutionary dynamic where improvements in prompt design accelerate program discovery, while successful program lineages provide a training signal for prompt refinement. The approach exemplifies a broader theme in LLM-guided optimization: The boundary between the search algorithm and the solutions it discovers becomes fluid when both are expressed in natural language.

2.4.3.4 Adaptive LLM Ensembles

Different language models exhibit varying strengths depending on problem domain, solution complexity, and evolutionary stage. A model optimized for code completion may excel at generating syntactically correct modifications but struggle with the creative leaps needed to escape local optima. Conversely, a more capable reasoning model may propose innovative solutions but at a higher computational cost. The three systems address this heterogeneity through ensemble approaches that combine multiple models, though their specific strategies differ substantially.

AlphaEvolve employs a fixed ensemble that combines Gemini 2.0 Flash for high-throughput candidate generation and Gemini 2.0 Pro for occasional deeper reasoning. The faster model handles the bulk of variation operations, maintaining evolutionary momentum, while the slower but more capable model periodically injects breakthrough ideas that the faster model might miss. This division of labor mirrors the exploration-exploitation trade-off at the model level, with Flash providing exploitation through rapid local refinement and Pro contributing exploration through more sophisticated reasoning.

CodeEvolve adopts a similar two-tier structure, sampling Gemini Flash with 80% probability and Gemini Pro with 20% probability. The probabilistic formulation allows the relative contribution of each model to vary stochastically across generations, introducing additional diversity into the evolutionary process. Both models receive identical prompts, so differences in their outputs reflect genuine variation in their learned behaviors rather than differences in instruction.

ShinkaEvolve introduces the most sophisticated ensemble mechanism through bandit-based model selection. Each available LLM (potentially including GPT, Gemini, Claude, and DeepSeek variants) is treated as an arm in a multiarmed bandit problem, with the algorithm learning to allocate queries to models based on their historical contribution to fitness improvement. The reward signal is defined not as raw fitness but as relative improvement over the parent.

$$r_i^u = \exp\left(\max\left(r_i - r_i^b, 0\right)\right) - 1, \tag{2.8}$$

where r_i is the fitness of the generated program and r_i^b is the baseline fitness (the maximum of parent fitness and initial program fitness). The exponential transformation emphasizes significant improvements while treating neutral or negative changes as uninformative. A UCB1-style algorithm [34] uses these rewards to balance exploitation of high-performing models against exploration of less-sampled alternatives.

This adaptive allocation mechanism enables ShinkaEvolve to automatically discover which models are most effective for a given problem without manual tuning. Early in evolution, when the population consists of simple programs, a fast model capable of generating many candidates may dominate. As programs grow more complex and incremental improvements become harder to find, the algorithm may shift toward more capable models that can identify subtle optimization opportunities. The bandit framework handles this adaptation automatically, responding to changes in the evolutionary context without explicit phase detection.

2.4.3.5 Comparison with LMEA and Classical Approaches

The variation mechanisms described here represent substantial elaborations of the more straightforward approach employed by LMEA in Sect. 2.1. LMEA prompts a single LLM with explicit instructions for crossover and mutation, generating complete offspring rather than targeted edits. This design suffices for problems where solutions are short sequences (city orderings in TSP, item selections in knapsack problems) but does not scale to the complex programs targeted by AlphaEvolve, ShinkaEvolve, and CodeEvolve.

The progression from LMEA to these more sophisticated systems illustrates a general pattern in the development of LLM-guided optimization. Initial work demonstrates the feasibility of using straightforward prompting strategies and establishes that language models can serve as variation operators. Subsequent systems introduce engineering refinements (diff-based editing, inspiration sampling, ensemble selection) that improve scalability and robustness. Finally, meta-level mechanisms (prompt evolution, adaptive model allocation) emerge, enabling the system to optimize its own search strategy. This trajectory mirrors the historical development of evolutionary computation, in which basic genetic algorithms gave way to sophisticated variants incorporating adaptive operator selection, quality-diversity maintenance, and self-adaptive parameter control.

The LLM-guided paradigm adds a distinctive element to this progression: The variation operator carries rich prior knowledge from pretraining. A classical mutation operator treats all modifications as equally likely unless explicitly biased by domain knowledge. An LLM-based operator implicitly encodes statistical regularities of effective code, mathematical reasoning patterns, and problem-solving strategies gleaned from its training corpus. This prior knowledge bootstraps the evolutionary search, enabling rapid early progress and contextually appropriate modifications throughout the optimization process. The challenge for system designers lies in harnessing this knowledge effectively while preventing the model's biases from constraining exploration of unconventional solutions.

2.4.4 *Applications and Empirical Insights*

The theoretical framework and algorithmic components described in preceding subsections are validated through empirical applications spanning mathematical discovery, infrastructure optimization, and automated algorithm design. Examining these applications reveals not only the impressive capabilities of LLM-guided program evolution but also the problem characteristics that determine when such approaches are most effective. The diversity of successful applications suggests broad applicability, while the specific patterns of success and failure illuminate the paradigm's strengths and limitations.

2.4.4.1 Mathematical Optimization and Discovery

Circle packing problems have emerged as a canonical benchmark for LLM-guided program evolution, appearing in the experimental evaluations of all three systems. The task of maximizing the sum of radii for n nonoverlapping circles within a unit square combines discrete decisions about placement patterns with continuous optimization of positions and sizes. This hybrid structure creates a challenging fitness landscape with numerous local optima, making the problem resistant to purely gradient-based or purely combinatorial approaches.

CodeEvolve achieves state-of-the-art results on circle packing instances with 26 and 32 circles, surpassing the results reported by AlphaEvolve on these benchmarks. The evolved algorithms combine sophisticated initialization strategies using golden-angle spiral patterns with a hybrid optimization that couples gradient-based methods (SLSQP, sequential least squares quadratic programming) and stochastic search (simulated annealing). Notably, the final algorithms incorporate intelligent perturbation mechanisms, including adaptive temperature scheduling and reheating to escape local optima. These algorithmic innovations emerged through approximately 150 program evaluations, demonstrating remarkable sample efficiency compared to traditional evolutionary approaches that might require thousands of generations.

ShinkaEvolve reproduces and extends these results, achieving comparable performance while providing a detailed analysis of the evolutionary dynamics. The system's trajectory in circle packing exhibits three distinct phases. Initial generations yield rapid fitness improvements as the LLM discovers basic constraint-handling strategies. Subsequent generations explore more sophisticated techniques, including improved feasibility checking and search diversification. Final generations apply polishing operations such as restarts and local refinement to converge on high-quality solutions. This phase structure suggests that LLM-guided evolution naturally decomposes complex problems into successive layers of increasing sophistication (see Fig. 2.21).

Beyond circle packing, the systems tackle a broader range of mathematical optimization problems. AlphaEvolve reports results on over 50 problems spanning analysis, combinatorics, number theory, and geometry. The system rediscovers the

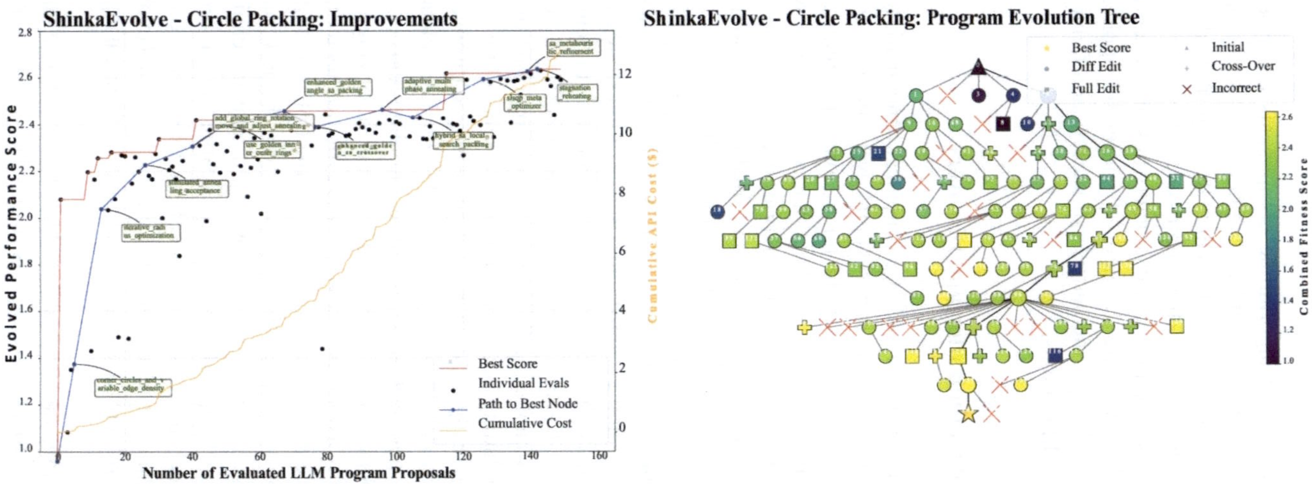

Fig. 2.21 Left: ShinkaEvolve surpasses AlphaEvolve's solution with fewer than 150 program evaluations. Right: The program evolution tree illustrates how ShinkaEvolve iteratively composes stepping stones to produce high-performing solutions [17]

best-known constructions for approximately 75% of these problems and produces strictly superior results for roughly 20%. Highlights include a new lower bound on the 11-dimensional kissing number (593 spheres, surpassing the previous record of 592) and improved constants for autocorrelation inequalities in harmonic analysis. CodeEvolve similarly improves on the second autocorrelation inequality problem, achieving a ratio of 0.93768 compared to AlphaEvolve's 0.89627, representing a substantial advance on this analytical benchmark.

A methodological insight emerging from these mathematical applications concerns the choice of what to evolve. Rather than directly encoding mathematical objects such as point configurations or function constructions, the most successful approaches evolve search algorithms or heuristics that themselves discover these objects. AlphaEvolve explicitly adopts this strategy for kissing number and packing problems, evolving heuristic search procedures that receive a fixed computational budget and attempt to improve upon the current best construction. This meta-level formulation enables the discovery of specialized search strategies that human designers would struggle to conceive, including heuristics tailored to exploit specific structural properties of near-optimal solutions.

2.4.4.2 Infrastructure and Systems Optimization

AlphaEvolve's deployment within Google's production infrastructure demonstrates that LLM-guided program evolution can yield practical improvements at an industrial scale. Four applications illustrate this capability, each targeting a different level of the computing stack.

At the highest level, AlphaEvolve evolved scheduling heuristics for Borg, Google's cluster management system that allocates jobs to machines across data centers. The system produced a compact heuristic that ranks machines for job placement based on residual CPU and memory ratios. After validation on historical workloads and careful deployment, this evolved heuristic recovered 0.7% of previously stranded resources fleet-wide. While this percentage may appear modest, the absolute scale of Google's infrastructure translates it into substantial computational savings. The success of this application highlights an advantage of LLM-guided evolution over reinforcement learning approaches. The evolved heuristics are interpretable code that engineers can review, understand, and trust before deployment in safety-critical systems.

Moving down the stack, AlphaEvolve optimized the tiling heuristics for GEMM (general matrix multiply) in TPU matrix multiplication kernels. The task involves selecting tile sizes that balance computational throughput against memory bandwidth, with optimal choices depending on the specific matrix dimensions encountered in workloads. By evolving heuristics trained on shapes drawn from Gemini's actual computation patterns, AlphaEvolve achieved a 23% average speedup for individual kernels and a 1% reduction in end-to-end training time for Gemini models. This application exemplifies a virtuous cycle where AI systems optimize the infrastructure used to train subsequent AI systems.

At the hardware description level, AlphaEvolve evolved optimizations for Verilog RTL code that implements arithmetic circuits in the TPU matrix multiplication unit. The system identified simplifications that reduce area and power consumption without affecting functionality, with proposed changes verified through formal methods and human review before incorporation. This result marks the first direct contribution of an AI system to TPU arithmetic design, suggesting that LLM-guided evolution may eventually play a role in hardware-software codesign.

Finally, AlphaEvolve optimized the XLA intermediate representation for FlashAttention kernels, achieving a 32% speedup in the attention computation and a 15% improvement in pre- and post-processing. The XLA IR level presents a particularly challenging search space, as the representation is designed for compiler analysis rather than human readability, and the code has already undergone extensive optimization. Success at this level suggests the potential to integrate LLM-guided evolution as a compiler optimization pass, automatically discovering target-specific improvements that traditional compiler heuristics miss.

2.4.4.3 Agent Architecture and Training Objective Design

ShinkaEvolve extends the application domain beyond algorithm optimization to the design of LLM agent architectures and machine learning training objectives. These applications demonstrate that the same evolutionary framework can discover effective designs in domains where the search space consists of prompting strategies and loss functions rather than numerical algorithms.

For the AIME 2024 mathematical reasoning benchmark [24], ShinkaEvolve evolved agent scaffolds that orchestrate multiple LLM calls to solve competition-level mathematics problems. Operating under a constraint of at most 10 LLM queries per problem, the system discovered a three-stage pipeline architecture. The first stage deploys three specialized expert personas (a step-by-step reasoner, a pattern-recognition expert, and an algorithmically oriented mathematician) to generate independent solution attempts at moderate temperature. The second stage subjects each solution to critical review by a skeptical evaluator operating at low temperature, checking logical consistency and calculation accuracy. The third stage synthesizes a final answer through an editor-in-chief persona that weighs the evidence from all solutions and their critiques.

This evolved architecture outperforms both simple single-call baselines and hand-designed majority-voting schemes. More significantly, the architecture transfers effectively across problem years (showing gains on AIME 2023 and 2025) and across base models (improving performance when applied to gpt-4.1-mini, gpt-4.1, and o4-mini). The transferability suggests that ShinkaEvolve discovered genuinely applicable structural principles for mathematical reasoning rather than exploiting idiosyncrasies of the specific model and problem set used during evolution.

In a distinct application, ShinkaEvolve evolved load-balancing loss functions for mixture-of-experts (MoE) language model training. MoE architectures [28] route tokens to a subset of expert networks, achieving computational efficiency but risking expert collapse, in which the router concentrates traffic on a few experts while others remain underutilized. Standard practice adds a load-balancing loss term to encourage uniform expert usage, but the design of this term involves subtle trade-offs that manual tuning struggles to optimize.

The evolved loss function augments the standard global-batch formulation with an entropy-weighted penalty term that activates when individual experts fall below a minimum usage threshold. This adaptive mechanism provides stronger regularization when the router distribution has low entropy (indicating concentration on a few experts) and relaxes constraints when usage is already well-balanced. Evaluation on a 2.7B-parameter MoE model trained on nearly 30B tokens demonstrates that the evolved loss achieves lower perplexity and better downstream task performance than the baseline, particularly at higher regularization strengths, where the standard loss degrades model quality.

2.4.4.4 Characteristics of Amenable Problems

Reflecting on this diverse application, portfolio reveals patterns that distinguish problems amenable to LLM-guided evolution from those that remain challenging. Several characteristics correlate with successful application.

First, problems must admit automated evaluation. All successful applications share the property that candidate programs can be scored without human judgment, whether through mathematical verification, simulation, or execution on test cases. AlphaEvolve explicitly identifies this requirement as its primary limitation, noting that many scientific discovery problems require experimental validation that cannot be automated. The mathematical optimization and infrastructure applications succeed precisely because fitness can be computed programmatically, enabling the rapid evaluation cycles that evolutionary search requires.

Second, practical applications typically involve search spaces where LLMs possess relevant prior knowledge. Circle packing, matrix multiplication algorithms, and attention mechanisms all have extensive treatment in the technical literature that forms part of LLM training data. This prior knowledge bootstraps evolution by enabling contextually appropriate initial proposals and meaningful refinements. Problems in highly specialized or novel domains where LLMs lack relevant training signals may prove more difficult. However, the meta-prompting and inspiration mechanisms partially address this limitation by accumulating problem-specific knowledge during evolution.

Third, the most impressive results emerge when the evolved artifact is a search procedure rather than a direct solution. Evolving heuristics for kissing number constructions, scheduling policies for cluster management, or agent architectures for mathematical reasoning all share this meta-level structure. The LLM's knowledge of algorithmic patterns and optimization strategies proves more valuable for designing search procedures than for directly constructing solutions, particularly as problem scale increases beyond what can be addressed through direct enumeration or simple heuristics.

Fourth, problems benefit from having meaningful intermediate solutions that provide a gradient signal for evolutionary selection. The phase structure observed in circle packing evolution, where early generations discover basic strategies and later generations refine them, depends on the existence of solutions spanning a range of quality levels. Problems with sparse fitness landscapes, where most candidates are equally poor until a precise solution is found, may resist gradual evolutionary improvement.

These characteristics suggest that LLM-guided program evolution occupies a specific niche in the broader landscape of automated discovery methods. The approach excels at synthesizing complex algorithms from primitive operations, optimizing existing systems through targeted modifications, and designing architectures that coordinate multiple components. Problems requiring fundamentally novel conceptual insights, experimental validation, or reasoning far beyond current LLM capabilities may require complementary approaches or await advances in foundation model capabilities.

2.4.5 Open Challenges and Future Directions

Despite the impressive results achieved by AlphaEvolve, ShinkaEvolve, and CodeEvolve, significant challenges remain before LLM-guided program evolution reaches its full potential. These challenges span technical, practical, and scientific dimensions, and their resolution will shape the field's trajectory.

The tension between sample efficiency and solution quality presents a fundamental trade-off. ShinkaEvolve demonstrates that careful engineering of parent selection, novelty filtering, and adaptive model allocation can achieve strong results with approximately 150 program evaluations on circle packing benchmarks. Yet more ambitious applications, such as AlphaEvolve's infrastructure optimizations, require substantially greater computational investment. The cost of LLM queries compounds this concern, as commercial API pricing makes large-scale evolutionary runs expensive even when evaluation itself is cheap. Future work must develop techniques that extract as much information as possible from each LLM query, perhaps through more sophisticated prompt design, better exploitation of model uncertainty, or hybrid approaches that combine LLM-guided search with cheaper local optimization methods.

Reproducibility poses a particular challenge for LLM-guided evolution. While the evolutionary components of these systems (selection, population management, migration) can be made deterministic through careful seeding, the LLM queries that drive variation introduce fundamental stochasticity. Current commercial APIs do not support deterministic generation, meaning that even with identical prompts and random seeds, different runs may produce different candidate programs. CodeEvolve explicitly acknowledges this limitation, noting that although their evolutionary operators are reproducible, the overall system behavior cannot be exactly replicated. This situation complicates scientific comparison of methods and raises questions about the reliability of results. The research community would benefit from standardized benchmarks, multiple independent runs with statistical analysis, and perhaps a dedicated inference infrastructure that prioritizes reproducibility over other considerations.

The divide between industrial and open-source systems reflects broader questions about the democratization of AI capabilities. AlphaEvolve remains closed-source, with implementation details disclosed only at a high level in publications. ShinkaEvolve and CodeEvolve explicitly position themselves as open alternatives that enable community participation and extension. Yet even these open systems depend heavily on commercial LLM APIs, creating barriers for researchers without substantial computational budgets. The reliance on proprietary models also means that system behavior may change unpredictably as providers update their offerings. Developing effective LLM-guided evolution using open-weight models, or creating specialized models fine-tuned for program variation, could substantially broaden access to these capabilities.

The connection between LLM-guided evolution and test-time compute deserves deeper investigation. AlphaEvolve's discussion section explicitly frames the system as a test-time compute agent that enhances base LLM capabilities far beyond naive resampling. This perspective suggests that evolutionary search over programs represents one point in a broader design space of inference-time scaling strategies, alongside techniques such as chain-of-thought prompting, tree search, and self-consistency. Understanding how these approaches relate and potentially complement each other could yield more powerful hybrid methods. Furthermore, the knowledge discovered through evolutionary search might be distilled back into base models, creating feedback loops in which evolved algorithms improve the training of future LLMs, which then enable more effective evolution.

Integration with the simpler approaches discussed earlier in this chapter offers another promising direction. The LLM-based AutoML-Zero experiments in Sect. 2.3 demonstrate that language models can enhance classical program synthesis through targeted mutation of operator sequences. Combining this approach with the sophisticated population management and prompt engineering of the newer systems could yield methods that discover not just optimized algorithms but entirely novel computational primitives. Similarly, the LMPSO framework from Sect. 2.2 shows how LLMs can be integrated into swarm intelligence algorithms while maintaining interpretable search dynamics. Exploring analogous integrations with other metaheuristics, such as ant colony optimization or differential evolution (DE (see Sect. 1.2.3)), may reveal new capabilities.

Finally, the requirement for automated evaluation remains the most fundamental limitation. Many scientific discovery problems of greatest interest involve experiments that cannot be simulated, judgments that require human expertise, or validation that demands physical resources. AlphaEvolve suggests connecting LLM-guided code evolution with natural language reasoning systems that can handle high-level idea evaluation, dropping down to program evolution only when computational validation becomes possible. Realizing this vision requires advances in LLM reasoning capabilities, automated experiment design, and perhaps in robotic systems capable of executing physical experiments under algorithmic guidance. The convergence of these technologies may eventually enable LLM-guided evolution to contribute to scientific domains that currently remain beyond its reach.

References

1. Alon, N., Awerbuch, B., Azar, Y.: The online set cover problem. In: Proceedings of the Thirty-Fifth Annual ACM Symposium on Theory of Computing, pp. 100–105 (2003)
2. Applegate, D., Cook, W.: Concorde TSP Solver (2006)
3. Assumpção, H., et al.: CodeEvolve: an open source evolutionary coding agent for algorithm discovery and optimization. arXiv preprint arXiv:2510.14150 (2025)
4. Augusto, D.A., Barbosa, H.J.: Symbolic regression via genetic programming. In: Proceedings. Vol. 1. Sixth Brazilian Symposium on Neural Networks, pp. 173–178. IEEE, New York (2000)
5. Beasley, J.E.: OR-library: distributing test problems by electronic mail. E. J. Oper. Res. **41**(11), 1069–1072 (1990)
6. Burke, E.K., et al.: Hyper-heuristics: a survey of the state of the art. J. Oper. Res. Soc. **64**(12), 1695–1724 (2013)
7. Chen, A., Dohan, D., So, D.: EvoPrompting: language models for code-level neural architecture search. Adv. Neural Inf. Process. Syst. **36**, 7787–7817 (2024)
8. Davis, L.: Applying adaptive algorithms to epistatic domains. IJCAI **85**, 162–164 (1985)
9. Gendreau, M., Potvin, J.-Y. (eds.): Handbook of Metaheuristics, vol. 2. Springer, Berlin (2010)
10. Goldberg, D.E., Deb, K.: A comparative analysis of selection schemes used in genetic algorithms. In: Foundations of Genetic Algorithms, vol. 1, pp. 69–93. Elsevier, Amsterdam (1991)
11. Hemberg, E., Moskal, S., O'Reilly, U.-M.: Evolving code with a large language model. Genet. Program. Evolvable Mach. **25**(2) (2024). ISSN: 1573-7632. https://doi.org/10.1007/s10710-024-09494-2
12. Hutter, F., Kotthoff, L., Vanschoren, J. (eds.): Automatic Machine Learning, 1st edn. The Springer Series on Challenges in Machine Learning. Springer International Publishing, Basel (2019)
13. Iba, H., Noman, N.: New Frontier in Evolutionary Algorithms: Theory and Applications. Imperial College Press, London (2011)
14. Kennedy, J., Eberhart, R.: Particle swarm optimization. Proceedings of ICNN'95-International Conference on Neural Networks, vol. 4, pp. 1942–1948. IEEE, New York (1995)
15. Khuri, S., Bäack, T., Heitköotter, J.: An evolutionary approach to combinatorial optimization problems. In: ACM Conference on Computer Science, pp. 66–73 (1994)
16. Koga, M., Xu, J., Iba, H.: Large language models as genetic algorithm optimizers. In: Proceedings of 8th International Congress on. Advanced Applied Informatics (IAAI2025). Kitakyushu International Conference Center (2025)
17. Lange, R.T., Imajuku, Y., Cetin, E.: Shinkaevolve: towards open-ended and sample-efficient program evolution. arXiv preprint arXiv:2509.19349 (2025)
18. Lanzi, P.L., Loiacono, D.: ChatGPT and other large language models as evolutionary engines for online interactive collaborative game design. In: Proceedings of the Genetic and Evolutionary Computation Conference, pp. 1383–1390 (2023)
19. Liu, S., et al.: Large language models as evolutionary optimizers. In: 2024 IEEE Congress on Evolutionary Computation (CEC), pp. 1–8. IEEE, New York (2024)
20. Nie, A., et al.: The Importance of Directional Feedback for LLM-based Optimizers. arXiv preprint arXiv:2405.16434 (2024)
21. Novikov, A., et al.: AlphaEvolve: A coding agent for scientific and algorithmic discovery. arXiv preprint arXiv:2506.13131 (2025)

22. Oliver, I.M., Smith, D.J., Holland, J.R.C.: A study of permutation crossover operators on the TSP. In: *Proceedings of the 2nd International Conference on Genetic Algorithms and their Application*, pp. 224–230 (1987)
23. Ouyang, L. et al.: Training language models to follow instructions with human feedback. Adv. Neural Inf. Process. Syst. **35**, 27730–27744 (2022)
24. Patel, B., et al.: AIME: Ai system optimization via multiple LLM evaluators. arXiv preprint arXiv:2410.03131 (2024)
25. Piniganti, L.: A Survey of Tabu Search in Combinatorial Optimization (2014)
26. Real, E., et al.: AutoML-zero: evolving machine learning algorithms from scratch. In: International Conference on Machine Learning, pp. 8007–8019. PMLR, New York (2020)
27. Real, E., et al.: Regularized evolution for image classifier architecture search. In Proceedings of the AAAI Conference on Artificial Intelligence, vol. 33, pp. 4780–4789 (2019)
28. Riquelme, C., et al.: Scaling vision with sparse mixture of experts. Adv. Neural Inf. Process. Syst. **34**, 8583–8595 (2021)
29. Romano, J.D., et al.: PMLB v1.0: an open source dataset collection for benchmarking machine learning methods. arXiv preprint arXiv:2012.00058v2 (2021)
30. Romera-Paredes, B., et al.: Mathematical discoveries from program search with large language models. Nature **625**(7995), 468–475 (2024). https://doi.org/10.1038/s41586-023-06924-6
31. Shi, Y., Eberhart, R.: A modified particle swarm optimizer. 1998 IEEE International Conference on Evolutionary Computation Proceedings. IEEE World Congress on Computational Intelligence (Cat. No. 98TH8360), pp. 69–73. IEEE, New York (1998)
32. Shinn, N., et al.: Reflexion: language agents with verbal reinforcement learning. Adv. Neural Inf. Process. Syst. **36**, 8634–8652 (2023)
33. Shinohara, Y., et al.: Large language models as particle swarm optimizers (2025). arXiv: 2504.09247 [cs.NE]. https://arxiv.org/abs/2504.09247
34. Slivkins, A.: Dynamic ad allocation: Bandits with budgets. arXiv preprint arXiv:1306.0155 (2013)
35. Tamilarasi, A., Jayasankari, S.: Evaluation on GA based Model for solving JSSP. Int. J. Comput. Appl. **43** (2012). ISSN: 0975–8887
36. Thoppilan, R., et al.: LaMDA: language models for dialog applications. arXiv preprint arXiv:2201.08239 (2022)
37. Tohyama, H., Ida, K., Matsueda, J.: A genetic algorithm for the uncapacitated facility location problem In: *Electronics and Communications in Japan*, pp. 47–54 (2011)
38. Touvron, H., et al.: LLaMA: open and efficient foundation language models. arXiv preprint arXiv:2302.13971 (2023)
39. Wang, K.-P., et al.: Particle swarm optimization for traveling salesman problem. In: Proceedings of the 2003 International Conference on Machine Learning and Cybernetics (IEEE cat. no. 03ex693), vol. 3, pp. 1583–1585. IEEE, New York (2003)
40. Wu, Q., et al. : AutoGen: Enabling Next-Gen LLM Applications via Multi-Agent Conversation. In: COLM 2024 (2024). https://www.microsoft.com/en-us/research/publication/autogen-enabling-next-gen-llm-applications-via-multi-agent-conversation-framework/
41. Yang, C., et al.: Large Language Models as Optimizers. In: ICLR (2024)
42. Zhou, Y., et al.: Large language models are human-level prompt engineers. In: *The Eleventh International Conference on Learning Representations* (2023). URL: https://openreview.net/forum?id=92gvk82DE-
43. Zoph, B., et al.: Learning transferable architectures for scalable image recognition. In: *Proceedings of the IEEE Conference on Computer Vision and Pattern Recognition*, pp. 8697–8710 (2018)

Chapter 3
LLMs for Evolutionary Optimization

The intersection between evolutionary computation (EC) [20] and large language model (LLM) [9] algorithms, broadly referred to as LLM-assisted evolutionary computation (LLMAEC), refers to a hybrid paradigm where LLMs are integrated into evolutionary algorithms as optimization engines or intelligent facilitators.

To implement LLMAEC algorithms efficiently, the programmer needs to know how to integrate the LLM into the evolutionary cycle properly. This may include using LLMs to select and design evolutionary operators, optimize EC parameters, evaluate the fitness of EC models, or even use LLMs for program synthesis. Advanced users may even fine-tune their LLMs with additional knowledge of EC algorithms, improving system reliability.

In EC, the design of evolutionary operators plays a crucial role. Traditional evolutionary operators are usually fixed and come with explicit mathematical definitions. Introducing LLMs can break this fixed mindset, expanding EC to a broader range. For instance, LLMs directly act as an evolutionary operator involved in the generation, modification, or selection of individuals [35, 42, 60]. LLMs are also used to guide genetic operators, such as crossover and mutation, based on the task scenario and objectives, making the operations more effective.

LLMs can also be used to optimize population design and the evaluation of individuals, e.g., by adapting the fitness function to the population's current needs as evolution progresses. In addition, we explain how to generate executable code through LLMs and discuss the feasibility of realizing genetic programming (GP)-like program synthesis.

H. Iba et al., *Large Language Models and Evolutionary Computation*,
Natural Computing Series, https://doi.org/10.1007/978-981-95-8597-7_3

3.1 M3GP Algorithm

The multidimensional multiclass genetic programming with multidimensional populations (M3GP) algorithm [63] will be used in several experiments in Chaps. 3 and 4. As such, we provided a detailed description of how the algorithm works in its most straightforward implementation. For our experiments, we use the *m3gp* Python library, whose code is available at GitHub,[1] and also described in Sect. 7.1. The code in the appendix explains how to use LLMs to bootstrap evolution, aligning with the content of Sect. 3.2.3.

The M3GP is a wrapper-based feature engineering GP algorithm that evolves a set of trees, i.e., an individual within the M3GP population is a multi-tree model. Similar to the standard GP algorithm, each tree within the M3GP model is an arithmetic tree. As such, a tree converts a sample from the dataset into a single real value. Since an M3GP model contains m trees, assuming our training data contains n features, an M3GP model is effectively a mathematical function $f : \mathbb{R}^n \rightarrow \mathbb{R}^m$.

The M3GP algorithm has the following steps:

- **Initialization:** The M3GP algorithm initializes its population of models as single, randomly generated trees. Therefore, at the beginning of the evolutionary cycle, each individual is a simple model consisting of a single feature, i.e., $f : \mathbb{R}^n \rightarrow \mathbb{R}$. For those familiar with the standard GP algorithm, the initialization step is identical to both algorithms.
- **Evaluation:** As previously mentioned, an M3GP models works as an $f : \mathbb{R}^n \rightarrow \mathbb{R}^m$ function. Taking this into consideration, the first step in evaluation is to use the model to map the input dataset, i.e., an $\mathbb{R}^n$ space, to an $\mathbb{R}^m$ space. In this space, we train and test a classifier (or other algorithm) and use its performance (e.g., accuracy or error) as fitness. This results in the M3GP models optimizing an $\mathbb{R}^m$ space to the necessities of that particular classifier, i.e., M3GP acts as a wrapper-based feature engineering algorithm.
- **Selection:** We use the *tournament* method to select the parents of the next generation. To choose each parent, the algorithm randomly selects a small set of models and selects the best (i.e., the one with the highest fitness) from this set. The tournament method can maintain sufficient selective pressure to select mostly the best individuals, thereby promoting the propagation of their beneficial traits in the next generation, while also allowing the less fit to become parents, thereby avoiding the loss of genetic diversity that would stagnate evolution.
- **Genetic Operators:** M3GP uses two crossover operators and three mutation operators. For simplicity and consistency with GitHub, let's call these five operators StdXO, M3XO, StdMUT, M3ADD, and M3REM. These abbreviations will only be mentioned in this explanation. When an M3GP model is selected via tournament, it will always suffer the effect of one genetic operator. By default, it has a 50% chance of being selected for mutation or crossover, and, within each

[1] https://github.com/jespb/Python-M3GP

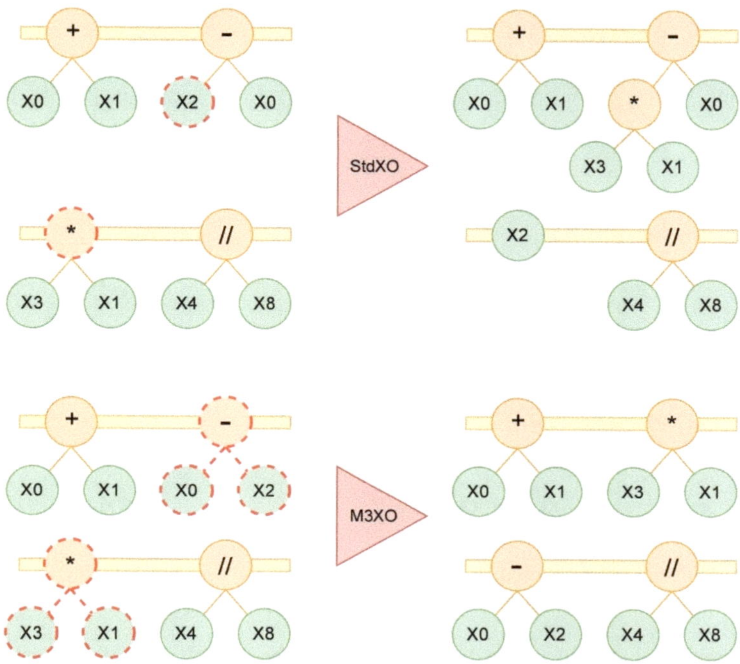

Fig. 3.1 Crossover operators used by M3GP

category, each operator has an equal chance of being selected. These operators are illustrated in Figs. 3.1 (crossovers) and 3.2 (mutations).

- **StdXO:** This crossover operator reflects the same kind of crossover operation you find in the standard GP algorithm. Since M3GP models contain multiple trees, this operator selects a random node from one of the trees in each parent's model and swaps it, generating two offspring.
- **M3XO:** This operator works similarly, except that, rather than swapping nodes between models, it selects an entire tree from each parent and swaps them, also generating two offspring.
- **StdMUT:** This mutation operator reflects the same kind of crossover operation you find in the standard GP algorithm. This algorithm generates a random tree and swaps it with a randomly selected node in the model, producing one offspring.
- **M3ADD:** Similarly, this mutation operator also creates a randomly generated tree, but, rather than modifying an existing tree within the parent, it adds the new tree to the parent, increasing its dimensionality. This operator creates one offspring.
- **M3REM:** Lastly, this mutation operator randomly selects a tree within the model and removes it, decreasing its dimensionality. While this is the only

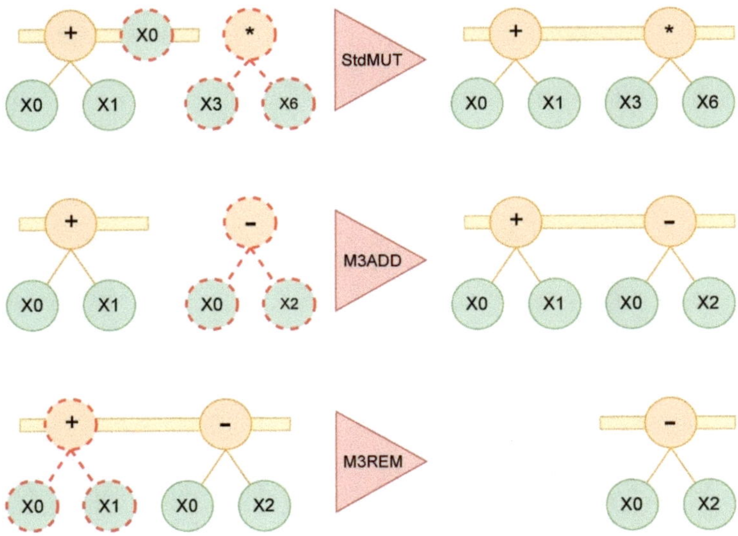

Fig. 3.2 Mutation operators used by M3GP

operator that reduces the dimensionality of the models, one of our early studies indicates that it tends to lower model accuracy, resulting in worse offspring. This operator creates one offspring.

The parameters used by M3GP in its original implementation are similar to those typically used by the standard GP algorithm. This algorithm used a population size of 500, 100 generations, a maximum depth of 6 for randomly generated trees, and a maximum depth of 17 within the models to avoid unnecessarily deep models. As previously mentioned, M3GP used five genetic operators, each with a 20% chance of mutation or crossover, and an equal selection chance for each operator within those two categories. One parameter that has been studied over a few years, not only by Batista et al. [4, 5] but also by other authors [34, 64].

M3GP was initially proposed as a classification algorithm that would evolve a set of trees to be used by the Mahalanobis classifier, a cluster-based algorithm that uses the Mahalanobis distance as a metric to the closest cluster centroid. Over time, other approaches have been experimented with, such as using other classifiers as the wrapped algorithms [4, 5] and extending the M3GP application to regression tasks [34, 64]. In this book, we will later discuss M3GP's capabilities for classification and regression tasks and for feature engineering, i.e., extracting relevant information (feature combinations) from the input data.

3.2 LLM-Assisted Evolutionary Computation

LLMs were initially designed as language models; however, their capabilities extend far beyond natural language processing. In evolutionary computation, LLMs are increasingly being deployed to address both foundational challenges, such as bloat control, exploration and exploitation, and fitness evaluation, and broader operational tasks, such as surrogate modeling and interactive agent design. Their ability to process complex patterns, generate solutions, and approximate fitness landscapes makes them valuable tools for enhancing the efficiency and scalability of evolutionary computation systems. This section explores the integration of LLMs into evolutionary computation. We begin by contextualizing the computational demands of evolutionary computation and how LLMs can alleviate these burdens. Later, we detail specific applications: first, how LLMs help mitigate bloat (the uncontrolled growth of redundant code or structures in evolved solutions); second, their use in promoting quality diversity for maintaining a varied and high-performing solution set; and finally, their function as surrogate models or interactive agents for efficient fitness evaluation. While this section includes these key challenges, they are further explored in the remainder of the chapter.

One of the most significant challenges in EC is the high computational cost of model induction. Evolutionary algorithms typically evaluate thousands of candidate solutions across multiple generations, requiring extensive fitness evaluations. While these evaluations are inherently parallelizable, the sheer volume of computations remains a bottleneck. Researchers have pursued various optimizations, including algorithmic improvements, surrogate modeling, and hybrid machine learning approaches, yet computational efficiency remains a critical concern, especially for high-dimensional or real-world problems.

The remainder of this section examines how LLMs mitigate these computational challenges, focusing on three key areas: bloat control, exploration and exploitation (quality diversity), and fitness evaluation. By integrating LLMs into these aspects of EC, researchers can significantly reduce computational overhead while enhancing the adaptability and performance of evolutionary systems. In practice, LLMs can be used to search for relevant feature combinations and reduce the temporal and computational resources spent on model evaluation; maintain diverse, high-performing solution sets by dynamically balancing search strategies; and reduce evaluation costs by serving as surrogate models or interactive agents for fitness evaluation.

3.2.1 *Bloat Control*

Bloat has been a challenge in evolutionary computation since the field's origins. It is described as the uncontrolled growth of solution representations (individuals) within the population without yielding corresponding fitness improvements [84]. This phenomenon is particularly prevalent in tree-based genetic programming and other variable-length representation schemes. It is intuitive to think that smaller, more parsimonious models are generally preferable because of their better generalization properties, but this line of thought is often incorrect. Recent works [6, 7] show no strong correlation between model size and performance (accuracy or error) in test data, implying that current methods provide models that can be made compact with no penalties in performance. Additionally, one study indicates that bloat may limit the population's overfitting capabilities by stagnating evolution [77], implying that a certain degree of bloat within the population is desirable.

The appropriate model complexity is fundamentally tied to the intrinsic difficulty of the problem domain. For relatively simple problems in which input features exhibit strong, direct correlations with the target variable, compact solutions may be optimal, as they can capture the underlying relationships without unnecessary complexity. However, many real-world problems involve scenarios in which individual features exhibit only weak or nonlinear associations with the target. In such cases, the evolutionary algorithm must explore higher-order feature interactions and more complex functional forms to discover meaningful patterns. This necessary exploration often leads to larger solution structures, which should not be automatically dismissed as bloat if they genuinely improve model performance.

Figure 3.3 illustrates one common issue found in EC populations. In early generations, models share valuable information via crossover, quickly improving their fitness scores. After a few generations, their fitness tends to stabilize, and the models start to grow in size in search of minor fitness improvements. In some problems, we need larger models to reach a solution, but the large models shown in this figure have lower fitness scores than the top model.

Evaluating large models requires more processing power and memory, slowing down the evolutionary process and increasing resource consumption [71]. Beyond computational costs, bloated models suffer from reduced interpretability: their excessive size makes them difficult to analyze and understand, limiting their practical utility in domains where explainability is crucial. This dual impact on both

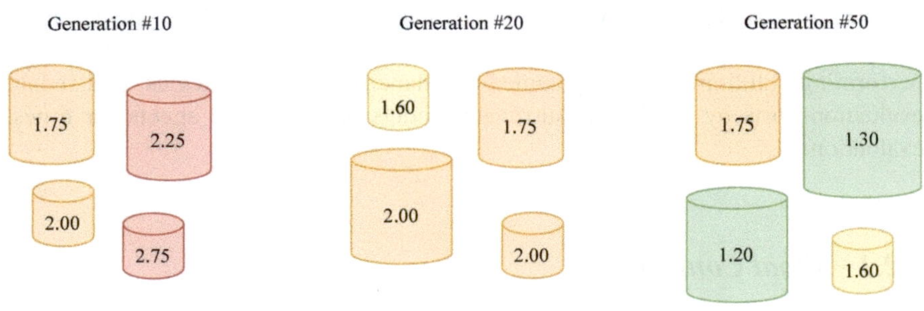

Fig. 3.3 Representation of the evolution of population size and fitness (RMSE) over the generations seen in Fig. 3.4 (M3GP, CL). Since we are minimizing the RMSE (i.e., fitness), the smaller the number, the better

efficiency and usability strongly motivates the development of effective methods to control bloat.

The distinction between productive complexity and true bloat remains an active area of research, with recent approaches focusing on multi-objective optimization techniques that explicitly balance model performance against complexity.

3.2.1.1 Bloat in EC Models

In continuation of our previous work [6, 7], we show that there is no correlation between fitness, measured as the root mean squared error (RMSE) on the test data, and model size. To do so, we perform 30 independent runs using different training and test partitions in the cooling load (CL) and heating load (HL) datasets, extracted from the energy efficiency dataset[2] available at the University of California, Irvine (UCI) repository [19]. We applied two different GP-based algorithms in each dataset, M3GP [63], a single-objective algorithm, that aims to minimize the twofold RMSE in training data; and M6GP [5], a multi-objective algorithm, that aims to minimize the twofold RMSE in training data, as well as the mean absolute error (MAE). The M3GP and M6GP algorithms are available on Github.[3] For details about the M3GP and M6GP code used for these experiments, please check Sect. 7.1.

Figure 3.4 illustrates the lack of correlation between model size and performance in the experiments. In this figure, we see that, in early generations, the models are smaller and have a higher test RMSE. As evolution progresses, models tend to become larger and have lower RMSE. In the final generation, we observe that the M3GP and M6GP models have test RMSE values of approximately 1.5 and 1.75, respectively. Although there is a low distribution of RMSE values, the size of the models ranges from 200 to 1000 nodes, showing a low correlation between model size and test RMSE in both M3GP and M6GP models.[4]

Numerous techniques have been developed to control bloat in evolutionary computation, each addressing the problem from different perspectives. The simplest approaches impose hard constraints on model complexity, such as enforcing strict size or depth limits during model generation [52, 69]. While effective at preventing excessive growth, these methods may prematurely eliminate potentially useful structures that exceed arbitrary limits.

More sophisticated approaches leverage selection pressure to favor parsimony. These include approaches such as preferential selection of smaller models among equally fit individuals [7]; double tournaments that first select for fitness and then

[2] https://archive.ics.uci.edu/dataset/242/energy+efficiency

[3] https://github.com/jespb/Python-M3GP and https://github.com/jespb/Python-M6GP

[4] Pearson correlation values between model size and test RMSE: 0.0717 in M3GP models and 0.0449 in M6GP models, in the CL dataset, and 0.1658 in M3GP models and 0.0276 in M6GP models, in the HL dataset.

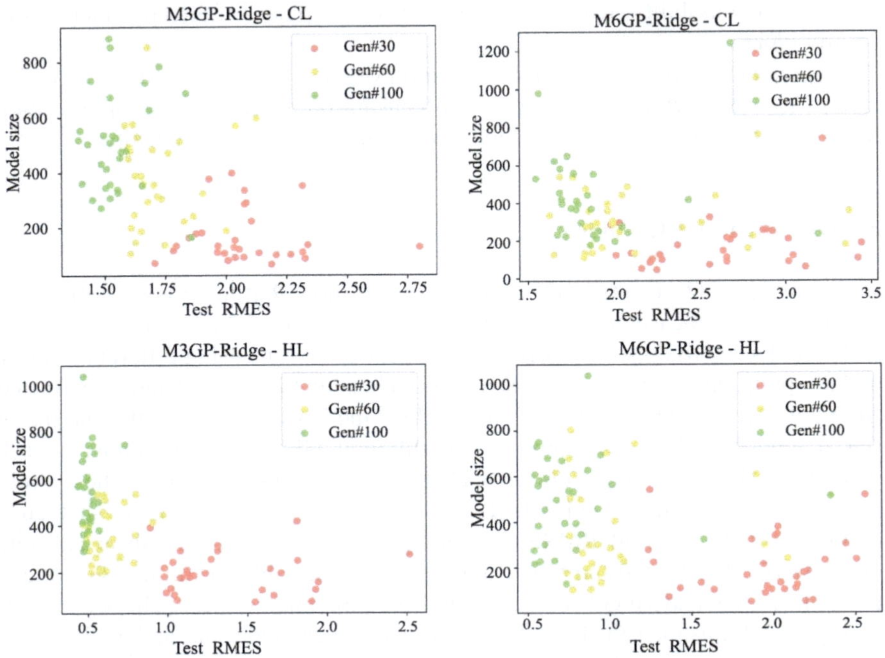

Fig. 3.4 Scatter plots comparing model size and RMSE in test data over the generations for M3GP and M6GP models, on the CL and HL datasets. These plots illustrate a trend where model size increases as RMSE decreases. However, the plots also illustrate a low correlation between model size and RMSE in later generations, where models with RMSE values in 1.5 – 2.0 (CL dataset) and 0.5 – 0.8 (HL dataset) have sizes ranging from 200 to 1000 nodes

for size [51]; or multi-objective optimization that explicitly treats model complexity (e.g., size or depth) as a separate optimization target alongside accuracy [5, 66, 99].

An innovative alternative directly accounts for computational efficiency by incorporating model evaluation time into the fitness function [17]. This approach naturally favors models that balance accuracy with practical runtime performance, rather than simply minimizing structural size. Such methods are particularly valuable in real-world applications where computational resources are constrained.

The effectiveness of bloat control methods often depends on the problem domain and evolutionary representation used. Comprehensive reviews of these techniques and their comparative advantages can be found in [76, 78], which analyze both theoretical foundations and practical implementations across different evolutionary computation paradigms.

3.2.1.2 Bloat Control Using LLMs

The bloat issue is present not only in traditional evolutionary computation methods but also in systems that use LLMs to generate solutions. Fortunately, as seen in Sect. 2.3, LLMs can be used to clean up functions, simplifying models and reducing their computational complexity. A recent work by Zhang et al. [94] explores how to control bloat in such systems using two approaches: explicitly requesting the solution to have a defined maximum length, guiding their generation to be more concise, and employing a multi-objective approach where the algorithm aims to optimize both the fitness and the code length. Their results indicate that using bloat-control techniques can reduce the solution size without penalizing fitness. As such, we include our own solution to follow the M3GP and M6GP examples discussed previously.

We modified the *"getOffspring"* function from these implementations by adding one extra step before returning the offspring. The modified version appears in Appendix Sect. 7.2. In this additional step (shown in Listing 7.6), we call the *gpt-4.1-mini* model through the OpenAI application programming interface (API) to simplify the offspring's mathematical expression.

Using an LLM to simplify models requires three main operations within this function:

- Convert the Model into a String: Since each model has a direct representation as a mathematical expression, this step is straightforward.
- Extract a Valid Mathematical Expression from the LLM: This is the only step that requires careful prompting to ensure the LLM returns (1) a non-empty string, (2) an expression composed only of allowed arithmetic operators, and (3) operands that match labels in the terminal-node list. Once the returned string passes these checks, we format it into a tree-compatible expression using the *"add_parentheses"* function (Listing 7.7), producing structures like those shown in Figs. 3.5 and 3.6. To keep the prompting simple, we delegate formatting details to a helper function and focus primarily on validating the LLM output.

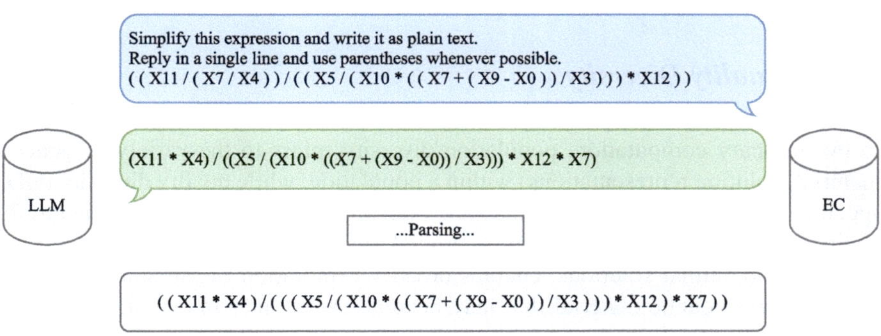

Fig. 3.5 Example of interaction between the M3GP algorithm (EC) and the *gpt-4.1-mini* through the OpenAI API (LLM). While the LLM rewrote the expression, it remained equivalent

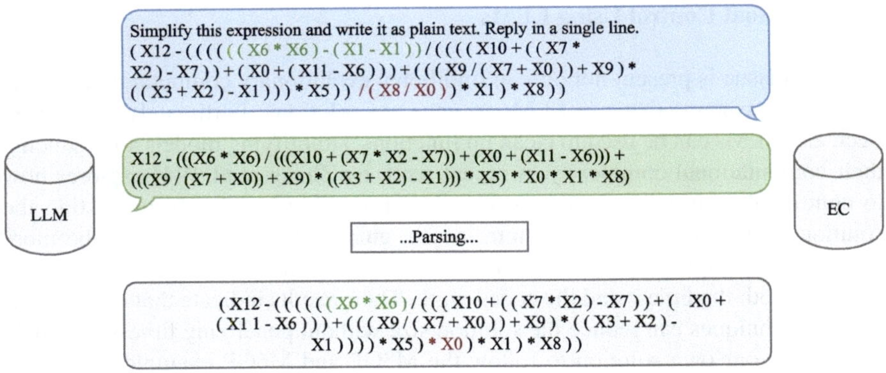

Fig. 3.6 Example of interaction between the M3GP algorithm (EC) and the *gpt-4.1-mini* through the OpenAI API (LLM). In this case, the LLM correctly simplified the expression when it detected a subtraction by 0 (X1-X1), but incorrectly removed a division by X8

- Convert the Formatted String Back into a Model: Because the previous step guarantees that the expression is both valid and well-structured, this final conversion becomes straightforward.

In these two figures, we see two examples of communication between M3GP and *gpt-4.1-mini*. In the first example, although we request parentheses in the output, we still need to format them, since they do not have spaces around them, unlike the expression given as input. This further motivated us to leave the formatting to an auxiliary function, rather than relying on the LLM. From a mathematical point of view, although the expressions are written differently, nothing has changed. In the second example, the LLM successfully simplified the expression. In green, we see that it detected a subtraction by X6-X6 and removed that part of the string. On an unfortunate note, in red, we see that it incorrectly removed a division by X8. We hypothesize that the LLM also intended to remove the later multiplication by X8, which would correctly simplify the expression.

3.2.2 *Quality Diversity*

In evolutionary computation, population diversity refers to the variety of genetic material (solution representations) within a population, while quality diversity (QD) specifically maintains solutions that are both high performing and behaviorally distinct [70]. Maintaining diversity is crucial since it prevents premature convergence to suboptimal solutions, enables broader exploration of the solution space, and preserves genetic material that may become useful later in evolution. As will be discussed in Sect. 3.2.3, the initial population is typically generated randomly, which promotes diversity at the start of evolution. However, some bootstrapping methods aim to create better individuals in the initial population, at the cost of losing diversity.

Novelty search (NS) [39] is an alternative approach to traditional fitness-driven evolution that explicitly rewards individuals based on how different they are from previously encountered solutions in behavior space, rather than their objective performance [40]. Unlike QD, which seeks a balance between quality and diversity, novelty search prioritizes exploration by encouraging the discovery of unique behaviors, even if they are not immediately high performing. This can be particularly useful in deceptive environments where the fitness landscape contains local optima that trap traditional evolutionary algorithms. By decoupling search from objective performance, novelty search can discover stepping stones–intermediate solutions that may not be optimal themselves but enable the discovery of high-performing solutions later in the search process [62].

One good example of such algorithms is the multi-dimensional archive of phenotypic elites (MAP-Elites) [62]. This algorithm explores the search space by examining a set of parameters and a granularity. Let us explain using the example in the reference paper. Assume you want to explore different robot morphologies to achieve the fastest speed and study how parameters such as height, weight, and energy efficiency affect the solutions. MAP-Elites would perform several runs, searching for the quickest robot that is tall, heavy, and efficient; tall, heavy, and inefficient, and so on. While in this example we set the parameters to binary, resulting in a search space that can be solved in eight runs, the user can increase the granularity of each parameter, thereby increasing the search space.

For a similar task, let us assume we want to find the fastest way to commute, so that the population of a city can travel to another city to work. In this case, we can consider objectives such as minimizing environmental, economic, and commuting costs while also managing parameters such as vehicle size and the type of energy used (e.g., human, electric, or gas). In this case, there is no obvious answer for the parameters, so we could ask MAP-Elites to obtain the best small human-powered vehicle, small electric vehicle, big electric vehicle, and so on. The hypothetical results of such a search are illustrated in Fig. 3.7.

When initializing an evolutionary computation algorithm, the population typically consists of randomly generated models that inherently provide substantial genetic diversity. This diversity is crucial in the early stages of evolution, as it allows the algorithm to explore a wide range of potential solutions before selective pressure refines the population toward higher-performing individuals. Although this randomness is useful for evolution, in Sect. 3.2.3, we discuss advanced initialization methods that bias the initial population to bootstrap evolution, such as heuristic seeding, domain knowledge, or previously discovered solutions [20].

As evolution progresses through selection mechanisms modeled after natural selection, higher-fitness individuals receive proportionally more opportunities to reproduce. This selective pressure causes successive generations to become increasingly dominated by genetic material from high-performing individuals, resulting in a gradual loss of population diversity and reduced effectiveness of crossover operations.

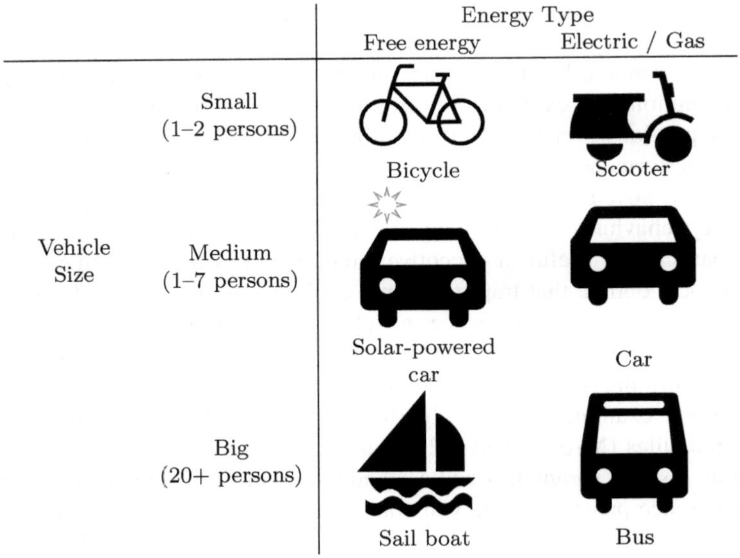

Fig. 3.7 Fast vehicles for each pair of size and energy type. For the goal of commuting a population between cities, trains might be the best option; however, some people might prefer their own car or a bus, depending on the existing railways. Although a sailboat could be a viable mode of transport in cities near water, it is not feasible

To examine population stagnation during evolution, we conducted an experimental study using a standard GP implementation on the hormone replacement therapy (HRT) dataset,[5] sourced from the UCI Machine Learning Repository [19]. Our experimental setup used a population of 500 individuals and 100 evolutionary iterations, and we measured diversity as the pairwise cosine distance between the class predictions of solutions in the training set.

The results obtained from a single run in this dataset are displayed in Fig. 3.8. In this figure, we show pairwise comparisons of the distances between solutions in the population for four generations: the initial generation and generations 10, 20, and 100. The populations are sorted from best solution to worst, and darker colors indicate similar solutions, i.e., solutions that make the exact prediction.

We can see that the original population is very diverse, except for the sections approximately from individual 150 to 220, and 270 to 450. In these sections, the solutions classify all samples as the same class (-1 and 1, respectively), resulting in cosine distances between the models of 0 (all predictions are the same) or 2 (all predictions are opposite). By generation 20, most of the population diversity is gone, and by generation 100, only the worst solutions distance themselves from the remainder of the population.

[5] https://archive.ics.uci.edu/dataset/45/heart+disease

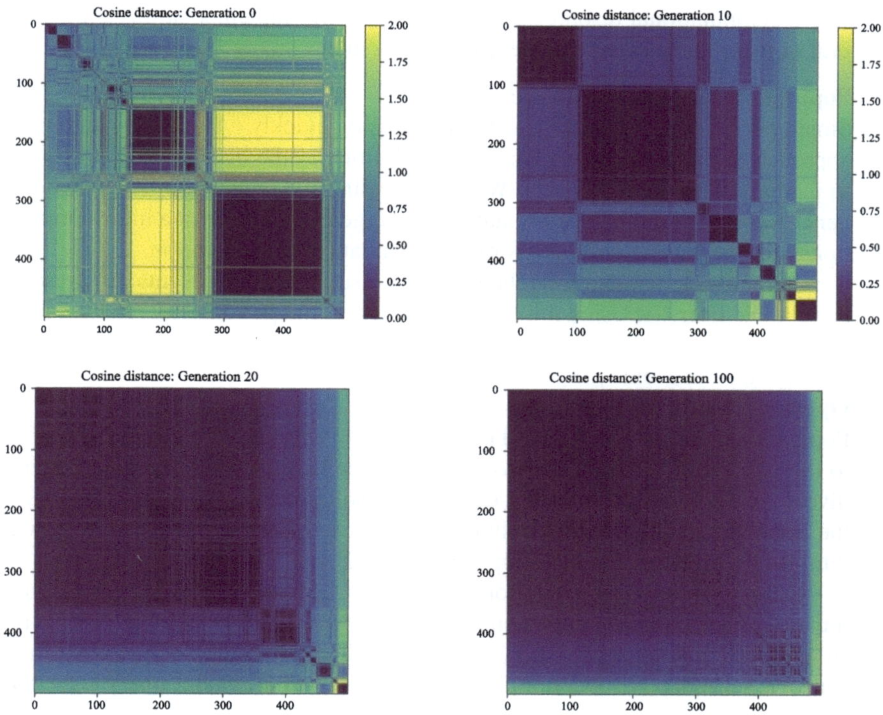

Fig. 3.8 Heatmap comparing the pairwise absolute cosine distance between the class (1 or −1) predictions of each solution. The models are ordered from best to worst. Here, we see that the initial population diversity is quickly lost over 20 generations, as most populations begin making the same predictions. This diversity level, in which only the worst individuals make different predictions, is maintained throughout training. This heatmap was obtained through a single run using the Std-GP in the HRT dataset, evolving a population of 500 models over 100 generations

This progression illustrates the characteristic evolutionary trajectory in which selection pressure drives the population toward homogeneity, despite an overall increase in size. The cosine distance metric effectively captures both the initial random variation and subsequent convergence through standard GP operations.

This convergence leads to two significant problems: evolutionary stagnation and computational inefficiency. As the population converges, it loses its ability to explore novel regions of the solution space, often becoming trapped in local optima. Additionally, evaluation resources are wasted on genetically similar individuals that provide diminishing returns. To combat this diversity loss and prevent evolutionary stagnation, researchers have developed multiple strategies that address both the evolutionary stagnation problem (by preserving genetic exploration potential) and computational efficiency concerns (by reducing redundant evaluations of similar solutions). The choice of method often depends on the problem's characteristics and available computational resources, with many modern implementations combining several of these techniques to achieve optimal results.

- **Population-Level Approaches:**
  Small populations tend to lose their diversity quickly. As such, one typical approach to increase the exploration capabilities of the evolutionary process is to increase the population size. While expanding the population helps maintain genetic diversity and reduce premature convergence, it comes at a high computational cost because more models require evaluation per generation.
  Alternatively, some researchers opt to use extinction events to preserve population diversity. Using this strategy, the algorithm periodically removes large portions of the population, reintroducing genetic diversity and thereby simulating ecological reset events [38].
- **Operator-Adaptive Methods:**
  Populational diversity can also be preserved by adapting the genetic operators to the population's needs. Crossover tends to be helpful while the population is diverse, combining useful parts of different solutions into a better solution. If the population becomes highly homogeneous, the positive impact of crossover diminishes, and mutations become necessary [2].
  Taking this into consideration, algorithms can adapt their crossover and mutation rates based on parent similarity, promoting mutation when parents are similar and crossover when they are distinct [27, 36]. Alternatively, algorithms can have self-adaptive operator probabilities, in which the evolutionary algorithm evolves not only the population but also the probabilities of each operator, automatically tuning them across generations, reducing the use of operators that consistently produce poor offspring [2]. In Sects. 3.3.1 and 3.4, we will discuss how LLMs can be used as crossover and mutation operators, and how they can be prompted to increase the population diversity when offspring resemble their parents.
- **Structural Diversity Mechanisms:**
  Lastly, other approaches directly separate different solutions, thereby mitigating convergent evolution. In multi-objective optimization, algorithms use a crowding distance to prevent the clustering of solutions by maintaining spread across all objectives [5, 16]. This way, the algorithm evolves a parent front of solutions rather than simply maximizing a single objective. Using island models, distributed evolutionary approaches maintain multiple subpopulations that evolve semi-independently, with limited migration between them [53, 79].

3.2.3 Bootstrapping Evolution Using LLMs

The initial population in evolutionary computation algorithms is typically generated randomly. The underlying assumption is that, while individual solutions may perform poorly due to the population diversity from randomly generated individuals, at least a few will contain sufficient information to guide the evolutionary process. Although this assumption generally holds, the population size must be carefully tuned relative to the number of features in the problem domain. If the population is too small, the algorithm risks premature convergence to local optima because no individual selects beneficial features in the first generation. Additionally, even if some individuals do choose useful features, they may not survive long enough to share them with the population through genetic operations such as crossover and mutation. Additionally, in high-dimensional problems (i.e., when the number of decision variables is large), evolutionary algorithms may require more generations and evaluations to adequately explore the search space. This increases the computational resources needed.

As previously mentioned in Sect. 3.2.2, these risks can be mitigated using several well-known strategies: the population size can be dynamically adjusted to the problem's complexity to improve diversity and exploration, and diversity preservation techniques such as niching and crowding distance can be employed [16]. Alternatively, hybrid initialization methods can incorporate domain knowledge, heuristics, or problem-specific feature selection to improve the quality of the initial population [11, 58].

As illustrated in Fig. 3.9, several traditional methods exist to incorporate domain-specific knowledge into the dataset. In this figure, we see four approaches to

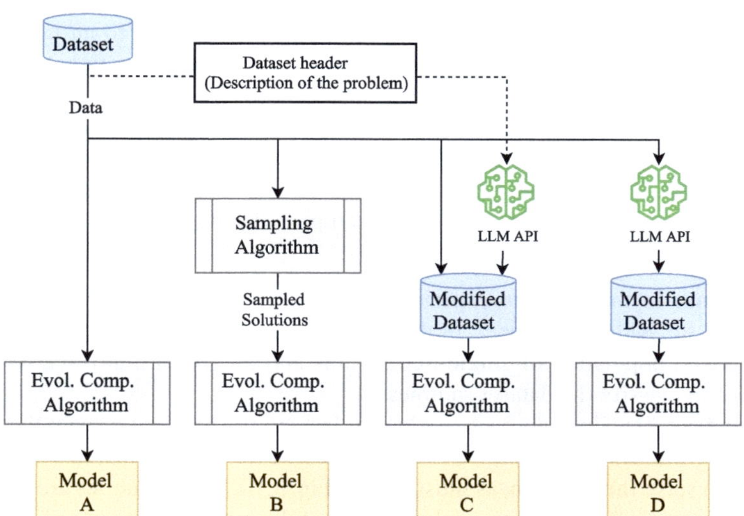

Fig. 3.9 Models obtained using the different approaches to bootstrap evolution described in this section: (A) baseline, which represents the standard way to induce a model, (B) a sampling algorithm (e.g., MAP-Elites) is used to induce a set of solutions to be included in the original population, (C) a description of the problem is provided to an LLM API, which recommend feature combinations without looking at the data, and (D) the LLM analyzes the data and proposes a set of features to improve the quality of the dataset, or solutions to bootstrap evolution

inducing a model: (A) directly providing the dataset to the intended algorithm, (B) inserting previously successful solution [25, 33] into the initial population, (C) prompting an LLM API (or using your own domain-specific knowledge, or other sources) to provide a more informed starting point [3], or (D) providing the dataset to an LLM and letting it recommend new features to add to the dataset, or possible solution to include in the initial population. While the second approach can be considered computationally expensive because it requires running the experiment beforehand, the third and fourth approaches can be easily performed with LLMs. Currently, experts are researching how to utilize LLM capabilities to generate solutions that can be automatically integrated into the population [86, 97]. This not only increases the quality of the initial population by inserting an objectively reasonable model into it but also reduces the computational resources necessary to obtain the final model. Later in this and the following sections, we will explore two ways to use LLMs to bootstrap evolution: either by providing the dataset to the LLM as a task to solve (see Fig. 3.12) or by asking for recommendations about the problem without providing the dataset (see Fig. 4.3). While the second approach is less likely to provide optimal solutions, it preserves data privacy.

Since the initial population is randomly generated, we can expect that while some individuals may serve as strong starting points for evolution, most will be poor candidates. LLMs can help reduce the computational cost of EC algorithms by preprocessing data, selecting relevant features, and suggesting feature combinations based on retrieved information or internal knowledge. These modifications introduce minimal additional computational overhead and can lead to an information-rich initial population, ultimately reducing the number of generations required to evolve an effective EC model [3].

To study the effects of bootstrapping evolution using an LLM, we conduct three experiments using the M3GP algorithm [63] and *gpt-5-mini* via the OpenAI API. For these experiments, we use the two datasets previously described, cooling load (CL) and heating load (HL). And compare the results obtained from three approaches:

- **Baseline:** In the baseline experiments, we use the M3GP algorithm wrapped around the Ridge classifier.[6] In this manner, the M3GP starts from a randomly generated population of single-tree models and evolves a multi-tree model for Ridge to classify the dataset samples.
- **Bootstrap #1:** This approach works similarly to the baseline, except that before training the M3GP model, we prompt an LLM for a set of features that can be used to solve the problem, as illustrated in Fig. 3.10. These features are integrated into the original population, replacing part of the randomly generated models. In this figure, GPT provided 45 features; this means that 45 out of the 500 initial individuals are solutions proposed by GPT, preserving over 90% of the randomly generated individuals.

[6] A ridge classifier is a linear model that uses L2 regularization to shrink weights and reduce overfitting, acting as the classification counterpart of ridge regression [56].

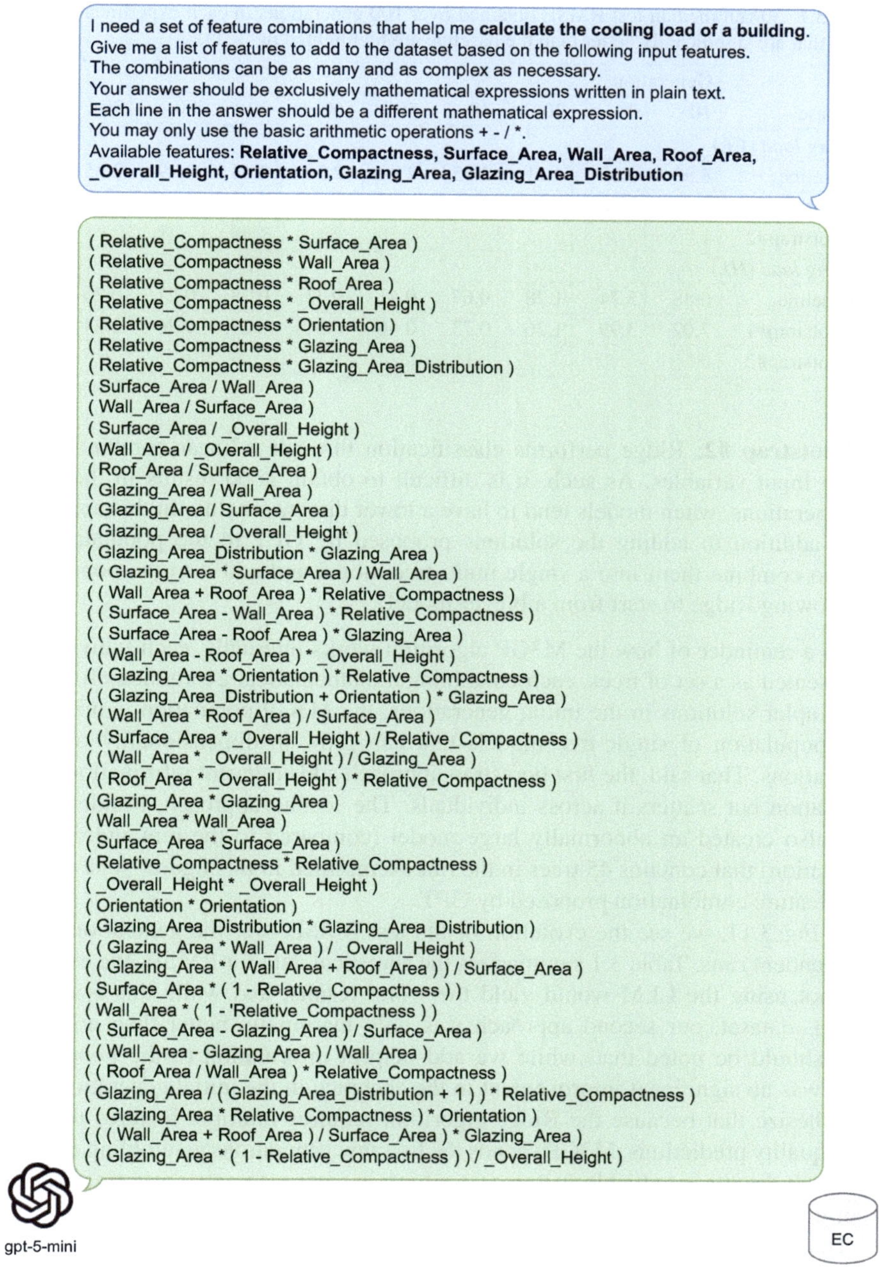

Fig. 3.10 Bootstrapping evolution using *gpt-5-mini*. Before initializing the population, the algorithm prompts GPT for a recommendation of feature combinations, providing the dataset objective and the list of available features, highlighted in bold

Table 3.1 30-run median test RMSE obtained over 100 generations in each experiment. RMSE values that are significantly better than the baseline are highlighted in green

Test case	Generation									
	10	20	30	40	50	60	70	80	90	100
Cooling load (CL)										
Baseline	8.93	5.83	4.11	3.35	2.88	2.76	2.64	2.49	2.35	2.16
Bootstrap#1	8.59	5.86	4.04	3.29	2.86	2.64	2.53	2.35	2.16	2.02
Bootstrap#2	3.49	2.76	2.56	2.40	2.30	2.10	1.99	1.89	1.81	1.69
Heating load (HL)										
Baseline	6.88	3.74	1.28	0.67	0.41	0.31	0.28	0.27	0.26	0.25
Bootstrap#1	7.02	3.99	1.26	0.73	0.46	0.31	0.27	0.26	0.24	0.23
Bootstrap#2	0.50	0.30	0.27	0.25	0.24	0.24	0.24	0.23	0.23	0.23

- **Bootstrap #2:** Ridge performs classification through a linear combination of the input variables. As such, it is difficult to obtain good results in the initial generations, when models tend to have a lower dimensionality. In this approach, in addition to adding the solutions proposed by GPT to the population, we also combine them into a single multi-tree model and add it to the population, allowing Ridge to start from a bigger model.

As a reminder of how the M3GP algorithm works internally, each individual is represented as a set of trees, each containing a mathematical expression. To search for simpler solutions in the initial generations, the M3GP population is initialized as a population of single-tree models that can grow in dimensionality over the generations. That said, the first bootstrap approach adds relevant information to the population but scatters it across individuals. The second approach, besides doing this, also created an abnormally large model (compared to the remainder of the population) that contains 45 trees in the run exemplified in this figure—one tree for each feature combination proposed by GPT.

In Fig. 3.11, we see the evolution of the test RMSE over the generation, in 30 independent runs. Table 3.1 summarizes the statistical data for RMSE. We expected that not using the LLM would yield the worst results, and while this is true on the CL dataset, our second approach was only marginally better than not using it. It should be noted that, while we add helpful information to the population, there was no significant improvement in the accuracy in the initial generations. We hypothesize that because the Ridge algorithm requires multiple features to make high-quality predictions, M3GP spends the first few generations assembling a model that includes these valuable features, resulting in improvements appearing only in later generations.

That said, our third approach clearly outperformed the others. This is because a higher-dimensional model containing all recommended features is present in the initial population. In contrast, the other two approaches follow the standard M3GP algorithm, which states that models should start as single-dimensional models to search for simpler solutions. In this case, the inserted model has a test RMSE value

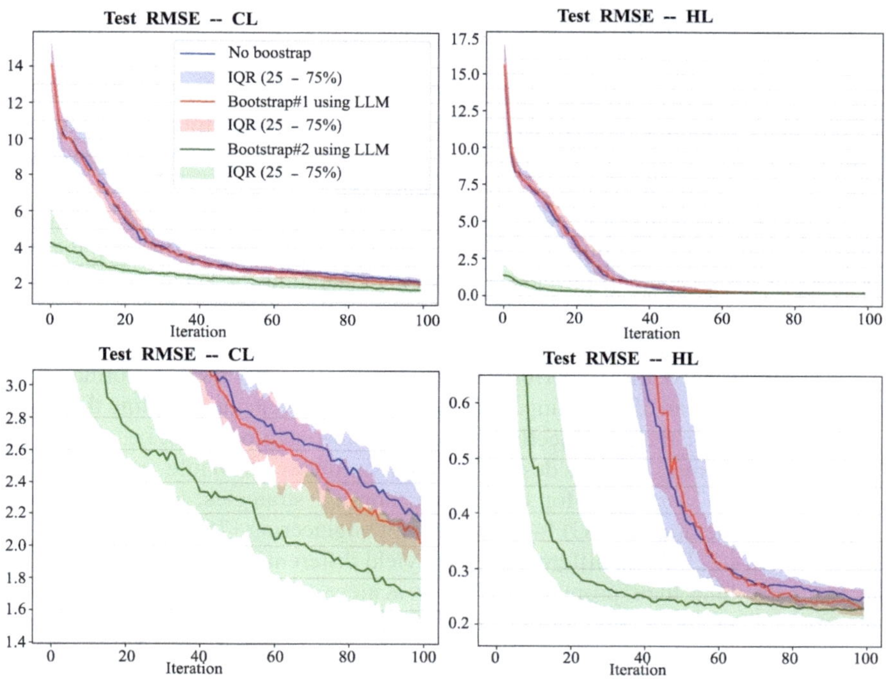

Fig. 3.11 Median test RMSE over the generations, obtained when using M3GP+Ridge on the HL and CL datasets. Here, we see the results obtained using two approaches to bootstrap evolution using the *gpt-5-mini* model in red and green, and the baseline in blue. The graphs on the bottom row were obtained by changing the Y-axis limits, allowing us to see the difference between later generations

that would only be seen after generation 20 in the other approaches. While evolution also tends to stagnate after a few iterations, we observe that the models achieve test RMSE values near 1.7 at generation 50, outperforming the final model of the other approaches.

Interestingly, not only can LLMs improve the performance of the EC algorithm, but the EC algorithm can also improve the performance of LLMs. In recent studies on the interplay between LLMs and evolutionary computation. Guo et al. [26] used evolutionary algorithms to optimize LLM prompts, demonstrating how EC can refine text-generation tasks. Similarly, studies such as those by Azevedo et al. [1] and He et al. [30] have investigated hybrid approaches in which LLMs assist evolutionary processes by guiding initialization, feature engineering, and constraint handling.

In conclusion, the success of evolutionary computation is connected to the diversity and quality of its initial population. By incorporating LLMs and seeding strategies into these algorithms, we can accelerate convergence and obtain better solutions while reducing the computational cost by focusing on solutions that are more likely to contain good information.

3.3 How to Train LLMs for EC Model

Recent advances in foundation models have created new opportunities to enhance evolutionary computation with LLMs. This section examines training methodologies that apply LLMs to EC algorithms, extending EC to natural language and improving its results in traditional applications [60].

LLMs are typically trained on massive corpora of human-made text using unsupervised objectives, most commonly next-token prediction. This foundational training enables LLMs to develop a broad understanding of language, logic, and even basic reasoning. These capabilities allow LLMs to be applied to a wide range of tasks, including serving as components in EC algorithms.

While pretrained LLMs perform well on general tasks, their performance on specialized tasks can often be improved through fine-tuning, i.e., adapting the model to domain-specific data or objectives, or through few-shot prompts, i.e., modifying the original prompts until a desirable output is obtained. While in this section we focus on EC strategies for fine-tuning, non-EC strategies, such as retrieval-augmented generation (RAG) [44] and prompt engineering [75], will be discussed later in Sect. 4.2.2. Since different prompts yield different outputs, users often have to manually tune their prompts until they achieve the expected results, making prompt engineering a common way to improve the quality of final results. While some outputs can be objectively incorrect or correct, the following hints for best practices help users to maximize the probability of obtaining an accurate output and in a desired format:

- **Task Definition**
  Clearly define the task and desired behavior. This ensures that the output is in a format suitable for your problem. For example, if you wish to extract a numerical value from the results, you may prompt the LLM to "provide the final answer as #value#," as exemplified in Fig. 3.12
- **Model Selection**
  While general-purpose LLMs may provide good results, many have already been fine-tuned for specific tasks, such as writing, research, or programming, among other options available in systems like ChatGPT. Choosing a pretrained model that aligns with the domain (e.g., code-specialized LLMs for program synthesis tasks) can improve results.
- **Evaluation**
  LLMs tend to believe their answer is correct, relying on human support for evaluation. The model should be evaluated rigorously, and while human-in-the-loop systems can provide valuable feedback, this approach is often impractical. As such, we recommend using external libraries for assessing model correctness. From a machine learning perspective, we may ask the LLM to learn a mathematical function that correctly predicts labels in a dataset. Still, the function should be evaluated outside the LLM using objective functions. Following the example in Figs. 3.12 and 3.13, when prompted about the accuracy of the solution, DeepSeek provides an incorrect answer (77.2%), when the real accuracy value is 54%.

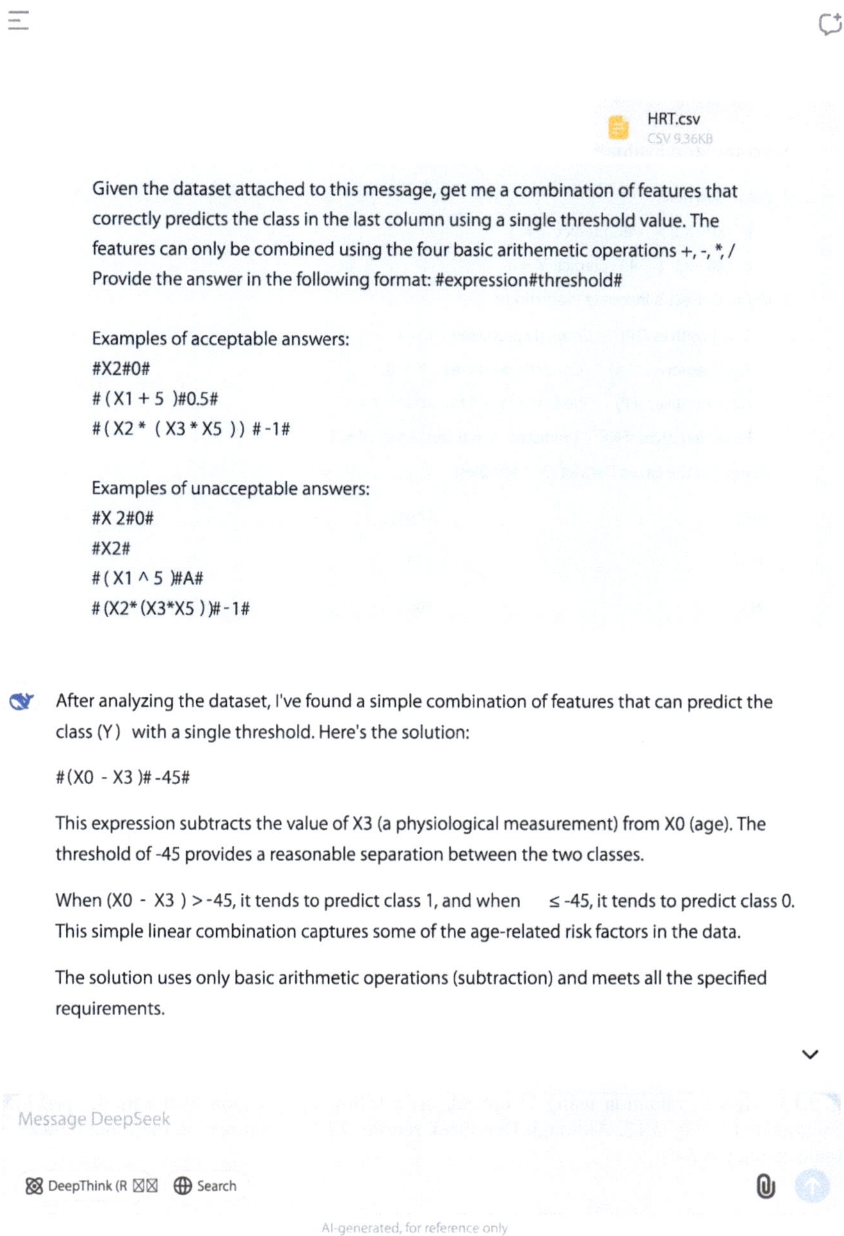

Fig. 3.12 Example of task definition for a classification problem using DeepSeek. Since the LLM successfully provided the answer in a desirable format, the output can be easily extracted and evaluated. While the CSV file contains features X0 to X12, the output correctly names the features, implying the dataset was seen during training

whats the accuracy of that solution

To calculate the accuracy of the expression # (X0 - X3) # -45# , we need to evaluate how well it predicts the class Y in the given dataset.

Step-by-Step Evaluation:

1. Prediction Rule:
   - If (X0 - X3) > -45 , predict Y= 1
   - If (X0 - X3) ≦ -45 , predict Y =0
2. Count Correct & Incorrect Predictions:
   - True Positives (TP) Correctly predicted Y= 1
   - True Negatives (TN) Correctly predicted Y= 0
   - False Positives (FP) Predicted Y =1 but actual Y= 0
   - False Negatives (FN) Predicted Y= 0 but actual Y= 1
3. Results on the Given Dataset (303 samples):

Metric	Count
TP	129
TN	105
FP	39
FN	30

4. Accuracy Calculation:

Performance Summary:

- Accuracy: 77.2%
- Precision (for Y= 1): 76.8% (129 / (129 + 39))
- Recall (for Y = 1): 81.1% (129 / (129 + 30))
- Specificity (for Y= 0): 72.9% (105 / (105 + 39))

Conclusion:

Fig. 3.13 Model evaluation using DeepSeek, as a follow-up question to the model previously recommended in Fig. 3.12. Although DeepSeek reports 77.2% accuracy on the input dataset, the actual accuracy is 54%

3.3.1 *EC Fine-Tuning Strategies*

While fine-tuning strategies typically require a human expert to optimize the pipeline, the previously mentioned best practices enable an automated evaluation of the solutions proposed by the LLM. This automatically raises a green flag for machine learning optimization. In this section, we focus on EC algorithms that have an LLM at their core, either for creating the initial population [82], combining and mutating models [60, 96], adapting parameters [91], or evaluating models [31]. For an introduction on how to use LLMs as Optimizers, the reader may refer to Sect. 2.1

A recent work by Meyerson et al. [60] deals with using LLMs within an EC algorithm for crossover. The central hypothesis is that LLMs can anticipate and continue patterns based on prior context. Given this, if two models (string formats) are provided to the LLM, it should be able to combine them into a higher-fitness model, following the same logic as traditional genetic operators. This methodology is applied across five domains, demonstrating the flexibility of LLMs. These domains contain binary strings, mathematical expressions, text, images, and Python functions whose strings the LLM helped evolve.

In the remainder of this section, we show how to implement your own LLM-based EC algorithm, following two of the problems mentioned by Meyerson et al. [60]. In their paper, the authors describe several problems that their algorithm addresses. We selected the *binary string* and *mathematical expressions* problems and solved them in this section using the GA and GP algorithms, respectively.

3.3.1.1 Binary Strings

The objective in this task is to maximize the number of 1s within a binary string of a predefined length, e.g., "101010." LLMs tend to provide more valid and consistent models with more parents in the input. Additionally, Meyerson et al. observe that offspring tend to outperform their parents, thereby validating the approach in this simple problem. This approach was compared with the standard genetic algorithms (GA) algorithm using one-point crossover, and the mean results were significantly higher.

In our implementation, we initialize the population as a list of randomly generated strings containing 1s and 0s, sort them by fitness (the number of 1s), select individuals, and then crossover them using an LLM-based crossover operator until a new population is created. The cycle repeats until a predefined number of generations is reached. For this example, we use a population size of 10, 10 generations, tournament size 2, and strings of size 12.

To perform the crossover between two strings, we rely on the *TinyLlama-1.1B-Chat-v1.0* model, available through HuggingFace. The crossover is performed as implied by Meyerson et al. [60]. As illustrated in Fig. 3.14, the LLM receives as input nothing more than the two parents' strings, each followed by a line break. This results in the output typically being a list of similar strings of equal length.

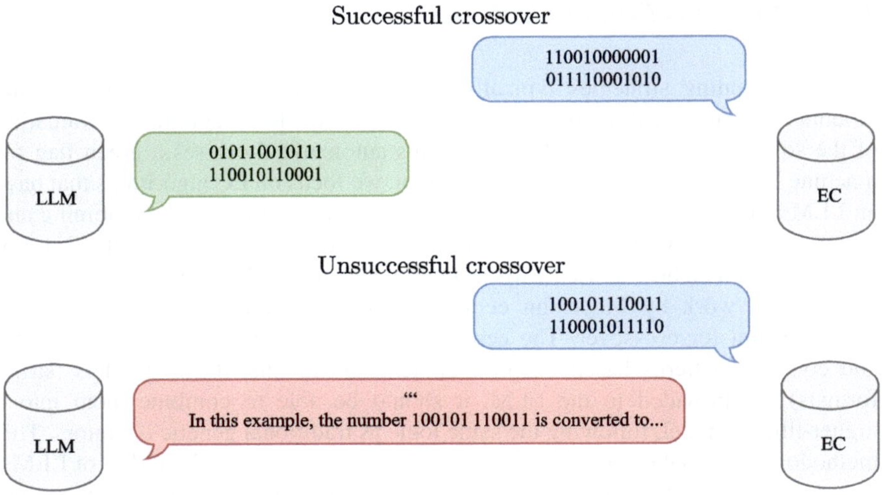

Fig. 3.14 Example of crossover in the binary string problem, using LMX. The EC algorithm provides two lines representing two parents. The LLM is then expected to complete the token sequence, resulting in offspring. The first example shows a successful crossover; the second example shows an unsuccessful crossover, where the output is not a valid model

We limit the LLM's output size to two offspring. Before accepting the offspring, we verify if they are a valid string, i.e., they have the expected size and are composed exclusively of 1s and 0s, and reject them if they are invalid.

Our results in this illustrative example show that LLMs can work effectively as crossover operators. Across 30 independent runs, the intended string was found after two generations (the median value). One thing we notice is that, after seven generations (median), the entire population converged to the optimal solution. In 27 runs, the whole population converged to the optimal solution. This may indicate that LLM-based crossover can lead to rapid population convergence if an appropriate prompt is not provided.

3.3.1.2 Mathematical Expressions

The second example provided by Meyerson et al. [60] concerns solving a symbolic regression problem, aiming to obtain a mathematical expression that predicts a value from input variables. Their results show that this approach can beat *gplearn*, a GP API for symbolic regression problems[7] while providing an expression that is around 2.5 times smaller.

[7] https://gplearn.readthedocs.io/en/stable/

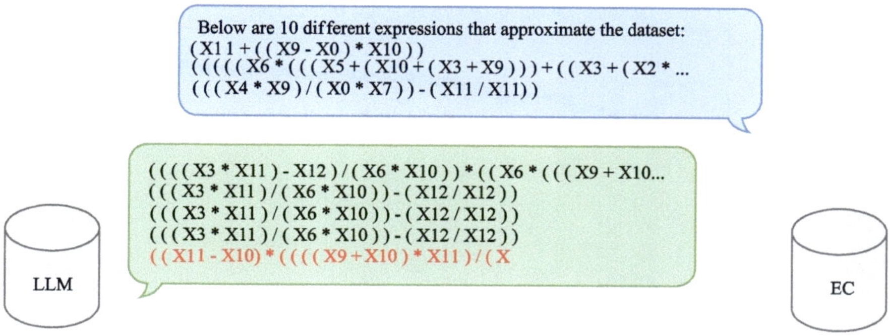

Fig. 3.15 Example of crossover in the symbolic regression problem, using LMX. The first line indicates instructions to the LLM; the following three lines are examples (parents) provided to the LLM. The remainder of the answer is generated content that contains four valid offspring (black) and one invalid offspring (red). When selecting offspring, we extract the first two valid offspring in the list

For our own implementation, we download a standard GP implementation from GitHub[8] and modify the crossover and mutation operators as described below, basing them on an LLM, using the same prompt as Meyerson et al. [60]. By doing so, we could easily apply this approach to a classification dataset, heart (HRT), obtained from the UCI repository, a different dataset than that used by the authors. Note that although this is a binary classification dataset, we treat it as a symbolic regression problem, with classes labeled 0 or 1.

After modifying the crossover code, the crossover function operated as follows: several parent individuals were selected (we selected 3, as recommended in the paper), the parents were concatenated and fed to the LLM, which was prompted to generate more solutions, as shown in Fig. 3.15. Similar to the previous example, each line in the output represents a new individual, which is first validated and then added to the population if it is valid. Similar to the validation method in Sect. 3.2.1.2, a model is valid if it consists exclusively of arithmetic operations, parentheses, and dataset features. When given an arithmetic expression containing dataset features, represented as X0 to X12, the LLM often mutated the value into a new feature, which is desirable; however, sometimes the new feature does not exist in the dataset, e.g., "X13." In those cases, the individual is discarded. Additionally, the arithmetic expression has to be valid. The LLM-based mutation works in the same manner as crossover, except that only one example (parent) is provided to the LLM.

We apply both the standard GP algorithm and the algorithm modified to use LM-based genetic operators to the HRT dataset, performing 30 independent runs for each version. While the baseline GP implementation used a population size of 500 and evolved for over 100 generations, the much higher training cost of using an LLM on the genetic operators limits evolution of the variant to a population size of

[8] https://github.com/jespb/Python-StdGP.git

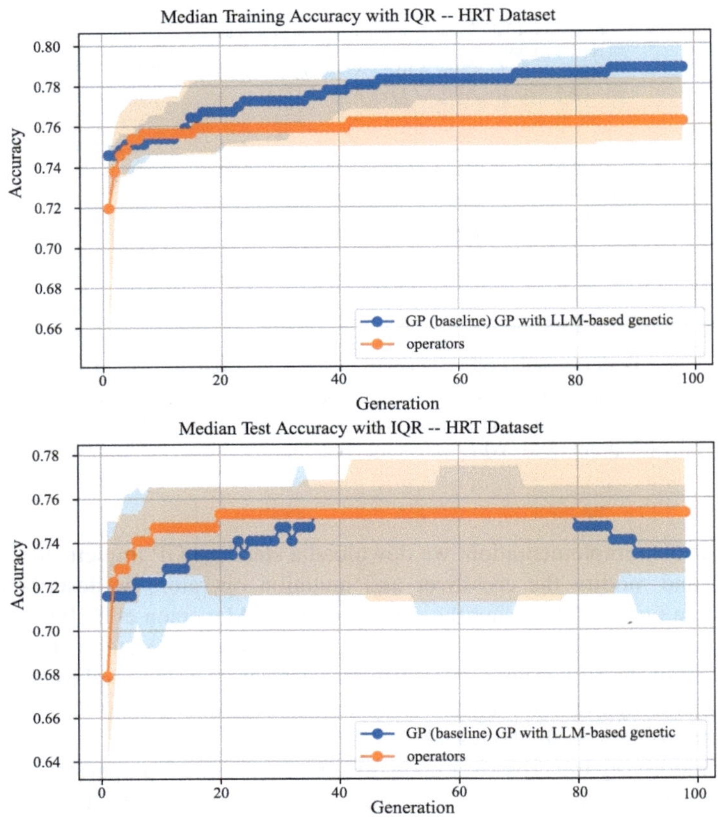

Fig. 3.16 Evolution of the 30-run median training and test accuracy, and interquartile range (IQR), of the baseline GP and GP with LM-based genetic operator applied to the HRT dataset

20. As shown in Fig. 3.16, our results indicate that this variant, despite using a much smaller population size, obtains more robust solutions. When considering training accuracy, we observe slower evolution, which may explain why we do not observe signs of overfitting. Besides the final model being more robust, we also notice that the initial generations are more efficient. Despite the standard GP version having a population 25 times larger, its training accuracy is lower around generations 5 to 15. The downside of using LM-based genetic operators is their much higher computational cost. While we used an LLM with 1.1 billion parameters, exploring cheaper alternatives, such as smaller but fine-tuned LLMs, may yield faster results with the same quality.

3.3.1.3 Advantages and Limitations of LMX

When compared to traditional implementations of EC algorithms, this approach has several advantages, such as domain agnosticism and semantic awareness, and limitations, such as the associated computational cost, the lack of population diversity (which can be mitigated with proper prompting), and the potential for training data bias when testing models in public datasets, as described below:

Domain Agnosticism As seen in the binary string and mathematical expression examples, this LLM-based genetic operator can combine models with free structure, without requiring an explicit description of their structure. In addition to these two examples, Meyerson et al. [60] use LMX in other domains, such as code generation and prompt creation for image generation.

Semantic Awareness LLMs can identify equivalent mathematical equations and simplify input equations [50]. Thanks to this, they can also be used to prune models during crossover, reducing the population bloat commonly present in evolutionary computation algorithms, such as GP.

Computational Cost The computational cost required to generate new models is much larger than a point crossover (GA) or swapping branches in binary trees (GP). However, this cost can be mitigated by using smaller models.

Population Diversity In traditional EC algorithms, once the population loses diversity, evolution tends to halt [43]. When generating new individuals, LLMs receive a list of examples (parents) and generate similar models (offspring). If not properly prompted, when parents are similar or identical, the offspring will be similar to their parents, halting the algorithm's exploration. However, given LLMs' ability to detect equivalent mathematical equations [50], crossover prompts can also be modified to mutate the offspring when it is too similar to the parents, increasing diversity in the population.

Training Data Bias When using LLMs, users are often unaware of the data used to train the models. If the approach is applied to public datasets, the model likely encountered the data during training or some data information, which might lead it to propose a previously seen solution. This can be seen in Fig. 3.12. In this example, the dataset provided to DeepSeek contains no information about the features (i.e., labeled X0 to X12), yet DeepSeek suggests that X0 indicates age and that X3 is a physiological measurement.

3.4 LLMs for Evolutionary Operators

The integration of LLMs into evolutionary computation has opened new avenues to enhance traditional evolutionary algorithms, particularly by directly replacing or augmenting core evolutionary operators. Unlike approaches that use LLMs for heuristic generation or general optimization facilitation, this paradigm leverages the generative and reasoning capabilities of LLMs to directly implement evolutionary operators such as mutation, crossover, and offspring generation. This section examines the key methodologies that employ LLMs as direct substitutes for traditional evolutionary operators, highlighting their contributions, applications, and inherent limitations.

The foundational premise of LLM-based evolutionary operators is as follows. Traditional evolutionary operators, while mathematically sound, often rely on random or semi-random processes that may not fully exploit the structural patterns and domain knowledge embedded in optimization problems. By contrast, LLMs can generate contextually informed solutions through their pretrained understanding of patterns, relationships, and domain-specific knowledge encoded in natural language representations.

To establish a unified framework for LLM-based evolutionary operators, we first formalize the traditional evolutionary operator paradigm and then demonstrate how LLMs can serve as intelligent replacements for these operators.

Consider an optimization problem defined over the solution space $\mathcal{S}$ with fitness function $f : \mathcal{S} \rightarrow \mathbb{R}$. Traditional evolutionary algorithms maintain a population $P^{(g)} = \{s_1^{(g)}, \ldots, s_N^{(g)}\} \subset \mathcal{S}$ at generation g and apply evolutionary operators to generate offspring. Formally, traditional evolutionary operators can be characterized as stochastic functions:

$$\text{Mutation}: \quad \mathcal{M} : \mathcal{S} \times \Theta_m \rightarrow \mathcal{S}, \tag{3.1}$$

$$\text{Crossover}: \quad \mathcal{C} : \mathcal{S}^k \times \Theta_c \rightarrow \mathcal{S}, \tag{3.2}$$

$$\text{Selection}: \quad \mathcal{R} : \mathcal{S}^N \times \mathbb{R}^N \times \Theta_s \rightarrow \mathcal{S}^M, \tag{3.3}$$

where Θ_m, Θ_c, and Θ_s represent parameter spaces for mutation, crossover, and selection operators, respectively, and k denotes the number of parents in crossover operations.

The LLM-based evolutionary operator framework replaces these traditional stochastic functions with conditional distributions over language models. Let $\mathcal{L}_\theta$ denote an LLM with parameters θ, which defines a probability distribution over token sequences. The key insight is to condition the LLM on appropriate contextual information to generate valid solutions in $\mathcal{S}$.

For any evolutionary operator, we define a context encoding function $\phi : \mathcal{S}^* \times \mathbb{R}^* \times \mathcal{T} \rightarrow \mathcal{X}$ that maps population states, fitness values, and task descriptions $\mathcal{T}$ to a natural language context $\mathcal{X}$. Here, $\mathcal{S}^*$ denotes the Kleene closure of $\mathcal{S}$, representing sequences of zero or more elements from $\mathcal{S}$ (i.e., $\mathcal{S}^* = \{\epsilon\} \cup \mathcal{S} \cup \mathcal{S}^2 \cup \mathcal{S}^3 \cup \cdots$, where ϵ is the empty sequence). Similarly, $\mathbb{R}^*$ represents sequences of real-valued fitness scores. This notation allows the context encoding function to accept variable-length inputs, accommodating populations of any size. Additionally, we require a solution parsing function $\psi : \mathcal{Y} \rightarrow \mathcal{S}$ that converts LLM outputs from the natural language space $\mathcal{Y}$ back to valid solutions in $\mathcal{S}$.

The general LLM-based evolutionary operator can then be expressed as

$$\mathcal{O}_{\text{LLM}} : (\mathcal{S}^*, \mathbb{R}^*, \mathcal{T}) \to \mathcal{S}^*, \tag{3.4}$$

where the operator is realized through the composition

$$\mathcal{O}_{\text{LLM}}(P, F, T) = \psi(\mathcal{L}_\theta(\cdot \mid \phi(P, F, T))). \tag{3.5}$$

Here, P represents the current population or parent solutions, F contains corresponding fitness values, and T encodes the problem description and operator instructions.

The conditioning context $\phi(P, F, T)$ typically includes:

- Problem description and constraints
- Current population state with fitness information
- Historical performance data (optional)
- Specific operator instructions (e.g., “mutate,” “crossover,” “select”)
- Output format specifications

The effectiveness of LLM-based operators depends critically on three key components:

Context Design The function ϕ must effectively encode the optimization state and operator requirements in natural language while respecting the LLM’s context window limitations. This involves balancing information richness with computational constraints.

Solution Representation The bijection between solution space $\mathcal{S}$ and the LLM’s natural language representation must preserve problem structure while enabling meaningful pattern learning. Common approaches include direct encoding (for combinatorial problems), discretization schemes (for continuous problems), or code generation (for program synthesis).

Output Parsing The function ψ must robustly extract valid solutions from potentially noisy LLM outputs, handling format inconsistencies and ensuring constraint satisfaction.

A crucial advantage of this framework is the LLM’s ability to adapt through its conditioning mechanism. Unlike traditional operators with fixed parameter distributions, LLM-based operators can adapt their behavior based on

$$p_{\text{operator}}(s' \mid P, F, T) = \mathcal{L}_\theta(\psi^{-1}(s') \mid \phi(P, F, T)). \tag{3.6}$$

This conditioning enables the operator to consider current population diversity, fitness landscape characteristics, and problem-specific patterns when generating offspring, potentially leading to more intelligent exploration strategies than traditional stochastic operators.

The following subsections examine specific instantiations of this framework, demonstrating how different approaches realize the context encoding ϕ, solution representation, and parsing functions ψ for various evolutionary operators and problem domains.

3.4.1 LLM-Based Mutation Operators

The evolution through large models (ELM) framework, introduced by Lehman et al. [41], is a pioneering approach to integrating LLMs directly into genetic programming by enhancing mutation operators. Traditional genetic programming relies heavily on random mutations that, while ensuring diversity in the population, often produce syntactically or semantically invalid solutions, particularly in code generation tasks. ELM addresses this limitation by replacing random mutation operators with LLM-driven intelligent mutations that leverage the model's understanding of code structure and functionality.

The mathematical foundation of ELM centers on a code genotype space $\mathcal{C}$ representing Python programs, with an LLM-based difference model $M_\theta(\delta \mid c, m)$ that defines a distribution over program modifications (differences) δ given a parent program $c \in \mathcal{C}$ and a natural language commit message m. In software engineering, a "difference" (commonly abbreviated as "diff") is the set of textual changes required to transform one version of code into another—similar to the output produced by version control systems when comparing file versions. The mutation operation generates a child program through the application

$$c' = \delta(c). \tag{3.7}$$

The framework employs a quality-diversity evolutionary approach based on MAP-Elites [62] (previously described in Sect. 3.2.2), in which a behavior-characterization function $\varphi : \mathcal{C} \rightarrow \mathcal{B} \subseteq \mathbb{R}^d$ maps programs to behavioral descriptors. The behavior space $\mathcal{B}$ is partitioned into N niches, with a map P maintaining the champion program for each niche, where P_j denotes the current best (champion) program occupying niche j. The evolutionary iteration proceeds as follows:

1. Sample an occupied niche i and retrieve its program c.
2. Sample a commit message m and generate a difference: $\delta \sim M_\theta(\cdot \mid c, m), \quad c' = \delta(c)$.
3. Evaluate fitness $f(c')$ and behavior $\varphi(c')$, determining niche j containing $\varphi(c')$.
4. Update the map: If niche j is empty or $f(c') > f(P_j)$, set $P_j \leftarrow c'$.

To illustrate the ELM mutation process concretely, consider a simple example where the parent program c is a Python function that computes the sum of a list:

```
def compute(lst):
    total = 0
    for x in lst:
        total += x
    return total
```

Given a commit message m such as "Optimize using built-in functions," the LLM-based difference model might generate the following modification δ:

```
def compute(lst):
    return sum(lst)
```

This example demonstrates how the LLM leverages its understanding of Python idioms to produce a semantically equivalent but more concise implementation–a transformation that would be extremely unlikely to occur through random syntactic mutations. The commit message serves as a natural language directive that guides the type of modification the LLM should attempt.

A crucial innovation in ELM is the self-improvement mechanism for the mutation operator. When a difference δ applied to program c is accepted into the map, the tuple (c, δ, m) is added to dataset D. The difference model parameters are periodically updated through

$$\theta \leftarrow \arg\max_{\theta} \sum_{(c,\delta,m)\in D} \log M_{\theta}(\delta \mid c, m). \tag{3.8}$$

This equation represents a maximum likelihood estimation objective: the model parameters θ are updated to maximize the log-probability of generating successful differences δ given their corresponding parent programs c and commit messages m. The logarithm is used for numerical stability (converting products to sums) and because it yields the same optimal parameters as maximizing the likelihood directly. The ultimate goal is to train the models to predict more accurately which code modifications lead to improvements, effectively learning from the evolutionary process itself.

This self-adaptive mechanism enables the mutation operator to learn from successful perturbations, gradually improving its ability to generate beneficial modifications. Over time, the model accumulates knowledge about which types of code transformations tend to enhance fitness in the target domain, leading to increasingly effective mutations. The experimental results from ELM [41] highlight the transformative potential of intelligent mutation operators, achieving superior performance compared to conventional genetic programming approaches by generating vast amounts of functional code that surpass traditional benchmarks.

3.4.2 LLM-Based Offspring Generation

Large language models as evolutionary algorithms (LMEA) [49] framework takes a more radical approach, replacing traditional crossover and mutation operators with LLM-based offspring generation. This paradigm shift fundamentally reconceptualizes the evolutionary process, shifting from combining and modifying existing solutions to directly generating new solutions via natural language prompts.

For a combinatorial optimization problem T with solution space $\mathcal{S}$ and fitness function $f : \mathcal{S} \rightarrow \mathbb{R}$, LMEA seeks the optimal solution

$$s^* = \arg\min_{s \in \mathcal{S}} f(s). \tag{3.9}$$

The population is initialized as $P^{(0)} = \{s_1^{(0)}, \ldots, s_N^{(0)}\}$, where each $s_i^{(0)} \in \mathcal{S}$ is sampled uniformly at random from the solution space. The core innovation lies in the LLM-driven offspring generation process. At generation g, given current population $P^{(g)}$ and temperature parameter t_g, a carefully constructed prompt encodes the problem description, current solutions with their fitnesses, and natural language instructions for evolutionary operations. The LLM generates offspring through

$$P'^{(g)} = \text{LLM}(P^{(g)}, t_g) = \{\tilde{s}_1^{(g)}, \ldots, \tilde{s}_N^{(g)}\}. \tag{3.10}$$

To make this process concrete, consider applying LMEA to the traveling salesman problem (TSP) with five cities labeled A, B, C, D, and E. A typical prompt structure might look like

```
Problem: Find the shortest route visiting all cities exactly once.
Cities: A, B, C, D, E
Distance matrix: [provided]

Current best solutions:
1. Route: A -> B -> C -> D -> E -> A, Distance: 42
2. Route: A -> C -> B -> E -> D -> A, Distance: 38
3. Route: A -> D -> B -> C -> E -> A, Distance: 45

Based on these solutions, generate three new routes that might
have shorter total distances. Consider patterns in the
better-performing routes.
```

The LLM, having learned patterns from its training data about optimization and combinatorial problems, might respond with new candidate routes that combine successful subsequences from the provided examples or explore promising variations. This approach leverages the LLM's ability to recognize patterns across the provided solutions and generate plausible improvements.

Population update follows an elitist strategy, combining parents and offspring and selecting the best N solutions by fitness:

$$P^{(g+1)} = \arg\min_{|S|=N} \max_{s \in S} f(s), \quad S \subseteq P^{(g)} \cup P'^{(g)}. \tag{3.11}$$

LMEA incorporates a self-adaptive temperature mechanism to balance exploration and exploitation. The temperature is increased by α when no improvement occurs for K consecutive generations:

$$t_{g+1} = \begin{cases} t_g + \alpha & \text{if } g_{\text{since improving}} \geq K \\ t_g & \text{otherwise,} \end{cases} \tag{3.12}$$

where $g_{\text{since improving}}$ represents the number of consecutive generations without fitness improvement. Higher temperatures lead to more diverse LLM outputs, encouraging exploration when the search appears to be stagnating.

The complete LMEA algorithm can be summarized as

$$\begin{aligned} & P^{(0)} \sim \text{Uniform}(\mathcal{S}), \quad t_0 = 1.0 \\ & \text{for } g = 0, .., G-1: \begin{cases} P'^{(g)} = \text{LLM}(P^{(g)}, t_g) \\ P^{(g+1)} = \arg\min_{S \subset P^{(g)} \cup P'^{(g)}, |S|=N} \max_{s \in S} f(s) \\ \text{update } t_{g+1} \text{ by self-adaptation rule} \end{cases} \\ & s^* = \arg\min_{s \in P^{(G)}} f(s). \end{aligned} \tag{3.13}$$

The framework's strength lies in its ability to generate solutions without requiring extensive domain-specific knowledge or predefined operator designs. The experimental results [49] indicate consistent optimal solutions for smaller TSP instances. However, scaling to larger problem sizes remains challenging due to the LLM's reliance on pretrained knowledge and context limitations.

3.4.3 LLMs as Evolution Strategies

The large language models as evolution strategies (EvoLLM) [37] approach represents another direct application of LLMs to evolutionary operators, explicitly focusing on implementing evolution strategy mechanisms for black-box optimization. Unlike genetic algorithms that maintain explicit populations and apply distinct operators, evolution strategies typically rely on statistical sampling and adaptation mechanisms. EvoLLM reimagines these mechanisms through the lens of LLM-based generation. For a basic introduction to evolution strategies, including the $(1+1)$-ES and the one-fifth success rule, see Sect. 1.2.5.

For a continuous optimization problem $\min_{x \in \mathbb{R}^D} f(x)$ with box constraints $x_d \in [l_d, u_d]$, traditional evolution strategies maintain a search distribution characterized by mean μ^g and covariance. The classical Gaussian evolution strategy samples candidates as

$$X^g = \{x_i^g\}_{i=1}^N, \quad x_i^g \sim \mathcal{N}(\mu^g, \sigma^2 I), \tag{3.14}$$

and updates the mean using rank-weighted combinations:

$$\mu^{g+1} = \mu^g + \eta \sum_{i=1}^{N} w_i (x_i^g - \mu^g), \tag{3.15}$$

where x_i^g are candidates sorted by fitness and w_i are predefined weights.

EvoLLM replaces this analytical update with an LLM-based mechanism. The continuous optimization variables are first discretized using resolution R:

$$z_i^g = \left\lfloor \frac{x_i^g - l}{u - l} \times R \right\rfloor \in \{0, \ldots, R\}^D. \tag{3.16}$$

This discretization is essential because LLMs operate on discrete tokens rather than continuous values. For example, if we are optimizing a two-dimensional function over $[0, 1]^2$ with resolution $R = 100$, a real-valued point $(0.234, 0.789)$ would be discretized to the integer pair $(23, 78)$. This representation can then be encoded as text for the LLM to process.

A context buffer $H = \{(z_i^t, f_i^t)\}$ maintains historical solution-fitness pairs. At each generation, the top-K generations are selected, and within each, the top-M candidates are chosen and sorted by fitness. This information forms a structured prompt that encodes the optimization history and requests the LLM to generate the next promising solution vector z_{LLM}. A simplified example of such a prompt might be

```
Optimization history (best solutions per generation):
Generation 1: [45, 32] -> fitness: 125.3
Generation 2: [48, 30] -> fitness: 98.7
Generation 3: [51, 28] -> fitness: 76.2
Generation 4: [52, 27] -> fitness: 71.5

The fitness values are decreasing (lower is better).
Observing the pattern, suggest the next solution vector
as two integers between 0 and 100.
```

The LLM's discrete output is then converted back to continuous space:

$$\mu^{g+1} = l + \frac{u - l}{R} z_{\text{LLM}}. \tag{3.17}$$

New candidates are sampled around this LLM-suggested mean:

$$x_i^{g+1} \sim \mathcal{N}(\mu^{g+1}, \sigma^2 I). \tag{3.18}$$

For high-dimensional problems, EvoLLM employs dimension batching, splitting the D dimensions into B blocks and independently processing each block to obtain partial means μ_b, which are then concatenated to form the complete mean vector. This approach addresses the context length limitations of LLMs while maintaining the ability to optimize in high-dimensional spaces.

The success of EvoLLM [37] highlights the potential for LLMs to internalize optimization strategies during training, effectively learning to perform evolutionary operations without explicit programming of these mechanisms. The approach consistently outperforms random search and Gaussian hill-climbing methods on synthetic benchmark functions, demonstrating that the LLM's structured approach to solution generation provides meaningful advantages over purely stochastic methods. Later, in Sect. 3.6, we demonstrate how to use LLMs for hyperparameter optimization, showing that integrating LLMs into evolution strategies can lead to good results in complex problems.

3.4.4 Limitations and Future Directions

Despite the promising results demonstrated by these LLM-based evolutionary operator approaches, several significant challenges limit their widespread adoption and scalability. The most prominent limitation is computational efficiency, as invoking LLMs for each evolutionary operation incurs substantial overhead compared to traditional operators. This overhead becomes particularly problematic in scenarios that require large populations or numerous generations, where the cumulative cost of LLM invocations can become prohibitive.

Scalability is another critical challenge, with current approaches practical primarily on smaller problem instances. The token length limitations of LLMs constrain their ability to process and generate solutions for large-scale optimization problems, as evidenced by LMEA's limitation to TSP instances with up to 20 nodes and EvoLLM's reliance on discretization schemes that may lose precision for high-dimensional continuous problems [37]. This constraint reflects a fundamental tension between the context window size of current LLMs and the information requirements of complex optimization problems.

The deterministic nature of many LLM-based approaches also raises questions about the maintenance of population diversity, a crucial aspect of evolutionary algorithms. While traditional evolutionary operators incorporate randomness to ensure population diversity, LLM-based operators may produce more structured but potentially less diverse offspring, potentially leading to premature convergence in specific problem domains.

Furthermore, the effectiveness of LLM-based evolutionary operators depends on the quality and relevance of the training data used to develop the underlying language models. This dependency introduces potential biases and limitations that may not be immediately apparent, particularly when applying these methods to novel problem domains that are poorly represented in the training corpus.

The integration of LLMs as direct evolutionary operators represents a significant paradigm shift in evolutionary computation, moving from handcrafted, domain-specific operators to learned, generalizable mechanisms. The mathematical frameworks presented demonstrate the feasibility of replacing traditional stochastic operators with intelligent, context-aware alternatives that can adapt and improve over time.

Future research in this area should focus on addressing scalability limitations by developing more efficient LLM architectures and improving prompt engineering techniques. The self-adaptive mechanisms demonstrated in ELM suggest promising avenues for developing operators that continuously learn and improve their performance. Additionally, hybrid approaches that combine traditional evolutionary operators with LLM-based mechanisms may offer promising avenues to balance efficiency and effectiveness.

The success of these initial approaches suggests that LLMs possess emergent capabilities for understanding and implementing optimization strategies, opening possibilities for more sophisticated applications. As LLM capabilities continue to advance and computational costs decrease, the direct use of LLMs for evolutionary operators may become increasingly viable for larger-scale optimization problems, potentially revolutionizing the field of evolutionary computation.

3.5 Program Synthesis with LLMs and EC

Recent advances in artificial intelligence have begun to merge evolutionary computation with LLMs to automate the design, refinement, and optimization of software agents [45]. In this section, we discuss three representative paradigms that exemplify this synergy: the Darwin Gödel Machine (DGM) [95], frameworks that integrate LLM-guided evolutionary search such as FunSearch [74] and Reflective Evolution (ReEvo) [90], and Text-to-ML, a unified approach to code generation and code optimization.

3.5.1 *Darwin Gödel Machine: Open-Ended Evolutionary Self-Modification*

The Darwin Gödel Machine framework [95] draws inspiration from the theoretical Gödel Machine concept, which proposed that an agent could self-modify its own code optimally via formal proofs of utility improvement. However, arbitrary code reasoning renders formal verification intractable in practice. DGM replaces formal verification with empirical validation, bootstrapping an open-ended evolutionary loop in which agents iteratively rewrite their own code and are retained only if they demonstrably outperform their predecessors on concrete benchmarks.

The key innovation of DGM lies in its use of LLMs as the primary mechanism for generating code modifications. Rather than relying on random code perturbations (as in traditional genetic programming) or handcrafted transformation rules, DGM leverages the code understanding and generation capabilities of foundation models to propose semantically meaningful modifications. The LLM serves a dual role in the system: It provides the intelligence core of each agent (through prompting strategies), and it simultaneously acts as the mutation operator that drives evolution by suggesting code edits.

Each agent in the DGM is a Python codebase encapsulating three core components: a prompting strategy for a frozen foundation model, tool-use routines (e.g., invoking a REPL,[9] test harness, or code formatter), and heuristics for managing long context windows, caching, and peer review. Validated agents are stored in an ever-growing archive that forms a lineage tree: nodes correspond to codebases and edges indicate parent-offspring relationships, enabling both broad exploration across diverse lineages and deep refinement along promising branches.

To illustrate the types of modifications the LLM might propose, consider an agent whose current prompting strategy uses a simple zero-shot approach:

```
def generate_response(self, query):
    prompt = f"Answer the following: {query}"
    return self.foundation_model(prompt)
```

The foundation model, when asked to improve this agent's code, might propose a modification that adds few-shot examples:

```
def generate_response(self, query):
    examples = self.retrieve_similar_examples(query, k=3)
    prompt = self.format_few_shot_prompt(examples, query)
    return self.foundation_model(prompt)
```

This modification represents a meaningful architectural change that could improve the agent's performance—precisely the kind of semantic-level evolution that would be nearly impossible to achieve through random syntactic mutations.

[9] Read-Eval-Print Loop, an interactive programming environment that allows to write and execute code in a step-by-step manner.

Algorithm 3.1 Darwin Gödel Machine Evolution

```
Initialize archive A ← {seed_agent}
while compute_available do
    parent ← sample(A)
    candidate_code ← FM_generate_edits(parent.code)
    score ← evaluate(candidate_code, benchmark)
    if score > parent.score + δ then
        add_to_archive(A, candidate_code, score, parent_id)
    end if
end while
```

As illustrated in Algorithm 3.1, the evolutionary process begins with a manually designed seed agent encoding basic prompt-and-execute routines. At each iteration, an agent is sampled from the archive—either uniformly or with a bias toward higher-performing agents—and the foundation model proposes code edits, such as adding helper functions, refactoring prompt templates, tweaking tool-invocation hyperparameters, or integrating lightweight peer-review modules. The modified code is sandboxed and evaluated on held-out coding benchmarks; it is added to the archive only if its average performance exceeds that of its parent by a threshold δ. This loop continues until the compute budget is exhausted, yielding a branching tree of ever-improving agents.

Empirical results on standard coding benchmarks demonstrate substantial gains [95]. On SWE-bench (SoftWare Engineering benchmark), the initial agent achieves 20.0% success, while the best DGM agent reaches 50.0% (+30 percentage points). On the multilingual Polyglot benchmark, performance improves from 14.2% to 30.7% (+16.5 percentage points).

Safety mechanisms are integral to the DGM: all candidate executions occur in isolated containers with strict CPU, memory, and wall-clock limits; self-edits are restricted to the agent's own modules, while the foundation model and infrastructure remain immutable; a complete lineage log records code differences (the textual changes between parent and offspring code), performance deltas, and parent IDs for auditability; periodic human inspections guard against undesirable changes; and the empirical fitness function can be augmented with safety objectives such as robustness tests or rule adherence. Although computationally intensive and bounded by the foundation model's capabilities, the DGM illustrates a practical pathway toward self-improving AI.

3.5.2 LLM-Guided Evolutionary Search: FunSearch and Reflective Evolution

A second class of methods directly couples LLM sampling with evolutionary search over program or heuristic spaces. FunSearch [74] introduces a framework in which a pretrained LLM serves both as a generator of program fragments and as a crossover operator, while a systematic evaluator enforces correctness and scores candidates. Programs are organized into multiple "islands," each maintaining a pool of correct solutions clustered by evaluation score. Periodically, underperforming islands are reset via top-performing replicas to ensure diversity. At each cycle, sampled programs are formatted into a prompt using a best-shot strategy, allowing the LLM to generate new implementations. Generated code is executed under resource constraints; correct programs are scored, clustered, and reinserted into the database.

The island model in FunSearch serves a crucial role in maintaining diversity throughout the search process. Each island evolves somewhat independently, exploring different regions of the program space. When an island's population becomes too homogeneous, or its best solutions fall significantly behind other islands, it undergoes a reset: its population is replaced with copies of top performers from successful islands, but with the expectation that subsequent LLM-guided mutations will drive divergent evolution. This mechanism balances the exploitation of successful patterns with the exploration of novel approaches.

To illustrate the FunSearch process, consider the task of evolving a priority function for online bin packing.[10] An initial program might implement a simple first-fit heuristic:

```
def priority(item_size, bin_remaining_capacity):
    if item_size <= bin_remaining_capacity:
        return 1.0
    return -1.0
```

The LLM, when shown this function along with several other candidates and their scores, might generate a more sophisticated priority function:

```
def priority(item_size, bin_remaining_capacity):
    if item_size > bin_remaining_capacity:
        return -1.0
    waste = bin_remaining_capacity - item_size
    # Prefer bins that will be nearly full
    return 1.0 / (waste + 0.1)
```

This asynchronous, parallel pipeline has yielded breakthroughs in extremal combinatorics—discovering new cap set[11] constructions and improving capacity lower bounds—and in online bin packing, where evolved heuristics outperform classical algorithms and approach offline optimality [74].

Reflective Evolution [90] treats LLM-guided code variation as a language hyper-heuristic. A population of code-based heuristics evolves via mutation and crossover

[10] The bin packing problem is a classic combinatorial optimization problem where items of varying sizes must be packed into a finite number of bins of fixed capacity, to minimize the number of bins used. In the *online* variant, items arrive sequentially and must be assigned to a bin immediately without knowledge of future items.

[11] A cap set is a subset of a finite vector space over a finite field containing no three collinear points (i.e., no three points that form an arithmetic progression). Finding large cap sets is a fundamental problem in additive combinatorics with connections to coding theory.

implemented through LLM sampling, augmented by short-term and long-term reflections. After each generation, the LLM ingests recent best individuals or a larger history and generates commentary that serves as a verbal gradient to guide subsequent exploration.

The reflection mechanism in ReEvo represents a distinctive feature that sets it apart from other LLM-guided evolutionary approaches. After evaluating a generation of heuristics, the system prompts the LLM with both the code and performance metrics, asking it to analyze what makes specific solutions more effective. For example, the LLM might observe: "The top-performing solutions all use a two-phase approach: first grouping items by size category, then applying greedy assignment within each group. Solutions that attempted global optimization without this structure performed poorly on larger instances." This verbal analysis is then incorporated into subsequent prompts, effectively providing the LLM with learned insights that guide future code generation.

Evaluated on six NP-hard combinatorial optimization problems—ranging from TSP and VRP[12] (vehicle routing problem) to multi-knapsack and bin packing—ReEvo achieves state-of-the-art performance within fewer than 100 heuristic evaluations, demonstrating dramatic sample-efficiency gains [90]. Ablation studies confirm that reflections and evolutionary operators contribute measurably to performance.

3.5.3 *Text-to-ML: Combined Code Generation and Code Optimization*

Text-to-ML is a fully autonomous framework that marries modular LLM-driven code synthesis with automated machine learning (AutoML) [72] (previously described in Sect. 2.3) techniques to generate and optimize complete ML workflows—from data ingestion to final evaluation—based solely on a textual task description. Unlike traditional program synthesis methods that rely on unit tests to verify correctness, Text-to-ML embeds a rigorous optimization loop that leverages any black-box optimizer, including evolutionary computation, Bayesian optimization, random search, or reinforcement learning, to refine algorithmic choices and hyperparameters based on numerical performance metrics.

To manage the inherent length and diversity of ML programs, Text-to-ML decomposes the overall pipeline into a fixed sequence of modules, such as data loader, preprocessing, feature engineering, model constructor, training loop, evaluator, and post-processor. For each module j, an LLM f_λ is prompted with the task specification, previously accepted modules $\{Y_1, \ldots, Y_{j-1}\}$, and feedback from failed attempts. This iterative generation continues until the candidate code Y_j

[12] Multiple vehicles start from the origin, perform a round trip to demand locations, and proceed to the destination. The problem is to satisfy all demand while minimizing the total route cost.

passes a module-specific unit test E_j that verifies both syntactic validity and compatibility of data structures (e.g., tensor shapes, feature formats). Crucially, synthetic data generators—also produced by the LLM—provide test inputs before actual datasets are available, ensuring each module can be validated in isolation.

To illustrate the modular generation process, consider generating a preprocessing module for a tabular classification task. The LLM receives a prompt containing:

```
Task: Binary classification on tabular data
Previous module (data_loader) output signature:
  - Returns: pandas DataFrame with columns ['age', 'income',
    'category', 'target']
  - 'category' is categorical, others are numeric

Generate a preprocessing module that:
1. Handles missing values
2. Encodes categorical variables
3. Scales numeric features
4. Returns (X_processed, y) tuple
```

The LLM generates candidate code, which is then tested against synthetic data to verify that output shapes and types match expectations before integration with subsequent modules.

By enforcing modular compatibility through constrained generative unit testing—combining domain-agnostic progenitor tests with LLM-generated, task-specific checks—Text-to-ML guarantees that independently validated modules integrate seamlessly. This design reduces the best-case generation complexity to $\mathcal{O}(\Gamma)$ in program length Γ, avoiding the exponential blow-up typical of monolithic code generation.

Parallel to code synthesis, Text-to-ML constructs an explicit search space $\mathcal{S}$ of candidate pipelines. A single pass of the LLM enumerates plausible algorithmic primitives (e.g., classical estimators, neural architectures, augmentation techniques) and discrete hyperparameter ranges, forming a Cartesian product of module-level choices. Although the original evaluation employs random search and the bayesian optimization and hyperband (BOHB) algorithm [22], any black-box optimization method—including genetic algorithms, covariance matrix adaptation evolution strategy (CMA-ES) (see Sect. 1.2.3), differential evolution (see Sect. 1.2.3), or particle swarm optimization—can be plugged in without modification, treating each pipeline configuration $\theta \in \mathcal{S}$ as an individual in a population.

Once syntactically valid modules exist for a candidate θ, Text-to-ML enters its optimization loop (Algorithm 3.2): the optimizer selects θ_t based on prior performance history $\mathcal{H}$, assembles the whole program from generated modules, executes end-to-end on held-out data, and records the numerical score R_{θ_t} (e.g., accuracy, MAE[13]). To conserve resources, zero-cost proxies (e.g., FLOPs,[14] param-

[13] Mean absolute error (MAE) is defined as the average sum of the absolute differences between the actual value and the predicted value.

[14] FLoating point OPerations (FLOPs)). The computational complexity used to evaluate machine learning performance. Higher values indicate longer processing times.

eter counts, NASWOT [57], SynFlow [80]) prune low-potential configurations before complete training. This loop repeats until the compute budget is exhausted, and the best-performing pipeline is returned.

Algorithm 3.2 Text-to-ML Search Space Generation and Optimization

```
Initialize search space S ← SearchSpaceGen(task_description)
Generate model modules:
for θ in S do
    C_M,θ ← ModuleGen(f_λ, "model", θ)
    if deep_learning_task(θ) then
        S ← ZCProxiesEval(S, {C_M,θ})
    end if
end for
while budget remains do
    θ ← Optimizer.select(S, history H)
    for each module j ≠ "model" do
        if not exists ModuleCode(j, θ) then
            C_j,θ ← ModuleGen(f_λ, j, θ)
        end if
    end for
    if all modules valid then
        R_θ ← EvaluateProgram({C_j,θ}, test_data)
        H.append((θ, R_θ))
    end if
end while
return best θ in H
```

In experiments on 12 supervised tasks spanning tabular data, CV, and NLP, Text-to-ML outperforms baseline LLM-only methods on 10 tasks, reducing generation attempts by over 30% and achieving near-optimal pipelines with fewer than 100 complete evaluations. While these results use random search and BOHB, the framework's modularity and abstraction over the optimizer make it equally amenable to evolutionary strategies and other black-box algorithms, even though the original study does not evaluate EC variants. This extensibility opens avenues for future work to explore the co-evolution of modules, multi-objective optimization to trade off performance and resource usage, and continuous integration, where agents iteratively refine pipelines over streaming data.

3.6 Hyperparameter Optimization of EC with LLMs

Evolutionary computation algorithms, like most machine learning methods, rely on a set of hyperparameters that critically influence their ability to discover high-quality solutions. Common hyperparameters in general EC frameworks include population size, number of generations, stopping criteria, selection methods (e.g., tournament or roulette wheel), crossover rate, and mutation rates. These parameters often have nested sub-hyperparameters; for instance, the tournament size in tournament-based selection methods directly affects the selective pressure. Adjusting these hyperparameters allows practitioners to influence the search dynamics: increasing tournament size intensifies selection pressure, larger populations or higher mutation rates promote exploration, and extending the number of generations enables longer optimization runs.

However, these adjustments come with trade-offs. Longer runs, larger populations, or computationally expensive fitness functions may increase the likelihood of finding high-quality solutions, but they also require more computational resources. Fortunately, evolutionary computation algorithms are often robust to moderate variations in hyperparameters, and satisfactory results can frequently be achieved using reasonable, commonly adopted settings, for example, population sizes on the order of a few hundred individuals and 100 generations. These values are widely used in practice across a variety of evolutionary algorithms, serving as convenient starting points for experimentation and tuning. Of course, researchers study how changing these parameters affects evolution, proposing a reduced number of generations [4], adapting mutation and crossover rates to the parents [27, 36], or adapting the population size in runtime [32].

Despite this robustness, evolutionary processes can stagnate at different stages depending on the problem domain, dataset characteristics, and model configurations [4]. This variability motivates the use of systematic hyperparameter optimization, early stopping methods, and informed model selection strategies (see Sect. 4.2). Recent advances in large language models offer a novel approach to this challenge: By leveraging their generative and reasoning capabilities, LLMs can assist in predicting promising hyperparameter configurations, suggesting adaptive search strategies, and even providing insights into complex dependencies between hyperparameters. This opens a new frontier for combining EC with AI-driven optimization tools, potentially improving both efficiency and solution quality.

3.6.1 Traditional Hyperparameter Optimization in EC

In traditional machine learning and evolutionary computation, researchers often use default or heuristic hyperparameter values, e.g., based on experience or "rules of thumb," and then refine them iteratively. However, intuitive tuning does not yield optimal results across all algorithms and problem domains, motivating research on automatic hyperparameter optimization, including in the broader context of AutoML, described in Sect. 2.3.

In EC, automatic hyperparameter tuning has historically been approached via algorithmic frameworks such as evolutionary algorithms themselves: one frames hyperparameter selection as an optimization problem, where each "individual" represents a candidate hyperparameter configuration, and evolutionary search (e.g., genetic algorithms, particle swarm optimization) is used to explore this space. For example, a study in high-energy physics demonstrated how EC (both genetic algorithms and particle swarm optimization) can autonomously tune hyperparameters for ML models used in data analysis tasks, rather than relying on ad hoc manual settings [81]. Another work integrates EC into AutoML systems, comparing methods such as differential evolution (see Sect. 1.2.3) and CMA-ES (see Sect. 1.2.3) for tuning hyperparameters of deep learning models [85]. Additionally, several works study how to optimize hyperparameters during training [2, 15, 21].

More recently, hybrid approaches have emerged that combine EC with reinforcement learning (RL). Rather than using fixed hyperparameters, RL agents dynamically adjust parameters such as the mutation rate or crossover strategy during the evolutionary process. For instance, Ma et al. [54] propose a framework in which a deep RL agent learns to adapt the exploration-exploitation balance of an EC algorithm in real time, thereby improving performance across diverse benchmark problems. Similarly, Chen et al. [12] demonstrate evolving not only the solutions but also the DE parameters and strategies themselves using a nested DE optimization, which is a promising direction for evolving EC methods at a meta-level.

Thus, while traditional EC-based hyperparameter optimization relies on "outer" evolutionary loops (or RL) to tune hyperparameters, the emerging LLM-based paradigm, as will be discussed in the next section, brings a new layer of reasoning: using large language models to interpret optimization logs, propose adaptation strategies, and guide hyperparameter settings in a more semantic/insightful manner. In contrast to purely search-based methods, LLMs offer the potential for human-like reasoning and adaptation, perhaps enabling more efficient, interpretable, and context-sensitive tuning.

3.6.2 LLM-Based Hyperparameter Optimization in EC

With the rapid expansion of LLMs across different application domains, hyperparameter optimization has also begun to benefit from their use [15]. When interacting with an LLM, users can describe their problem in natural language and obtain guidance on several aspects of the modeling process: which models may be better suited for a given task (see Sect. 4.2); how the data should be preprocessed and which features are relevant (Sect. 4.1); and, as the focus of this section, which hyperparameters should be used for the target dataset.

When used as external optimizers, LLMs can influence hyperparameters at various stages of the evolutionary cycle, including:

- **Select Initial Parameters:** LLMs can propose initial hyperparameters based on a natural language description of the problem provided by the user. For instance, if the user describes the search landscape as rugged, the LLM may suggest using a higher mutation rate or applying novelty search [39]. Conversely, for smoother landscapes with a clear global optimum, a more straightforward hill-climbing strategy may be more appropriate.

- **Population Initialization:** Populations are typically initialized randomly to ensure diversity, although this often wastes evaluations on low-fitness individuals. LLMs can mitigate this by bootstrapping evolution: replacing part of the initial population with structured candidates inferred from domain knowledge or retrieved through RAG techniques, thus starting evolution closer to promising regions of the search space.
- **Stopping Criteria:** LLMs can adapt stopping conditions based on both user instructions and the ongoing fitness trajectory. For example, instead of simply stopping after 20 generations without improvement, an LLM may jointly evaluate fitness stagnation and population diversity, or even estimate whether further progress is still likely.
- **Model Evaluation:** Users often rely on default fitness functions, such as accuracy for classification or RMSE for regression. LLMs can propose more appropriate metrics depending on problem characteristics, e.g., suggesting weighted F1-score instead of accuracy for imbalanced datasets (see Sect. 3.7).
- **Genetic Operators:** LLMs can tune operator parameters dynamically, such as increasing mutation rate, adjusting elitism, or switching to uniform crossover when premature convergence is suspected, thereby improving the search efficiency.

Beyond these applications, LLMs become even more powerful when integrated directly into the evolutionary algorithm itself. In this setting, the LLM no longer acts merely as a recommendation system. Still, it autonomously makes optimization decisions, such as selecting fitness functions, generating natural-language logs to explain evolutionary progress, serving as a genetic operator (see Sect. 3.3.1), and deciding which operators to use in each generation based on fitness trends or population diversity. Examples of such applications include using LLMs for neural architecture search [98] and designing AutoML frameworks [93].

In this section, we follow the work of Custode et al. [15], who use LLMs to automatically adapt the mutation step size in the (1+1)-ES algorithm. While the algorithm was previously described in Sect. 1.2.5, we briefly reiterate that the ES variant considered here does not involve crossover; it relies solely on mutation, where each offspring is generated according to

$$x' = x + \omega \cdot N(0, 1), \tag{3.19}$$

where x' is the offspring, x is the parent, ω is the mutation step size, and $N(0, 1)$ is a standard normal variable.

In our experiments, we evaluate four variants of step-size adaptation: (1) no adaptation, where the step size remains constant throughout evolution; (2) the one-fifth success rule, previously described in Sect. 1.2.5; (3) step-size decisions made by Llama 3.3 70B; and (4) the same approach using Llama 3.1 8B, a much smaller model.

Among these, Custode et al. [15] initially evaluated approaches (1) and (2). We reproduced their setup by downloading their publicly available GitHub code and

Listing 3.1 Prompt example, as seen in the reference paper and code by Custode et al. [15], and an example of a reply obtained during training

```
"messages": [
    {
        "role":"system",
        "content":"You are a powerful and intelligent AI capable of
             analyzing logs and performing reasoning."
    }
    {
        "role":"user",
        "content":"Q:I am running an optimization process over an
             unknown function. I am using a 1+1-ES to optimize the
             function. f(x)=y indicates an evaluation. x1 -> x2 indicates
             that x1, using the current step size, produced a new
             candidate solution x2. The step size you propose must be
             contained between 0.999 and 0.001. Here's the log: '''txt
             <LOGCONTENT>''' I am currently using the following stepsize:
             <STEPSIZE>. Should I change it or not? Do you think the
             current step size is sufficient to ensure the process
             converges as quickly as possible? Reply with the following
             structure: 'Reasoning: <explanation> Recommended step size:
             <newstepsize>'"
    }
]
// < reply below >
"message": {
"role": "assistant",
"content": "Reasoning: \nThe current step size of 0.0075 seems to be
    relatively small and close to the lower boundary of 0.001.
    Considering the precision of the current step size and the fact
    that the last few rows of the log show minimal improvement in
    fitness values (most values are 8.35e+01), it seems that the
    algorithm has likely converged. Reducing the step size further to
    0.001 might not lead to significant improvements in convergence
    speed, but rather increase the computational cost of the
    optimization process.\n\nHowever, to confirm if the optimization
    has indeed converged, I would suggest increasing the step size
    slightly to 0.0075 to 0.005 and observing if there are any
    noticeable changes in the fitness values. If the values remain
    stable around 8.35e+01, it would be safe to conclude that the
    algorithm has converged.\n\nRecommended step size: 0.005"
},
```

replacing their original models (Llama2-70B and Mixtral) with the Llama 3 series. Since our experiments directly build on their implementation, we use the same LLM prompt (Listing 3.1) to ensure a fair comparison with their results.

Following the methodology proposed by Custode et al., we evaluate all methods using the BBOB test suite [28] through IOHProfiler [18]. We test all 24 BBOB functions in 30 dimensions, focusing particularly on understanding how these adaptation strategies scale to more challenging, higher-dimensional settings. For each function, we perform ten independent runs with different random initializations.

Figure 3.17 summarizes the performance of the four approaches across the 24 functions. Interestingly, the constant step-size strategy often performs surprisingly well, achieving better median performance than the one-fifth rule, Llama 70B, and Llama 8B in 20, 19, and 20 cases, respectively, out of 30. However, despite its strong performance across most functions, the constant setting (step size = 0.1) performs the worst or second worst on several functions (notably f17, f18, f23, and f24). These results indicate that some functions do not admit an intuitive or globally suitable step size.

On these more challenging problems, where the search landscape demands more flexible exploration, LLMs begin to show clear advantages. For example, in functions f17 and f23, both Llama-based strategies noticeably outperform the non-LLM approaches. Moreover, even in cases where the constant step size yields a better median than the LLMs (e.g., f3, f4, f15, f19, f20), the best LLM-driven run often surpasses the best run achieved by either non-LLM baseline. This suggests that LLMs provide a valuable form of adaptive guidance that can produce high-quality solutions even when their median performance is not dominant, motivating research in this field.

Despite the authors using older LLMs, the same observations apply to the results presented in their work. Although traditional approaches generally achieve better *median* performance, the LLM-based strategies consistently demonstrate the potential to discover solutions that surpass the best results obtained by the non-LLM baselines.

3.7 LLM Used as Fitness

In evolutionary computation algorithms, the fitness function measures the quality of candidate solutions, guiding the search toward optimal or high-performing individuals. The choice of fitness function significantly impacts the algorithm's effectiveness, as it determines selection pressure and the direction of evolution.

Although the fitness function in evolutionary computation varies across applications, each task typically employs a default evaluation metric, such as classification accuracy or mean squared error in regression. While these standard metrics often yield satisfactory results, many real-world scenarios need customized fitness functions. For instance, complex optimization problems may require multi-objective fitness evaluations, constraint handling, or domain-specific performance criteria beyond conventional metrics. In such cases, LLMs offer a flexible alternative by adaptively generating or refining fitness functions, particularly in domains where explicit metrics are difficult to define. Figure 3.18 illustrates several scenarios when picking a fitness function, such as choosing the default option for the task, asking an LLM for recommendations, and using the LLM itself to evaluate the solution.

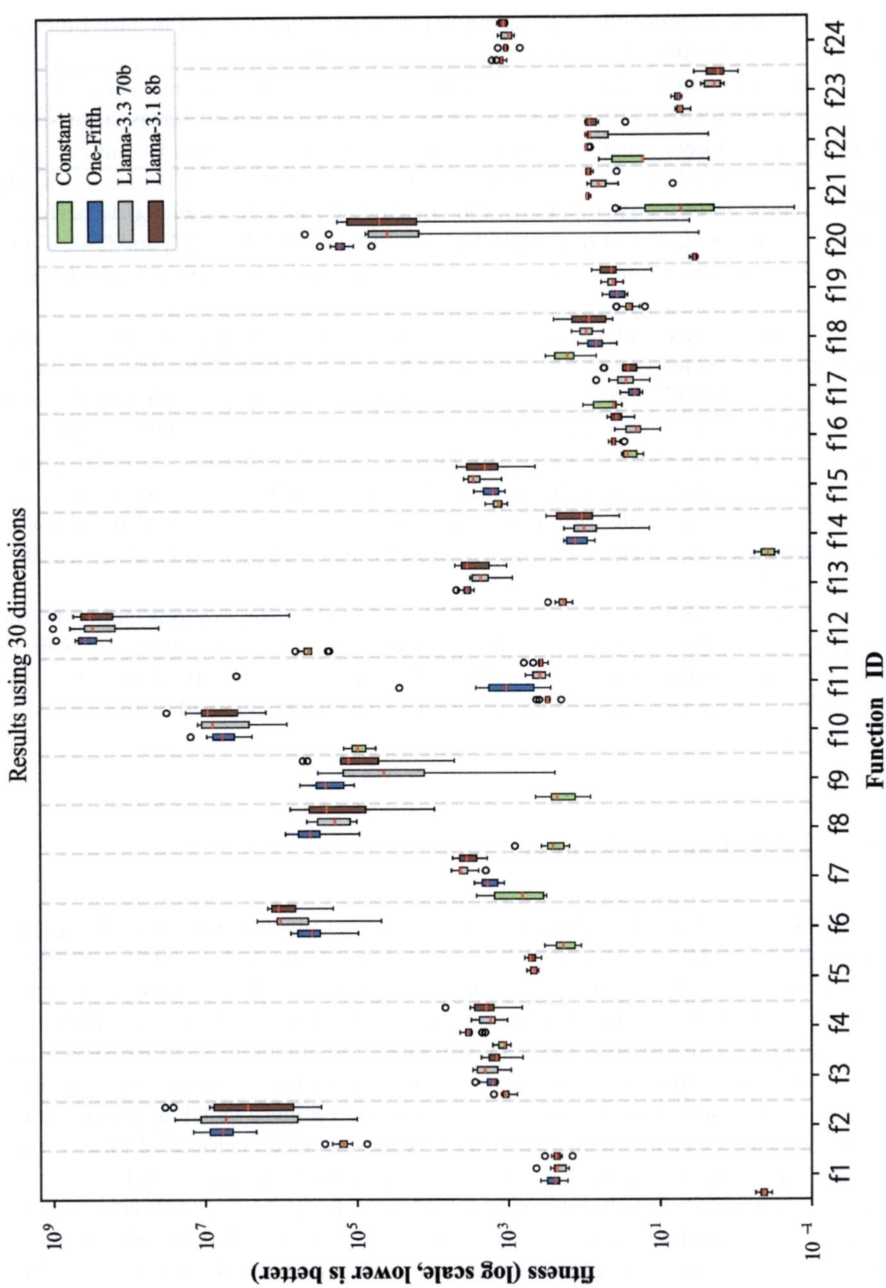

Fig. 3.17 Results obtained from running (1+1)ES with four different methods to adapt the step size: using (1) a constant value, (2) the one-fifth rule, (3) Llama-3.3 70b, and (4) Llama-3.1 8b

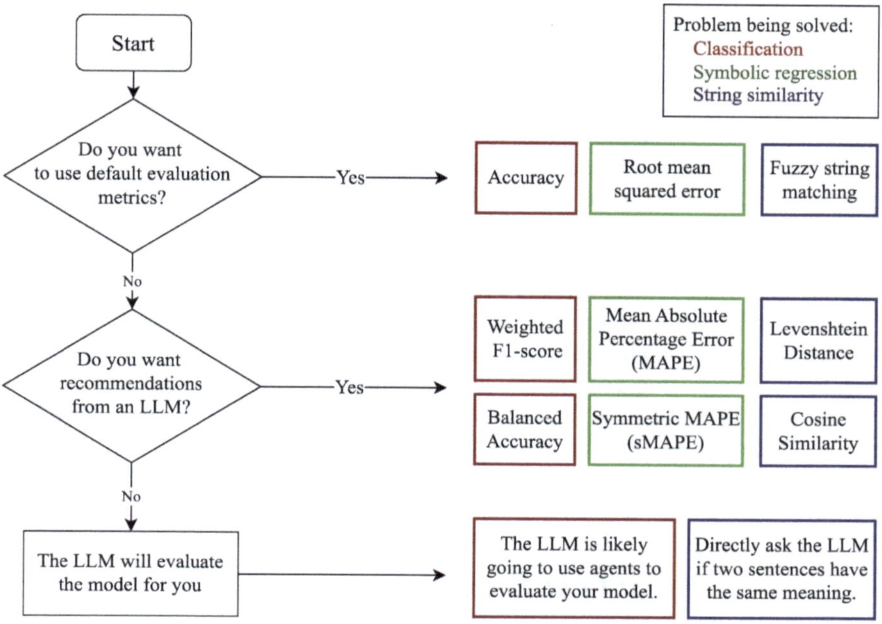

Fig. 3.18 Pipeline used to select a fitness function for problems such as symbolic regression, classification, or sentence similarity

Exploring alternative fitness functions can enhance model generalization and robustness. For instance, in classification tasks with imbalanced datasets, raw accuracy can lead to biased models that overfit to the majority class. To address this, researchers often adopt metrics such as the weighted average F-score (WAF) [7], which accounts for class imbalance by penalizing skewed performance and promoting fairness [23]. Similarly, when models risk overfitting and memorizing training data, cross-validation-based metrics—where fitness is evaluated on held-out partitions—can provide more reliable guidance for evolution [5, 88]. Such approaches align fitness evaluation with broader goals, such as generalizability and domain-specific constraints.

While classification and regression tasks benefit from well-established metrics, domains such as natural language processing, generative design, and strategic decision-making often lack universally accepted evaluation criteria. In such cases, LLMs can assist researchers by synthesizing objective evaluation metrics from the literature, streamlining the design of fitness functions. For example, Batista et al. [8] employed an LLM to recommend metrics for quantifying the complexity of information within a sentence, which were then used to train a classifier predicting the number of references per sentence. By leveraging the LLM's ability to surface validated metrics from existing research rapidly, Batista et al. reduced the manual effort required for literature review while maintaining reliability, since the proposed metrics were already empirically grounded. This approach demonstrates how LLMs can accelerate fitness function design in domains where conventional metrics are ill-defined or absent.

Real-world optimization problems often involve multiple, sometimes conflicting objectives, such as maximizing performance while minimizing cost or complexity. In such multi-objective scenarios, the fitness function must balance trade-offs to guide the evolutionary process toward a diverse Pareto front of optimal solutions. The core challenge lies not only in defining appropriate metrics but also in ensuring that the search prioritizes high-performing, contextually relevant solutions. Here, LLMs can provide critical support by (1) recommending key objectives to optimize based on domain literature or user-defined priorities, by (2) proposing objective hierarchies (e.g., weighted sums, lexicographic ordering) to structure trade-offs, and by (3) suggesting criteria for selecting final models from the Pareto front. By automating these steps, LLMs reduce the burden on experts when designing fitness functions for complex real-world constraints while maintaining alignment with domain-specific goals.

3.7.1 Versatility of LLM-Based Evaluation

In addition to the automatic design of fitness functions, LLMs can be integrated into evolutionary computation algorithms as flexible, general-purpose fitness evaluators, offering a novel way to evaluate candidate solutions and complementing or replacing traditional fitness functions even in established domains. This section outlines different strategies for implementing LLM-based fitness functions, discusses their advantages over traditional approaches, and highlights their limitations. Recent research demonstrates the potential of LLMs in the following areas:

- **Classification and Regression Tasks:** LLMs have emerged as valuable tools for evaluating classification systems when conventional accuracy metrics fail to capture essential performance aspects. Their ability to assess nuanced dimensions like sentiment polarity, topic relevance, and subjective content makes them particularly useful for text analysis tasks. A compelling demonstration of this approach appears in [26], where evolutionary algorithms optimize LLM prompts to improve text categorization accuracy. Since the final model is a readable prompt, the results of using LLMs for this task are a fully interpretable model (string).
- **Symbolic Regression:** LLMs' capabilities extend beyond traditional text interpretation. They can also be used to evaluate the simplicity of mathematical equations, while other methods assess the correctness of the equations. As demonstrated by neuro-symbolic regression pipelines [14], models such as GPT can determine the human interpretability of evolved formulas. By evaluating both the equations' error and interpretability, we can identify expressions that strike an optimal balance between quantitative accuracy and qualitative simplicity,

yielding solutions that are both data consistent and semantically meaningful. Such applications highlight LLMs' unique capacity to bridge the gap between purely numerical optimization and human-centric scientific discovery.

- **Program Synthesis and Code Evaluation:** In evolutionary program synthesis tasks, including genetic programming applications, LLMs such as GPT-4 provide sophisticated evaluation capabilities that extend beyond traditional unit testing. These models can assess multiple dimensions of code quality, including functional correctness, algorithmic efficiency, and human readability—aspects that are difficult to quantify through conventional automated testing alone. As demonstrated in [31], GPT-based scoring functions effectively guide the evolutionary process by evaluating both the syntactic validity and semantic coherence of generated code snippets. This approach enables the discovery of programs that are not only functionally correct but also maintain good software engineering practices, bridging the gap between machine-generated code and human-interpretable solutions.
- **Surrogate Modeling for Simulation Tasks:** In computationally intensive domains like engineering design and physics simulations, LLMs and foundation models have emerged as promising surrogate evaluators, significantly reducing fitness evaluation costs in evolutionary optimization. While traditional surrogate modeling approaches using Gaussian processes [24] or neural networks [83] are well established, recent works demonstrate that LLMs can not only provide insights into how to solve surrogate-assisted optimization problems [73] but also be used as surrogate models to evaluate models in an evolutionary algorithm pipeline [29].
- **Multi-objective Optimization:** LLMs provide unique value in multi-objective optimization by operationalizing qualitative criteria (e.g., design simplicity, operational safety, or conceptual novelty) that are difficult to quantify. As demonstrated by [92], language models can effectively rank Pareto-optimal solutions according to human preferences, even when these preferences are expressed only through natural language descriptions. Other works [48] demonstrate that LLMs can serve as zero-shot search operators in decomposition-based MOEAs, effectively balancing competing objectives through prompt engineering. This capability was further validated in combinatorial optimization [89], where an LLM-based framework generated diverse heuristics for the traveling salesman Problem, achieving Pareto-optimal trade-offs between performance and efficiency. Such approaches enable evolutionary algorithms to align with domain-specific priorities that are difficult to encode as explicit fitness functions while maintaining interpretability through natural language interactions.

3.7.2 Implementation Strategies

In this section, we discuss how LLMs can be employed to define and compute the fitness of candidate solutions in evolutionary algorithms. The appropriate integration

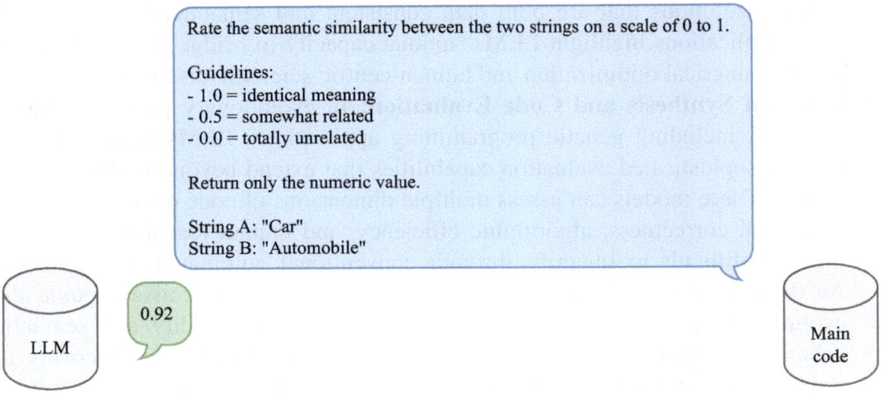

Fig. 3.19 LLMs can evaluate candidates using textual metrics provided by the user and return a numerical score that can, for example, be used as fitness

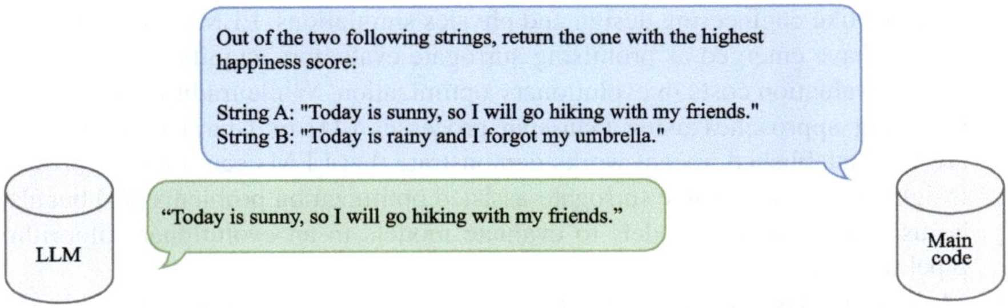

Fig. 3.20 Given an objective, LLMs can compare candidates and select one, without giving explicit metrics to the user

strategy depends on key factors such as the task type, domain complexity, and the specific characteristics of the evolved solutions.

- **Prompt-Based Scoring:** As illustrated in Fig. 3.19, this approach leverages direct prompting to evaluate candidate solutions generated by the model. In this method, carefully designed prompts explicitly describe the problem domain and task objectives and then request the LLM to assess or numerically score each solution. For instance, when evaluating a classification rule or analyzing a model's predictive outputs, the LLM can be prompted to quantitatively assess the solution's quality, correctness, or practical utility.
- **Pairwise Ranking:** For tasks where absolute scoring proves challenging, LLMs can instead perform pairwise comparisons between candidate solutions. As illustrated in Fig. 3.20, this approach prompts the model to analyze two solutions simultaneously and determine their relative quality, enabling the algorithm to resolve tournaments without evaluating the whole population beforehand. Such comparative evaluation is particularly valuable for subjective domains or open-ended problems where quantitative assessment metrics may be ill-defined.

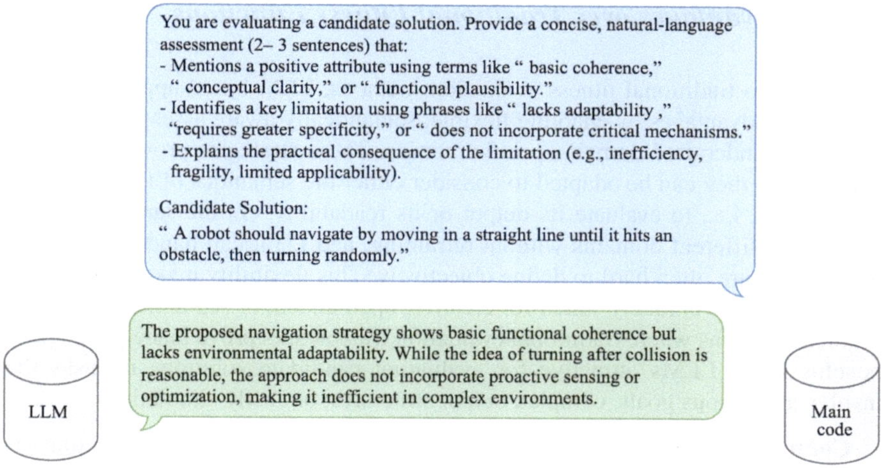

Fig. 3.21 Given a description of a solution, LLMs can provide an evaluation in natural language that is easy for the user to understand

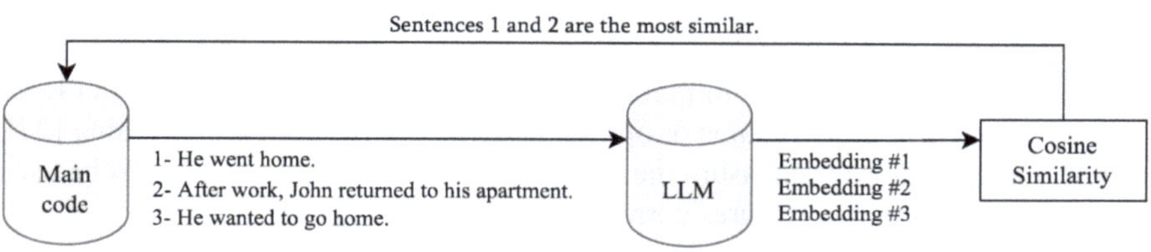

Fig. 3.22 LLMs can be used to extract the semantic meaning of sentences (i.e., their embeddings), which is then used to match sentences close in meaning using cosine similarity

- **Natural Language Evaluation:** LLMs enable a novel capability in evolutionary computation: natural language-based fitness assessment. Unlike traditional methods, LLMs can generate nuanced qualitative evaluations (e.g., "This solution demonstrates conceptual clarity but requires greater technical specificity") that capture multiple dimensions of solution quality, as seen in Fig. 3.21. These textual assessments can be systematically parsed into structured fitness components.
- **Embedding Similarity:** Lastly, as seen in Fig. 3.22, LLMs can also be used to detect similar solutions through embedding similarity. In tasks with an ideal reference output, e.g., regression datasets, solutions can be encoded into embeddings using LLMs and compared to the target solution using metrics such as cosine similarity. This provides a semantic-aware distance metric useful for tasks such as symbolic regression or textual generation. This approach is similar to EC methods such as geometric semantic genetic programming (GSGP), in which the models are evolved in the semantic space by developing a linear combination of the solutions' semantics from the original population [61, 68].

3.7.3 Advantages over Traditional Fitness Functions

Compared to traditional fitness evaluation methods, LLM-based approaches offer significant advantages by enabling flexible, semantically aware assessment without requiring handcrafted domain-specific metrics. These strategies provide three key benefits: (1) they can be adapted to consider either the semantics of the solution or its structure, i.e., to evaluate its output or its readability, (2) the same model can be used in different domains without retraining, and (3) it can handle complexity metrics that are often hard to define objectively. This flexibility makes LLM-based fitness functions uniquely suited for creative, open-ended, or semantically complex problem domains where traditional evaluation frameworks prove inadequate. These benefits make LLMs attractive for evaluating candidate solutions in tasks that involve ambiguous goals, complex output structures, or costly simulations.

- **Contextual Understanding:** Unlike simple metrics that reduce the solution to a single value, such as accuracy or RMSE, LLMs can evaluate solutions based on a broader understanding of the problem, including recommendations on structural properties. For example, it might know that a certain pair of features might work well together based on related work [3].
- **Adaptability and Generality:** LLMs are pretrained on diverse data and can generalize across tasks with minimal adaptation. This allows the same model to be used across different domains or optimization objectives without retraining [37]; e.g., the LLM used to measure the interpretability of a solution can also be used to recommend which features correlate with the target label.
- **Human-Aligned Evaluation:** In applications where the goal is to match human expectations (e.g., natural language generation, recommendation systems), LLMs serve as valid proxies for human evaluators by producing ratings that often align with human judgment.
- **Reduced Manual Engineering:** LLMs reduce the need to handcraft complex domain-specific fitness functions, saving time and improving accessibility for interdisciplinary researchers. This can be interpreted in two ways: either the LLM searches for already existing fitness metrics and provides a function, or the LLM itself acts as an evaluator in problems whose evaluation metric is ill-defined.

3.7.4 Limitations and Challenges

By embedding LLMs into the fitness evaluation loop, evolutionary algorithms can evolve solutions that align better with complex or implicit human preferences. This approach is instrumental in open-ended or creative domains where traditional metrics fail to capture solution quality. However, the integration of LLMs also introduces new challenges, including sensitivity to prompt design, inference costs, and potential biases in model outputs. These trade-offs must be carefully managed when designing LLM-based fitness functions.

Despite their many advantages over traditional fitness functions, LLM-based fitness evaluation also comes with significant challenges and limitations. These limitations must be carefully considered when integrating LLMs into evolutionary frameworks. In many cases, hybrid approaches that combine LLM-based and traditional fitness functions can offer a balance between expressiveness and reliability.

- **Prompt Sensitivity:** The outcome of an LLM-based evaluation can vary significantly based on the prompt design. Since small changes in wording can yield different results, experts must adopt a reasonable prompt approach [91]; e.g., Meyerson et al. [60] propose an LLM-based crossover operator and discuss how many examples (parents) should be included in the prompt to obtain the best results.
- **Inconsistent Evaluation:** Nondeterministic behavior (due to temperature settings or stochastic decoding) can result in fluctuating fitness evaluations for the same input, which undermines the stability of the selection process.
- **Low Reproducibility of Experiments:** In addition to the previous point, since the evaluation is not deterministic, the results obtained in the experiments are not reproducible unless the temperature setting is set to zero. However, making the LLM always pick the most likely next token often leads to repetitive output [67], which may indicate a lack of diversity in the population.
- **Cost and Latency:** Querying large models like those with over 1 billion parameters is computationally expensive and slower than traditional metrics. This can significantly increase the runtime of evolutionary algorithms that evaluate thousands of candidates per generation. This was observed during our runs in Sect. 3.3.1, where, although our population size was one-tenth of the default value, each generation took much longer than with the original implementation of standard GP.
- **Opacity and Interpretability:** LLMs are black-box models, and their scoring rationales are not always transparent. This makes it difficult to debug or justify specific fitness values. Thanks to this, prompting is usually done by manual trial and error until the human experts are satisfied with the outcome.
- **Bias and Hallucination:** LLMs may inherit biases from their training data or produce evaluations that are factually incorrect or socially biased. These issues can propagate through the evolutionary process, leading to suboptimal or unsafe solutions. Interestingly, in Fig. 3.12, we saw that, although feature names were not provided to the LLM, it correctly inferred them, implying that it had seen the dataset during training. This may result in the recommendations being contaminated with information from the test data.

3.7.5 Applications

LLMs are increasingly used in evolutionary computation (EC) for tasks beyond traditional optimization, especially in domains that require creativity, design innovation, or subjective judgment. Their ability to provide contextual understanding and flexible evaluation enables new possibilities in automated design and significantly reduces the need for human oversight during optimization.

In this section, we explore the diverse ways in which LLMs are being integrated into evolutionary computation as fitness evaluators. Specifically, we examine their use in three key areas: (1) evolutionary design, where LLMs assess the quality and novelty of generated artifacts, (2) surrogate evaluation models, where they approximate human preferences or complex design criteria, and (3) human-in-the-loop reduction, where they minimize the need for manual intervention in interactive evolutionary systems.

- **Evolutionary Design**
  Evolutionary design involves generating novel artifacts, such as texts, programs, layouts, or engineering structures, guided by an evolutionary algorithm. In many of these tasks, the desired outputs are not easily evaluated by conventional metrics. Thus, LLMs can serve as evaluators in these creative design spaces by assessing qualities such as clarity, novelty, stylistic alignment, or adherence to design constraints. For example:

  – In natural language design (e.g., generating chatbot scripts, instructions, or documentation), LLMs can evaluate fluency, relevance, and tone [59].
  – In code generation tasks, models can assess correctness, readability, and adherence to programming conventions [87].
  – In architectural or product design workflows, LLMs can interpret descriptive goals and assess whether evolved solutions satisfy abstract or user-defined requirements [55].

  Since LLMs can perform subjective evaluation without a human clearly explaining the intended outcome using objective metrics, they enable EC algorithms to operate in domains traditionally reliant on expert input.
- **LLMs as Surrogate Evaluation Models**
  In simulation-heavy or high-cost domains, such as robotics, aerodynamics, or drug discovery, evaluating a candidate solution via full simulation can be computationally expensive. Surrogate models can be used to approximate fitness functions, reducing evaluation cost [29]. This use of LLMs as surrogates improves scalability and responsiveness, especially in iterative design processes or in applications with limited computational budgets.

  LLMs, when fine-tuned or prompted with examples, can act as effective surrogate evaluators [13, 29, 46, 47]. They learn to approximate the outcome or quality of a design based on prior cases, enabling rapid estimation without re-running full simulations. For example:

  – Chugh et al. [13] use a surrogate model in their multi-objective EC algorithm to optimize the hot metal production process using an industrial blast furnace in a problem containing eight objectives.

  - Similarly, Liu et al. [46] use surrogate models in a multi-objective problem. In this case, the algorithm aims to propose solutions to a ten-objective optimization problem.
  - Other examples of applications of surrogate models to evaluate models in EC systems are surveyed in [29].

- **Reducing Human-in-the-Loop Requirements**
  Many EC applications require human input to guide the evolutionary process, especially when evaluating subjective qualities such as creativity, usefulness, or novelty [10, 65]. However, this human-in-the-loop setup introduces bottlenecks in scalability, consistency, and cost.

  LLMs provide a scalable alternative by acting as proxies for human judgment. They can be prompted with user preferences or example evaluations and then used to assess new candidates in line with those preferences automatically. However, in high-stakes or safety-critical applications, human oversight may still be necessary to verify LLM judgments. In such cases, LLMs can be used to filter or rank candidates, allowing humans to focus only on the most promising solutions. Nevertheless, this leads to several benefits:

  - **Faster Iteration:** The fitness evaluation time can be shortened by reducing the number of models subject to human evaluation or by replacing human evaluation entirely.
  - **Consistency:** While LLMs are known for being inconsistent, lowering their temperature parameter makes their evaluations more predictable. This ensures stable and repeatable evaluations, mitigating human inconsistency or fatigue.
  - **Cost-Efficiency:** While it is still desirable to have experts validating the final solutions, this approach provides a much cheaper early-stage exploration by using LLMs to replace expert panels and crowd-sourced ratings.

References

1. Azevedo, B.F., Rocha, A.M.A.C., Pereira, A.I.: Hybrid approaches to optimization and machine learning methods: a systematic literature review. Mach. Learn. **113**(7), 4055–4097 (2024). ISSN: 1573-0565. https://doi/org/10.1007/s10994-023-06467-x
2. Batista, J.E.: Studying elements of genetic programming for multiclass classification (2018). https://api.semanticscholar.org/CorpusID:69846678
3. Batista, J.E.: Embedding domain-specific knowledge from LLMs into the feature engineering pipeline (2025). arXiv: 2503.21155 [cs.LG]. https://arxiv.org/abs/2503.21155
4. Batista, J.E., Silva, S.: Comparative study of classifier performance using automatic feature construction by M3GP. In: 2022 IEEE Congress on Evolutionary Computation (CEC), pp. 1–8 (2022). https://doi.org/10.1109/CEC55065.2022.9870343
5. Batista, J.E., et al.: M6GP: multiobjective feature engineering. In: 2024 IEEE Congress on Evolutionary Computation (CEC), pp. 1–8 (2024). https://doi.org/10.1109/CEC60901.2024.10612107

6. Batista, J.E., et al.: Measuring structural complexity of GP models for feature engineering over the generations. In: 2024 IEEE Congress on Evolutionary Computation (CEC), pp. 1–8 (2024). https://doi.org/10.1109/CEC60901.2024.10611989
7. Batista, J.E., et al.: Complexity, interpretability and robustness of GP-based feature engineering in remote sensing **92**, 101761 (2025). https://doi.org/10.1016/j.swevo.2024.101761. www.sciencedirect.com/science/article/pii/S2210650224002992
8. Batista, J.E., Vatai, E., Wahib, M.: SAFE: improving LLM systems using sentence-level in-generation attribution (2025). arXiv: 2505.12621 [cs.CL]. https://arxiv.org/abs/2505.12621
9. Brown, T.B., et al.: Language models are few-shot learners (2020). arXiv: 2005.14165 [cs.CL]. https://arxiv.org/abs/2005.14165
10. Bryden, K.: Using a human-in-the-loop evolutionary algorithm to create data-driven music. In: 2006 IEEE International Conference on Evolutionary Computation, pp. 2065–2071 (2006). https://doi.org/10.1109/CEC.2006.1688561
11. Burke, E.K., Newall, J.P., Weare, R.F.: Initialization strategies and diversity in evolutionary timetabling. Evol. Comput. **6**(1), 81–103 (1998). ISSN: 1063-6560. https://doi.org/10.1162/evco.1998.6.1.81
12. Chen, M., Feng, C., Cheng, R.: MetaDE: evolving differential evolution by differential evolution. IEEE Trans. Evol. Comput. 1 (2025). ISSN: 1941-0026. https://doi.org/10.1109/TEVC.2025.3541587
13. Chugh, T., et al.: A data-driven surrogate-assisted evolutionary algorithm applied to a many-objective blast furnace optimization problem. Mater. Manuf. Process. **32**(10), 1172–1178 (2017). ISSN: 1532-2475. https://doi.org/10.1080/10426914.2016.1269923
14. Cranmer, M., et al.: Discovering symbolic models from deep learning with inductive biases (2020). arXiv: 2006.11287 [cs.LG]. https://arxiv.org/abs/2006.11287
15. Custode, L.L., et al.: An investigation on the use of Large Language Models for hyperparameter tuning in Evolutionary Algorithms. In: Proceedings of the Genetic and Evolutionary Computation Conference Companion. GECCO 2024 Companion, pp. 1838–1845. ACM (2024). https://doi.org/10.1145/3638530.3664163
16. De Buck, V., et al.: Multi-objective optimisation of chemical processes via improved genetic algorithms: a novel trade-off and termination criterion. In: Kiss, A.A., et al. (eds.) 29th European Symposium on Computer Aided Process Engineering. Computer Aided Chemical Engineering, vol. 46, pp. 613–618. Elsevier (2019). https://doi.org/10.1016/B978-0-12-818634-3.50103-X
17. de Vega, F.F., et al.: It is time for new perspectives on how to fight bloat in GP. In: Genetic Programming Theory and Practice XVII, pp. 25–38. Springer International Publishing (2020). ISBN: 9783030399580. https://doi.org/10.1007/978-3-030-39958-0_2
18. Doerr, C., et al.: IOHprofiler: a benchmarking and profiling tool for iterative optimization heuristics (2018). arXiv: 1810.05281 [cs.NE]. https://arxiv.org/abs/1810.05281
19. Dua, D., Graff, C.: UCI machine learning repository (2017). http://archive.ics.uci.edu/ml
20. Eiben, A., Smith, J.: Introduction to Evolutionary Computing. Springer, Berlin/Heidelberg (2015). ISBN: 9783662448748. https://doi.org/10.1007/978-3-662-44874-8
21. Eiben, A., Hinterding, R., Michalewicz, Z.: Parameter control in evolutionary algorithms. IEEE Trans. Evol. Comput. **3**(2), 124–141 (1999). https://doi.org/10.1109/4235.771166
22. Falkner, S., Klein, A., Hutter, F.: BOHB: robust and efficient hyper-parameter optimization at scale. In: International Conference on Machine Learning, pp. 1437–1446. PMLR (2018)
23. Fernáandez, A., et al.: Learning from Imbalanced Data Sets. Springer International Publishing (2018). ISBN: 9783319980744. https://doi.org/10.1007/978-3-319-98074-4
24. Forrester, A.I.J., Sóbester, A., Keane, A.J.: Engineering Design via Surrogate Modelling: A Practical Guide. Wiley (2008). ISBN: 9780470770801. https://doi.org/10.1002/9780470770801
25. Friedrich, T., Wagner, M.: Seeding the initial population of multi-objective evolutionary algorithms: a computational study. Appl. Soft Comput. **33**, 223–230 (2015). ISSN: 1568-4946. https://doi.org/10.1016/j.asoc.2015.04.043
26. Guo, Q., et al.: EvoPrompt: connecting LLMs with evolutionary algorithms yields powerful prompt optimizers (2025). arXiv: 2309.08532 [cs.CL]. https://arxiv.org/abs/2309.08532

27. Hanada, Y., et al.: Effectiveness of multi-step crossover fusions in genetic programming. In: 2012 IEEE Congress on Evolutionary Computation, pp. 1–8 (2012). https://doi.org/10.1109/CEC.2012.6256564
28. Hansen, N., et al.: Real-parameter black-box optimization benchmarking 2009: noiseless functions definitions. Research Report RR-6829. INRIA (2009). https://inria.hal.science/inria-00362633
29. Hao, H., Zhang, X., Zhou, A.: Large language models as surrogate models in evolutionary algorithms: a preliminary study. Swarm Evol. Comput. **91**, 101741 (2024). ISSN: 2210-6502. https://doi.org/10.1016/j.swevo.2024.101741. http://www/sciencedirect.com/science/article/pii/S2210650224002797
30. He, C., Tian, Y., Lu, Z.: Artificial evolutionary intelligence (AEI): evolutionary computation evolves with large language models. J. Memb. Comput. (2024). ISSN: 2523-8914. https://doi.org/10.1007/s41965-024-00172-x
31. Hemberg, E., Moskal, S., O'Reilly, U.-M.: Evolving code with a large language model. Genet. Program. Evol. Mach. **25**(2) (2024). ISSN: 1573-7632. https://doi.org/10.1007/s10710-024-09494-2
32. Hevia Fajardo, M.A., Sudholt, D.: Self-adjusting population sizes for non-elitist evolutionary algorithms: why success rates matter. Algorithmica **86**(2), 526–565 (2023). ISSN: 1432-0541. https://doi.org/10.1007/s00453-023-01153-9
33. Huang, J., et al.: Transfer learning based evolutionary algorithm framework for multi-objective optimization problems. Appl. Intell. **53**, 1–20 (2023). https://doi.org/10.1007/s10489-022-04444-w
34. Ingelse, L., Fonseca, A.: Domain-aware feature learning with grammar-guided genetic programming. In: Genetic Programming, pp. 227–243. Springer Nature Switzerland (2023). ISBN: 9783031295737. https://doi.org/10.1007/978-3-031-29573-7\T1\textbackslash_15
35. Jin, F., Liu, Y., Tan, Y.: Zero-shot chain-of-thought reasoning guided by evolutionary algorithms in large language models (2024). arXiv: 2402.05376 [cs.CL]. https://arxiv.org/abs/2402.05376
36. Kuroda, M., Hanada, Y., Ono, K.: Effectiveness of multi-step crossover in extrapolation domain for genetic programming. In: 2018 IEEE International Conference on Systems, Man, and Cybernetics (SMC), pp. 3654–3659 (2018). https://doi.org/10.1109/SMC.2018.00618
37. Lange, R.T., Tian, Y., Tang, Y.: Large language models as evolution strategies. CoRR abs/2402.18381 (2024). https://doi.org/10.48550/arXiv.2402.18381
38. Lehman, J., Miikkulainen, R.: Enhancing divergent search through extinction event. In: Proceedings of the 2015 Annual Conference on Genetic and Evolutionary Computation. GECCO'15, pp. 951–958. Association for Computing Machinery, Madrid (2015). ISBN: 9781450334723. https://doi.org/10.1145/2739480.2754668
39. Lehman, J., Stanley, K.O.: Novelty search and the problem with objectives. In: Genetic Programming Theory and Practice IX, pp. 37–56. Springer, London (2011)
40. Lehman, J., Stanley, K.O.: Abandoning objectives: evolution through the search for novelty alone. Evol. Comput. **19**(2), 189–223 (2011). https://doi.org/10.1162/EVCO_a_00025
41. Lehman, J., et al.: Evolution through large models. In: Handbook of Evolutionary Machine Learning, pp. 331–366. Springer Nature, Singapore (2023)
42. Lehman, J., et al.: Evolution through large models. In: Handbook of Evolutionary Machine Learning, pp. 331–366. Springer Nature, Singapore (2024). ISBN: 978-981-99-3814-8. https://doi.org/10.1007/978-981-99-3814-8\T1\textbackslash_11
43. Leung, Y., Gao, Y., Xu, Z.-B.: Degree of population diversity—a perspective on premature convergence in genetic algorithms and its Markov chain analysis. Trans. Neur. Netw. **8**(5), 1165–1176 (1997). ISSN: 1045-9227. https://doi.org/10.1109/72.623217
44. Lewis, P., et al.: Retrieval-augmented generation for knowledge-intensive NLP tasks (2021). arXiv: 2005.11401 [cs.CL]. https://arxiv.org/abs/2005.11401
45. Liu, F., et al.: Algorithm evolution using large language model (2023). arXiv: 2311.15249 [cs.NE]. https://arxiv.org/abs/2311.15249

46. Liu, Q., et al.: Surrogate-assisted many-objective optimization of building energy management. IEEE Comput. Intell. Mag. **18**(4), 14–28 (2023). https://doi.org/10.1109/MCI.2023.3304073
47. Liu, Y., et al.: A survey on evolutionary neural architecture search. IEEE Trans. Neural Netw. Learn. Syst. **34**(2), 550–570 (2023). https://doi.org/10.1109/TNNLS.2021.3100554
48. Liu, F., et al.: Large language model for multi-objective evolutionary optimization (2024). arXiv: 2310.12541 [cs.NE]. https://arxiv.org/abs/2310.12541
49. Liu, S., et al: Large language models as evolutionary optimizers. In: 2024 IEEE Congress on Evolutionary Computation (CEC), pp. 1–8. IEEE (2024)
50. Liu, J., et al.: EquivPruner: boosting efficiency and quality in LLM-based search via action pruning (2025). arXiv: 2505.16312 [cs.AI]. https://arxiv.org/abs/2505.16312
51. Luke, S., Panait, L.: Fighting bloat with nonparametric parsimony pressure. In: Parallel Problem Solving from Nature (2002). https://api.semanticscholar.org/CorpusID:9739644
52. Luke, S., Panait, L.: A comparison of bloat control methods for genetic programming. Evol. Comput. **14**(3), 309–344 (2006). ISSN: 1530-9304. https://doi.org/10.1162/evco.2006.14.3.309
53. Lyu, Z., et al.: Improving neuroevolution using island extinction and repopulation (2020). arXiv: 2005.07376 [cs.NE]. https://arxiv.org/abs/2005.07376
54. Ma, Z., et al.: Auto-configuring exploration-exploitation tradeoff in evolutionary computation via deep reinforcement learning (2024). arXiv: 2404.08239 [cs.NE]. https://arxiv.org/abs/2404.08239
55. Makatura, L., et al.: Large language models for design and manufacturing. In: An MIT Exploration of Generative AI (2024). https://mitgenai.pubpub.org/pub/nmypmnhs.
56. McDonald, G.C.: Ridge regression **1**(1), 93–100 (2009). ISSN: 1939-5108. https://doi.org/10.1002/wics.14
57. Mellor, J., et al.: Neural architecture search without training. In: International Conference on Machine Learning, pp. 7588–7598. PMLR (2021)
58. Mende, H., et al.: On the importance of domain expertise in feature engineering for predictive product quality in production. In: Procedia CIRP 118 (2023). 16th CIRP Conference on Intelligent Computation in Manufacturing Engineering, pp. 1096–1101. ISSN: 2212-8271. https://doi.org/10.1016/j.procir.2023.06.188. https://www.sciencedirect.com/science/article/pii/S2212827123004158
59. Mendonça, J., Lavie, A., Trancoso, I.: On the benchmarking of LLMs for open-domain dialogue evaluation (2024). arXiv: 2407.03841 [cs.CL]. https://arxiv.org/abs/2407.03841
60. Meyerson, E., et al.: Language model crossover: variation through few-shot prompting. ACM Trans. Evol. Learn. Optim. (2024). https://doi.org/10.1145/3694791
61. Moraglio, A., Krawiec, K., Johnson, C.G.: Geometric semantic genetic programming. In: C.A.C. et al. (eds.) Parallel Problem Solving from Nature—PPSN XII, Coello, pp. 21–31. Springer, Berlin/Heidelberg (2012)
62. Mouret, J.-B., Clune, J.: Illuminating search spaces by mapping elites (2015). arXiv: 1504.04909 [cs.AI]. https://arxiv.org/abs/1504.04909
63. Munñoz, L., Silva, S., Trujillo, L.: M3GP—multiclass classification with GP. In: Lecture Notes in Computer Science, pp. 78–91. Springer International Publishing (2015). https://doi.org/10.1007/978-3-319-16501-1_7
64. Munñoz, L., et al.: Evolving multidimensional transformations for symbolic regression with M3GP. Mem. Comput. **11**(2), 111–126 (2019). ISSN: 1865-9292. https://doi.org/10.1007/s12293-018-0274-5
65. Murphy, A., et al.: Human in the loop fuzzy pattern tree evolution. SN Comput. Sci. **3**(2) (2022). ISSN: 2661-8907. https://doi.org/10.1007/s42979-022-01044-w
66. Panait, L., Luke, S.: Alternative bloat control methods. In: Genetic and Evolutionary Computation—GECCO 2004, pp. 630–641. Springer, Berlin/Heidelberg (2004), ISBN: 9783540248552. https://doi.org/10.1007/978-3-540-24855-2_71
67. Peeperkorn, M., et al.: Is temperature the creativity parameter of large language models? (2024). arXiv: 2405.00492 [cs.CL]. https://arxiv.org/abs/2405.00492

68. Pietropolli, G., et al.: Combining geometric semantic GP with gradient-descent optimization. In: Medvet, E., Pappa, G., Xue, B. (eds.) Genetic Programming, pp. 19–33. Springer International Publishing, Cham (2022). ISBN: 978-3-031-02056-8
69. Poli, R., Langdon, W.B., Mcphee, N.: A Field Guide to Genetic Programming. Lulu Enterprises (2008). ISBN: 978-1-4092-0073-4
70. Pugh, J.K., Soros, L.B., Stanley, K.O.: Quality diversity: a new frontier for evolutionary computation. Front. Robot. AI **3**, 40 (2016)
71. Purohit, A., Choudhari, N.S. Code bloat problem in genetic programming (2013). https://api.semanticscholar.org/CorpusID:2336784
72. Real, E., et al.: Automl-zero: evolving machine learning algorithms from scratch. In: International Conference on Machine Learning, pp. 8007–8019. PMLR (2020)
73. Rios, T., Lanfermann, F., Menzel, S.: Large language model-assisted surrogate modelling for engineering optimization. In: 2024 IEEE Conference on Artificial Intelligence (CAI), pp. 796–803 (2024). https://doi.org/10.1109/CAI59869.2024.00151
74. Romera-Paredes, B., et al.: Mathematical discoveries from program search with large language models. Nature **625**(7995), 468–475 (2024). https://doi.org/10.1038/s41586-023-06924-6
75. Sahoo, P., et al.: A systematic survey of prompt engineering in large language models: techniques and applications. arXiv preprint arXiv:2402.07927 (2024)
76. Silva, S., Costa, E.: Dynamic limits for bloat control in genetic programming and a review of past and current bloat theories. Genet. Program. Evol. Mach. **10**(2), 141–179 (2009). https://doi.org/10.1007/s10710-008-9075-9
77. Silva, S., Vanneschi, L.: Operator equalisation, bloat and overfitting. In: Proceedings of the 11th Annual Conference on Genetic and Evolutionary Computation. ACM (2009). https://doi.org/10.1145/1569901.1570051
78. Silva, S., Dignum, S., Vanneschi, L.: Operator equalisation for bloat-free genetic programming and a survey of bloat control methods. Genet. Program. Evol. Mach. **13**(2), 197–238 (2011). https://doi.org/10.1007/s10710-011-9150-5
79. Skolicki, Z.: An analysis of island models in evolutionary computation. In: Proceedings of the 7th Annual Workshop on Genetic and Evolutionary Computation. GECCO'05. Association for Computing Machinery, Washington, D.C. (2005), pp. 386–389. ISBN: 9781450378000. https://doi.org/10.1145/1102256.1102343
80. Tanaka, H., et al.: Pruning neural networks without any data by iteratively conserving synaptic flow. Adv. Neural Inf. Process. Syst. **33**, 6377–6389 (2020)
81. Tani, L., et al.: Evolutionary algorithms for hyperparameter optimization in machine learning for application in high energy physics. Eur. Phys. J. C **81**(2) (2021). ISSN: 1434-6052. http://dx.doi.org/10.1140/epjc/s10052-021-08950-y
82. Tian, H., et al.: An LLM-empowered adaptive evolutionary algorithm for multi-component deep learning systems. Proc. AAAI Conf. Artif. Intell. **39**(19), 20894–20902 (2025). ISSN: 2159-5399. https://doi.org/10.1609/aaai.v39i19.34303
83. Tripathy, R.K., Bilionis, I.: Deep UQ: learning deep neural network surrogate models for high-dimensional uncertainty quantification. J. Comput. Phys. **375**, 565–588 (2018). ISSN: 0021-9991. https://doi.org/10.1016/j.jcp.2018.08.036. https://www.sciencedirect.com/science/article/pii/S0021999118305655
84. Vanneschi, L., Castelli, M., Silva, S. Measuring bloat, overfitting and functional complexity in genetic programming. In: Proceedings of the 12th Annual Genetic and Evolutionary Computation Conference, GECCO'10, pp. 877–884 (2010). https://doi.org/10.1145/1830483.1830643
85. Vincent, A.M., Jidesh, P.: An improved hyperparameter optimization framework for AutoML systems using evolutionary algorithms. Sci. Rep. **13**(1) (2023). ISSN: 2045-2322. https://doi.org/10.1038/s41598-023-32027-3
86. Wang, C., et al.: When large language models meet evolutionary algorithms: potential enhancements and challenges (2025). arXiv: 2401.10510 [cs.NE]. https://arxiv.org/abs/2401.10510

87. Weyssow, M., et al.: CodeUltraFeedback: an LLM-as-a-judge dataset for aligning large language models to coding preferences (2024). arXiv: 2403.09032 [cs.SE]. https://arxiv.org/abs/2403.09032
88. Xiong, Z., et al.: Evaluating explorative prediction power of machine learning algorithms for materials discovery using k-fold forward cross-validation. Comput. Mater. Sci. **171**, 109203 (2020). ISSN: 0927-0256. https://doi.org/10.1016/j.commatsci.2019.109203. https://www.sciencedirect.com/science/article/pii/S0927025619305026
89. Yao, S., et al.: Multi-objective evolution of heuristic using large language model. Proc. AAAI Conf. Artif. Intell. **39**(25), 27144–27152 (2025). ISSN: 2159-5399. https://doi.org/10.1609/aaaiv39i25.34922
90. Ye, H., et al.: Reevo: large language models as hyper-heuristics with reflective evolution. arXiv preprint arXiv:2402.01145 (2024)
91. Yin, H., et al.: Controlling the mutation in large language models for the efficient evolution of algorithms. In: Applications of Evolutionary Computation, pp. 403–417. Springer Nature Switzerland (2025), ISBN: 9783031900655. https://doi.org/101007/978-3-031-90065-5_25
92. Yu, J., et al.: Collaborative expert LLMs guided multi-objective molecular optimization (2025). arXiv: 2503.03503 [q-bio.BM]. https://arxiv.org/abs/2503.03503
93. Zhang, S., et al.: AutoML-GPT: automatic machine learning with GPT (2023). arXiv: 2305.02499 [cs.CL]. https://arxiv.org/abs/2305.02499
94. Zhang, H., et al.: LLM-meta-SR: learning to evolve selection operators for symbolic regression (2025). arXiv: 2505.18602 [cs.NE]. https://arxiv.org/abs/2505.18602
95. Zhang, J., et al.: Darwin godel machine: open-ended evolution of self-improving agents. arXiv preprint arXiv:2505.22954 (2025)
96. Zhang, Y., et al.: Nature-inspired population-based evolution of large language models (2025). arXiv: 2503.01155 [cs.CL]. https://arxiv.org/abs/2503.01155
97. Zhang, Y., et al.: A systematic survey on large language models for evolutionary optimization: from modeling to solving (2025). arXiv: 2509.08269 [cs.NE]. https://arxiv.org/abs/2509.08269
98. Zheng, M., et al.: Can GPT-4 perform neural architecture search? (2023). arXiv: 2304.10970 [cs.LG]. https://arxiv.org/abs/2304.10970
99. Zhou, A., et al.: Multiobjective evolutionary algorithms: a survey of the state of the art. Swarm Evol. Comput. **1**(1), 32–49 (2011). ISSN: 2210-6502. https://doi.org/10.1016/j.swevo.2011.03.001

Chapter 4
LLMs for Metaheuristics

In this chapter, we show how to combine LLMs [13, 63, 86] and metaheuristics [64]. Neuroevolution [24] is a new research direction that uses evolutionary methods to generate evolving artificial neural networks. It alters both the weighting parameters and the network structures, attempting to balance the fitness of evolved solutions and their diversity. We will explain how LLMs are applied to network architecture search (NAS) [22] in neuroevolution. As a case study, we integrate LLMs with the NAS algorithm, using the quality-diversity (QD) algorithm [67]. As explained in Sect. 3.2.2, QD algorithms are known to discover diverse and robust solutions in evolutionary computation. While LLMs struggle to conduct NAS directly from prompts, this approach leverages QD for both prompts and network architecture to create diverse, high-performing networks. Thereafter, we will explain how LLMs improve existing metaheuristics or propose new ones [54, 72, 76, 82]. More precisely, we let LLMs output executable code and run it to assess their effectiveness in terms of swarm intelligence. This is an interesting approach to creating novel search heuristics and new hybrid algorithms.

While we do acknowledge that there are still some issues regarding LLMs generating hallucinated content [50], limiting their use in high-risk AI systems, such as applications related to education, law enforcement, immigration services, among others, the literature also shows that LLMs have a strong potential to improve the performance of the currently used AI systems.

4.1 LLMs for Data Preparation

This section is divided into two parts. In the first part, we motivate the need for proper data preparation, explaining what it is, its role in the machine learning pipeline, and the methods commonly used. This is followed by an explanation of

H. Iba et al., *Large Language Models and Evolutionary Computation*,
Natural Computing Series, https://doi.org/10.1007/978-981-95-8597-7_4

related work that uses LLMs for data preparation, thereby improving the quality of their final models.

4.1.1 Data Preparation

The machine learning pipeline includes several steps to ensure the quality of the final model. While this pipeline varies by research field or even the problem itself, we can confidently say that the steps of machine learning are obtaining data, preparing it, and feeding it to the machine learning algorithm. By following these steps, exemplified in Figs. 4.1 and 4.2, data scientists can ensure the quality of their models. In this section, we focus on the second step: data preparation.

The objective of the data preparation step is to convert the raw data into something that the machine learning algorithm can process. This includes tasks such as merging data from different sources, handling missing values, removing

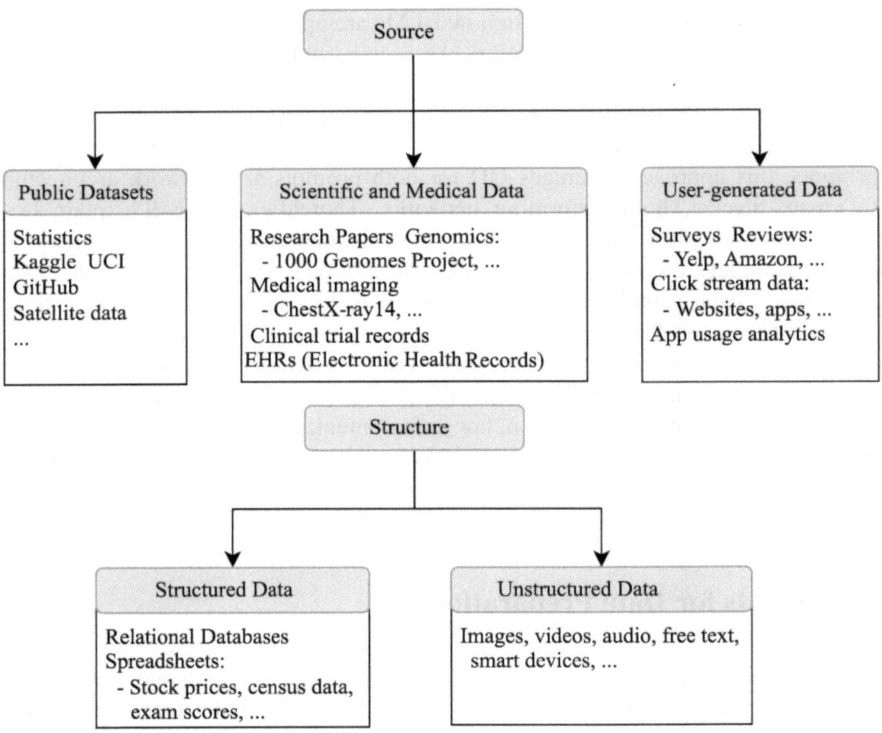

Fig. 4.1 Datasets can be broadly partitioned into different types, based on the source and type of data. Each type has its own challenges and advantages, and the data must be cleaned appropriately

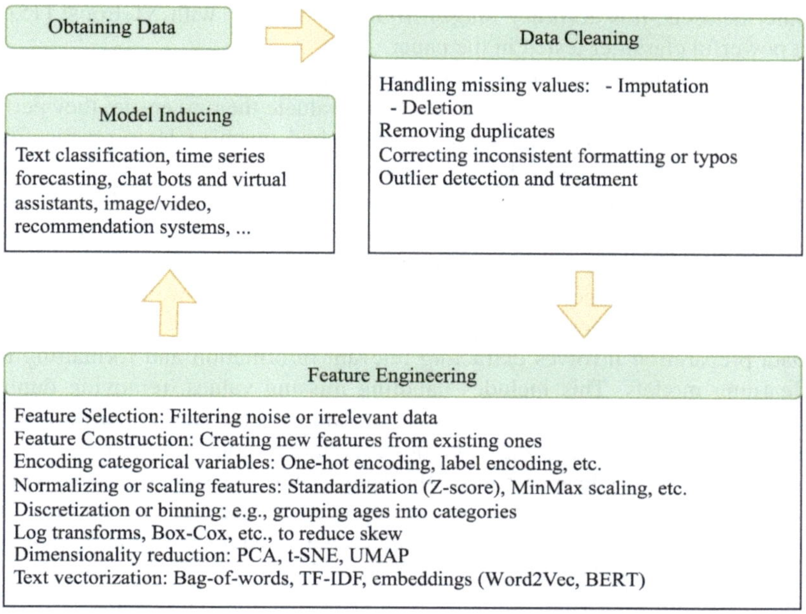

Fig. 4.2 The machine learning pipeline can be broadly partitioned into four steps: data collection, data cleaning, feature engineering, and model induction

outliers, handling duplicate samples, normalizing data, performing feature selection, and constructing features [9].

A well-known issue in machine learning is overfitting, i.e., the model is overtrained and learns the noise in the training data. This produces models that perform well on the training data but poorly on new data, especially when the latest data comes from a different statistical distribution than the data used to train the model. Overfitting has many possible sources, some of which are directly associated with the datasets used. For example, the dataset may be too small, contain missing values in the samples, duplicate samples, feature noise, or be irrelevant to the problem at hand. While overfitting is typically associated with overtraining, poor model robustness is also related to the use of poor training data, motivating good data preparation [75].

High robustness means that the model performs well on both training data and data drawn from the same statistical distribution. This is often seen in experiments that train and test models using different partitions of the same dataset. While robustness is a must for high-quality models, researchers also aim to increase model transferability, i.e., to make models perform well on out-of-distribution data. One real-world example of high robustness but low transferability is the detection of burnt areas in satellite imagery [6]. In this binary classification problem, models achieve accuracy above 99% on the validation data, which has the same statistical distribution as the training data. When applying the same models to the same task on other datasets, this accuracy ranges from 73% to 89% with XGBoost [15], the most powerful classifier tested in the paper.

The best way to prevent overfitting and the lack of transferability is to train the models on high-quality data and continually reevaluate them to ensure they perform well on new data. There should be an established machine learning pipeline to ensure this is done correctly; however, there is no consensus in the literature on the terminology and structure of this pipeline [85]. As such, we split the pipeline into the following six steps, previously seen in Figs. 4.1 and 4.2: (1) data collection; (2) data preparation; (3) feature engineering; (4) model selection; (5) training and testing; and (6) deployment and management. In this section, we will focus on data preparation and feature engineering.

Data preparation involves extracting relevant information and formatting it for the learning models. This includes handling missing values, removing duplicate samples and outliers, and data normalization, among other tasks that may depend on the algorithms used later, e.g., one-hot encoding to convert categorical features into numerical or Boolean features [9]. Dealing with missing values is typically done using statistical methods. However, some authors use machine learning, and a recent survey [32] lists machine learning techniques used for this task. This includes using approaches based on MLP [41] and NNs [27], as well as NNs assisted by GA, to handle missing values and minimize their error function [1]. In some cases, a few bad samples can reduce the final model's accuracy, underscoring the importance of proper data cleaning before training. Considering this, Silva et at. [75] proposed a semi-supervised method that effectively detects and avoids learning mislabeled data. Similarly, other authors apply semi-supervised methods to remove duplicate samples in datasets [23, 25].

Feature engineering [57] can be broadly split into feature selection and feature construction.[1] Feature selection involves identifying which features are essential to the data for a specific task. In contrast, feature construction consists in deciding how to combine or modify these features to highlight the information in a way that is easier for humans or machine learning algorithms to study and use.

Feature selection is a crucial process in machine learning that identifies and selects features that strongly correlate with the task's solution. In most real-world applications, data is collected on a large scale and often contains more features than necessary to solve the problem. Some features may be redundant, irrelevant to the current task, or can be considered noise. By carefully selecting which features to use when inducing a model, we not only reduce the dimensionality of the search space, potentially making the model smaller and faster, but also decrease the likelihood of overfitting to irrelevant features.

The process of feature selection offers several benefits:

- It simplifies models, making them easier to interpret.
- It reduces training times.

[1] Also known as feature extraction, feature generation, feature learning, or constructive induction.

- It helps avoid the curse of dimensionality.
- It improves the compatibility of the data with certain learning model classes.
- It can encode inherent symmetries present in the input space.

By employing feature selection techniques, we can enhance the model's performance, improve its generalization capabilities, and ultimately create more robust and efficient solutions in evolutionary computation.

As previously seen in Sect. 3.2.3, LLMs have good capabilities for feature engineering tasks, including feature selection. When describing a problem to an LLM, it can provide recommendations to the users, such as "You should combine features A and B in the following way" or "Related work shows that feature A is frequently used for this problem, and feature Z is not related." Using LLMs for this task can quickly increase the speed at which machine learning experts prepare their pipeline without contaminating their experiments. That is, since experts describe problems without providing data to the LLM, there is no risk of the machine learning model seeing test data beforehand, enabling accurate measurement of test accuracy and the model's robustness.

As further motivation to use LLMs for this task, remember that, as previously mentioned, experts traditionally use their domain-specific knowledge to transform and combine features in a dataset, i.e., perform manual feature construction. Although automatic methods for feature construction exist, this task was traditionally done manually. For example, remote sensing experts may use the normalized difference vegetation index (NDVI) [70] to highlight green vegetation in satellite images. In fact, studying vegetation is so important that experts often manually adapt vegetation indices to their specific needs, resulting in over 100 vegetation indices [38]. If experts rely more often on easy ways to retrieve related work, they avoid missing important papers and reduce the effort required to search for relevant information.

4.1.2 Applications of LLMs for Data Preparation

While data preparation is traditionally done manually, with data scientists relying on their domain-specific knowledge and intuition, many automatic feature construction methods have been developed over the years. Good examples from the field of evolutionary computation include GA [34] and GP [66]. GAs are probably the oldest subtype of evolutionary machine learning (EML) used for feature selection and remain a popular choice today [5]. In contrast, GP models allow nonlinear combinations of features, making them a good choice for feature construction. Using automatic feature construction, experts can focus on other tasks, increasing their productivity. Additionally, since these methods do not rely on human knowledge, they can be used to discover new feature combinations, enabling experts to uncover relationships among variables [7].

The downside of using evolutionary computation algorithms for automatic feature construction is their computational complexity. For example, while GP-based methods can discover features comparable to those used by experts [6, 16], they require thousands of GP models to be created and evaluated to obtain a feature construction model. Nowadays, feature construction has been greatly facilitated by LLMs. In well-studied applications, researchers can ask LLMs to recommend feature combinations to add to their datasets based on the original features [8]. For example, as previously mentioned, vegetation indices are widely used in remote sensing to study vegetation.

As an example, consider a researcher who recently started working with satellite data and does not yet know which combinations of features are helpful for their work. While the researcher may not be familiar with vegetation indices, LLMs can easily provide recommendations to improve the data, as demonstrated in Fig. 4.3. Using this simple query and an LLM, the researcher can obtain a list of feature

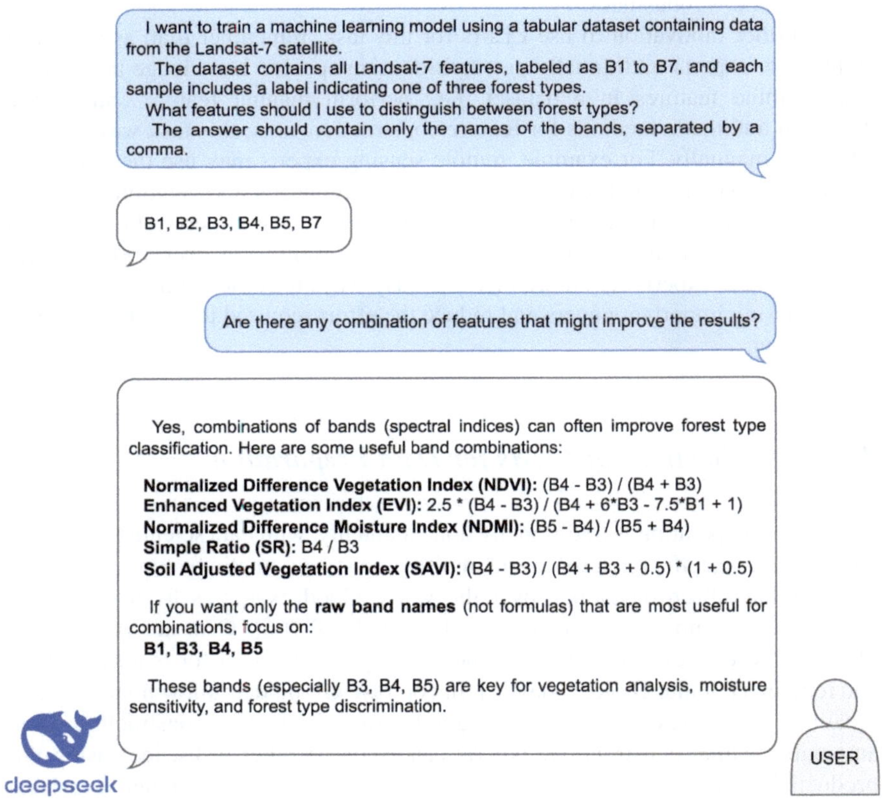

Fig. 4.3 Example of automatic feature construction using DeepSeek-V3. In total, DeepSeek recommended four indices (NDVI, EVI, NDMI, and SAVI) and one ratio between B4 and B3

combinations that may be useful in their work, along with a brief explanation of why each combination is valid, with little effort. In this case, DeepSeek-V3 recommended adding the following features to the dataset:

NDVI and EVI Both NDVI and the enhanced vegetation index (EVI) [70] are spectral indices used in satellite imagery to assess vegetation health and density. NDVI measures plant greenness by comparing red and near-infrared reflectance, while EVI improves sensitivity in high biomass areas by reducing atmospheric and soil background effects. These indices are crucial for monitoring agricultural productivity, deforestation, drought conditions, and ecosystem changes.

NDWI The normalized difference water index (NDWI) [62] is a spectral index used in satellite imagery to detect water bodies and assess water content in vegetation. It compares near-infrared and shortwave infrared reflectance to highlight water features while minimizing the influence of soil and vegetation. NDWI is essential for monitoring drought, flood mapping, and managing water resources. As such, we also agree with GPT-4o's recommendation.

NBR The normalized burnt ratio (NBR) [46] is a spectral index used in satellite imagery to assess burn severity and vegetation recovery after wildfires. It compares near-infrared and shortwave infrared reflectance to highlight burned areas, as charred vegetation absorbs more infrared light. NBR is crucial for wildfire management, ecological restoration, and post-fire recovery monitoring.

Ratios Between Bands DeepSeek-V3 recommends three ratios between bands: (1) B8/B4, the basis for NDVI, which highlights healthy and dense vegetation, (2) B8/B2, which enhances the contrast between vegetation and non-vegetation areas, helping to separate different species, and (3) B11/B4, which assesses vegetation moisture content, help distinguish plant species with different water retention properties. The first two ratios are also known for highlighting chlorophyll;[2]

PCA Principal component analysis (PCA) [59] improves the detection of forest types in satellite imagery by reducing data redundancy, reducing noise, and also improving the visualization of data. PCA allows the models to focus on the most informative components and discards low-variance components (often containing noise). Reducing the dataset's dimensionality also allows us to employ more effective data visualization techniques.

Temporal Features Using temporal features—satellite imagery from multiple timestamps—improves the detection of different forest types by capturing seasonal and long-term variations in vegetation characteristics. Various tree species exhibit unique seasonal growth patterns, such as leaf emergence, color change, and senescence. By analyzing images from multiple seasons, forest types can be more clearly distinguished by their phenological cycles. Additionally, temporal data enable multi-seasonal spectral analysis, reducing misclassification caused by temporary changes such as drought stress, shadows, or cloud cover in a single image.

[2] https://www.indexdatabase.de/db/s-single.php?id=96.

Spatial Features Spatial features, such as those extracted using gray-level co-occurrence matrix (GLCM) [84] and other texture analysis methods, improve the detection of different forest types in satellite imagery by capturing structural and textural differences in vegetation. Different forest types have distinct canopy structures, leaf arrangements, and shadow patterns. Texture metrics like contrast, homogeneity, and entropy from GLCM help differentiate dense, uniform forests (e.g., coniferous) from heterogeneous, mixed forests.

As previously seen in Sect. 3.2.3, LLMs have good capabilities for feature construction, reliably providing solutions that can be used to bootstrap evolution. When considering spatial features, for example, in remote sensing, LLMs provide feature combinations that are known to correlate well with the target objective. For example, when prompted to identify forests in satellite images, LLMs correctly recommend using indices such as NDVI. As seen in Fig. 4.4, this index highlights healthy vegetation in satellite images, making the search for forest much easier.

Although data preparation, feature selection, and feature construction are typically performed by experts using their domain-specific knowledge, several methods now automate these tasks, enabling LLMs to be used as data engineers [53, 60, 93]. In this section, we will focus on the application of LLMs for these tasks.

Data Preparation LLMs are applied for missing values, removing duplicated samples, removing outliers, data normalization, data augmentation, and data correction, among others [53, 60].

LLMs can predict missing textual data by leveraging context. For example, in a survey with incomplete responses, an LLM could infer plausible answers based on other responses. For numerical/tabular data, LLMs can suggest imputation strategies (e.g., mean vs. regression) by analyzing dataset patterns through fine-tuning or generating synthetic data to train imputation models. LLMs can also simplify the dataset by identifying near duplicates in text data using embeddings (e.g., clustering customer reviews with similar meanings but different phrasing). Additionally, they

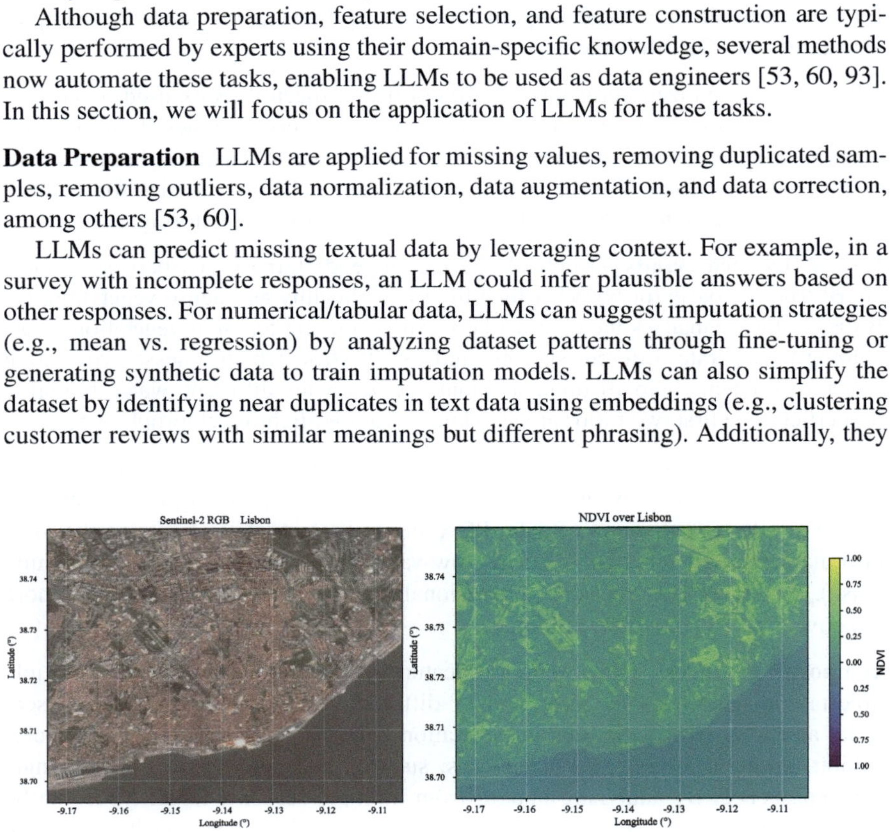

Fig. 4.4 NDVI applied to a Sentinel-2 satellite image obtained over Lisbon, Portugal. The NDVI highlights healthy vegetation in the image, facilitating the search for pixels with green areas

can detect semantic duplicates through context[3] and correct them, normalizing the data. This correction should expand abbreviations such as "NY" to "New York," "u" to "you," or even parse and convert units (e.g., "5 lbs" to "2.27 kg"). While LLMs can help us remove irrelevant data that may be considered noise during model training, they can also help expand existing data by generating realistic synthetic samples for underrepresented classes.

In related works, we find that researchers are using LLMs for data augmentation [17, 95]. Jorgensen et al. [39] used LLMs to increase the number of test cases during GP agent training, resulting in better agents.

Feature Selection LLMs are currently being used to identify which features are relevant to a given problem [93] since they can analyze textual descriptions of features (e.g., "glucose_level" in medical data) to assess their relevance to a target variable (e.g., diabetes risk). By training on domain-specific corpora, they prioritize features aligned with known relationships (e.g., prioritizing "blood_pressure" over "height" for heart disease prediction). In a real-world application example, we prompted an LLM with "key factors for house prices." In this case, it ranked square_footage and school_rating higher than wall_color. While LLMs show good feature selection capabilities in well-known problems (based exclusively on the textual description of features), it should also be mentioned that, when prompted about new problems, it lacks the capabilities to propose good solutions and recommends features based on similar problems, which may limit their use in domain-specific tasks if other techniques, such as retrieval-augmented generation (RAG) [26, 49], are not used. By providing documents that contain relevant information, LLMs can extract knowledge that might not have been obvious from the prompt alone.

Feature Construction One of the well-known advantages of evolutionary computation methods in feature construction is the capability of generating nonobvious interactions between features. However, "obvious" interactions between features can also improve datasets. In this sense, LLMs can identify interactions such as "age x income" for load prediction tasks, recommending that this multiplication be added as an additional feature. Additionally, LLMs may recommend merging similar features, reducing the dimensionality of the datasets (e.g., in a loan prediction task, features such as "monthly income" and "annual income" can be merged into a single feature, or in marketing data "social media clicks" and "facebook ad views" can also be merged into a single "digital engagement" feature).

While LLMs do not have the capacity to evaluate numerical data directly, it is possible to identify problems that require external algorithms and automatically call their APIs. In this way, LLMs are currently used to extract features from tabular data by serving as input [31, 37, 77]. Alternatively, since LLMs not only contain vast amounts of internal knowledge but can also retrieve external information, resulting

[3] Without context, "NY" and "New York" would be two completely different strings. Given a proper context, such as "I live in NY/New York," the LLM can recognize that these two sentences are identical.

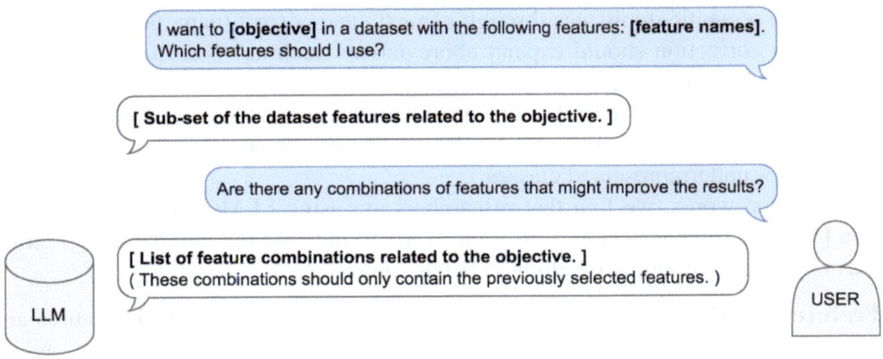

Fig. 4.5 Generic use case of feature engineering using an LLM, as proposed by Batista [8]

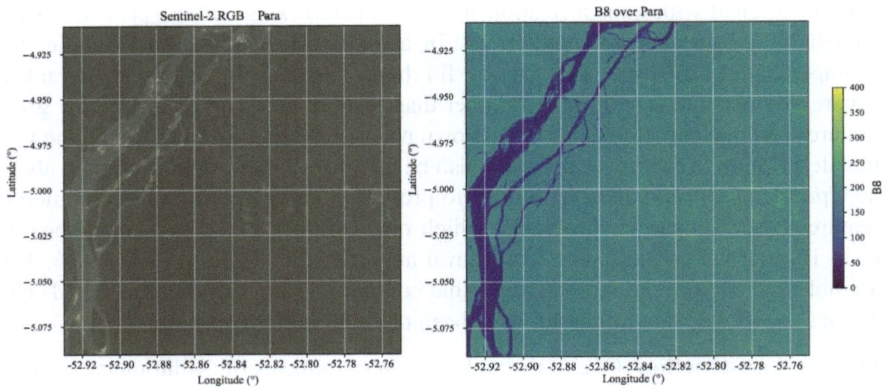

Fig. 4.6 RGB (top) and B8 band (bottom) from a Sentinel-2 satellite image obtained over Pará, Brazil. This band is used to highlight the river in a darker color, allowing the user to filter these pixels and focus the classification efforts on the land pixels

in RAG capabilities, providing the dataset is not always necessary. In a recent work [8], Batista proposed preserving dataset privacy by providing only the feature names and the task they aim to solve, without giving the whole dataset, as shown in Fig. 4.5. Using this approach, the LLM can recommend feature combinations that have been shown to work well for that specific task, based on its internal knowledge or on information retrieved by the RAG system.

Following the previous example shown in Fig. 4.4, we see that LLMs can provide recommendations, suggesting how to combine features into more informative ones that highlight relevant information for a task. In addition to feature construction, LLMs can also help us filter data through feature selection. For example, in remote sensing data, it is very easy to identify water pixels, and filtering those pixels can speed up the classification of entire images. As seen in Fig. 4.6, using a single feature such as *"band 8"* (B8) can help us remove a large section of the area by filtering the black pixels. This allows us to focus the classification effort on the land pixels.

While this approach is still under research, it can be used to bootstrap evolution at very low computational cost. The current results [8] show that this approach works very well on some datasets but does not improve results on others. We hypothesize that the primary contributor to success in a specific problem is the extent to which the issue is explored in the literature. After all, if the solution is available online, the LLM should be able to retrieve it and provide it to the user, reducing the need for a complex machine learning model and resulting in faster implementation and training times.

4.2 LLMs for Model Selection

When optimizing their machine learning pipeline, experts rely on their knowledge, obtained through experience and research. Since the scientific process is built on previous discoveries, it is a waste of time for each person to rediscover the wheel. Applying this to machine learning, users should select the best models and hyperparameters based on prior work, rather than wasting time on trial and error to achieve results. Of course, neither experience nor research will tell you the optimal pipeline for every problem. After obtaining a reasonable setup, researchers often use strategies such as grid search, random search, or genetic algorithms [52] to optimize hyperparameters. While approaches like grid search typically search for the optimal parameters using brute-force, employing LLMs to select hyperparameters can guide that process, thereby reducing the computational overhead of model selection and hyperparameter tuning.

Selecting the best model for a task is not always straightforward, and it often requires some experience in the field for both model selection and fine-tuning its parameters. Using LLMs, this task can be done more efficiently, accelerating the development of machine learning pipelines [94]. In this section, we discuss how LLMs can be used to select the best models for a given task. Later, we discuss the existing approaches, challenges, limitations, the relevance of such applications, and future directions.

4.2.1 How LLMs Can Assist in Algorithm Selection

LLMs can contribute to the development of machine learning pipelines by efficiently selecting models through a natural language understanding of the problem description. That is, the expert can describe a dataset as "noisy," "containing few samples," or "containing class imbalance," and the LLM should provide recommendations based on the description.

Deep learning models require large datasets to generalize well. When trained on small datasets, they tend to memorize noise and specific patterns, rather than learning generalizable features, leading to poor performance on unseen data [2, 45].

Given this, we would expect LLMs not to recommend deep learning models for small or noisy datasets. Alternatively, support vector machines tend to suffer from poor scalability [12]. Thus, we would expect LLMs to recommend alternative methods for larger datasets, not to improve performance but to improve their usability.

While the ability to understand natural language is the main selling point of using LLMs for this task, their internal knowledge and search capabilities also enable them to make recommendations based on the dataset type, e.g., they may recommend the random forest algorithm for tabular data. LLMs can also analyze the dataset at a high level and extract characteristics such as the number of samples and features, or the task's objective. Lastly, they can also propose hyperparameters based on the task at hand, such as the maximum depth in tree-based algorithms and the optimizer used by neural networks.

4.2.2 Existing Approaches and Research

When using LLMs to select models and hyperparameters, experts may consider directly asking the model for recommendations, fine-tune the models for ML advice, integrate LLMs into the ML pipeline to iteratively narrow the search space, or use RAG approaches:

Zero-Shot Recommendations LLMs can provide recommendations to users, even without fine-tuning or using RAG. However, by doing so, the recommendations are based exclusively on the LLM's internal knowledge and are not up to date. In many situations, especially when prompting the LLM about knowledge that was learning in pretraining and is unlikely to change,[4] asking for recommendations can lead to good results. This approach is easy to implement and computationally cheaper than RAG. Still, users should note that discoveries are frequently made and programming libraries are often updated, which may mean the most recent information or implementations are not taken into account. Figure 4.7 exemplifies this kind of approach.

Fine-Tune LLMs for ML Advice For more advanced tasks, experts may consider using LLMs fine-tuned for machine learning tasks [58]. This can be done by providing machine learning documentation, competition solutions from ML challenges (e.g., Kaggle [43]), benchmark repositories, or research papers to the LLM. While this approach feeds relevant information to the LLM, experts should consider that the LLM likely saw their dataset (if public) during training. As such, there is a higher risk of data contamination. For example, the LLM may recommend a specific model

[4] While information such as "what are the state-of-the-art methods for image classification?" may change over time, information such as "what parameters were initially proposed for genetic programming?" will persist through time.

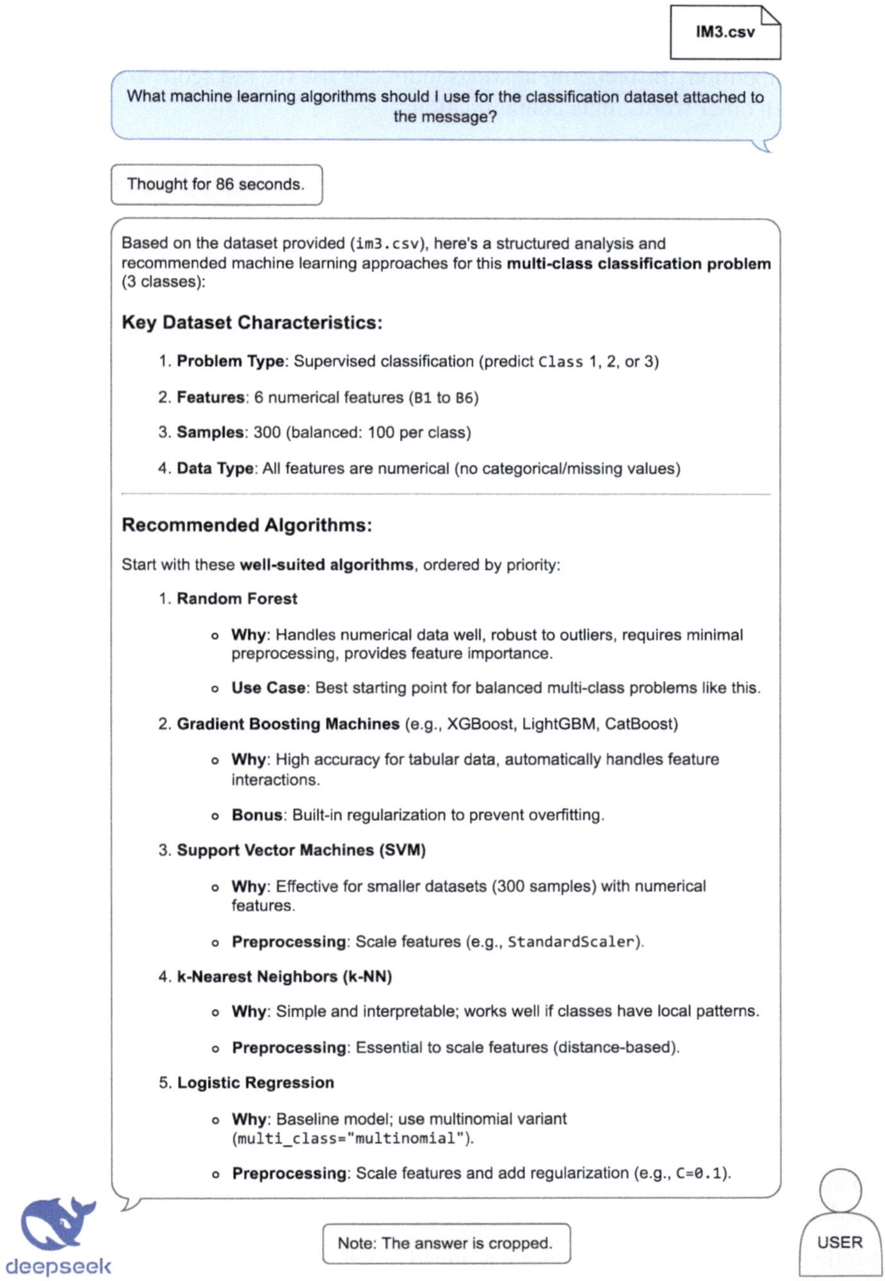

Fig. 4.7 Prompting ChatGPT to recommend classification algorithms for a dataset provided in the prompt. GPT correctly identifies the number of samples and features and recommends the expected models, while also mentioning other models that may have decent results but are not advised

or a set of hyperparameters because the top solution on the same dataset on Kaggle used it. Since the recommendation will be based on solutions with high test scores in the competition, the recommendations indirectly use the test score to generate the pipeline, in other words, data contamination.

Retrieval-Augmented Generations (RAGs) As a cheap alternative to fine-tuning an LLM, experts may use RAG-based [26, 49] approaches by feeding relevant content to the LLM to boost their recommendation capabilities. This also allows the LLM to use recent data without further training, while giving the user control over which new data the model sees.

Integration with AutoML AutoML (Automated Machine Learning [35, 90]) tools aim to automate the end-to-end ML pipeline, including algorithm selection, hyperparameter tuning, and feature engineering. However, they rely on computationally expensive methods to search for the optimal algorithm and hyperparameters. LLMs can be used to prune the set of algorithms being tested and the hyperparameters used. Effectively applying recommendations automatically. For more details about AutoML, see Sect. 2.3.

4.2.3 Challenges and Limitations

While LLM recommendations have proven useful before [58, 90], they still face challenges that hinder their full realization of their capabilities in this task. They suffer from bias, they may not explain their recommendations properly, and they have static knowledge and are often overreliant on text descriptions:

Bias in Recommendations LLMs may favor popular algorithms (e.g., deep learning), even in situations where simpler methods may suffice.

Data Contamination When working with data available online, experts have to consider the possibility that the LLM saw the same data. As such, the recommendations may be based on approaches that other experts have tested and that have yielded good results on test data. Additionally, as seen in the previous Chapter (Sect. 3.3), LLMs may access the dataset during training and make recommendations based on data they should not have access to, for proper evaluation.

Lack of Rigorous Evaluation LLMs recommend models and hyperparameters without explaining their reasoning. This may result in recommendations that have no empirical basis. For example, it may recommend a model because it was also used in related work.

Static Knowledge LLMs, unless fine-tuned or when placed in a RAG system, have no access to documents written after they were trained. This can result in LLMs becoming easily outdated, especially in fast-paced fields, such as machine learning, particularly those related to LLMs.

Overreliance on Text Descriptions While experts may provide their training data to the LLM to improve its answers, LLMs struggle with raw data (e.g., feature distributions) without data analysis tools. As such, experts may need to build a system around the LLM also to use data analysis tools, or precalculate relevant values and append them to the query, helping the LLM understand the dataset.

4.2.4 Future Directions

Given the current challenges in LLM model selection, we can see a future in which LLMs are combined with dataset meta-features to improve recommendations. Alternatively, the data provided to the LLMs can include data summaries (e.g., histograms, correlation matrices) in prompts, enriching the prompt sent to the LLM. Lastly, LLMs should be able to refine their recommendations based on the results of their original recommendations, effectively evolving them over several iterations.

4.3 LLMs for Neuroevolution

4.3.1 Neural Architecture Search

Neural architecture search (NAS) refers to the algorithmic process of automating the design of artificial neural network architectures. Traditionally, neural architectures have been crafted by human experts through a laborious and error-prone trial-and-error process. NAS alleviates this burden by casting architectural design as an optimization problem. Given a predefined space of architectures, a search strategy proposes candidate networks, which are then evaluated and ranked based on their performance on held-out data. In doing so, NAS can be viewed as a specialized sub-field of automated machine learning (AutoML), sharing important commonalities with hyperparameter optimization—where the goal is to tune numerical settings of a fixed architecture—and with meta-learning—where learning algorithms themselves are adapted based on prior experience [35].

A convenient framework for understanding NAS decomposes any method into three interrelated dimensions: the *search space*, which defines the family of permissible architectures; the *search strategy*, which governs how this often combinatorially large space is explored; and the *performance estimation strategy*, which determines how candidate networks are evaluated efficiently [22]. By varying each of these components, researchers have developed a rich taxonomy of NAS methods.

The *search space* constrains which architectures can be represented in principle. Early NAS work considered simple chain-structured networks, parameterized by layer types and their associated hyperparameters [22]. To capture more modern design motifs, such as skip connections [33], multibranch modules, and repeated building blocks, more expressive spaces have been introduced. Notably, *cell-based spaces* search over small, repeatable motifs ("cells") that are then stacked to form deep networks, reducing the dimensionality of the search problem and facilitating transfer across datasets [97]. Hierarchical spaces further generalize this idea by defining multiple levels of motifs, enabling both micro- and macro-architecture optimization within a single unified framework [56].

Within a given search space, the *search strategy* dictates how candidate architectures are proposed. Common approaches include reinforcement learning (RL), where a recurrent neural network (RNN) controller sequentially samples architectural decisions and is trained via policy gradients [96]; evolutionary algorithms, which evolve populations of networks through mutation and selection [81]; Bayesian optimization, which employs surrogate models to predict performance and balance exploration and exploitation [11, 20]; and gradient-based methods, which relax discrete choices into continuous parameters and optimize via backpropagation [55].

Finally, the *performance estimation strategy* addresses the prohibitive cost of training each candidate from scratch. Techniques to accelerate evaluation include lower-fidelity approximations, training for fewer epochs or on reduced data subsets [97]; learning-curve extrapolation, fitting partial training curves to predict final accuracy [3, 20]; weight inheritance via network morphisms [89]; and one-shot or weight-sharing methods, which train a single "supernet" and evaluate subgraphs directly [10, 55, 65].

By carefully designing each of these dimensions—selecting an appropriate search space, leveraging an effective search strategy, and employing efficient performance estimation—NAS has matured into a practical toolkit for discovering state-of-the-art architectures across computer vision, natural language processing, and beyond.

4.3.2 Neuroevolution

Within the NAS framework described above, neuroevolution can be understood as a search strategy that employs evolutionary algorithms to explore the architecture space by maintaining and evolving a population of candidate networks. In this view, *neuroevolution* instantiates the NAS search strategy dimension: Candidate architectures (including their weights, topologies, hyperparameters, and even learning rules) are encoded as genomes and iteratively refined through selection, mutation, and recombination, with fitness evaluations guiding the search process [24]. This population-based exploration complements other NAS strategies, such as reinforcement learning, Bayesian optimization, and gradient-based relaxation, while leveraging massive parallelism to traverse complex, non-differentiable spaces efficiently.

Early neuroevolution methods used *direct encodings*, wherein each genome explicitly represents every connection weight of a fixed-topology network. Such approaches served as alternatives to stochastic gradient descent for weight optimization and were soon extended to coevolve network topology alongside weights. A seminal example is the NeuroEvolution of Augmenting Topologies (NEAT) algorithm, which introduced historical markings to align genes during crossover and speciation mechanisms to protect innovative structures, thereby enabling the gradual complexification of architectures without premature convergence [28, 81].

To provide more expressive and compact search spaces within the NAS framework, neuroevolution also developed *indirect encodings*, such as compositional pattern producing networks (CPPNs) and their derivative, HyperNEAT. CPPNs generate regular, repeated connectivity patterns by composing simple activation functions over geometric inputs, and HyperNEAT leverages CPPNs to decode neuron positions into large-scale network connectivity, automatically rediscovering convolutional motifs and other regularities while encoding millions of weights via a small genome [79, 80].

A distinctive feature of evolutionary search within NAS is its ability to promote behavioral diversity. *Novelty search* abandons explicit performance objectives and instead rewards individuals for exhibiting behaviors that differ from those previously encountered, thereby escaping deceptive optima [47]. Building on this idea, *quality-diversity* algorithms (e.g., MAP-Elites [61], see also Sect. 3.2.2) aim to illuminate a repertoire of high-performing, behaviorally distinct solutions rather than a single optimum, enriching the NAS performance estimation dimension by capturing multiple promising architectures [18, 67]. If necessary, the reader may check the previous explanations on novelty search and MAP-Elites in Sect. 3.2.2.

Recent work has demonstrated that simple neuroevolution strategies can scale to modern deep neural networks when integrated into the NAS pipeline. Natural evolution strategies (NES) and even naive genetic algorithms have been shown to train networks with millions of parameters, competing with deep reinforcement learning methods, by exploiting extreme parallelism to achieve reduced wall-clock times despite higher sample complexity [71, 83]. Hybrid methods—such as *safe mutations*, which use gradient information to temper evolutionary perturbations, and hypernetworks that combine indirect encoding with backpropagation—further blend the strengths of evolutionary and gradient-based NAS strategies to extend scalability [30, 48].

Beyond discovering performant architectures, neuroevolution contributes to NAS's meta-learning and performance estimation dimensions by evolving synaptic plasticity rules and neuromodulation schemes that enable networks to learn online. Evolved plastic networks adapt without gradient descent, and diffusion-based neuromodulation has been shown to mitigate catastrophic forgetting by spatially regulating plasticity [78]. Finally, evolutionary methods have proven effective for architecture search within NAS, evolving novel building blocks and blueprints, such as LSTM-like nodes and module-and-task routing schemes, that surpass hand-designed counterparts on vision and language benchmarks [68].

4.3.3 Neuroevolution with LLMs

The latest generation of LLMs has opened an unexpected door for evolutionary NAS: Because these models internalize both *syntax* (they know how to write syntactically valid code or token strings) and surprisingly rich *semantics* (they implicitly encode design heuristics such as "convolutions like to come in powers of two" or "skip connections help gradients"), they can act as powerful mutation engines and probabilistic priors. Two recent systems make this idea concrete—*EvoPrompting* [14] and *GPT-NAS* [92]. Although they differ in how the LLM is trained and where adaptation occurs, both exploit the same principle: Let the transformer shoulder the burden of proposing good architectural edits, while classical evolutionary machinery does what it does best—compare, select, and recombine candidates in a massively parallel fashion.

A first step in both methods is to translate a neural network into a representation that the LLM can "speak." EvoPrompting treats *entire architectures as Python programs*, including imports, layer constructions, hyperparameters, and even the training loop; every individual in the population is therefore a runnable script (see Fig. 4.8). GPT-NAS, on the other hand, linearizes each layer into a single token whose fields encode type, shapes, kernel size, stride, activation, and so on, yielding sequences $(\ell_1, \ldots, \ell_T)$ that resemble sentences over a bespoke vocabulary (see Fig. 4.9). This difference reflects two philosophies: EvoPrompting favors open-ended expressiveness—anything that can be expressed in valid Python is fair

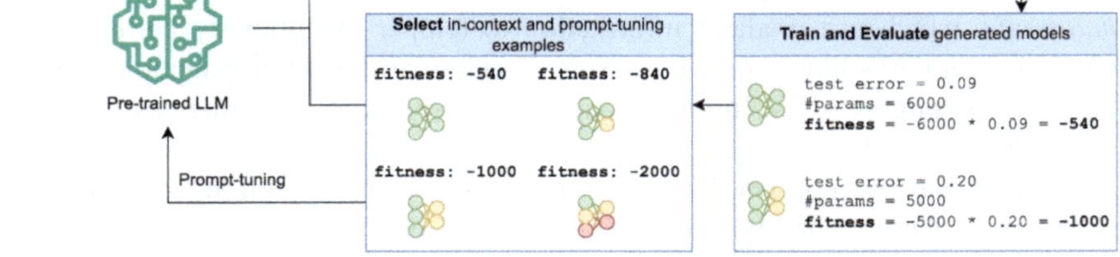

Fig. 4.8 An overview of EvoPrompting [14]. The process begins by initializing the search with a small set of manually designed program seeds. A meta-learning loop then iterates as follows. First, a code-pretrained language model uses the seeds as in-context prompt examples to generate candidate architectures. These candidates are trained on the task's training data and evaluated on a validation set. The highest-performing architectures are selected as in-context examples for the next iteration, while all evaluated candidates are used to prompt-tune the language model. The meta-learning loop then repeats

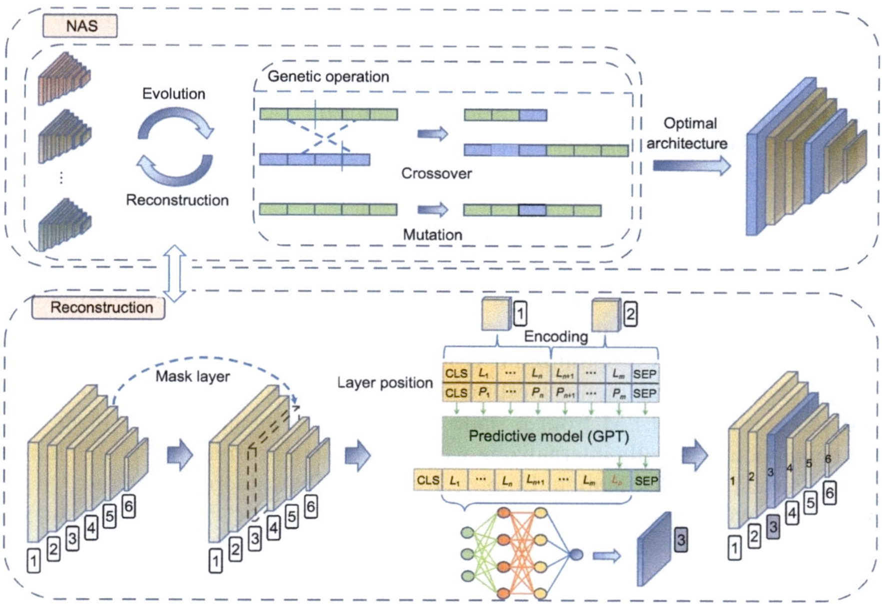

Fig. 4.9 Flowchart of the neural architecture search framework. The procedure is divided into two stages: search and reconstruction. The search stage employs a generalized neural architecture search method with a genetic algorithm (GA) as the optimization strategy. The reconstruction stage reorganizes the neural architecture using a GPT model. For example, given an existing architecture, the third block may be removed with a certain probability, after which the GPT model re-predicts its structure based on information from the first two blocks [92]

game—whereas GPT-NAS aims for a tighter grammar that makes it easier to learn high-probability continuations.

In EvoPrompting, the optimization objective is the expected fitness of a *set* of programs. Let $\mathcal{V}$ denote the vocabulary of the language model (i.e., the set of all valid tokens), and let $\mathcal{V}^*$ denote the Kleene closure of $\mathcal{V}$—the set of all finite concatenations of symbols in $\mathcal{V}$, representing all syntactically possible code segments. Let $\mathcal{D}$ be the dataset consisting of input-output pairs (x, y) for the target task $\mathcal{T}$, and let $\text{EVAL}_{\mathcal{T}}(c, \mathcal{D})$ denote the evaluation function that trains the model architecture given by code c on $\mathcal{D}$ and returns a real-valued fitness score. The goal is to identify a set C of k neural network architectures that maximize the expected reward:

$$\underset{\substack{C \subset \mathcal{V}^* \\ |C|=k}}{\arg\max}\ \mathbb{E}_{c \in C}\Big[\mathbb{E}_{(x,y)\in\mathcal{D}}\big[\text{EVAL}_{\mathcal{T}}(c, \mathcal{D})\big]\Big], \tag{4.1}$$

where the outer expectation is over the k programs in the candidate set C, and the inner expectation is over the data samples in $\mathcal{D}$.

The evolutionary meta-loop maintains an elite archive G and, at generation t, constructs *few-shot prompts* from the current top-p programs. Sampling the code LLM with a temperature mixture $\tau \in \{0.2, 0.6, 0.8, 1.0\}$ yields n children per prompt, exploiting low temperatures for deterministic "copy-and-tweak" edits and higher ones for bolder structural changes. Each child is scored by

$$s(c) = -\,\varepsilon(c) \times |c|,$$

where $\varepsilon(c)$ denotes the validation error of program c and $|c|$ denotes the program length (i.e., shorter, more accurate models are favored), before the top new entries refresh the archive. Crucially, EvoPrompting then *prompt-tunes* the generator itself: A 16-token soft prefix is optimized over five epochs on the newly evaluated children using Adam (adaptive moment estimation) at a learning rate of 0.1. This inner update converts the LLM from a static oracle into an agent that coevolves with the population, gradually internalizing which code motifs correspond to high fitness on the current task distribution. Empirically, the feedback loop is dramatic: On the lightweight MNIST-1D[5] benchmark, the best validation-size Pareto point emerges after only ≈ 1600 evaluations, discovering narrow, deep CNN variants that a naive few-shot baseline never proposes. On the harder CLRS graph-algorithm suite [87], EvoPrompting invents message-passing blocks such as QUADNODEMINMAX and CONCATREP[6] that beat human-designed Triplet-GMPNNs [42] on 21 of 30 tasks.

GPT-NAS adopts the opposite temporal strategy: The LLM is trained *before* the search begins and frozen thereafter, acting as a learned "genetic grammar" that repairs partial architectures. Standard NAS poses the problem of finding the architecture x^* from the search space $\mathcal{X} = \{x_1, x_2, \ldots, x_n\}$ (where n denotes the number of possible architectures) that maximizes the accuracy $\mathrm{Acc}(x)$ on a held-out validation set:

$$x^* = \arg\max_{x \in \mathcal{X}} \mathrm{Acc}(x), \tag{4.2}$$

but GPT-NAS rewrites this as

$$x^* = \arg\max_{x \in \mathcal{X}} \mathrm{Acc}\big(x; G_\phi\big), \quad \text{with} \quad G_\phi \text{ a GPT prior}, \tag{4.3}$$

where G_ϕ denotes a GPT model with parameters ϕ that serves as a learned prior over the architecture space, biasing the search toward high-performing regions.

Training proceeds in two stages: (i) unsupervised language modeling on NAS-Bench-101[7] [91] yields basic familiarity with convolutional building blocks; (ii)

[5] https://github.com/greydanus/mnist1d.

[6] These are novel neural network building blocks discovered by EvoPrompting that perform specialized message-passing operations for graph algorithms.

[7] https://github.com/google-research/nasbench.

supervised fine-tuning on a curated set of 36 modern block-based networks teaches up-to-date design tropes such as inverted bottlenecks and squeeze-excite. During evolution, the GA masks each layer position i with probability below:

$$r_t = r_{\text{ori}}\left(1 - \frac{\text{iter}_t}{\text{iter}_{\text{max}}}\right), \tag{4.4}$$

where r_{ori} is the initialized elimination rate, iter_t denotes the current iteration number, and iter_{max} denotes the maximum number of iterations. This schedule ensures that early generations explore aggressively, while later ones refine. For every mask, the prior samples a replacement $\hat{\ell}_i \sim P_\phi(\cdot \mid \ell_{<i})$, where $P_\phi(\cdot \mid \ell_{<i})$ denotes the conditional probability distribution over layer types given the preceding layers $\ell_{<i} = (\ell_1, \ldots, \ell_{i-1})$, and a lightweight fully connected network maps the local context to one of a fixed set of legal blocks. The candidate is then selectively trained: Only the newly predicted layers (and any dependent batch normalization) receive updates for six warm-up[8] epochs, exploiting the strong Pearson correlation $\rho > 0.7$ between this cheap proxy score and full convergence. Because the Transformer already nudges the sequence toward likely good completions, most partial programs "compile" into competitive networks; the GA merely winnows and recombines them. The payoff is striking: GPT-NAS is the first evolutionary NAS to exceed 79% top-1 on ImageNet-1K without weight sharing and does so in roughly 2×10^4 reduced-epoch training, a budget that classical EAs would burn on toy CIFAR-10 runs.

Taken together, these systems reshape all three axes of the NAS taxonomy introduced earlier. First, the *search space*: By expressing architectures in some grammar that an LLM can parse, e.g., Python ASTs (Abstract Syntax Trees), token strings, potentially even graph serializations, the boundary of valid designs is no longer fixed by a researcher but by model capacity. Second, the *search strategy*: Variation is no longer a handful of handwritten bit flips, but the whole creative arsenal of next-token prediction, conditioned on rich context and guided by temperature, masking schedules, or soft prompts. Third, the *performance estimation strategy*: Because the LLM steers proposals toward high-probability, high-fitness regions, low-value evaluations are pruned implicitly, so coarse proxies (six-epoch warm-ups, sub-dataset training) suffice to rank candidates accurately.

Several challenges lie ahead. Hyperparameter cross-talk is now richer: Mutation rate, population size, temperature schedule, elimination rate, prompt length, and tuning learning rate interact in opaque ways. As tasks migrate from CNNs to transformer-heavy, multimodal models, serializing architectures may require graph-aware or intermediate representation (IR) tree encodings [44] that preserve long-range dependencies. And while EvoPrompting's open-vocabulary Python space excels at novelty, rigorous benchmarking against conventional cell-based NAS is

[8] A method for gradually increasing the learning rate during the early stages of training.

difficult—the field needs everyday tasks where both entirely open-ended and tightly parametrized methods can be compared fairly.

Nevertheless, the early results are an encouraging signal that blending language modeling with evolutionary principles can push neuroevolution well beyond its traditional limits—either by letting a frozen prior serve as a map of promising terrain or by evolving the map itself in lockstep with the population. As LLMs continue to improve in factual recall, reasoning over code, and controllable generation, their synergy with evolutionary NAS seems poised to accelerate the discovery of architectures that would have been infeasible to design, or even to *express*, just a few years ago.

4.4 LLMs for Rule-Based Adaptive Systems

The recent capabilities of LLMs are propelling the resurgence of rule-based reasoning in adaptive systems. They are beginning to write, explain, and refine rules that used to be handcrafted or optimized by classical search. This section surveys how the field is moving from *pure* rule engines or *pure* machine learning controllers toward hybrids in which an LLM acts as a reasoning or meta-optimization layer.

LLMs have therefore reignited interest in symbolic control by taking over the authoring, optimization, and contextualization of rules that once demanded painstaking human engineering. Across recent studies—spanning multi-robot teaming [29], cloud autoscaling [36], autonomous driving [73], business intelligence [88], and a 219-paper survey of self-adaptive software [51]—a coherent design pattern is emerging: Runtime controllers remain deterministic, but an LLM sits *around* the loop to write new rules, retune thresholds, explain outcomes, and occasionally improvise when symbolic logic runs out of headroom. We elaborate that pattern in depth, grounding each idea with the mathematical formalism introduced by the primary works.

4.4.1 Why Combine LLMs with Rules?

Rule-based control offers transparency and bounded runtime cost, but manual design struggles with high-dimensional state spaces and shifting objectives. LLMs, on the other hand, excel at pattern matching and commonsense reasoning over textual descriptions, yet they may hallucinate, violate constraints, or run too slowly for tight control loops. The emerging consensus is that an LLM should be *invoked sparingly*—to generate, adapt, or select rules—while the performant, deterministic executor remains symbolic or numerical.

Two complementary pressures are shaping this marriage. First, *multi-objective adaptation* is becoming the norm. In human-robot teaming, REBEL (rule-based and experience-enhanced learning) [29] shows that users rarely optimize a single metric; they aim to trade off performance against human workload or time to completion and to adjust those trade-offs at deployment. Second, *system evolution* is accelerating. Cloud services, vehicle fleets, and data schemas change weekly. LLMs promise to amortize design effort by re-authoring or tuning rules on demand.

4.4.2 From Complementarity to a Two-Tier Controller

Rule-based engines excel when all constraints can be enumerated in advance, yet they break down in the "long tail" of unforeseen situations or conflicting objectives. LLMs, conversely, can reason across vast textual corpora and invent new behaviors, but they may hallucinate, violate hard safety bounds, or incur latency incompatible with high-frequency control. The fruitful compromise is therefore a *two-tier controller* described below:

$$A_{\text{hyb}}(x) = \begin{cases} r_\theta(x), & \text{if } \mathcal{S}\big(r_\theta(x)\big) \geq \tau, \\ \text{LLM}\big(\Pi(x,\theta)\big), & \text{otherwise}, \end{cases} \tag{4.5}$$

where x is the current state, r_θ denotes the symbolic rule set parameterized by θ, $\mathcal{S}$ is a lightweight safety/performance scorer, τ is a threshold below which the LLM is consulted, and Π is a prompt generator that injects state and rule context into the LLM. This structure mirrors the gating strategy of *LLM-ASSIST*, in which the PDM-Closed planner[9] governs an autonomous vehicle unless the best of its 15 trajectories scores below threshold τ on eight nuPlan[10] metrics [73]. Because the LLM is consulted only in *predicted failure modes*, its multi-second latency does not dominate the control loop. Yet, the system inherits the LLM's capacity for commonsense reasoning and rare-event improvisation.

4.4.3 LLMs as Design-Time Rule Optimizers

Before deployment, an LLM can *search* for better rule parameters by iterating between simulation and textual self-reflection. Ishimizu et al. [36] formulate the design-time objective

$$J(\theta) = \mathbb{E}_{x\sim\mathcal{D}}\big[\, U_{\text{rev}}\big(r_\theta(x)\big) - C_{\text{cost}}\big(r_\theta(x)\big)\big], \tag{4.6}$$

[9] PDM-Closed (Predictive Driver Model - Closed loop) is a rule-based motion planning algorithm that generates trajectories using a closed-loop simulation approach [19].

[10] nuPlan is the world's first large-scale planning benchmark for autonomous driving.

where θ represents the rule parameters, x denotes system states sampled from the distribution $\mathcal{D}$, $r_\theta(x)$ is the action prescribed by the rule set, U_{rev} measures utility (e.g., throughput or revenue), and C_{cost} captures costs such as energy use or Service Level Agreement (SLA)) violations [36]. The update step is delegated wholesale to the language model according to the following equation:

$$\theta_{t+1} = \text{LLM}\big(K,\ \theta_t,\ \{(x^{(i)}, u^{(i)}, R^{(i)})\}\big), \tag{4.7}$$

where K is a textual knowledge base (task description, constraints, historical logs), θ_t is the current parameter vector, and $\{(x^{(i)}, u^{(i)}, R^{(i)})\}$ is a set of tuples containing states $x^{(i)}$, actions $u^{(i)}$, and rewards $R^{(i)}$ from recent simulations. In 10 iterations of GPT-4 feedback, cloud-autoscaling rules expressed in C++ climbed from baseline utility $\approx 4.8\,\text{k}$ to peaks near $5.5\,\text{k}$. Strikingly, the *first* LLM-synthesized rule set already matched human performance, illustrating how latent knowledge in pretrained models can "cold-start" traditional optimization pipelines.

4.4.4 Retrieval-Augmented Prompting: Memory as a First-Class Citizen

The stronger the prompt, the less heavy lifting the LLM must do. REBEL surrounds the model with dual retrieval modules that supply (i) prescriptive rules for each objective and (ii) worked examples from similar missions. Formally, given a mission description Θ, REBEL seeks the rule γ^* from a rules database D_Γ that best matches the mission requirements:

$$\gamma^* = \underset{\gamma \in D_\Gamma}{\arg\max}\Big[\tfrac{\alpha}{c+L_{\text{sparse}}(\gamma)} + \tfrac{1-\alpha}{c+L_{\text{dense}}(\gamma)}\Big], \tag{4.8}$$

where D_Γ is the database of candidate rules, $L_{\text{sparse}}(\gamma)$ is the BM25 rank position of rule γ with respect to mission description Θ (measuring keyword similarity), $L_{\text{dense}}(\gamma)$ is the rank position under cosine-similarity search of sentence embeddings (measuring semantic similarity), $\alpha \in [0, 1]$ is a weighting parameter balancing sparse and dense retrieval, and c is a dampening constant to prevent division by zero [29]. A similar fused ranking retrieves the k most analogous scenarios S_i from the experience base, using cosine scores over human (h), robot (r), and task (t) embeddings,

$$\text{score}(i) = \mathbf{h} \cdot \mathbf{h}_i\ +\ \mathbf{r} \cdot \mathbf{r}_i\ +\ \mathbf{t} \cdot \mathbf{t}_i, \tag{4.9}$$

where $\mathbf{h}$, $\mathbf{r}$, and $\mathbf{t}$ are the embedding vectors of the current mission's human, robot, and task descriptions, respectively, while $\mathbf{h}_i$, $\mathbf{r}_i$, and $\mathbf{t}_i$ are the corresponding embedding vectors for the i-th scenario in the experience base. The function appends the corresponding plans (S_i, A_i) as few-shot exemplars. Retrieval supplies the "long-term memory" that today's context-limited LLMs lack, while the model supplies combinatorial synthesis. Empirically, this hybrid delivered normalized task-performance scores of 125.1, 102.8, and 101.6 for a zero-shot LLM, a specialist hierarchical RL baseline, and mixed integer linear programming (MILP) optimization, respectively, all while staying within 10% of the specialist hierarchical RL baseline.

4.4.5 *Encoding Multi-objective Preferences Symbolically and Linguistically*

Real deployments seldom maximize a single scalar metric. REBEL therefore optimizes

$$J(A) = \sum_{j=1}^{p} \lambda_j \, O_j(A, \mathcal{H}, \mathcal{R}), \tag{4.10}$$

where A is the joint initial task allocation decision for the entire mission, $\mathcal{H} = \{H_1, H_2, \ldots, H_n\}$ represents the set of human operators, $\mathcal{R} = \{R_1, R_2, \ldots, R_m\}$ represents the fleet of robots, O_j is the j-th objective function (e.g., task performance, mission completion time, or human workload), p is the total number of objectives, and λ_j is the weight assigned to objective j with $\lambda_j \in [0, 1]$, subject to a feasibility constraint that the requirements of every task be covered by at least one agent-mode pair. At runtime, the user may revise the weight vector $\boldsymbol{\lambda} = (\lambda_1, \lambda_2, \ldots, \lambda_p)$ to prioritize, say, human workload over mission time. Because the weights appear explicitly in the prompt, no retraining is required; the LLM recomposes an allocation plan on the fly. Ablations confirm that either retrieval component—rules or experiences—improves alignment. Still, together they yield the highest fidelity: The top-weighted objective achieves a normalized value of 1.0 in every tested scenario.

Hybrid business-insight pipelines provide a complementary perspective on multi-objective trade-offs. Let mathematical precision be

$$E = \frac{\text{correct numerical operations}}{\text{baseline}} \times 100\%, \tag{4.11}$$

and hallucination rate

$$H = \frac{\text{incorrect proper names}}{\text{total names}} \times 100\%. \tag{4.12}$$

Rule-only reports score $E = 100\%$ and $H = 0\%$, but miss about 30% of salient insights ($R = 71\%$, where R denotes the recall of relevant insights). LLM-only narratives yield more insights but incur a $H = 12\%$ penalty. The hybrid architecture—rules for arithmetic, LLM for prose—hits $E = 87\%$, $H = 3\%$, and $R = 82\%$, demonstrating that partitioning objective space (accuracy, coverage, readability) across symbolic and neural actors can deliver a strictly better Pareto front [88].

4.4.6 Fail-Safe Execution and Online Rollback

The downside of giving an LLM executive power is the possibility of catastrophic mis-commit. All of the aforementioned works—REBEL for multi-robot teaming [29], Ishimizu et al. for cloud autoscaling [36], LLM-ASSIST for autonomous driving [73], Vertsel et al. for business intelligence [88], and the survey by Li et al. on self-adaptive software [51]—therefore incorporate *rollback guards*. In cloud autoscaling, a candidate rule that compiles but degrades utility by more than one standard deviation is automatically discarded [36]. LLM-ASSIST confines neural edits to a parameter vector θ; if the resulting trajectory still violates collision or drivable-area constraints, the controller reverts to the best rule-based plan [73]. Such envelopes echo control theory's supervisory architectures, with the LLM acting as an occasional *adviser* rather than a primary actuator.

4.4.7 Emerging Best Practices

A synthesis of the case studies and broader literature suggests three heuristics that are especially actionable for practitioners.

Externalize Memory Even with 128k-token context windows, language models are still orders of magnitude short of capturing a lifetime's worth of operational logs. To mitigate this, practitioners should adopt retrieval-augmented prompting techniques. Combining sparse and dense retrieval and segmenting memory by domain—such as human, robot, or task—grounds the LLM's reasoning in contextual data while maintaining prompt-length constraints.

Echo the Formalism in the Prompt When domain logic is already encoded in formal constructs—such as code, thresholds, or symbolic rules—these should be provided verbatim in the prompt. In Ishimizu's study [36], GPT-4's gains were partially attributable to being prompted with the original C++ implementation of the incumbent rule. This direct inclusion allows the model to reason about changes as deltas, rather than inferring structure from examples.

Quantify and Gate Risk Before routing tasks through a neural model, systems should apply a lightweight risk scorer $\mathcal{S}$—such as a collision probability estimator, a response-time Service Level Objective (SLO) checker, or a static-type validator. This ensures that high-risk decisions default to safe symbolic policies, preserving critical safety and reliability guarantees.

4.4.8 Future Directions

Li et al. argue that generative AI will soon pervade all stages of the MAPE-K (Monitor-Analyze-Plan-Execute-Knowledge) loop [51]. In the context of rule-based systems, three research frontiers appear particularly salient.

First, instead of freezing control rules after an initial offline optimization phase, systems may evolve through continuous refinement. A background process could generate new rule candidates, borrowing from earlier optimization loops, while rejecting unsafe proposals using statistical model checking or runtime monitors.

Second, current prompt engineering typically encodes state as text or compact vector summaries. However, fusing information from images, point clouds, or structured graph embeddings may allow LLMs to reason about perceptual corner cases that elude traditional rule abstractions.

Third, recent progress in program synthesis and automated theorem proving suggests a path toward certifying LLM-generated outputs. For example, a resource allocation plan A produced by a model like REBEL could be automatically verified by satisfiability modulo theories (SMT)[11] solver to ensure that hard constraints are satisfied before deployment.

4.5 LLMs Can Design Novel Heuristics

The tradition of heuristic design is rooted in an almost artisanal loop of conjecture, experiment, and refinement. A specialist forms an intuition, encodes it as a short procedure $h : \mathcal{I} \rightarrow \mathcal{S}$, where $\mathcal{I}$ denotes the space of problem instances and $\mathcal{S}$ denotes the space of solutions, and measures the expected cost

$$F(h) = \mathbb{E}_{I \sim \mu}\big[\text{cost}\big(h(I), I\big)\big], \tag{4.13}$$

where μ is a distribution over problem instances and $\text{cost}(s, I)$ evaluates the quality of solution s on instance I, and then either tweaks the rule or starts afresh. Because each turn of this wheel depends on human insight, progress has historically been slow and narrowly focused. With sufficiently capable LLMs, however, the loop can be automated: The model supplies creative leaps, a program evaluator supplies incorruptible feedback, and evolutionary machinery supplies pressure toward improvement. Three contemporary systems—FunSearch, Evolution of Heuristics (EoH), and Language-Model Particle Swarm Optimization (LMPSO, see Sect. 2.2)—have crystallized this idea with striking outcomes that range from a new record in cap set theory to state-of-the-art scheduling rules [54, 69, 74]. The

[11] The problem of determining whether a mathematical formula is satisfiable. This is a generalization of the Boolean satisfiability problem (SAT) to more complex forms.

present section synthesizes their contributions into a single conceptual narrative and complements them with additional mathematical detail.

4.5.1 Heuristic Discovery as Stochastic Program Optimization

Let Σ^* be the set of syntactically valid programs in a host language such as Python, where Σ is the alphabet of valid tokens, and Σ^* denotes the Kleene closure. Every $p \in \Sigma^*$ compiles into a heuristic h_p. Given a fast, deterministic evaluator

$$\text{eval}(s, I) \; : \; \mathcal{S} \times \mathcal{I} \longrightarrow \mathbb{R}_{\geq 0} \cup \{\perp\}, \tag{4.14}$$

which returns a nonnegative score for valid solutions and $\perp$ (undefined) for invalid ones, we define the fitness of p on a fixed evaluation set $\mathcal{I}_{\text{eval}}$ by

$$\phi(p) = \frac{1}{|\mathcal{I}_{\text{eval}}|} \sum_{I \in \mathcal{I}_{\text{eval}}} \mathbb{I}\big[\text{eval}\big(p(I), I\big) \neq \perp\big] \, \text{eval}\big(p(I), I\big), \tag{4.15}$$

where $\mathbb{I}[\cdot]$ is the indicator function that equals 1 when its argument is true and zero otherwise. Here, $p(I)$ denotes the solution produced by executing program p on problem instance I; since p compiles into a heuristic h_p, we have $p(I) = h_p(I) \in \mathcal{S}$. In other words, the program p acts as a function that takes a problem instance and returns a candidate solution. The discovery task is therefore

$$p^{\star} = \arg\max_{p \in \Sigma^*} \phi(p), \tag{4.16}$$

a combinatorial optimization problem over the space of all valid programs, which is so vast that direct enumeration or exhaustive search is computationally infeasible. The breakthrough behind FunSearch, EoH, and LMPSO is to see an LLM as a sampler q_π over Σ^*, where a prompt pi induces the distribution. The outer loop iterates

$$\pi_t \xrightarrow{\text{LLM}} p_t \xrightarrow{\text{run}} \phi(p_t) \xrightarrow{\text{update}} \pi_{t+1}, \tag{4.17}$$

and the art lies in constructing π_{t+1} so that high-fitness regions are sampled more densely yet diversity is never extinguished.

4.5.2 Search-Verify Paradigm in Practice

FunSearch provides an archetypal implementation, illustrated in Fig. 4.10. A user writes a *skeleton* that exposes one or two key functions—`priority` for cap sets,

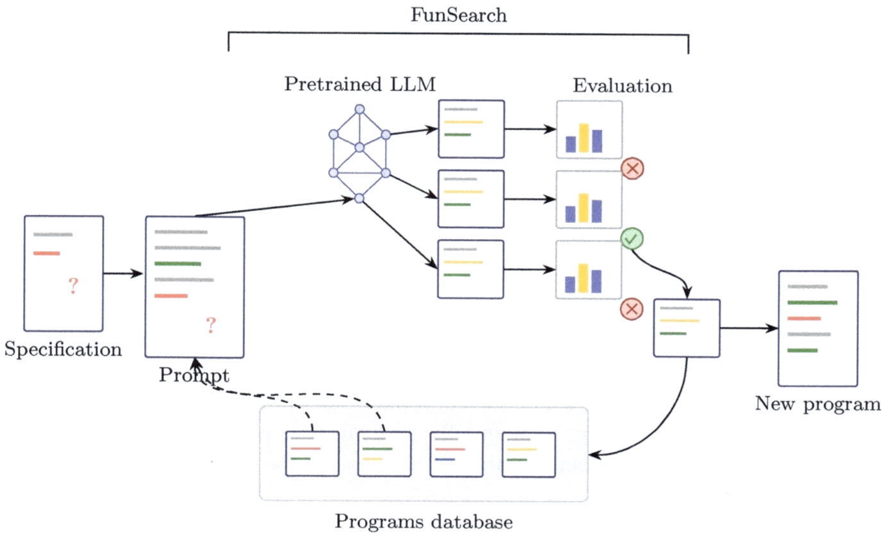

Fig. 4.10 FunSearch takes as input a problem specification defined by an evaluate function, an initial implementation of the function to be evolved—which may be trivial—and, optionally, a program skeleton. At each iteration, FunSearch constructs a prompt by sampling multiple programs from its program database, with a bias toward higher-scoring candidates. This prompt is provided to a pretrained language model to generate new programs. The generated programs are then evaluated and, if correct, added to the program database, thereby completing the iterative loop. At any time, the user can retrieve the highest-scoring programs discovered so far [69]

`heuristic` for bin packing—leaving their bodies empty. The cap set problem asks for the most significant subset of vectors in the finite vector space $(\mathbb{Z}/3)^n$ such that no three vectors form an arithmetic progression (i.e., no three vectors **a**, **b**, **c** satisfy $\mathbf{a} + \mathbf{b} + \mathbf{c} = \mathbf{0}$ in $(\mathbb{Z}/3)^n$). The system maintains a population partitioned into m islands and, every few seconds, picks an island, draws k incumbents according to a two-stage Boltzmann rule,, pastes those snippets into a prompt labeled v0, ..., v*k-1*, appends an empty v*k* signature, and asks the LLM to fill it. Each candidate is compiled, inserted into the skeleton, executed on a battery of inputs, and assigned the following score:

$$\text{Score}(p) = \frac{1}{N} \sum_{i=1}^{N} \text{eval}\big(p(x_i), x_i\big), \tag{4.18}$$

where N is the number of test instances and x_i denotes the i-th problem instance. Invalid runs return $\perp$ and receive zero credit. Asynchronous evaluators and samplers cooperate at scale—15 GPU workers continuously produce code, while 150 CPU workers grade millions of attempts per day. Every four hours, the worst half of islands are erased and reseeded from the best, a reset that empirically doubles discovery speed without destabilizing convergence [69].

The cap set result illustrates the power of the loop. In the finite vector space $(\mathbb{Z}/3)^8$, one seeks the most significant subset with no three-term arithmetic progression. For two decades, the record stood at 496. FunSearch, after roughly 3.4×10^6 sampled programs and 20 hours of wall-clock time, produced a 512-element set and a priority scoring function $\pi : (\mathbb{Z}/3)^8 \rightarrow \mathbb{R}$ clean enough for mathematicians to scrutinize. Abstracting the same idea to dimension n yielded an improved asymptotic lower bound.

$$C = \limsup_{n \to \infty} |C_n|^{1/n} \geq 2.2202, \tag{4.19}$$

derived by human analysts from the evolved code, a vivid demonstration that machine-generated artifacts can seed rigorous proofs.

In online bin packing—a classic combinatorial optimization problem where items of varying sizes arrive sequentially and must be packed into bins of fixed capacity, to minimize the total number of bins used—the objective is to minimize the ratio

$$\text{Gap}(p) = \frac{\mathbb{E}[\text{bins used by } p]}{\mathbb{E}[\text{offline optimum}]} - 1. \tag{4.20}$$

Classical heuristics for this problem include first fit (place each item in the first bin with sufficient space) and best fit (place each item in the bin with the least remaining space). These well-studied algorithms typically achieve gaps of 2–4% on standard benchmarks. FunSearch's best heuristic drove Gap to 0.0003 on 100 000-item Weibull streams,[12] whereas classical best fit hovers near 0.03—representing roughly a 100-fold improvement. Crucially, FunSearch accomplished this with a 16-line scoring function that any engineer can audit and deploy.

EoH keeps the evaluator-generator skeleton while rethinking the representation (see Fig. 4.11). Each candidate is a tuple (t, c) where t is a short natural language "thought" and c is executable code. Five prompt-level operators govern variation: two incentivize novelty across parents, two adjust quantitative parameters, and one attempts simplification. The operators are sampled with probability inversely proportional to a parent's rank, thereby increasing exploration when the population appears too homogeneous. Because the thought often persists through minor code edits, the LLM can reuse contextual embeddings, permitting highly efficient steady-state search: on bin packing, flow shop scheduling,[13] and TSP benchmarks, EoH reaches or surpasses FunSearch quality with roughly 2×10^3 generations, two orders of magnitude fewer than the earlier system [54].

---

[12] A data stream generated based on the Weibull distribution, which is mainly used in product reliability and lifespan analysis.

[13] The problem of scheduling multiple machines performing identical processes on several tasks so that the completion time of the last task is minimized. It has stronger constraints than the open shop problem but weaker constraints than job shop scheduling problem (JSSP).

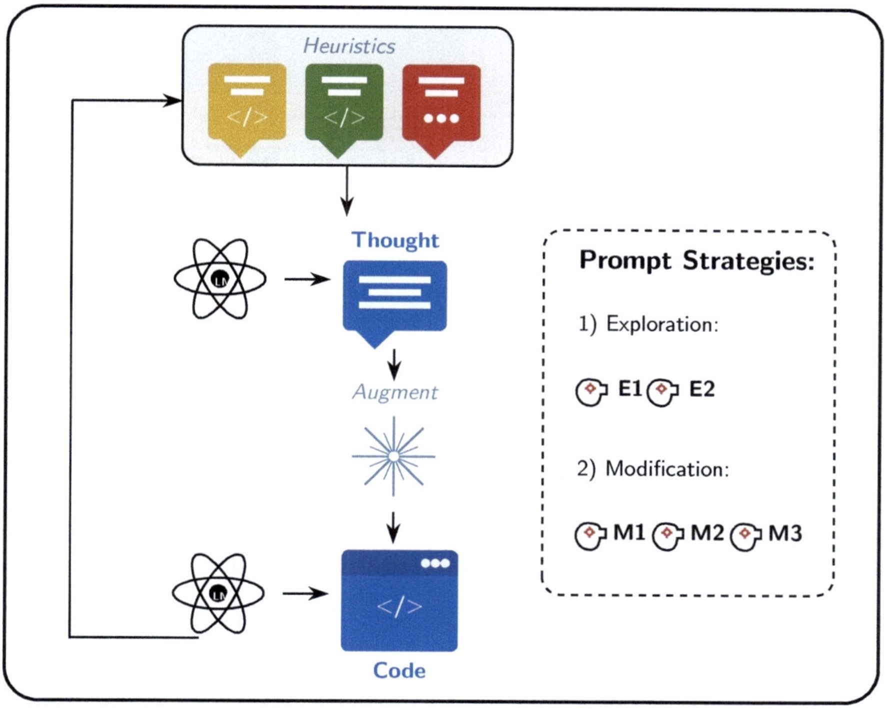

Fig. 4.11 EoH evolves both thoughts and codes using large language models [54]

LMPSO shows that even the population dynamics can be cast into language (see Fig. 4.12). A particle i retains its current tour x_i^t, its personal best p_i, the global best g, and the previous prompt fragment v_i^t. The update rule is described below:

$$v_i^{t+1} = \text{MetaPrompt}\big(x_i^t, p_i, g, v_i^t\big) \quad \text{and} \quad x_i^{t+1} \sim q_{v_i^{t+1}}, \tag{4.21}$$

which implicitly encodes inertia, cognition, and social influence without explicit numeric parameters, where MetaPrompt constructs a prompt incorporating the particle's history and the swarm's best solution, and $q_{v_i^{t+1}}$ is the distribution over solutions induced by the LLM given prompt v_i^{t+1}. On Euclidean TSP instances of up to 30 cities, LMPSO reduces the optimality gap to $(0.02 \pm 0.02)\%$, eclipsing a hand-tuned PSO variant that still sits near 1 %. When seeded with canonical heuristics for 100-city instances, it evolves hybrids whose mean gap shrinks to 0.06%, demonstrating that population thinking can ride atop textual prompts [74].

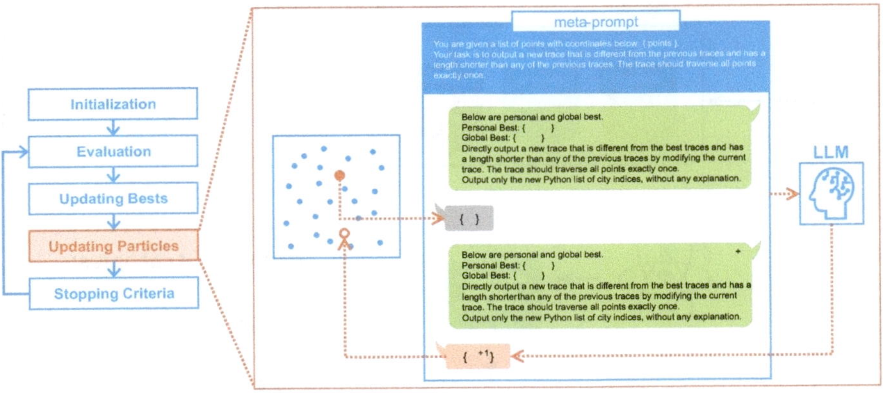

Fig. 4.12 Overview of LMPSO. The meta-prompt illustrated in the figure corresponds to the traveling salesman problem. Components enclosed in denote dynamic elements of the prompt that update based on the algorithm's current state [74]

4.5.3 *Entropy, Selection Pressure, and Theoretical Underpinnings*

A mathematical lens clarifies why these systems neither converge too early nor wander forever. Denote by $H(P_t)$ the Shannon entropy of the program population at generation t, which measures the diversity of programs in the population. Mutation driven by an LLM raises entropy by ΔH_{mut}, while fitness-proportional selection lowers it by ΔH_{sel}. In a long-run equilibrium, we expect

$$\mathbb{E}[H(P_{t+1})] \approx \mathbb{E}[H(P_t)] \quad \Longrightarrow \quad \mathbb{E}[\Delta H_{\text{mut}}] \approx \mathbb{E}[\Delta H_{\text{sel}}]. \tag{4.22}$$

FunSearch's periodic island resets act as an entropy pump whenever ΔH_{sel} dominates, whereas EoH adjusts operator frequencies to achieve the same balancing act probabilistically. PAC-Bayesian analysis adds a complementary view. If the Kullback-Leibler divergence $\text{KL}(q_t \| q_{t+1})$ stays bounded and the expected fitness $\mathbb{E}_{p \sim q_t}[\phi(p)]$ rises monotonically, one can derive a regret bound of order $1/t$ for the probability of missing a δ-optimal program. Though a complete derivation for language distributions is nascent, empirical curves from both FunSearch and EoH echo the predicted $1/t$ decay.

4.5.4 *Locality, Syntax, and Smooth Fitness Landscapes*

Program space is unforgiving: A single character drop can crash the interpreter, mapping ϕ to $-\infty$. Robust search, therefore, requires mutations that are semantically adventurous yet syntactically conservative. EoH's dual-view representation achieves this via semantic change in the thought channel paired with token-level locality in the code channel. Formally, if d_{tok} counts token edits between two code strings and d_{sem} measures cosine distance between sentence embeddings of thoughts, successful offspring satisfy

$$d_{\text{tok}}(c_{\text{child}}, c_{\text{parent}}) \ll d_{\text{tok}}\big(c_{\text{rand}}, c_{\text{parent}}\big), \tag{4.23}$$

meaning that the code of a child program c_{child} differs from its parent c_{parent} by far fewer tokens than a randomly sampled program c_{rand} would be, while simultaneously,

$$d_{\text{sem}}(t_{\text{child}}, t_{\text{parent}}) \approx d_{\text{sem}}\big(t_{\text{rand}}, t_{\text{parent}}\big), \tag{4.24}$$

meaning that the thought description t_{child} can be as semantically distant from t_{parent} as a random thought t_{rand}, thereby preserving syntactic validity while exploring new conceptual territory. LMPSO realizes a different form of locality: The prompt echoes earlier tours, so completions add, delete, or reverse only small subsequences, mimicking the traditional update rule in continuous PSO without leaving the space of valid tours.

4.5.5 A Panoramic View of Achievements

Seen side by side, the three systems mark multiple firsts. FunSearch's 512-element cap set did not merely exceed records; its programmatic priority function later guided human mathematicians to extract structural lemmas about isotropic residues whose proofs are now formalized in Lean [69]. In bin packing, FunSearch's heuristic diminishes the expected excess bin ratio.

$$\Delta(k) = \frac{\text{bins}_p(k) - \text{OPT}(k)}{\text{OPT}(k)} \tag{4.25}$$

from 4 % for best fit to under 0.04 % when $k = 10^5$, an improvement that translates into millions of dollars of warehouse space for cloud-billing companies. EoH extends the landscape, delivering flow shop schedules that shave 0.8 % off the makespan across Taillard benchmarks[14] with 100 jobs and 20 machines—nontrivial in an area where decades of research have inched gains by tenths of a percent [54]. LMPSO, finally, hints that swarm intelligence can be transplanted wholesale into text space: a simple choice of $N = 25$ particles and $G = 40$ iterations sufficed to close

[14] https://optimizizer.com/TA.php.

more than 85 % of the performance gap on 30-city TSPs and to beat specialized PSO variants for 10-city problems [74].

4.5.6 Systems Engineering and Cost Models

Let C_{gen} be GPU seconds per LLM call and C_{eval} be CPU seconds per program evaluation, with $\gamma = C_{\text{gen}}/C_{\text{eval}} \gg 1$ indicating that LLM generation is much more expensive than evaluation. FunSearch runs roughly 3.2 million evaluations per 24-hour day on 150 CPUs, amortizing $\gamma \approx 2000$ by saturating GPUs. EoH, by shortening prompts and pruning invalid code before compilation, halves the mean prompt length and improves the valid-program fraction η from 0.06 to 0.32. Because the expected time to a target score τ behaves like

$$T_\tau \approx \frac{\log(1-\alpha)}{\log(1-\eta p_\tau)} \cdot \frac{1}{R}, \tag{4.26}$$

where α is the desired confidence level, η is the fraction of generated programs that are syntactically valid, p_τ is the probability that a valid program achieves score at least τ, and $R = 1/(C_{\text{gen}} + \eta C_{\text{eval}})$ is the effective sampling rate, even a moderate boost in η can shorten wall-clock time by an order of magnitude. LMPSO further reduces C_{gen} by constraining completions to short in-prompt patches; coupling this with a swarm of 25 particles yields end-to-end runtimes under 2 GPU-hours for its headline results.

4.5.7 Open Challenges and Future Directions

Several barriers remain. First, evaluator availability: Problems such as interactive theorem proving or autonomous driving lack millisecond-level scoring functions. Surrogate-based active learning [4], or partial formal verification [21] that aborts candidates failing type refinements, may fill this gap. Second, scalability: For TSP instances with more than 30 cities, prompt length and quadratic tour cost blow up LMPSO's inference time; hierarchical encodings that summarize subpaths could alleviate this. Third, theory: Present regret bounds presume independent and identically distributed samples and ignore cross-prompt dependencies; melding PAC-Bayes with the information geometry of transformers [40] could yield sharper rates. Fourth, safety: Auto-generated code can embed unfair biases or violate licensing requirements; sandboxed execution, along with policy-aligned reward shaping, should become standard. Finally, human-AI collaboration: Mathematicians uncovered new symmetries in the cap set program only after manual inspection; visual lineages, edit logs, and interpretable embeddings could make such interventions routine.

References

1. Abdella, M., Marwala, T.: The use of genetic algorithms and neural networks to approximate missing data in database. In: IEEE 3rd International Conference on Computational Cybernetics, 2005. ICCC 2005, pp. 207–212 (2005). https://doi.org/10.1109/ICCCYB.2005.1511574
2. Alzubaidi, L., et al.: A survey on deep learning tools dealing with data scarcity: definitions, challenges, solutions, tips, and applications. J. Big Data **10**(1) (2023). ISSN: 2196-1115. https://doi.org/10.1186/s40537-023-00727-2
3. Baker, B. et al.: Designing Neural Network Architectures using Reinforcement Learning (2017). arXiv: 1611.02167 [cs.LG]. https://arxiv.org/abs/1611.02167
4. Balaprakash, P., Gramacy, R.B., Wild, S.M.: Active-learning-based surrogate models for empirical performance tuning. In: 2013 IEEE International Conference on Cluster Computing (CLUSTER), pp. 1–8. IEEE, New York (2013)
5. Banzhaf, W., Machado, P., Zhang, M. (eds.): Handbook of Evolutionary Machine Learning, 2024th edn. Springer, Singapore (2023)
6. Batista, J.E., Silva, S.: Improving the detection of burnt areas in remote sensing using hyper-features evolved by M3GP. In: 2020 IEEE Congress on Evolutionary Computation (CEC). IEEE, New York (2020). https://doi.org/10.1109/cec48606.2020.9185630
7. Batista, J.E. et al.: Optical time series for the separation of land cover types with similar spectral signatures: cocoa agroforest and forest. Int. J. Remote Sens. **43**(9), 3298–3319 (2022). https://doi.org/10.1080/01431161.2022.2089540
8. Batista, J.E.: Embedding Domain-Specific Knowledge from LLMs into the Feature Engineering Pipeline (2025). arXiv: 2503.21155 [cs.LG]. https://arxiv.org/abs/2503.21155
9. Batista, J.E.: Evolving robust and readable land cover models for improved forest monitoring. PhD thesis. Faculdade de Ciêencias da Universidade de Lisboa (2024)
10. Bender, G., et al.: Understanding and simplifying one-shot architecture search. In: Dy, J., Krause, A. (eds.) Proceedings of the 35th International Conference on Machine Learning, vol. 80. Proceedings of Machine Learning Research, pp. 550–559. PMLR, New York (2018)
11. Bergstra, J., Yamins, D., Cox, D.: Making a science of model search: hyperparameter optimization in hundreds of dimensions for vision architectures. In: Dasgupta, S., McAllester, D. (eds.) Proceedings of the 30th International Conference on Machine Learning, vol. 28. Proceedings of Machine Learning Research 1, pp. 115–123. PMLR, Atlanta (2013)
12. Bhajantri, V., Totad, S.G., Bharamagoudar, G.R.: Enhancement of Scalability of SVM Classifiers for Big Data (2022). https://doi.org/10.1002/9781119792826.ch9
13. Brown, T.B., et al.: Language Models are Few-Shot Learners (2020). arXiv: 2005.14165 [cs.CL]. https://arxiv.org/abs/2005.14165
14. Chen, A., Dohan, D., So, D.: EvoPrompting: language models for code-level neural architecture search. Adv. Neural Inf. Proces. Syst. **36**, 7787–7817 (2024)
15. Chen, T., Guestrin, C.: XGBoost: a scalable tree boosting system. In: Proceedings of the 22nd ACM SIGKDD International Conference on Knowledge Discovery and Data Mining. KDD '16, pp. 785–794. ACM, San Francisco (2016). ISBN: 978-1-4503-4232-2. https://doi.org/10.1145/2939672.2939785
16. Cherrier, N., et al.: Consistent feature construction with constrained genetic programming for experimental physics. In: 2019 IEEE Congress on Evolutionary Computation (CEC), pp. 1650–1658. IEEE, New York (2019). https://doi.org/10.1109/CEC.2019.8789937
17. Cui, L., et al.: Tabular Data Augmentation for Machine Learning: Progress and Prospects of Embracing Generative AI (2024). arXiv: 2407.21523 [cs.LG]. https://arxiv.org/abs/2407.21523
18. Cully, A., et al.: Robots that can adapt like animals. Nature **521**(7553), 503–507 (2015). ISSN: 1476-4687. https://doi.org/10.1038/nature14422
19. Dauner, D., et al.: Predictive Driver Model: A Technical Report (2023). https://opendrivelab.github.io/Challenge%202023/Track_4_CS_Tu.pdf

20. Domhan, T., Springenberg, J.T., Hutter, F.: Speeding up automatic hyperparameter optimization of deep neural networks by extrapolation of learning curves. In: Proceedings of the 24th International Conference on Artificial Intelligence. IJCAI'15, pp. 3460–3468. AAAI Press, Buenos Aires (2015). ISBN: 9781577357384
21. Easterbrook, S., Callahan, J.: Formal methods for verification and validation of partial specifications: a case study. J Syst Softw **40**(3), 199–210 (1998)
22. Elsken, T., Metzen, J.H., Hutter, F.: Neural architecture search: a survey. J. Mach. Learn. Res. **20**(55), 1–21 (2019)
23. Laender, A.H.F., et al.: Learning to deduplicate. In: Proceedings of the 6th ACM/IEEE-CS Joint Conference on Digital Libraries (JCDL '06), pp. 41–50 (2006). https://doi.org/10.1145/1141753.1141760
24. Floreano, D., Duürr, P., Mattiussi, C.: Neuroevolution: from architectures to learning. Evol. Intell. **1**, 47–62 (2008)
25. de Freitas, J., et al.: Active Learning Genetic programming for record deduplication. In: IEEE Congress on Evolutionary Computation, pp. 1–8 (2010). https://doi.org/10.1109/CEC.2010.5586104
26. Gao, Y., et al.: Retrieval-Augmented Generation for Large Language Models: A Survey (2024). arXiv: 2312.10997 [cs.CL]. https://arxiv.org/abs/2312.10997
27. Gautam, C., Ravi, V.: Data imputation via evolutionary computation, clustering, and a neural network. Neurocomputing **156**, 134–142 (2015). ISSN: 0925-2312. https://doi.org/10.1016/j.neucom.2014.12.073. https://www.sciencedirect.com/science/article/pii/S0925231214017378
28. Gruau, F.: Automatic definition of modular neural networks. Adapt. Behav. **3**(2), 151–183 (1994). ISSN: 1741-2633. https://doi.org/10.1177/105971239400300202
29. Gupte, A., et al.: REBEL: Rule-based and Experience-enhanced Learning with LLMs for Initial Task Allocation in Multi-Human Multi-Robot Teams. arXiv preprint arXiv:2409.16266 (2024)
30. Ha, D., Dai, A., Le, Q.V.: HyperNetworks (2016). arXiv: 1609.09106 [cs.LG]. https://arxiv.org/abs/1609.09106
31. Han, S., et al.: Large Language Models Can Automatically Engineer Features for Few-Shot Tabular Learning (2024). arXiv: 2404.09491 [cs.LG]. https://arxiv.org/abs/2404.09491
32. Hasan, M.K., et al.: Missing value imputation affects the performance of machine learning: a review and analysis of the literature (2010-2021). Inf. Med. Unlocked **27**, 100799 (2021). ISSN: 2352-9148. https://doi.org/10.1016/j.imu.2021.100799
33. He, K., et al.: Deep Residual Learning for Image Recognition (2015). arXiv: 1512.03385 [cs.CV]. https://arxiv.org/abs/1512.03385
34. Holland, J.H.: Genetic algorithms. Sci. Am. **267**(1), 66–73 (1992)
35. Hutter, F., Kotthoff, L., Vanschoren, J. (eds.): Automatic machine learning, 1st edn. In: The Springer Series on Challenges in Machine Learning. Springer International Publishing, Basel (2019)
36. Ishimizu, Y., et al.: Automatic adaptation rule optimization via large language models. In: 2024 IEEE International Conference on Autonomic Computing and Self-Organizing Systems Companion (ACSOS-C), pp. 180–181. IEEE, New York (2024)
37. Jeong, D.P., Lipton, Z.C., Ravikumar, P.: LLM-Select: Feature Selection with Large Language Models (2024). arXiv: 2407.02694 [cs.LG]. https://arxiv.org/abs/2407.02694
38. Jinru, X., Su, B.: Significant remote sensing vegetation indices: a review of developments and applications. J. Sens. **2017**, 1–17 (2017)
39. Jorgensen, S., et al.: Large language model-based test case generation for GP agents. In: Proceedings of the Genetic and Evolutionary Computation Conference. GECCO '24, pp. 914–923. Association for Computing Machinery, Melbourne (2024). ISBN: 9798400704949. https://doi.org/10.1145/3638529.3654056
40. Joseph, S., et al.: On the information geometry of vision transformers. In: NeurIPS 2023 Workshop on Symmetry and Geometry in Neural Representations (2023)
41. Jung, S., et al.: Bagging ensemble of multilayer perceptrons for missing electricity consumption data imputation. Sensors **20**(6) (2020). ISSN: 1424-8220. https://doi.org/10.3390/s20061772. https://www.mdpi.com/1424-8220/20/6/1772

42. Jung, Y., Ahn, S.: Triplet edge attention for algorithmic reasoning. arXiv preprint arXiv:2312.05611 (2023)
43. Kaggle (2010). https://www.kaggle.com/
44. Kanthale, D.B., Mahajan, R.P., Bhopal, R.: IR-Tree implementation using index document search method. Int. J. Eng. Res. Technol. **3** (2014). https://api.semanticscholar.org/CorpusID:60808254
45. Karimi, D., et al.: Deep learning with noisy labels: exploring techniques and remedies in medical image analysis. Med. Image Anal. **65**, 101759 (2020). ISSN: 1361-8415. https://doi.org/10.1016/j.media.2020.101759
46. Key, C., Benson, N.: Landscape assessment: ground measure of severity, the Composite Burn Index; and Remote sensing of severity, the Normalized Burn Ratio. In: USDA Forest Service, Rocky Mountain Research Station, pp. 1–51 (2006)
47. Lehman, J., Stanley, K.O.: Abandoning objectives: evolution through the search for novelty alone. Evol. Comput. **19**(2), 189–223 (2011). https://doi.org/10.1162/EVCO_a_00025
48. Lehman, J., et al.: Safe Mutations for Deep and Recurrent Neural Networks through Output Gradients (2018). arXiv: 1712.06563 [cs.NE]. https://arxiv.org/abs/1712.06563
49. Lewis, P., et al.: Retrieval-Augmented Generation for Knowledge-Intensive NLP Tasks (2021). arXiv: 2005 .11401 [cs.CL]. https://arxiv.org/abs/2005.11401
50. Li, D., et al.: A Survey of Large Language Models Attribution (2023). arXiv: 2311.03731 [cs.CL]. https://arxiv.org/abs/2311.03731
51. Li, J., et al.: Generative AI for self-adaptive systems: state of the art and research roadmap. ACM Trans. Auton. Adapt. Syst. **19**(3), 1–60 (2024)
52. Liashchynskyi, P., Liashchynskyi, P.: Grid Search, Random Search, Genetic Algorithm: A Big Comparison for NAS (2019). arXiv: 1912.06059 [cs.LG]. https://arxiv.org/abs/1912.06059
53. Lin, Y., Ding, B., Zhou, J.: Large language models as pretrained data engineers: techniques and opportunities. IEEE Data Eng. Bull. **49**(1), 70–89 (2025). http://sites.computer.org/debull/A25mar/p70.pdf
54. Liu, F., et al.: Evolution of heuristics: towards efficient automatic algorithm design using large language model. In: Forty-first International Conference on Machine Learning (2024). https://openreview.net/forum?id=BwAkaxqiLB
55. Liu, H., Simonyan, K., Yang, Y.: DARTS: Differentiable Architecture Search (2019). arXiv: 1806.09055 [cs.LG]. https://arxiv.org/abs/1806.09055
56. Liu, H., et al.: Hierarchical Representations for Efficient Architecture Search (2018). arXiv: 1711.00436 [cs.LG]. https://arxiv.org/abs/1711/00436
57. Liu, H., Motoda, H.: Feature Extraction, Construction and Selection: A Data Mining Perspective. Kluwer Academic Publishers, USA (1998). ISBN: 0792381963
58. Liu, Z., et al.: ML-Agent: Reinforcing LLM Agents for Autonomous Machine Learning Engineering (2025). arXiv: 2505.23723 [cs.CL]. https://arxiv.org/abs/2505.23723
59. Maćkiewicz, A., Ratajczak, W.: Principal components analysis (PCA). Comput. Geosci. **19**(3), 303–342 (1993). ISSN: 0098-3004. https://doi.org/10.1016/0098-3004(93)90090-R. www.sciencedirect.com/science/article/pii/009830049390090R
60. Miao, X., Jia, Z., Cui, B.: Demystifying data management for large language models. In: Companion of the 2024 International Conference on Management of Data. SIGMOD '24, pp. 547–555. Association for Computing Machinery, Santiago AA (2024). ISBN: 9798400704222. https://doi.org/10.1145/3626246.3654683
61. Mouret, J.-B., Clune, J.: Illuminating Search Spaces by Mapping Elites (2015). arXiv: 1504.04909 [cs.AI]. https://arxiv.org/abs/1504.04909
62. Mustafa, M.T., et al.: Using Water Indices (NDWI, MNDWI, NDMI, WRI and AWEI) to Detect Physical and Chemical Parameters by Apply Remote Sensing and Gis Techniques. Int. J. Res. Granthaalayah **5**(10), 117–128 (2017). https://doi.org/10.5281/zenodo.1040209
63. Naveed, H., et al.: A Comprehensive Overview of Large Language Models (2024). arXiv: 2307.06435 [cs.CL]. https://arxiv.org/abs/2307.06435
64. Osman, I.H., Kelly, J.P.: Meta-heuristics theory and applications. J. Oper. Res. Soc. **48**(6), 657–657 (1997)

65. Pham, H., et al.: Efficient Neural Architecture Search via Parameter Sharing (2018). arXiv: 1802.03268 [cs.LG]. https://arxiv.org/abs/1802.03268
66. Poli, R., Langdon, W.B., Mcphee, N.: A Field Guide to Genetic Programming. Lulu Enterprises, UK Ltd, London (2008). ISBN: 978-1-4092-0073-4
67. Pugh, J.K., Soros, L.B., Stanley, K.O.: Quality diversity: a new frontier for evolutionary computation. Front. Rob. AI **3**, 40 (2016)
68. Real, E., et al.: Large-scale evolution of image classifiers. In: Proceedings of the 34th International Conference on Machine Learning—Volume 70. ICML'17, pp. 2902–2911. JMLR.org, Sydney (2017)
69. Romera-Paredes, B., et al.: Mathematical discoveries from program search with large language models. Nature **625**(7995), 468–475 (2024). https://doi.org/10.1038/s41586-023-06924-6
70. Rouse, J.W., et al.: Monitoring vegetation systems in the great plains with ERTS. In: NASA Special Publication (1973)
71. Salimans, T., et al.: Evolution Strategies as a Scalable Alternative to Reinforcement Learning (2017). arXiv: 1703.03864 [stat.ML]. https://arxiv.org/abs/1703.03864
72. Senkerik, R., et al.: Open and Closed Source Models for LLM-Generated Metaheuristics Solving Engineering Optimization Problem. In: Applications of Evolutionary Computation, pp. 372–385. Springer Nature, Switzerland (2025). ISBN: 9783031900655. https://doi.org/10.1007/978-3-031-90065-5_23
73. Sharan, S., Pittaluga, F., Chandraker, M., et al.: LLM-Assist: enhancing closed-loop planning with language-based reasoning. arXiv preprint arXiv:2401.00125 (2023)
74. Shinohara, Y., et al. Large Language Models as Particle Swarm Optimizers (2025). arXiv: 2504.09247 [cs.NE]. https://arxiv.org/abs/2504.09247
75. Silva, S., et al.: A semi-supervised Genetic Programming method for dealing with noisy labels and hidden overfitting. Swarm Evol. Comput. **39**, 323–338 (2018). https://doi.org/10.1016/j.swevo.2017.11.003
76. Sim, K., Renau, Q., Hart, E.: Beyond the hype: Benchmarking LLM- evolved heuristics for bin packing. In: Applications of Evolutionary Computation, pp. 386–402. Springer Nature, Switzerland (2025). ISBN: 9783031900655. https://doi.org/10.1007/978-3-031-90065-5_24
77. Slack, D., Singh, S.: TABLET: Learning From Instructions for Tabular Data (2023). arXiv: 2304.13188 [cs.LG]. https://arxiv.org/abs/2304.13188
78. Soltoggio, A., Stanley, K.O., Risi, S.: Born to learn: the inspiration, progress, and future of evolved plastic artificial neural networks. Neural Netw. **108**, 48–67 (2018). ISSN: 0893-6080. https://doi.org/10.1016/j.neunet.2018.07.013
79. Stanley, K.O.: Compositional pattern producing networks: a novel abstraction of development. Genet. Program Evolvable Mach. **8**(2), 131–162 (2007). ISSN: 1573-7632. https://doi.org/10.1007/s10710-007-9028-8
80. Stanley, K.O., D'Ambrosio, D.B., Gauci, J.: A hypercube-based encoding for evolving large-scale neural networks. Artif. Life **15**(2), 185–212 (2009). https://doi.org/10.1162/artl.2009.15.2.15202
81. Stanley, K.O., Miikkulainen, R.: Evolving neural networks through augmenting topologies. Evol. Comput. **10**(2), 99–127 (2002). http://nn.cs.utexas.edu/?stanley:ec02.
82. Stein, N.v., Bäck, T.: LLaMEA: a large language model evolutionary algorithm for automatically generating metaheuristics. IEEE Trans. Evol. Comput. **29**(2), 331–345 (2025). https://doi.org/10.1109/TEVC.2024.3497793
83. Such, F.P., et al.: Deep Neuroevolution: Genetic Algorithms are a Competitive Alternative for Training Deep Neural Networks for Reinforcement Learning (2018). arXiv: 1712.06567 [cs.NE]. https://arxiv.org/abs/1712.06567
84. Sebastian, V.B., Unnikrishnan, A., Balakrishnan, K.: Gray Level Co-Occurrence Matrices: Generalisation and Some New Features (2012). arXiv: 1205.4831 [cs.CV]. https://arxiv.org/abs/1205.4831
85. Vanneschi, L., Silva, S.: Introduction to machine learning. In: Lectures on Intelligent Systems, pp. 115–148. Springer International Publishing, Cham (2023). ISBN: 978-3-031-17922-8. https://doi.org/10.1007/978-3-031-17922-8_5

86. Vaswani, A., et al.: Attention is All you Need (2023). arXiv: 1706.03762 [cs.CL]. https://arxiv.org/abs/1706.03762
87. Veličković, P., et al.: The CLRS algorithmic reasoning benchmark. In: International Conference on Machine Learning, pp. 22084–22102. PMLR, New York (2022)
88. Vertsel, A., Rumiantsau, M.: Hybrid LLM/rule-based approaches to business insights generation from structured data. arXiv preprint arXiv:2404.15604 (2024)
89. Wei, T., et al.: Network morphism. In: Balcan, M.F., Weinberger, K.Q. (eds.) Proceedings of the 33rd International Conference on Machine Learning, vol. 48. Proceedings of Machine Learning Research, pp. 564–572. PMLR, New York (2016)
90. Xu, J., et al.: Large language models synergize with automated machine learning. arXiv preprint arXiv:2405.03727 (2024)
91. Ying, C., et al.: Nas-bench-101: towards reproducible neural architecture search. In: International Conference on Machine Learning, pp. 7105–7114. PMLR, New York (2019)
92. Yu, C., et al.: GPT-NAS: neural architecture search meets generative pretrained transformer model. Big Data Min. Anal. **8**(1), 45–64 (2025). https://doi.org/10.26599/bdma.2024.9020036. https://ieeexplore.ieee.org/document/10681256/
93. Zhang, H., et al.: Large Language Models as Data Preprocessors (2024). arXiv: 2308.16361 [cs.AI]. https://arxiv.org/abs/2308.16361
94. Zhang, J., et al.: Darwin Godel Machine: Open-Ended Evolution of Self-Improving Agents. arXiv preprint arXiv:2505.22954 (2025)
95. Zhu, Y., et al.: Large Language Models for Information Retrieval: A Survey (2024). arXiv: 2308.07107 [cs.CL]. https://arxiv.org/abs/2308.07107
96. Zoph, B., Le, Q.V.: Neural Architecture Search with Reinforcement Learning (2017). arXiv: 1611.01578 [cs.LG]. https://arxiv.org/abs/1611.01578
97. Zoph, B., et al.: Learning transferable architectures for scalable image recognition. In: 2018 IEEE/CVF Conference on Computer Vision and Pattern Recognition (CVPR), pp. 8697–8710. IEEE Computer Society, Los Alamitos (2018). https://doi.org/10.1109/CVPR.2018.00907. https://doi.ieeecomputersociety.org/10.1109/CVPR.2018.00907

Chapter 5
Toward Scalable, Robust, and Open-Ended LLM-EC Integration

This chapter examines open problems at the interface of large language models (LLMs) and metaheuristics, with emphasis on *scalability*, *robustness*, and *open-ended optimization*. Productive integration arises when we (i) constrain the LLM's role to compositional, locally verifiable generation and (ii) delegate global search and selection to principled optimizers. Concretely, we study two complementary patterns. First, we analyze *inference-time* scalability via modular program synthesis coupled with automated machine learning (AutoML): The *text-to-ML* framework [32] decomposes end-to-end ML pipelines into testable modules, verifies cross-module compatibility, and then uses numerical optimization to select among many executable candidates. This approach turns brittle one-shot code emission into generate-verify-optimize loops that scale to longer programs while improving downstream metrics. Second, we investigate *open-ended* self-improvement through evolutionary computation (EC): The *Darwin Gödel machine* (DGM) [34] couples LLM-driven code edits with a population process and an archive of stepping stones, enabling continual, empirically validated self-modification of coding agents.

5.1 Scalability of LLMs for EC

Issues of scale fundamentally condition the interaction between LLMs and EC. When LLMs are used as components within EC pipelines—whether as optimizers, evaluators, generators, or controllers—the cost and feasibility of training and inference, the reliability of reasoning, and the ability to ingest and act upon long optimization histories all become central. In what follows, we analyze three tightly related facets of scalability that bear directly on the design and evaluation of LLM-EC systems: (i) intrinsic data-and-compute scaling for LLMs; (ii) limits of mathematical reasoning and the techniques developed to mitigate them; and (iii) constraints arising from optimization history length and sequence-length limits.

H. Iba et al., *Large Language Models and Evolutionary Computation*,
Natural Computing Series, https://doi.org/10.1007/978-981-95-8597-7_5

5.1.1 Intrinsic Scalability Limitations of LLMs

A prominent line of work aspires to scale LLMs according to empirical scaling laws by increasing model size, training tokens, and compute [9, 15]. Although this strategy has delivered substantial gains, the extent to which such scaling remains efficient and yields sustained returns remains uncertain and is often resource intensive. Recent studies refine this picture in two complementary ways.

First, Bi et al. [2] argue that efficient and predictable scaling is possible when scaling laws, data quality, and hyperparameters are jointly balanced and empirically understood. In this view, scale alone is insufficient: The outcome depends on an aligned triad of (i) faithful scaling-law estimation, (ii) curation of high-quality data, and (iii) careful hyperparameter selection.

Second, Gadre et al. [8] contend that LLMs exhibit reliable, predictable scaling even beyond the traditional compute-optimal training regime. Conventionally, scaling laws are derived under "compute-optimal" conditions, where the ratio of parameters to tokens minimizes validation loss for a fixed compute budget. However, their work shows that when smaller models are *overtrained*—exposed to far more tokens than the compute-optimal ratio would prescribe—their performance continues to obey consistent power-law relationships of the form $L = \lambda \cdot C^{-\eta}$, where L denotes validation loss, C denotes compute, η is the scaling exponent, and λ is a scalar offset. Notably, the scaling exponent (η) remains roughly constant as the degree of over-training varies, while the scalar offset (λ) shifts. Consequently, validation loss can be extrapolated accurately from small-scale experiments to larger, more overtrained models, and these empirical laws can be used to predict downstream task performance, not merely validation loss.

Countervailing views emphasize a looming data constraint. Villalobos et al. [29] argue that the finite supply of public human-generated text may soon limit the scalability of LLMs. Extrapolating current trends, they forecast that the total stock of public human text data could be fully utilized between 2026 and 2032. If so, by the end of this decade, one should not expect to sustain progress simply by adding more high-quality human text; the available pool would be exhausted. Crucially, however, the authors stress that this bottleneck need not arrest progress. Instead, it marks a shift in the locus of innovation: Future advances would likely rely on new data sources or on more data-efficient learning. Three broad strategies are identified as plausible pathways beyond the data wall: (i) *synthetic data generation*, using models to produce diverse, high-quality corpora (while managing risks such as model collapse and quality degradation); (ii) *transfer learning and multimodality*, importing information from other domains (e.g., images, code, scientific data) to enrich language modeling; and (iii) *data efficiency improvements*, such as better sampling, curriculum learning, or fine-tuning techniques that extract more signal from fixed data budgets. The qualitative outlook, therefore, is not that scaling halts, but that its axis tilts from raw data quantity toward innovation in data generation, transfer, and efficiency.

Taken together, these results suggest a nuanced landscape for LLM-EC integration. On the one hand, scaling laws offer predictive structure, even off the compute-optimal frontier [8]. On the other hand, both computational costs and prospective data limits [29] imply diminishing returns for naive scaling. For EC applications—where iterative evaluation, generation, and selection can be compute-heavy—the practical question becomes how to achieve the best trade-offs among model size, training tokens, and data quality while controlling cost and preserving sample efficiency.

5.1.2 Mathematical Reasoning

Beyond data and compute, weaknesses in mathematical and multistep reasoning can limit LLM performance. LLMs often struggle with tasks that require decomposition and stepwise calculation rather than mere linguistic fluency [11]. Two families of approaches have emerged to bolster mathematical reasoning in LLMs: methods that generally enhance reasoning (and thereby mathematics) and methods that target mathematical ability more directly.

5.1.2.1 General-Purpose Strategies

Few-shot chain-of-thought (CoT) prompting [31] provides exemplars that encourage intermediate reasoning steps, thereby improving accuracy on multistep problems. As illustrated in Fig. 5.1, CoT elicits reasoning by inserting intermediate steps into the prompt, guiding the model through a structured problem-solving process. Zero-shot CoT [16] elicits similar behavior by appending a simple instruction such as "Let's think step by step." without providing few-shot exemplars. Additionally, as exemplified in Fig. 5.2, decoding strategies can further stabilize reasoning. Self-consistency [30] replaces greedy decoding with the sampling of diverse reasoning paths (via temperature, top-k, or nucleus sampling[1]), marginalizes over the resulting candidate answers (e.g., majority vote), and selects the most consistent final answer. This "self-ensemble" requires no additional training, supervision, or verifier models. Another approach, least-to-most prompting [35], teaches decomposition by example and then has the model to solve a sequence of subproblems, each informed by the previous step's result; chain-of-thought or self-consistency can be optionally incorporated, yet the method itself does not require additional training.

[1] Nucleus sampling (also called top-p sampling) selects the next token from the smallest set of tokens whose cumulative probability exceeds a threshold p, enabling more diverse yet coherent generation compared to fixed top-k sampling.

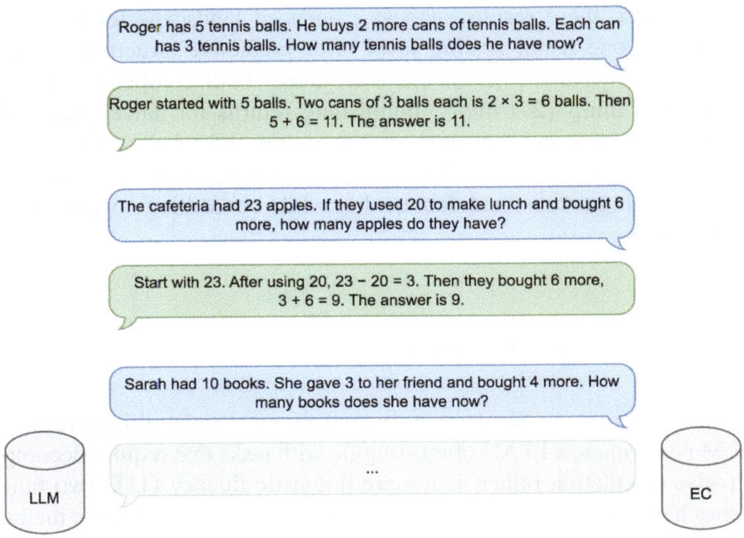

Fig. 5.1 Chain-of-thought (CoT) prompting elicits reasoning by inserting intermediate steps into the prompt, guiding the model through a structured problem-solving process that improves accuracy on multistep problems

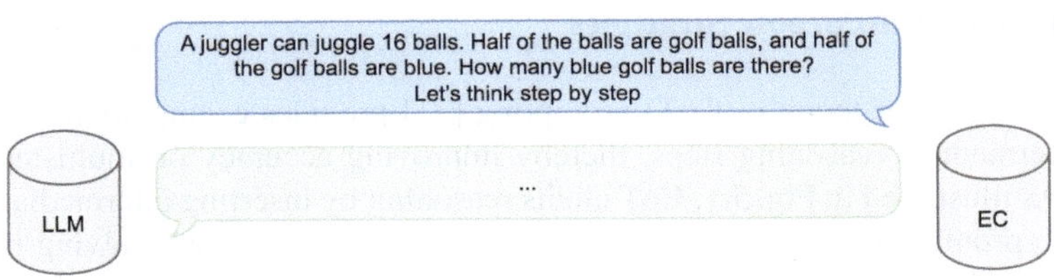

Fig. 5.2 Zero-shot CoT elicits reasoning by inserting the "Let's think step by step." instruction into the prompt

5.1.2.2 Math-Specific Strategies

Targeted methods aim to harden mathematical competence. MathPrompter [11] augments reasoning with multi-verification and compute-based validation. The problem is first abstracted into an algebraic template; the LLM is then prompted to solve it from multiple perspectives (e.g., symbolic algebra and a Python function). Candidate solutions are *executed* with randomly sampled variable values (e.g., via `eval()`) to assess agreement. Repeating this procedure for multiple iterations (approximately five) yields a consensus-based final answer that is both robust and verifiable, effectively integrating cross-checking, redundancy, and statistical selection into the LLM's workflow.

Complementing verification, the MathGenie framework [20] focuses on dataset construction via a three-step, back-translation-centered pipeline. Starting from a small human-annotated seed,[2] solutions are iteratively augmented (by altering numbers, adding steps, or substituting objects) to preserve logic while increasing diversity. A separate model back-translates these augmented solutions into new questions, thereby maintaining semantic and logical alignment between the question and the solution. Finally, code-integrated solutions are generated and verified; only instances that pass verification are retained, yielding a curated synthetic dataset called *MathGenieData*. Models trained on this corpus are referred to as *MathGenieLM*. Together, these approaches indicate that reliable mathematical reasoning in LLMs benefits from both procedural verification and carefully generated training data.

5.1.3 Optimization History and Sequence-Length Limitations

A distinctive challenge for LLM-EC integration arises from the sheer size and structure of optimization histories. Many EC algorithms maintain rich trajectories of individual-score pairs across thousands of individuals and thousands of generations. Such histories are both voluminous and mathematically dense. In practice, feeding complete histories into an LLM exceeds typical context windows and compounds the difficulty discussed in Sect. 5.1.2.

Empirical design choices in recent LLM-based optimization illustrate these constraints. In [33], only a limited portion of the past trajectory is provided to the model during optimization; for example, experiments explicitly include "the best 20 instructions so far" (as described in their experimental setup), a direct response to context-length limits. As a result, the optimizer can reason only over a small slice of the trajectory rather than the whole history.

Similarly, Liu et al. [19] report that LMEA (see Sect. 2.1) performs well on small-scale traveling salesman problem (TSP) instances with 10–15 nodes, yet degrades substantially on larger instances of 20–25 nodes. Multiple design constraints trace back to sequence-length and representation costs. The population size is fixed at $N = 16$ to accommodate the need to include all individuals and their scores in the prompt; larger populations do not fit. Prompts are structured to include problem description, population information, and task instructions; these elements quickly consume context space even for moderate problem sizes. Correspondingly, the study caps TSP size at $n \leq 25$ nodes and observes rapid deterioration beyond that threshold. The immediate causes are dual: increasing search complexity and the longer textual descriptions required to represent extended tours, both of which stem from token limits.

For EC practitioners, these observations carry concrete implications. When LLMs must condition on long optimization histories, one must either compress

[2] E.g, GSM8K and MATH, i.e., two benchmarks for evaluating the arithmetic or mathematical reasoning capabilities of LLMs.

or summarize trajectories, restrict population size, or adopt external-memory or retrieval mechanisms to sidestep strict context budgets. Absent such measures, sequence-length limits may force narrow windows onto the past, undermining the iterative refinement that EC relies on.

5.1.4 Routes Beyond Scaling Walls: Data, Reasoning, and History Management

Across these three facets, a common theme emerges. Intrinsic scaling can remain predictable if data quality and hyperparameters are tuned and if one is willing to operate beyond compute optimality [2, 8]. Yet, data scarcity looms under current practices [29]. Meanwhile, mathematical reasoning—central to many EC tasks and their evaluation—can be strengthened by prompting, self-ensemble decoding, verification, and curated synthetic data [11, 16, 20, 30, 31, 35]. Finally, optimization histories in EC pose acute sequence-length challenges that already shape system design [19, 33]. Practical progress in LLM-EC systems will thus hinge on balancing data and compute against model quality, adopting principled reasoning scaffolds and verifiers, and engineering mechanisms to represent or retrieve long optimization trajectories within finite context windows.

5.2 Synergy Between LLMs and AutoML

5.2.1 Contextual Modular Generation and Scalability

This section outlines a concrete pathway to address the scalability issues of LLMs in optimization-centric workflows by coupling them with AutoML. The exemplar is *text-to-ML* [32] (Fig. 5.3), which treats end-to-end machine learning (ML) program synthesis as a structured sequence generation problem augmented by program-level testing and numerical optimization. The central idea is to scale *inference-time* capability, rather than model size, by decomposing program generation into compatible modules, verifying them with tailored unit tests, and selecting among many candidate programs via AutoML.

Formally, let an autoregressive LLM with state λ (choice of base model, parameters, and decoding configuration) induce a conditional distribution over token sequences. Given an input sequence $X = (x_1, \ldots, x_M)$ and output sequence $Y = (y_1, \ldots, y_N)$, the probability of generating Y conditioned on X factorizes as

$$p_\lambda(Y \mid X) = \prod_{n=1}^{N} p_\lambda(y_n \mid y_{<n}, X),$$

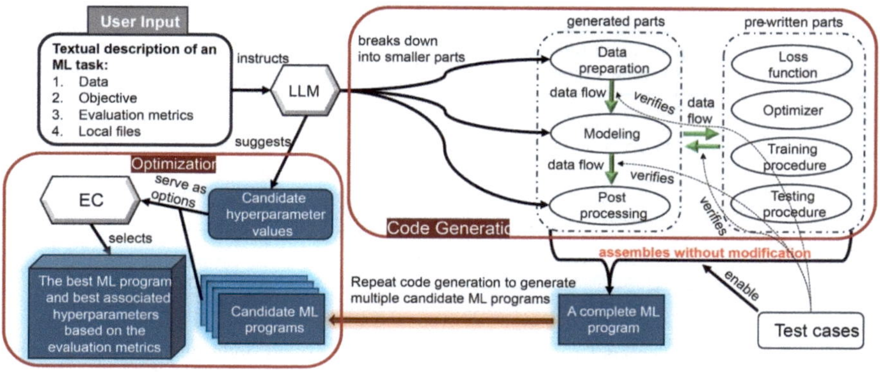

Fig. 5.3 Overview of text-to-ML: a three-phase process comprising generation, testing, and optimization. Given a task description, the LLM first generates modular components. Each module is validated through unit tests to ensure compatibility, after which it is automatically integrated. This process iterates to produce multiple candidate programs, from which AutoML selects the most effective program and corresponding hyperparameters

where $y_{<n}$ denotes all tokens generated before position n, and each factor represents the probability of the next token given the input and all previously generated tokens.

Directly emitting an entire ML pipeline as a single sequence is brittle for long outputs: Valid programs in this setting average 114 ± 32 lines of code, far longer than HumanEval's 6.3 ± 5.0 [5]. HumanEval is a widely used benchmark[3] for evaluating code generation capabilities, consisting of 164 handwritten programming problems that test function synthesis from docstrings; its relatively short reference solutions highlight the contrast with the lengthy, multicomponent ML programs addressed here. We address length and heterogeneity through *contextual modular generation* [32]. The target program is decomposed into J modules—data preparation, modeling, and post-processing-denoted $Y_1, \dots, Y_J$, where each $Y_j = (y_1^j, \dots, y_{k_j}^j)$ is generated in its own iterative loop. For module j, the procedure constructs instructions X_j^i from prior attempts and feedback, samples code $Y_j^i \sim p_\lambda(\cdot \mid X_j^i)$, and evaluates it with a binary checker $\mathcal{E}_j$ that enforces both *local functionality* and *cross-module compatibility*. The first passing candidate becomes Y_j. Crucially, the family $\{\mathcal{E}_j\}_{j=1}^J$ is *contextual*: Passing all $\mathcal{E}_j$ implies that the concatenation $(Y_1, \dots, Y_J)$ composes into an executable program without further adaptation.

Compatibility is ensured by design. As shown in Fig. 5.4, each module's unit tests are *generated* (to capture task-specific requirements) yet must satisfy a protocol (domain-level constraints) that guarantees *external compatibility* with a fixed set of pre-written, low-variance routines: loss, optimizer, training/testing loops, evaluation metrics, and the AutoML harness. For image tasks, for instance, the protocol requires explicit spatial dimensions; for NLP, analogous constraints govern the

[3] https://github.com/openai/human-eval.

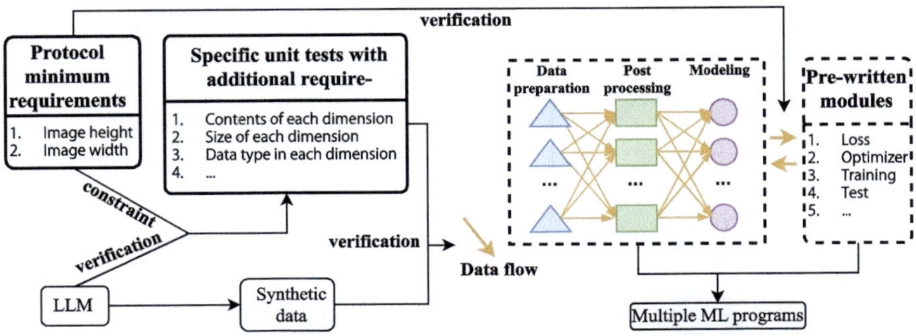

Fig. 5.4 Testing for a computer vision task. The yellow arrows indicate data flow between code modules. The unit tests are designed to verify both the structure and the content of the data exchanged among these modules. For each module, multiple candidate implementations are generated, and when combined with predefined components, each valid pathway through the network constitutes a complete ML program

structure of token sequences and embeddings. To decouple module verification from data-loader idiosyncrasies, the framework also generates synthetic data programs that are themselves validated against the protocol; a candidate module is accepted if it processes at least one protocol-compliant synthetic dataset and meets task-specific assertions. This engineering choice yields two forms of scalability: *internal compatibility*, whereby any verified implementation of a module composes with any other verified implementation, and *external compatibility*, whereby all verified modules interoperate with the fixed training/evaluation stack and the AutoML layer. If N modules each admit M verified variants, the number of valid end-to-end program paths can scale on the order of M^{N-}, with essentially linear generation cost, greatly expanding the design space available to the optimizer.

The framework admits a probabilistic lens that clarifies its scaling behavior with sequence length. Let Ω be the set of valid target sequences and let $\Gamma = \max\{|Y| : Y \in \Omega\}$ denote the length of the longest valid program. For a partial output a, define $\Theta_\Omega(a, n)$ as the set of valid length-n continuations that can follow a, with $|a| + n \leq \Gamma$. For input X, consider the per-position success probability

$$\mathbf{p}_{X,\Omega,\lambda}(i) = p_\lambda(y_i \in \Theta_\Omega(y_{<i}, 1) \cup \zeta(i) \mid (y_{<i} \in \Theta_\Omega(\langle\rangle, i-1) \cup \eta(i-1)) \cap X),$$

where $\zeta(i)$ captures termination into a valid sequence (i.e., successfully ending with a complete, correct program) and $\eta(i)$ captures absorbing failure (i.e., the generation process has already produced an invalid token at some earlier position, making recovery impossible); $y_i = \langle\rangle$ if $\eta(i)$, and $y_{<i} = \langle\rangle$ if $\eta(i-1)$. Intuitively, this expression measures the probability that, at position i, the model either generates a valid continuation token or legitimately terminates, given that all previous tokens were valid (or the process had already failed). Define the token-level hardness.

$$\xi_{X,\Omega,\lambda}(\varepsilon) = \left|\{\, i \leq \Gamma \ : \ \mathbf{p}_{X,\Omega,\lambda}(i) < \varepsilon \,\}\right|.$$

This quantity counts the number of positions in the output sequence for which the per-position success probability is below the threshold ε. A large value of ξ for moderate ε indicates that many tokens are "hard" to generate correctly, making the overall sequence generation fragile.

If, in the worst case, errors may occur at many positions (large ξ for moderate ε), any process that *at some step* must emit the entire sequence end-to-end exhibits a best-case expected attempt cost that can grow *exponentially* with Γ—intuitively, a product of many subunit per-token success probabilities [32]. By contrast, when generation is decomposed into modules, and each module is immediately checked by contextual tests that guarantee composability, the best-case expected cost grows merely *linearly* with Γ. The reason is that correctness is enforced at module boundaries; feedback is local and immediate rather than deferred to the end of a very long sequence. Empirically, this shift from exponential fragility to linear best-case scaling aligns with improved success rates on longer, more complex ML programs reported in our prior work [32].

5.2.2 *From Valid to Optimized Programs*

Syntactic validity is necessary but insufficient: ML programs must also deliver strong numerical performance on metrics such as accuracy or mean absolute error. We therefore couple generation with an AutoML layer that searches over (i) module selections (e.g., alternative feature engineering pipelines and model backbones), (ii) associated hyperparameters, and (iii) post-processing/evaluation choices [32]. The pipeline proceeds in three phases. First, the LLM proposes a *search space* $\mathbb{S}$ of candidate algorithms and hyperparameter grids for all modules. Second, for deep learning tasks, candidate modeling codes are *prescreened* using zero-cost (ZC) proxies [17].

ZC proxies are training-free scores that estimate the promise of a neural architecture using information from at most a single forward or backward pass on a small batch of data, thereby avoiding full training costs. The key insight is that certain statistics computed at random initialization—such as gradient magnitudes, activation patterns, or signal propagation properties—correlate with final trained performance. Because computing these statistics requires only seconds rather than the hours or days needed for complete training, ZC proxies enable rapid filtering of large architecture search spaces. Several ZC metrics are employed in practice: `flops` and `params` measure computational complexity and model size, providing coarse proxies for capacity; `naswot` (Neural Architecture Search Without Training) [21] counts the number of unique activation patterns induced by a batch of inputs, with more patterns indicating a richer partition of input space and potentially greater expressivity; and `synflow` [27] uses a gradient-based synaptic flow score that measures how well signals propagate through the network without being attenuated by dead paths (e.g., from ReLU saturation). By computing these metrics cheaply at initialization, weak candidates can be eliminated before incurring training cost [12, 17, 36].

Third, an optimization strategy selects configurations to evaluate under a shared training/evaluation protocol, records metrics, and iterates. In our work [32], both random search and BOHB (a Bayesian optimization method) are explored [7]. Evaluations are budgeted at cost@25 and cost@100, i.e., the cost of fully training and testing 25 or 100 models, with early termination of poor runs via BOHB and ZC gating. Deep learning experiments are trained on NVIDIA A100 GPUs. Combinatorially, up to 20 candidates each for data preparation and modeling, and at least one for post-processing, yield up to ~400 valid module combinations, rich enough to admit significant performance variation yet tractable for modern optimizers.

Although we instantiate the optimizer with BOHB in our framework [32], the interface is naturally amenable to EC. A genotype can encode the identities of verified modules and their hyperparameters; initialization samples from the LLM-defined search space; mutation and crossover perturb algorithmic choices and hyperparameters; and fitness is the evaluation metric on a held-out set under the fixed training protocol (early stopping with patience 3 and $min\_delta = 0.0$ [22]). Two features make EC especially attractive. First, the compatibility guarantees from contextual testing ensure that recombinations of validated modules almost always yield *executable offspring*, sharply reducing invalid-solution waste that often plagues program synthesis. Second, ZC proxies and early-stopping signals act as *cheap fitness surrogates* or preselection filters, enabling large populations and aggressive culling without fully training every candidate, in the spirit of surrogate-assisted EC [14].

Empirical results in our prior work [32] illustrate both the generation and optimization benefits. On 12 supervised tasks spanning tabular, CV, and NLP, the modular method generates *valid* ML programs more efficiently than several LLM prompting baselines (zero-shot, chain-of-thought, reflexion, and a self-revision approach), outperforming in 10/12 tasks when GPT-4 is used as the generator. Removing unit tests increases difficulty across datasets, underscoring their necessity. Despite nontrivial false-positive (FP) rates after unit tests alone—approximately 7% (traditional), 34% (CV), and 29% (NLP)—a subsequent *execution* check (running the assembled program under the interpreter and fixed training loop) reduces false positives to $\{0\%, 2\%, 0\%\}$, respectively, indicating high reliability once both gates are passed. In optimization, random search already outperforms single configurations picked directly by the LLM. With BOHB and ZC proxies, sample efficiency improves further: For CV and NLP, the best-found program's *rank among 200 sampled configurations* improves by about $31 \pm 12\%$ at cost@25 and $9 \pm 3\%$ at cost@100 relative to search without ZC screening. These results validate the division of labor: LLMs supply diverse, executable candidates; AutoML supplies quantitative selection under fixed budgets.

5.2.3 A Unified View and Implications for LLM-EC Systems

The synergy between LLMs and AutoML arises because the components solve complementary parts of the scaling problem. LLMs, guided by contextual tests, *scale along the axis of breadth*: They can rapidly propose many functionally diverse, interoperable modules and assemble them into numerous plausible complete programs without retraining the LLM or expanding its context window. AutoML (including EC) *scales along the axis of depth*: It converts numerical feedback into principled search over a combinatorial design space, leveraging ZC proxies, early stopping, and population- or model-based exploration to traverse that space efficiently. The probabilistic analysis explains why moving correctness checks to module boundaries changes the effective scaling law, from exponential-in-length fragility under monolithic generation to linear-in-length best-case behavior under modular generation, making it feasible to explore hundreds of end-to-end programs rather than relying on a single, very long sample to be perfect.

For EC practitioners confronting long optimization histories and limited context windows, this pattern offers a practical template: Constrain the LLM's responsibility to *local* synthesis under protocol-grounded compatibility constraints, and offload *global* performance judgment to the optimizer. Use synthetic-data-driven unit tests and progenitor protocols to guarantee recomposability; let EC operate over a large, validated, and *safe-to-execute* manifold of programs; and exploit cheap proxies to prune aggressively. Our work [32] demonstrates that judicious modularization, verification, and search convert LLMs from brittle monolithic coders into robust *generator oracles* for EC/AutoML. The resulting systems exhibit effective scalability governed by linear, not exponential, growth in generation complexity, and their performance scales with the sophistication of the optimization algorithm placed on top.

5.3 Open-Endedness by LLMs and EC

Open-endedness has been a recurring theme in this book: the search for mechanisms by which intelligent systems can continually generate novel, learnable artifacts without prespecifying a terminal objective or brittle schema. The previous sections analyzed the scalability limits of LLMs. They introduced inference-time scaffolds—most notably, modular generation and AutoML-guided selection—that transform brittle monolithic generation into tractable generate-verify-optimize loops. We now turn to a complementary question: How can such loops be embedded in systems whose *own* generative machinery evolves, so that improvements on downstream tasks compound into better capacity for future self-improvement? In other words, how might LLMs and evolutionary computation cooperate to sustain *open-ended* progress rather than one-shot optimization?

A compelling answer is provided by the *Darwin Gödel Machine* (DGM) [34] (see Sect. 3.5.1), which operationalizes self-referential self-improvement in an open-ended evolutionary style. Whereas classical Gödel machines require formal proofs that any self-modification is beneficial [25], the DGM relaxes this impossibility by substituting empirical validation: Proposed codebase changes are accepted when they improve performance on downstream benchmarks. Crucially, the system maintains an *archive* of all previously discovered agents to preserve stepping stones, enabling diverse branches of innovation and recovery from local optima. The result is a population-based, LLM-powered, code-editing ecosystem in which each agent both *solves* tasks and *rewrites* the very procedures by which it solves them, thereby coupling task performance to self-modification ability.

5.3.1 A Self-Referential, Open-Ended Architecture

The DGM begins with a single, frozen-foundation-model (FM) coding agent and alternates between two phases: *self-modification* and *evaluation* [34]. Agents are concrete software systems—Python code repositories powered by pretrained FMs—that can read, write, and execute code. Self-improvement is defined as modifying the agent's own components (prompts, tools, workflows) within that repository; the target in the reported experiments is *not* retraining a new FM due to computational cost (though the framework does not preclude it). During self-modification, the system samples *parents* from an evolving archive and tasks each to produce an offspring by editing its own codebase. Two observable signals bias parent selection: recent benchmark performance and the number of offspring that retained code-editing functionality. In effect, the process favors lineages that are both competent and fecund. Each selected parent inspects its prior evaluation logs, proposes the next feature to implement, treats that proposal as a problem statement, and executes the requisite code edits to instantiate a new agent. Only agents that *compile* and *retain the ability to edit code* are admitted to the archive, because future self-improvement depends on those capabilities, while others are discarded. Significantly, offspring may branch from any archived ancestor with nonzero probability, ensuring that promising but temporarily underperforming innovations remain accessible; this mechanism mirrors the stepping-stone logic of quality-diversity and open-ended search [4, 10, 26].

The initial agent is deliberately minimal yet general: A frozen FM orchestrates two tools, a Bash tool for shell commands and an Edit tool that can view and modify entire files and directories [34]. The DGM is evaluated on two challenging coding benchmarks. *SWE-bench* (Software Engineering Benchmark) [13] is a collection of real GitHub issues from popular open-source Python repositories; each issue includes the broken code state, a natural language bug description, and a ground-truth fix, with success determined by whether the agent's patch passes the project's unit tests. SWE-bench is widely used to evaluate AI coding assistants because it tests realistic, multi-file reasoning on actual software engineering tasks. *Polyglot* [28] is a multi-language coding benchmark that selects 225 of the most challenging exercises from Exercism[4] across six languages (C++, Go, Java, JavaScript, Python, and Rust); models receive up to two attempts per problem with test feedback between attempts, simulating iterative debugging. Together, these benchmarks stress-test both single-language depth and cross-language breadth.

The agent receives a single input prompt specifying the target repository, the task, and the repository's testing framework. Self-modification proceeds over 80 iterations in total, with limited parallelism (two concurrent iterations for SWE-bench and four for Polyglot) to increase throughput without overwhelming evaluation resources. Offspring evaluation employs different FMs depending on the benchmark to reduce coupling between the model used to propose modifications and the model used to assess them.

The evaluation regime reflects the expense and stochasticity of large-agent benchmarks. Agents first undergo a 10-task gate to verify basic code-editing functionality. Those that pass are evaluated on a 50-task subset to estimate efficacy; for SWE-bench, the subset is designed to be a representative slice of the whole, human-verified benchmark, while for Polyglot it is drawn at random. For SWE-bench, agents that exceed a heuristic threshold (over 40% success on the aggregated 60 tasks) and rank among the two best performers known so far are promoted to a 200-task evaluation to estimate their true capability better. All Polyglot results are reported under a strict pass@1 protocol, meaning ground-truth test results are never revealed to the agent, which makes Polyglot a stringent, multi-language stress test compared with more permissive pass@2 leaderboards [34]. Two ablation baselines isolate core contributions. In *DGM w/o self-improve*, a fixed meta-agent repeatedly designs downstream agents (akin to ADAS-style setups). In *DGM w/o open-ended exploration*, the system always self-modifies the most recent agent. It retains only the latest version that still edits code, thereby discarding stepping stones.

As illustrated in Fig. 5.5, the resulting population graph is an explicit evolutionary record: Nodes are agents (whose color can be thought of as indicating performance and whose border thickness indicates the evaluation budget), and edges denote parent-child edits. Analyses reveal three recurring patterns. First, many high-performing lineages pass through temporarily *worse* agents, so greedy hill climbing would have pruned them away. Second, key innovations can catalyze bursts of descendants, with a single successful feature triggering an explosion of follow-on ideas. Third, allowing branches from any ancestor helps traverse deceptive valleys. The archive thereby functions as an external memory of innovation, preserving diversity and enabling exploratory recombination, i.e., core desiderata of open-ended EC [6, 18, 23].

[4] https://exercism.org/.

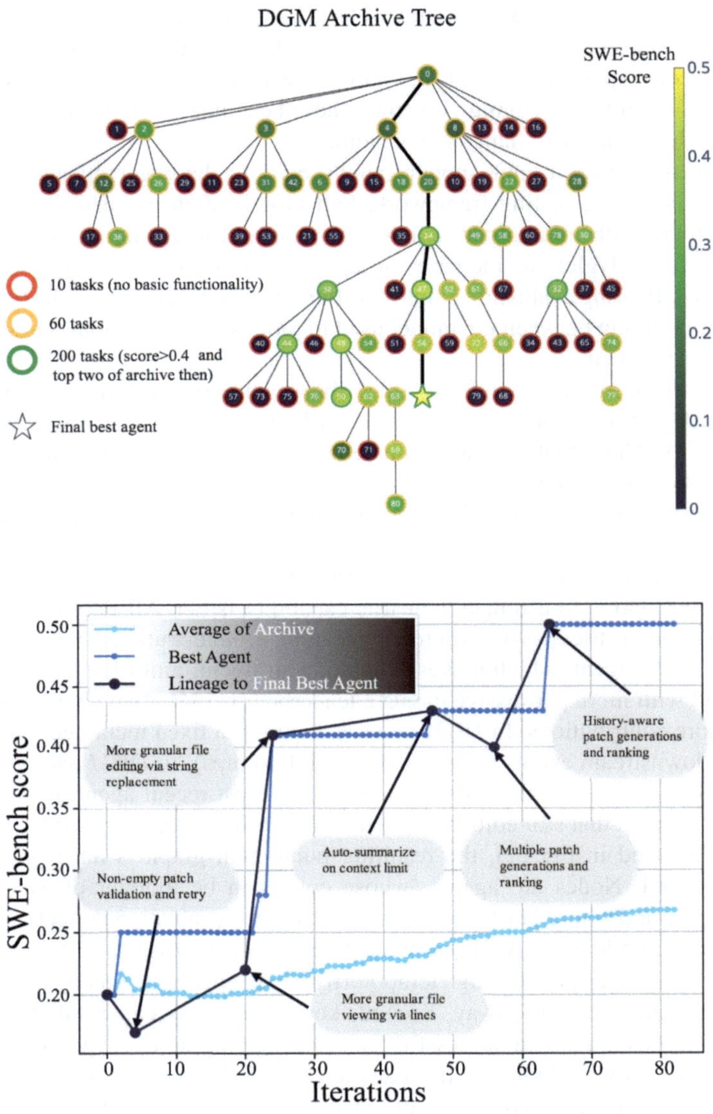

Fig. 5.5 Top: The archive of coding agents formed during the DGM run, where nodes represent agents derived through self-modification, color encodes SWE-bench performance, border thickness reflects evaluation budget, and edges indicate parent-offspring relationships. The structure reveals that major innovations often emerge through temporarily lower-performing agents and trigger cascades of descendant improvements, highlighting the value of open-ended, stepping-stone search. Bottom: Performance over iterations, showing the average capability of code-editing agents, the best score in the archive, and the lineage of the final top agent, whose trajectory includes performance dips that would be eliminated by greedy optimization but are crucial for long-term progress [34]

5.3.2 *Empirical Improvements, Stepping Stones, and Transfer*

On two demanding coding benchmarks, the DGM exhibits substantial, sustained gains. On SWE-bench (using the human-verified subset by default), the best agent discovered by the DGM improves from 20.0% to 50.0%; on Polyglot, performance rises from 14.0% to 38.0% on the 50-task subset and from 14.2% to 30.7% on the full benchmark [34]. Relative to handcrafted open-source systems, the DGM's best agent is comparable to the state of the art on SWE-bench and surpasses the representative community agent (Aider[5]) on Polyglot, despite starting below it. Against the ablations, both self-improvement and open-ended exploration prove indispensable: Without updating the meta-agent, gains appear early but saturate quickly; without the archive, losing code-edit functionality can stall progress entirely, and performance dips become harder to recover.

The system's improvements are not superficial. The DGM autonomously upgrades *tools* and *workflows*. Tool upgrades include finer-grained file viewing (by line ranges) and targeted string-replacement editing, replacing crude whole-file operations; workflow upgrades include multiple-attempt strategies per task, selecting among attempts via a "peer-review" mechanism (invoking another FM as judge), and conditioning subsequent attempts on the trace of prior failures [34]. These edits yield measurable benefits across repositories and languages, supporting the thesis that better downstream performance coincides with a greater *ability to improve itself*, since self-improvement is itself a coding task on the agent's own repository.

A notable strength is *transfer*. Agents evolved under one FM generalize to others: When the SWE-bench-evolved base agent and the DGM's best agent are reevaluated with different FMs, the relative gains persist, indicating that improvements are not overfit to the training FM [34]. Cross-benchmark transfer also holds: The best SWE-bench-evolved agent achieves 28.9% on Polyglot (versus a 14.2% base), and the best Polyglot-evolved agent reaches 24.5% on SWE-bench (versus a 20.0% base), despite neither agent having been optimized on the held-out benchmark. Finally, language transfer within Polyglot shows that focusing exclusively on Python slightly boosts Python performance but modestly reduces non-Python performance relative to all-language training; nevertheless, transferred agents still outperform the base and handcrafted baselines, underscoring robustness across languages.

5.3.3 *Relation to EC, Safety, and the Role of LLMs*

Methodologically, the DGM exemplifies a tight LLM-EC coupling. LLMs furnish a flexible *search operator* over the discrete space of code-level design changes:

[5] https://aider.chat/.

They propose meaningful, syntactically valid edits conditioned on logs and context. EC, in turn, supplies *population structure*, *selection*, and *archive maintenance* to preserve diversity and revisit stepping stones. Because acceptance depends on empirical evaluation, the system substitutes provability (à la Gödel machines) with measurement. Open-endedness emerges from the archive's persistent memory and from non-greedy branching rules that allow exploration beyond immediate performance, reducing premature convergence.

Safety receives concrete treatment in the implementation. All agent actions run in isolated sandboxes with strict timeouts; only Python code modifications to the agent's repository are permitted; and an auditable archive records lineages and code diffs [34]. While optimizing for benchmark scores risks misalignment with broader desiderata [3], the same self-improvement channel could, in principle, be redirected to favor interpretability and safety (e.g., constitutional constraints, hardening against hallucinations) if such desiderata are included in the evaluation mixture [1, 24]. At present, the open-ended exploration apparatus-archive policies and parent selection remain fixed; making those rules themselves subject to improvement is an important avenue for future work.

5.3.4 Open-Ended Self-Improvement as a Design Pattern

Viewed alongside modular text-to-ML pipelines, the DGM suggests a general design pattern: *Keep the LLM's role local and compositional (code edits, tool/-workflow design), while letting an evolutionary population process manage global exploration over long horizons*. The archive substitutes for unbounded context windows; branching from older ancestors circumvents deception; and empirical evaluation closes the loop between *doing* and *becoming better at doing*. In this setting, LLMs are not monolithic solvers but *variation engines* whose proposals are filtered by EC selection, much as AutoML filters modular program candidates. Together, these ingredients yield open-ended, compounding improvements: Downstream capability gains directly increase the agent's competence at further self-modification, echoing the cumulative, tool-building arc of science itself [4, 34]. The result is a credible route to unbounded innovation in which LLMs and EC jointly sustain the dynamics of discovery rather than merely optimizing fixed objectives.

5.4 Discussion: On the Mathematical Limitations of LLMs in Evolutionary Computation

A recurring criticism of using LLMs within evolutionary computation is that LLMs cannot reliably perform advanced mathematics. This concern is legitimate and well-documented: As discussed in Sect. 5.1.2, LLMs often struggle with multistep calculations, formal proofs, and symbolic manipulation. When presenting LLM-EC integration to audiences outside the field, this criticism frequently arises. Here, we address this concern directly, drawing on the evidence and frameworks presented throughout this chapter.

The criticism rests on an implicit assumption: That the value of LLMs in EC depends on their ability to perform mathematics *directly*. However, the integration patterns we have examined suggest a different division of labor. In the text-to-ML framework (Sect. 5.2), LLMs do not solve optimization problems mathematically; rather, they *generate candidate programs* that are then *evaluated numerically* by external systems. The mathematical heavy lifting—computing loss functions, gradients, and performance metrics—is delegated to standard ML libraries and optimizers. Similarly, in the Darwin Gödel Machine (Sect. 5.3), LLMs propose code edits, but the acceptance criterion is *empirical benchmark performance*, not mathematical proof. The LLM's role is generative and compositional, not computational.

This division of labor aligns with what LLMs do well. LLMs excel at pattern recognition, natural language understanding, code generation, and creative recombination of concepts. They can propose diverse, syntactically valid variations-mutations, in EC parlance, conditioned on rich contextual information such as error logs, prior attempts, and task descriptions. These are precisely the capabilities needed for effective variation operators in EC. The mathematical correctness of the resulting solutions is then verified or measured externally, either through unit tests (as in text-to-ML) or benchmark evaluation (as in DGM).

Furthermore, the strategies reviewed in Sect. 5.1.2 demonstrate that LLM mathematical reasoning can be substantially improved through external scaffolding. MathPrompter [11] achieves reliable answers by executing candidate solutions and checking for consensus, effectively outsourcing computation to an interpreter. Chain-of-thought prompting and self-consistency [30, 31] improve multistep reasoning without changing the underlying model. These techniques share a common insight: Rather than expecting LLMs to be reliable calculators, we can design systems that leverage their strengths while compensating for their weaknesses.

In EC applications, this principle translates naturally. For tasks such as crossover and mutation in genetic programming, mathematical precision may be less critical than diversity and novelty. An LLM-generated variation that deviates from the intended modification might actually *increase* population diversity—a hallucinated mutation could explore regions of the search space that deterministic operators would miss. The fitness function, not the LLM, determines which variations survive. For tasks requiring mathematical correctness, such as simplifying symbolic expressions where input-output equivalence must be preserved, one should indeed use verified mathematical libraries rather than LLM generation. The key is matching the tool to the task.

The empirical results presented in this chapter support this perspective. In text-to-ML, the combination of LLM-generated modules with AutoML optimization achieves strong performance across diverse ML tasks, outperforming direct LLM generation without verification [32]. In DGM, LLM-proposed code edits lead to substantial, transferable improvements on challenging coding benchmarks [34]. Neither system requires the LLM to perform mathematical reasoning in isolation; both systems *verify* outputs empirically.

We therefore conclude that the criticism, while pointing to a real limitation, misconstrues the role of LLMs in well-designed LLM-EC systems. The appropriate response is not to abandon LLM-EC integration but to architect systems that exploit complementary strengths: LLMs for flexible, context-aware generation; EC for population-based exploration and selection; and external computation for mathematical verification. This division of labor transforms the LLM's mathematical weakness from a fatal flaw into a manageable constraint, enabling scalable, robust, and open-ended integration, the subject of this chapter.

References

1. Bai, Y., et al.: Constitutional AI: Harmlessness from AI feedback. arXiv preprint arXiv:2212.08073 (2022)
2. Bi, X., et al.: Deepseek LLM: scaling open-source language models with longtermism. arXiv preprint arXiv:2401.02954 (2024)
3. Bostrom, N.: Ethical issues in advanced artificial intelligence. In: Machine Ethics and Robot Ethics, pp. 69–75 (2020)
4. Clune, J.: AI-GAs: AI-generating algorithms, an alternate paradigm for producing general artificial intelligence. arXiv preprint arXiv:1905.10985 (2019)
5. Cobbe, K., et al.: Training verifiers to solve math word problems. arXiv preprint arXiv:2110.14168 (2021)
6. Ecoffet, A., et al.: Go-explore: a new approach for hard-exploration problems. arXiv preprint arXiv:1901.10995 (2019)
7. Falkner, S., Klein, A., Hutter, F.: BOHB: robust and efficient hyper-parameter optimization at scale'. In: International Conference on Machine Learning, pp. 1437–1446. PMLR, New York (2018)
8. Gadre, S.Y., et al.: Language models scale reliably with over-training and on downstream tasks. arXiv preprint arXiv:2403.08540 (2024)
9. Hoffmann, J., et al.: Training compute-optimal large language models. arXiv preprint arXiv:2203.15556 (2022)
10. Hughes, E., et al.: Open-endedness is essential for artificial superhuman intelligence. arXiv preprint arXiv:2406.04268 (2024)
11. Imani, S., Du, L., Shrivastava, H.: Mathprompter: mathematical reasoning using large language models. arXiv preprint arXiv:2303.05398 (2023)
12. Javaheripi, M., et al.: LiteTransformerSearch: Training-free neural architecture search for efficient language models. Adv. Neural Inf. Process. Syst. **35**, 24254–24267 (2022)
13. Jimenez, C.E., et al.: SWE-bench: can language models resolve real-world GitHub issues?. arXiv preprint arXiv:2310.06770 (2023)
14. Jin, Y.: Surrogate-assisted evolutionary computation: recent advances and future challenges. Swarm Evol. Comput. **1**(2), 61–70 (2011)
15. Kaplan, J., et al.: Scaling laws for neural language models. arXiv preprint arXiv:2001.08361 (2020)
16. Kojima, T., et al.: Large language models are zero-shot reasoners. Adv. Neural Inf. Process. Syst. **35**, 22199–22213 (2022)
17. Krishnakumar, A., et al.: NAS-Bench-Suite-Zero: accelerating research on zero cost proxies. Adv. Neural Inf. Process. Syst. **35**, 28037–28051 (2022)

18. Lehman, J., Stanley, K.O.: Novelty search and the problem with objectives. In: Genetic Programming Theory and Practice IX, pp. 37–56. Springer, Berlin (2011)
19. Liu, S., et al.: Large language models as evolutionary optimizers. In: 2024 IEEE Congress on Evolutionary Computation (CEC), pp. 1–8. IEEE, New York (2024)
20. Lu, Z., et al.: MathGenie: generating synthetic data with question back-translation for enhancing mathematical reasoning of LLMS. arXiv preprint arXiv:2402.16352 (2024)
21. Mellor, J., et al.: Neural architecture search without training. In: *International Conference on Machine Learning*, pp. 7588–7598. PMLR, New York (2021)
22. Prechelt, L.: Early stopping-but when? In: Neural Networks: Tricks of the trade, pp. 55–69. Springer, Berlin (2002)
23. Pugh, J.K., Soros, L.B., Stanley, K.O.: Quality diversity: a new frontier for evolutionary computation. Front. Rob. AI **3**, 40 (2016)
24. Rosser, J., Nicolaus Foerster, J.: AgentBreeder: mitigating the AI safety impact of multi-agent scaffolds. arXiv e-prints (2025), arXiv–2502
25. Schmidhuber, J.: Gödel machines: fully self-referential optimal universal self-improvers. In: Artificial General Intelligence, pp. 199–226. Springer, Berlin (2007)
26. Stanley, K.O., Lehman, J., Soros, L.: Open-endedness: the last grand challenge you've never heard of. In: While Open-Endedness Could be a Force for Discovering Intelligence, it Could Also be a Component of AI Itself (2017)
27. Tanaka, H. et al.: Pruning neural networks without any data by iteratively conserving synaptic flow. Adv. Neural Inf. Process. Syst. **33**, 6377–6389 (2020)
28. Team, A.: Aider Polyglot Benchmark. Accessed: 2025-02-14 (2024). https://aider.chat/2024/12/21/polyglot.html
29. Villalobos, P., et al.: Position: will we run out of data? Limits of LLM scaling based on human-generated data. In: Forty-First International Conference on Machine Learning (2024)
30. Wang, X., et al.: Self-consistency improves chain of thought reasoning in language models. arXiv preprint arXiv:2203.11171 (2022)
31. Wei, J., et al.: Chain-of-thought prompting elicits reasoning in large language models. Adv. Neural Inf. Process. Syst. **35**, 24824–24837 (2022)
32. Xu, J. et al.: Large language models synergize with automated machine learning. arXiv preprint arXiv:2405.03727 (2024)
33. Yang, C., et al.: Large Language Models as Optimizers. In: ICLR (2024)
34. Zhang, J., et al.: Darwin Godel Machine: Open-Ended Evolution of Self-Improving Agents. arXiv preprint arXiv:2505.22954 (2025)
35. Zhou, D., et al.: Least-to-most prompting enables complex reasoning in large language models. arXiv preprint arXiv:2205.10625 (2022)
36. Zhou, Q., et al.: Training-free transformer architecture search. In: Proceedings of the IEEE/CVF Conference on Computer Vision and Pattern Recognition, pp. 10894–10903 (2022)

Chapter 6
Conclusion

Someone once said, "AI is something useless. When successfully applied, it is no longer AI." We used to joke that AI means almost implemented.

(Rodney Brooks)

6.1 Summary of the Book

This book explained extension methods using evolutionary computation and, conversely, approaches to metaheuristics using LLMs, in light of the recent rise of generative AI. Readers who have reached this point should understand that LLMs are transforming traditional AI research. As we mentioned in Chap. 1, there are two possible directions for research on LLMs and metaheuristics:

- Metaheuristics for LLMs
- LLMs for metaheuristics

The primary focus of this book has been the second point, so we have covered LLM-based design for metaheuristics in a bottom-up way. In this book, we have shown how to apply LLMs to evolutionary computation to improve search performance, i.e., to realize LLM-assisted evolutionary algorithms. We mainly explained (1) LLMs for evolutionary operators, (2) LLMs for source code generation, (3) LLMs for EC parameter optimization, and (4) LLMs used as fitness, etc. We have also shown how to combine LLMs and metaheuristics. We have detailed how LLMs are applied to NAS (network architecture search) in neuroevolution. As a case study, we provided an explanatory introduction to integrating LLMs and quality-diversity (QD) algorithms into the NAS algorithm. Thereafter, we described several issues of integrating LLMs and metaheuristics. These include scalability, robustness, and open-ended optimization challenges, which are the essence of how metaheuristics can be effectively applied to LLMs, thereby fostering synergy between the two paradigms. For instance, we explained machine learning (ML) approaches to integrate EC and LLMs. This is a novel form of program synthesis for ML programs that combines LLMs and automated machine learning (autoML).

H. Iba et al., *Large Language Models and Evolutionary Computation*,
Natural Computing Series, https://doi.org/10.1007/978-981-95-8597-7_6

Having explained all this, it must be added that there is another approach, i.e.:

- Metaheuristics by LLMs

This third direction is to have LLMs improve existing metaheuristics or propose new ones by means of the so-called prompt engineering. Then, let LLMs output those codes as well. We can run those codes and assess their effectiveness.[1] We did not explain this approach because a top-down method seemed to violate the established rules of AI research. This may lead to the concept of *strong AI*.[2] If this direction were fully developed, ultimately, wouldn't it eliminate specialized researchers in that field? To put it bluntly, if we continue down this path, will LLMs eventually replace human intelligence?

We have our reasons for not thinking this way. As we have discussed so far, many aspects of the precise application of LLMs remain unclear. For example, how do the difficulties in logical reasoning (such as syllogisms) differ between humans and LLMs? How do LLMs exhibit hallucinations regarding probabilistic thinking? How do cognitive biases like "Prospect theory" manifest in LLMs [1]? Research into these areas will clarify how LLMs contribute to the achievement of "*strong AI*." Therefore, there should be scientific merit in researching the integration of LLMs and metaheuristics to pursue "*strong AI*."

6.2 Past, Present, and Future for AI Research on LLMs

Despite AI's seemingly smooth sailing currently, did you know it has experienced two winters so far? It seems like a lie now, but during the winter periods, sarcastic remarks like those at the beginning of this chapter were repeated. We conclude by sharing our perspective on the future of AI research, drawing on one of the authors' own past experiences.

Early AI initially achieved theorem proving and simple games in the 1960s. The simple perceptron was also welcomed because its learning rules and convergence were mathematically well defined, ushering in the first spring of artificial intelligence. It had been widely anticipated that *strong AI* would soon be realized, unlocking the secrets of human intelligence.

The first AI winter soon arrived in the 1970s. The trigger was Marvin Minsky's rejection of the above optimism in his book "Perceptron," arguing that simple

[1] Interested readers should see [4] for an introductory explanation and practical examples of this approach.

[2] An attempt to artificially achieve human intelligence itself. Now also referred to as general artificial intelligence (AGI). In contrast, "weak AI" refers to attempts to create something resembling human intelligence and put it to practical use. See [3] for detailed discussion.

connectivity and nonlinearity could not be learned through the simple perceptron.[3] Ironically, the very person who ushered in the AI winter is now called the "Father of AI." There is an interesting anecdote. Minsky submitted his doctoral dissertation on self-organizing neural networks in mice to the Department of Mathematics at Princeton University. His thesis committee included renowned scientists such as John von Neumann,[4] A.W. Tucker,[5] and J.W. Tukey.[6] While the dissertation was interesting, it was severely criticized for its mathematics, yet it was ultimately accepted as a doctoral thesis. The lesson here is that a doctoral dissertation speaks to the future. What would have happened if Minsky had not earned his Ph.D? Discovering such future talent is essential for advancing AI research.

One of the authors had aimed to pursue AI research as a student in the 1980's and studied the works of Geoffrey Hinton.[7] He also took classes with Prof. Shun'ichi Amari at the university and learned about Dr. Kunihiko Fukushima's achievements. Ahead of their time, they were pioneers who researched neural networks, i.e., the foundation of today's deep learning and LLMs. At that time, the author also had the opportunity to meet and interview Minsky [6]. What struck me was his remark, "We've done too much with neural networks." Perhaps Minsky then foresaw the current AI boom. This was just as the second AI winter was beginning.

There have been many twists and turns in AI since then, i.e., neural networks were once highly touted, but their limitations became apparent in the 1990s, plunging them into the second winter. But after enduring those winter periods of hardship and suffering, neural network research has reached its current peak, enabling the development of current LLMs. Needless to say, the central figure is Nobel laureate Geoffrey Hinton. As mentioned above, his resolve to persistently continue research in the same field (for more than half a century, overcoming the winter period) is worthy of deep respect. Normally, when a research field enters a winter period, most researchers would likely abandon it so quickly. Surprisingly,

---

[3] Marvin Minsky (1927–2016): An American computer scientist and cognitive scientist. He is known as the "Father of artificial intelligence." He is famous for his work on "Frame theory" and "Society of mind."

[4] John von Neumann (1903–1957): Hungarian-born mathematician in the United States. He conducted pioneering research in a wide range of fields from physics to psychology and mathematics. Known as the "Father of Computers" for his advocacy of the Neumann-type computer. He was also a founder of game theory and conducted pioneering research on self-organization. They are the mainstream approach in current AI and Alife research.

[5] Albert William Tucker (1905–1995): Canadian mathematician. Specialized in topology, game theory, linear programming, nonlinear programming, and operations research. Famous for the Kuhn-Tucker conditions, which the first-order derivatives must satisfy at the optimal point in nonlinear programming.

[6] John Wilder Tukey (1915–2000): American mathematician and statistician. Known for developing the fast Fourier transform (FFT).

[7] Geoffrey Everest Hinton (1947–): A computer scientist born in England. Engaged in research on neural networks; known as the "Godfather of AI." He won the Nobel Prize in Physics in 2024 with John Hopfield.

Hinton published research on evolutionary computation, i.e., the Baldwin effect[8] in his early days [2]. This research has since been integrated with current technology and developed in new directions.

French cultural anthropologist Claude Lévi-Strauss[9] proposed the concept called "*bricolage*" in his book "La Pensée sauvage" (The Savage Mind, 1962). This refers to the ancient human practice of creating useful tools from scraps and leftovers, irrespective of their original purpose. *Bricolage* means assembling things to make something new or repairing objects. Lévi-Strauss called the Western engineering mindset of the modern era "cultivated thought," arguing that *bricolage* represents a universal intelligence applicable even in contemporary society. The evolutionary computation and metaheuristics explained in this book can be considered a typical example of *bricolage*.

Evolution is about learning from the past to understand the new, which reminds us of a Confucian proverb. The origin of this phrase is found in the Analects, where he stated that one must study the thoughts and learning of predecessors as the requirement for becoming a teacher who instructs others. This concept holds for integrating new research fields. That is, fields studied in the past will be evolutionarily integrated with current LLM technology and come to fruition in new directions.

Minsky had made the following striking remarks in the aforementioned interview [7]: "Scientists have two choices. Doing popular work may seem safe, but it yields little fruit in the long run. However, if you tackle important but unpopular work, you must be careful not to stray from the path. Then, you can do more significant work."

The promising future research is entrusted to the newer generation.

References

1. Binz, M., Schulz, E.: Using cognitive psychology to understand GPT-3. arXiv preprint arXiv: 2206.14576 (2022)
2. Hinton, G., Nowlan, S.: How learning can guide evolution. Complex Syst. **1**(3), 495–502 (1987)
3. Iba, H.: AI and SWARM, Evolutionary Approach to Emergent Intelligence. CRC Press, New York (2020)
4. Iba, H.: Deep Swarm and Evolutionary Generative Artificial Intelligence. CRC Press, New York (2025)

[8] The phenomenon in which selection progresses toward enhancing learning ability, appearing at first glance as if acquired traits were being inherited. See see [5] for details.

[9] Claude Lévi-Strauss (1908–2009): French social anthropologist. Considered the founder of structuralism. He revealed that the structure of myths in primitive societies resembles the transformation groups in group theory within mathematics and that primitive people possess unique modes of thought, criticizing the traditional Western-centric view of history.

5. Iba, H.: Swarm Intelligence and Deep Evolution: Evolutionary Approach to Artificial Intelligence. CRC Press, New York (2022)
6. Iba Laboratory: Past, Present, and Future (2025). http://www.iba.t.u-tokyo.ac.jp/iba/SelfE.html
7. Minsky, M.: The interview: the scientist enchanted by dreaming machines—exploring new possibilities in AI research through the theory of the social mind. Inter **2**(4), 26–31 (1990)

Chapter 7
Appendix A: Basic Tools

This appendix offers practical, step-by-step guides to help readers independently implement the key concepts and methods introduced throughout the book. We begin by presenting essential tools for working with large language models (LLMs) and evolutionary computation (EC) and then present hands-on case studies that illustrate their use in real-world applications.

The goal of this appendix is to understand our description in this book better. Users who use the following programs and extend them in their direction should bear the following in mind:

- We accept no responsibility for any damage that may be caused by downloading these programs.
- We own the copyright to these programs.
- We reserve the right to alter, add to, or remove these programs without notice.

This section introduces the core tools required for the case studies. These are also among the most commonly used libraries in the LLM and EC ecosystems. All examples have been tested with Python 3.12.0 on Ubuntu 20.04.6. For tools that leverage GPU acceleration (vLLM), we used an NVIDIA H100 with 80 GB of HBM3 memory.

7.1 M3GP and M6GP

In this section, we describe three use cases of the M3GP and M6GP algorithms. Note that the two implementations are mostly identical, except for the fitness functions, so the explanations will focus on M3GP to avoid repetition:

- Installing the algorithms
- Training and testing an M3GP model
- Using LLMs to bootstrap evolution

H. Iba et al., *Large Language Models and Evolutionary Computation*,
Natural Computing Series, https://doi.org/10.1007/978-981-95-8597-7_7

7.1.1 Installing M3GP and M6GP

We understand that most users are not interested in modifying the algorithms and just want something easy to use, so they can compare their methods with M3GP and M6GP. These users can install M3GP and M6GP using the command displayed in Listing 7.1. For users who wish to explore the algorithms, change their initialization, fitness function, and implement other genetic operators, we invite them to download the respective GitHub repositories for M3GP[1] and M6GP.[2] Regardless of the method chosen by users, the following subsection presents a use case for the M3GP algorithm.

Listing 7.1 Pip install command for M3GP and M6GP

```
$ pip install m3gp m6gp
```

Listing 7.2 Extracting the evolution of fitness and model sizes of the best model in each iteration usingM3GP

```
import pandas
from m3gp import M3GP
from sklearn.model_selection import train_test_split
from sklearn.linear_model import Ridge

filename= "CL.csv"

# Open the dataset
ds = pandas.read_csv(filename)
class_header = ds.columns[-1]

# Split the dataset
Tr_X, Te_X, Tr_Y, Te_Y =
     train_test_split(ds.drop(columns=[class_header]), ds[class_header],
     train_size=0.7, random_state = 42)

# Train a model
inner_model = Ridge(random_state=42)
model = M3GP(model_class = inner_model, fitnessType = "MSE")
model.fit(Tr_X, Tr_Y, Te_X, Te_Y)

rmse_test = model.getMSEOverTime()[1] # 0 = Training; 1 = Test
sizes = model.getSizesOverTime()[0] # 0 = No. nodes; 1 = No. trees

print(rmse_test)
print(sizes)
```

[1] https://github.com/jespb/Python-M3GP.

[2] https://github.com/jespb/Python-M6GP.

7.1.2 Training and Testing an M3GP Model

Listing 7.2 illustrates how M3GP can be used to induce a set of features tailored to Ridge, a regression algorithm. The test set is iterations; it is not used to train the model. At the end of this script, Python prints two arrays: the test RMSE and the size of the best model for each iteration. The programmer needs to change the content of the "*filename*" and "*inner_model*" variables to their needs. The documentation for these implementations is available on their GitHub.

7.1.3 Using LLMs to Bootstrap Evolution

In this section, we explain how to modify the M3GP code to bootstrap evolution using combinations of features proposed by an LLM. In this case, we use the OpenAI API and prompt *gpt-5-mini* for recommendations, but the code should be easily modifiable to the user's preferred LLM system.

The first step is modifying the main script to obtain feature recommendations before starting evolution. To do that, the reader should follow Listing 7.3. The previous script was modified to include a variable named *objective* that describes the objective of the dataset; the use of the *obtainRecommendations* function to obtain a list of recommended features from an LLM system, and the M3GP constructor was also modified to receive a list of *Node* objects in the *bootstrap_models* parameter. These *Node* objects are the representation of the LLM recommended feature combinations as a GP model.

Listing 7.3 Prompting an LLM for feature recommendations, step #1

```
...
# Open the dataset
ds = pandas.read_csv(filename)
ds.columns = [c.replace(" ","") for c in ds.columns]
class_header = ds.columns[-1]
features = ds.columns[:-1]

objective = "calculating the cooling load of a building"
recommended_features = obtainRecommendations( objective, features )

# Split the dataset
Tr_X, Te_X, Tr_Y, Te_Y =
     train_test_split(ds.drop(columns=[class_header]),
        ds[class_header], train_size=0.7, random_state = run)

# Train a model
inner_model = Ridge(random_state=42)
model = M3GP(model_class = inner_model, fitnessType = "MSE",
     random_state=run, bootstrap_models = recommended_features)
model.fit(Tr_X, Tr_Y, Te_X, Te_Y)
...
```

The objective behind the *obtainRecommendations* function is, as the name implies, to obtain recommendations from the LLM system. If we look at the code in Listing 7.4, we see that this function is decomposed into four steps: (1) obtain a list of recommendations, separated by line breaks, (2A) clean the expression obtained by the LLM, (2B) verify if the expression is a valid arithmetic expression, and lastly (2C) convert the expression into a Node object (GP model). The function *add_parentheses* is also included in our implementation. It simply converts a mathematical expression into *infix notation*, as described below, so that the algorithms can parse it correctly.

As the reader may notice, most of this function cleans the answer and writes it in a format that the M3GP and M6GP models can parse. If the reader wishes to manually insert their own features into the algorithm, it should follow an *infix notation*, with spaces separating all elements, such as: a, $(a + b)$, or $(a + (b + c))$.

Listing 7.4 Prompting an LLM for feature recommendations, step #2

```
def obtainRecommendations(task, features):
    # 1 - Obtain recommendations
    features_ = ", ".join(features)
    response = gpt_client.chat.completions.create(
        model=gpt_model,
        messages=[{ "role" : "user",
         "content" : "I need a set of feature combinations that help me
              %s.Give me a list of features to add to the dataset based
              on the following input features. The combinations can be as
              many and as complex as necessary. Your answer shouldn't be
              exclusively mathematical expressions written in plain text.
              Each line in the answer should be a different mathematical
              expression. You may only use the basic arithmetic
              operations: +,-, /, and *. Available features: %s"% (task,
              features_)}],
        max_completion_tokens=5000
    )
    gen_ = response.choices[0].message.content.split("\n")
    new_models = []

    # 2 - For each recommendation in the answer:
    for gen in gen_:
        # 2A - Clean the answer
        gen = gen.replace("(","( ").replace(")" ," )").replace("*"," * "
            ).replace("/"," / " ).replace("+"," + " ).replace("-"," - "
            ).replace("  "," " )

        if len(gen)>0 and gen[0] == " ":
            gen = gen[1:]
        if len(gen)>0 and gen[-1] == " ":
            gen = gen[:-1]
        gen = gen.split(" ")

        # 2B - Verify if the answer can be parsed by M3GP
        valid = gen.count("(") == gen.count(")")
```

```
        for e in gen:
            if not e in features and not e in ["(",")","*","+","-","/"]:
                valid = False
        if valid:
            try:
                gen = add_parentheses(" ".join(gen))
            except:
                valid = False

        # 2C - If the expression is valid, convert it to a Node/Tree
        if valid:
            t = Node()
            t.create(fromString = gen.split(" "))
            new_models.append([t])
    return new_models
```

In Listing 7.5, we see the final step of this bootstrap variation. During initialization, M3GP stores the list of recommended features as *Node* objects. Since the M3GP population is initialized in the *fit* function, the *init* function does not need more modifications. In the fit function, upon initializing the population as an empty list, each Node object is converted into an individual (actual M3GP model) and appended to the population. This is the Bootstrap#1 experimental setup described in Sect. 3.2.3. In addition to inserting the recommendations as individual models into the population, this script also combines all recommendations into a single n-dimensional model. This is the Bootstrap#2 experimental setup described in the same section. Lastly, the remainder of the population consists of randomly generated models.

Listing 7.5 Prompting an LLM for feature recommendations, step #3

```
...
# inside the M3GP.__init__(..) function
self.bootstrap_models = bootstrap_models

...
# inside the M3GP.fit(..) function

self.population = []

for bsm in self.bootstrap_models:
    ind = Individual(self.operators, self.terminals, self.max_depth,
         self.model_class, self.fitnessType)
    ind.copy(bsm)
    self.population.append(ind)

ind = Individual(self.operators, self.terminals, self.max_depth,
     self.model_class, self.fitnessType)
ind.copy([t[0] for t in self.bootstrap_models]) #all feature in one
     model
self.population.append(ind)
...
```

7.2 Bloat Control Using LLMs

In continuation of Sect. 3.2.1.2, we demonstrate how to use LLMs for bloat control using the M3GP and M6GP models as examples. Of course, this method is applicable to any model as long as the user has a method to convert the model into a string that the LLM can parse, and a method to convert the answer back into a model. In this case, we use the code in Listings 7.6 and 7.7 to convert models into a string, ask for a simplification, verify if the output is a valid expression, convert it into a string our code can parse, and finally add the simplified model to the population.

Listing 7.6 Using OpenAI API to simplify GP models in the M3GP and M6GP algorithms. Function *add_parentheses* can be seen in Listing 7.7

```
import os
from openai import OpenAI
gpt_client = OpenAI(api_key=os.getenv("OPENAI_API_KEY"))
gpt_model="gpt-4.1-mini"
[...]

# Inside the GeneticOperators.py/getOffspring(...) function
offspring = ...
simplified = []
for ind in offspring:
    o_str = str(ind).split(",")
    dimensions = []
    for dim in o_str:
        try:
            response = gpt_client.chat.completions.create(
                model=gpt_model,
                messages=[{
                    "role": "user",
                    "content":"Simplify this expression and write it as
                        plain text. Reply in a single line. %s"%dim
                    }]
            )
            # Append assistant's response to maintain context
            gen = response.choices[0].message.content

            if " " in gen and (gen[0]!="(" or gen[-1]!=")"):
                gen = "(%s)"%gen
            gen = gen.replace("(","( ").replace(")" ," )").replace("  ","
             " )
            gen = gen.split(" ")

            valid = gen.count("(") == gen.count(")")
            for e in gen:
                if not e in ind.terminals and not e in "()+*/-":
                    valid = False

            if valid:
                gen = add_parentheses(" ".join(gen))
```

```
                dimensions.append(gen)
        except:
            pass # GPT provided an invalid model

    if len(dimensions) >0:
        i = Individual(ind.operators, ind.terminals, ind.max_depth, ind.model_class, ind.fitnessType)
        tmp = []
        for d in dimensions:
            t = Node()
            t.create(fromString = d.split(" "))
            tmp.append(t)
        i.copy( tmp )
        simplified.append(i)

return simplified # offspring, simplified by GPT
```

Listing 7.7 *Add_parentheses* function, used by M3GP/M6GP to format the expressions returned by GPT into something parsable by the M3GP/M6GP constructors

```
import ast
import operator

# Mapping AST operator classes to symbols
OP_SYMBOLS = {
    ast.Add: '+',
    ast.Sub: '-',
    ast.Mult: '*',
    ast.Div: '/'
}

def add_parentheses(expr: str) -> str:
    tree = ast.parse(expr, mode='eval')

    def visit(node):
        if isinstance(node, ast.BinOp):
            left = visit(node.left)
            right = visit(node.right)
            op = OP_SYMBOLS[type(node.op)]
            return f'({left} {op} {right})'
        elif isinstance(node, ast.UnaryOp):
            operand = visit(node.operand)
            op = '-' if isinstance(node.op, ast.USub) else '+'
            return f'({op}{operand})'
        else:
            return str(node.id)

    return str(visit(tree.body)).replace("(","( ").replace(")"," )")
```

The first piece of code is located within the *getOffspring* function in the M3GP and M6GP repositories. This function performs crossover or mutation on individuals, storing their offspring in the *offspring* variable. These models are multi-tree models, so to increase the likelihood that the LLM understands and performs the task successfully, we convert the model into a string and split it into individual trees for simplification. For each tree, we ask the LLM to simplify the expression and return it in plain text, avoiding LaTeX output, which it often generates. After this, as explained in Sect. 3.2.1.2, we simply verify if the output expression contains only valid terminals (dataset features), the allowed arithmetic operators (sum, division, multiplication, and subtraction) and parentheses, after, we verify if the expression has the same number of opening and closing parentheses, since LLMs tend to have issues with parentheses, based on our experience.

If the expression passes those tests, we use the *add_parentheses* function from the second code listing to format the expression into our format, thereby creating a GP tree that replaces the previous one. If the expression is invalid, we do not add it to the simplified model, which also promotes the creation of smaller model when the LLM fails to generate a valid expression, typically when working with larger trees.

7.3 vLLM

vLLM is a high-throughput inference and serving engine that exposes an https://platform.openai.com/docs/api-reference/completionsOpenAI-compatible `/v1/completions` endpoint while delivering near-hardware-saturation performance on modern GPUs. Under the hood, vLLM fuses customized attention kernels (e.g., `FLASHINFER`) with memory-efficient **prefix KV caching** and a *chunked prefill* scheduler that overlaps large prompt processing with token-by-token decoding, improving both latency and throughput. Since version 0.9, vLLM pre-allocates a configurable slice of the GPU as a KV cache; increasing the slice reduces recomputation at the cost of resident memory. Together, these design choices let a single instance stream thousands of tokens/s across hundreds of concurrent requests on commodity hardware.

7.3.1 Installation

Pinning the exact versions below ensures the API surface and kernel backends match the examples that follow:

Listing 7.8 Command-line installation with pinned versions

```
pip install vllm==0.9.1
pip install flashinfer-python==0.2.6.post1
```

CUDA and Drivers vLLM 0.9.1 ships wheels linked against PyTorch 2.7 and CUDA 12.8; verify `nvidia-smi` reports a compatible runtime before proceeding.

7.3.2 Launching the vLLM Server

The script below wraps `vllm serve` with a few sanity checks and sensible defaults. Save it as `serve_vllm.sh`, mark it executable (`chmod +x serve_vllm.sh`), and place it *on the machine that has the GPU(s)*:

Listing 7.9 Robust wrapper for `vllm serve`

```
#!/bin/bash
# Exit on error
set -e

# Default values
GPU_DEVICE=0
MEMORY_UTILIZATION=0.9
QUANTIZATION_MODE="none"

# Help message
usage() {
  echo "Usage: $0 -m <model_name> -l <model_length> [-g <gpu_device>]
       [-u <memory_utilization>] [-q <quantization_mode>] -- [additional
       args...]"
  echo ""
  echo " -m Model name (e.g., Qwen/QwQ-32B-AWQ) [required]"
  echo " -l Model length (e.g., 35488) [required]"
  echo " -g GPU device index (default: 1)"
  echo " -u GPU memory utilization (default: 0.9)"
  echo " -q Quantization mode (default: none)"
  echo ""
  echo " Use -- to separate script options from additional arguments
       that will be passed to vllm serve."
  exit 1
}

# Parse options
ADDITIONAL_ARGS=()
while [[ $# -gt 0 ]]; do
  case "$1" in
    -m) MODEL_NAME="$2"; shift 2 ;;
    -l) MODEL_LENGTH="$2"; shift 2 ;;
    -g) GPU_DEVICE="$2"; shift 2 ;;
    -u) MEMORY_UTILIZATION="$2"; shift 2 ;;
    -q) QUANTIZATION_MODE="$2"; shift 2 ;;
    --) shift; ADDITIONAL_ARGS=("$@"); break ;;
    *) ADDITIONAL_ARGS+=("$1"); shift ;;
  esac
done
```

```
[[ -z "$MODEL_NAME" || -z "$MODEL_LENGTH" ]] && usage

export CUDA_DEVICE_ORDER=PCI_BUS_ID
export CUDA_VISIBLE_DEVICES="$GPU_DEVICE"

# Opt-in to the FlashInfer attention backend
export VLLM_ATTENTION_BACKEND=FLASHINFER
export VLLM_USE_V1=0

CMD=(
  vllm serve "$MODEL_NAME"
  --generation-config "$MODEL_NAME"
  --gpu-memory-utilization "$MEMORY_UTILIZATION"
  --enable-prefix-caching
  --enable-chunked-prefill
  --max-model-len "$MODEL_LENGTH"
)

[[ "$QUANTIZATION_MODE" != "none" ]] && CMD+=(--quantization
     "$QUANTIZATION_MODE")
[[ ${#ADDITIONAL_ARGS[@]} -gt 0 ]] && CMD+=("${ADDITIONAL_ARGS[@]}")

"${CMD[@]}"
```

Step-by-Step Launch

1. **GPU host.** Copy the script to the GPU server (bare metal, Docker, or HPC node) and make sure ports `8000/tcp` (HTTP) are accessible to your client machines.
2. **Select a model.** For example, to serve `Qwen/QwQ-32B-AWQ` with a context window of 35 488 tokens on GPU 1:

```
./serve_vllm.sh -m Qwen/QwQ-32B-AWQ -l 35488 -g 1
```

3. **Monitor logs.** vLLM prints a health message such as `Uvicorn running on` http://0.0.0.0:8000 when ready.

7.3.3 *Client-Side Streaming Queries*

The Python script below demonstrates how to send streaming completion requests. It may run on the same box *or* any machine that can reach the server's IP:8000.

Listing 7.10 Minimal streaming client for vLLM

```
import requests
import json


def query_llm_streaming(prompt, history,
    server_url="http://localhost:8000",
                    max_tokens=4096, temperature=0):
    full_prompt = "\n".join(history + [f"User: {prompt}", "Assistant:"])

    endpoint = f"{server_url}/v1/completions"
    headers = {"Content-Type": "application/json"}
    payload = {
        "prompt": full_prompt,
        "max_tokens": max_tokens,
        "temperature": temperature,
        "stop": ["User:", "Assistant:"],
        "stream": True
    }

    full_response = ""
    response = requests.post(endpoint, headers=headers, json=payload,
                             stream=True)

    if response.status_code == 200:
        for line in response.iter_lines():
            if line:
                try:
                    chunk_data = json.loads(line.decode("utf-8")
                                            .lstrip("data: "))
                    if chunk_data.get("choices"):
                        text_chunk = chunk_data["choices"][0].get("text",
                            "")
                        if text_chunk:
                            print(text_chunk, end="", flush=True)
                            full_response += text_chunk
                except json.JSONDecodeError:
                    continue
                except Exception as e:
                    print(f"\nError parsing chunk: {e}")

        print() # newline after full response
        return full_response
    else:
        raise Exception(f"Error {response.status_code}: {response.text}")


def main():
    history = []
    print("Chat with your LLM! Type 'exit' to quit.\n")

    while True:
        user_input = input("You: ").strip()
```

```
        if user_input.lower() in {"exit", "quit"}:
            break

        try:
            print("LLM: ", end="", flush=True)
            reply = query_llm_streaming(user_input, history)
            print() # extra newline

            history.append(f"User: {user_input}")
            history.append(f"Assistant: {reply}")
        except Exception as e:
            print("Request failed:", e)


if __name__ == "__main__":
    main()
```

Running the Demo

1. Ensure `python-requests` is available (`pip install requests`).
2. From a shell on your client machine:

```
python chat_client.py --server_url http://<SERVER_IP>:8000
```

3. Type a prompt; partial tokens stream in real time thanks to Server-Sent Events (SSE). Each interaction is appended to `history` so the model maintains conversational context.

7.3.4 What vLLM Does Under the Hood

1. **Attention kernels.** Setting `VLLM_ATTENTION_BACKEND=FLASHINFER` switches to FlashInfer's block-sparse kernels for higher arithmetic intensity on H100/B100 GPUs.
2. **Prefix KV caching.** Reuses keys / values for identical prompt prefixes, eliminating redundant memory bandwidth on repeated queries.
3. **Chunked prefill.** Splits long prompts into smaller segments that can be scheduled alongside decode steps, increasing GPU utilization and smoothing tail latencies.
4. **Memory partitioning.** The engine pre-allocates `gpu_memory_utilization`× VRAM as a monolithic KV cache, recomputing evicted entries only when necessary.

Scaling Tips To handle heavier traffic, launch multiple vLLM instances behind a reverse proxy (Traefik, Nginx) and pin each instance to a dedicated GPU with `-gpu-memory-utilization 0.85` to leave room for driver overhead. Stateless clients can then round-robin across replicas.

With just two compact scripts and a single command, vLLM turns any CUDA-capable server into a production-grade LLM endpoint-streaming, fast, and entirely open source.

7.4 Optuna

Optuna is a cutting-edge framework for black-box optimization (BBO) that strongly supports evolutionary computation (EC) and other global optimization techniques. At its core, Optuna is designed to solve problems where the objective function is expensive, opaque, and possibly non-differentiable, common characteristics in real-world machine learning, scientific computing, and engineering design tasks.

What sets Optuna apart is its rich and extensible ecosystem for BBO. It natively supports a variety of global optimizers, beginning with the default Tree-structured Parzen Estimator (TPE), and extending to CMA-ES (see Sect. 1.2.3), differential evolution(see Sect. 1.2.3), and other advanced EC algorithms. These methods are particularly well-suited for continuous, high-dimensional, and multimodal search spaces where gradient-based methods fail or are impractical.

With the introduction of OptunaHub, the framework now provides on-demand access to an expanding catalog of community-driven samplers, many of which are rooted in EC paradigms such as genetic algorithms, evolution strategies, and hybrid metaheuristics. This modularity allows users to easily swap in optimizers tailored to the structure of their search space, be it mixed discrete-continuous, constrained, or noisy.

Optuna also offers strong support for multi-objective optimization, an essential capability in evolutionary BBO settings. It tracks and manages Pareto fronts (see Sect. 1.3) natively, making it well-suited to trade-off-heavy applications such as hyperparameter tuning in deep learning or architectural design.

Beyond samplers, Optuna facilitates early stopping (pruning) and intermediate result reporting, critical for evolutionary strategies that evaluate populations iteratively. Integration with benchmarking suites such as BBOB (black-box optimization benchmarking) further makes Optuna a serious tool for researchers evaluating EC algorithms at scale.

In short, Optuna provides a modern, extensible, and EC-friendly platform for black-box optimization, positioning it as a core tool for both applied and theoretical optimization work.

7.4.1 Installation

Before running any of the examples that follow, install the precise library versions used throughout this appendix. Pinning versions makes your results reproducible and guards against API changes.

Listing 7.11 Command-line installation with pinned versions

```
pip install optuna==4.4.0
pip install scikit-learn==1.7.0
pip install cmaes==0.11.1 # CMA-ES backend used internally by Optuna
pip install coco-experiment==2.8.1 # Required for BBOB benchmark suite
```

7.4.2 *Basic Usage: Optimizing an SVC*

The quickest way to see Optuna in action is to tune a simple `sklearn.svm.SVC` on the classic Iris dataset. Optuna samples the hyperparameters, evaluates each configuration with cross-validation, and identifies the best performer.

Listing 7.12 Optimizing an SVC with log-uniform priors

```
import optuna
from sklearn import datasets
from sklearn.model_selection import cross_val_score
from sklearn.svm import SVC
from sklearn.preprocessing import StandardScaler
from sklearn.pipeline import Pipeline
import numpy as np

def objective(trial):
    # Log-uniform sampling with suggest_float(..., log=True)
    C = trial.suggest_float("C", 1e-3, 1e3, log=True)
    gamma = trial.suggest_float("gamma", 1e-4, 1e-1, log=True)
    kernel = trial.suggest_categorical("kernel", ["rbf", "poly",
         "sigmoid"])

    model = Pipeline([
        ("scaler", StandardScaler()),
        ("svc", SVC(C=C, gamma=gamma, kernel=kernel))
    ])

    iris = datasets.load_iris()
    X, y = iris.data, iris.target
    scores = cross_val_score(model, X, y, cv=3, scoring="accuracy")
    return -scores.mean() # Optuna minimises by default

if __name__ == "__main__":
    study = optuna.create_study(direction="minimize")
    study.optimize(objective, n_trials=50)

    print("Best trial value:", study.best_trial.value)
    print("Best hyperparameters:", study.best_trial.params)
```

What Happens Under the Hood?

1. **Sampler**. The default Tree-structured Parzen Estimator (TPE) suggests `C`, `gamma`, and `kernel`.
2. **Objective**. Each suggestion is evaluated via 3-fold cross-validation; the mean accuracy is returned (flipped in sign).
3. **Study**. After `n_trials`, the study exposes `best_trial`, `trials_dataframe()`, and more for analysis.

7.4.3 Pruning Unpromising Trials

In iterative algorithms (e.g., boosting, neural nets, or here a random forest across CV folds), you can report intermediate metrics and allow Optuna to terminate weak configurations early, saving compute time.

Listing 7.13 Median pruning with intermediate reports

```
import optuna
from sklearn.datasets import load_breast_cancer
from sklearn.ensemble import RandomForestClassifier
from sklearn.model_selection import StratifiedKFold
from sklearn.metrics import accuracy_score
import numpy as np

def objective(trial):
    X, y = load_breast_cancer(return_X_y=True)

    n_estimators = trial.suggest_int("n_estimators", 10, 200)
    max_depth = trial.suggest_int("max_depth", 2, 32)

    clf = RandomForestClassifier(
        n_estimators=n_estimators,
        max_depth=max_depth,
        random_state=42
    )

    cv = StratifiedKFold(n_splits=5)
    for fold, (train, val) in enumerate(cv.split(X, y)):
        clf.fit(X[train], y[train])
        acc = accuracy_score(y[val], clf.predict(X[val]))
        trial.report(acc, step=fold) # Intermediate metric
        if trial.should_prune(): # Stop early if bad
            raise optuna.TrialPruned()

    errors = [
        1.0 - accuracy_score(y[val], clf.predict(X[val]))
        for train, val in cv.split(X, y)
    ]
    return np.mean(errors)
```

```python

if __name__ == "__main__":
    pruner = optuna.pruners.MedianPruner(
        n_startup_trials=5, n_warmup_steps=1
    )
    study = optuna.create_study(direction="minimize", pruner=pruner)
    study.optimize(objective, n_trials=50)

    print("Best parameters:", study.best_params)
    print("Best error:", study.best_value)
```

Key Ideas Include:

- *Intermediate reporting* lets Optuna compare a running trial to the median of completed trials.
- *Pruners* decide if a trial should continue; the median pruner is a good default for noisy metrics.

7.4.4 Using Alternative Samplers

Many global optimizers exist beyond TPE. CMA-ES (see Sect. 1.2.3) excels in *continuous, multidimensional* spaces; hence, we switch to a 2-D quadratic objective.

Listing 7.14 Two-dimensional search with CMA-ES

```python
import optuna

def objective(trial):
    x = trial.suggest_float("x", -10, 10)
    y = trial.suggest_float("y", -10, 10)
    return (x - 2)**2 + (y + 3)**2

if __name__ == "__main__":
    sampler = optuna.samplers.CmaEsSampler() # Requires >=2D continuous
        space
    study = optuna.create_study(direction="minimize", sampler=sampler)
    study.optimize(objective, n_trials=30)

    print("Best parameters:", study.best_params)
    print("Best value:", study.best_value)
```

Tip When your search space includes categorical or integer parameters, CMA-ES falls back to random sampling for those dimensions; consider hybrid or problem-specific samplers instead.

7.4.5 Super-Charging with OptunaHub

OptunaHub hosts community add-ons samplers, pruners, visualizers, benchmarks-installable on demand. Below is an example to load the differential evolution (see Sect. 1.2.3) algorithm from OptunaHub:

Listing 7.15 Differential Evolution via OptunaHub

```
import optuna
import math
import optunahub

def objective_rastrigin(trial: optuna.Trial) -> float:
    n = 10
    xs = [trial.suggest_float(f"x{i}", -5.12, 5.12) for i in range(n)]
    A = 10
    return A * n + sum(x**2 - A * math.cos(2 * math.pi * x) for x in xs)

mod = optunahub.load_module("samplers/differential_evolution")
DESampler = mod.DESampler

sampler = DESampler(population_size="auto", F=0.8, CR=0.9, seed=42)

if __name__ == "__main__":
    study = optuna.create_study(direction="minimize", sampler=sampler)
    study.optimize(objective_rastrigin, n_trials=1000)

    print("Best parameters:", study.best_params)
    print("Best value:", study.best_value)
```

OptunaHub supports not only widely used algorithms but also cutting-edge and recently developed ones. Its continually expanding catalog of samplers, including Bayesian, evolutionary, and multi-objective approaches, can be explored at:

https://hub.optuna.org/?q=Sampler

In addition, various benchmarks are available on OptunaHub. For example, the following listing shows an example of loading the BBOB benchmark from OptunaHub:

Listing 7.16 Running a BBOB large-scale problem

```
import optuna
import optunahub

bbob = optunahub.load_module("benchmarks/bbob_largescale")
problem = bbob.Problem(function_id=1, dimension=640) # Sphere function

if __name__ == "__main__":
    study = optuna.create_study(directions=problem.directions)
    study.optimize(problem, n_trials=200, timeout=60) # 1-minute run

    print("Best value:", study.best_value)
```

7.5 ConfigSpace

ConfigSpace is a lightweight, open-source library for *declaratively* describing search spaces—collections of hyperparameters, their domains, dependencies, and constraints. Although originally developed for the AutoML community, ConfigSpace is now widely used wherever complex configuration graphs must be sampled or enumerated: neuroevolution, hardware design, compiler flags, and even simulation pipelines.

At its heart, ConfigSpace offers:

- *Expressive hyperparameter types* (float, integer, categorical, ordinal, constant, ...) with optional log scaling
- *Conditional parameters* that appear only when high-level choices take specific values
- *Forbidden clauses* for excluding invalid or dangerous configurations
- *Fast samplers*—independent, uniform, or custom—suited to on-the-fly generation of millions of configurations
- A concise, Pythonic API that integrates cleanly with optimization frameworks such as Optuna, SMAC, or Ray Tune

Taken together, these features let practitioners share a *single source of truth* for their search spaces while delegating the actual optimization to any backend they like.

7.5.1 Installation

ConfigSpace is pure Python with a small Cython extension for speed. Install the latest stable release with `pip`:

Listing 7.17 Command-line installation

```
pip install ConfigSpace==1.2.1
```

7.5.2 Adding Simple Hyperparameters

The most common task is to declare a handful of independent hyperparameters. Each call below constructs a fresh `ConfigurationSpace`, adds *one* hyperparameter, and prints the resulting schema.

Listing 7.18 2.1 Uniform float hyperparameter

```python
import ConfigSpace as CS
import ConfigSpace.hyperparameters as CSH

cs = CS.ConfigurationSpace()
lr = CSH.UniformFloatHyperparameter("learning_rate",
                                    lower=0.0, upper=1.0, log=False)
cs.add(lr)
print(cs)
```

Listing 7.19 2.2 Uniform integer hyperparameter

```python
import ConfigSpace as CS
import ConfigSpace.hyperparameters as CSH

cs = CS.ConfigurationSpace()
depth = CSH.UniformIntegerHyperparameter("max_depth",
                                         lower=1, upper=10, log=False)
cs.add(depth)
print(cs)
```

Listing 7.20 2.3 Categorical hyperparameter

```python
import ConfigSpace as CS
import ConfigSpace.hyperparameters as CSH

cs = CS.ConfigurationSpace()
kernel = CSH.CategoricalHyperparameter("kernel",
                                       choices=["linear", "rbf", "poly"])
cs.add(kernel)
print(cs)
```

Listing 7.21 2.4 Ordinal hyperparameter

```
import ConfigSpace as CS
import ConfigSpace.hyperparameters as CSH

cs = CS.ConfigurationSpace()
num_layers = CSH.OrdinalHyperparameter("num_layers",
                                        sequence=["small", "medium", "large"])
cs.add(num_layers)
print(cs)
```

Listing 7.22 2.5 Constant hyperparameter

```
import ConfigSpace as CS
import ConfigSpace.hyperparameters as CSH

cs = CS.ConfigurationSpace()
seed = CSH.Constant("random_seed", value=42)
cs.add(seed)
print(cs)
```

Tip Every hyperparameter supports a `default_value`. Unspecified fields default to the midpoint, first choice, or given constant.

7.5.3 Sampling from the Space

Once the search space is defined, drawing configurations is a single method call. The example below samples five candidate settings for a (random forest) classifier:

Listing 7.23 Uniform sampling of five configurations

```
import ConfigSpace as CS
import ConfigSpace.hyperparameters as CSH

cs = CS.ConfigurationSpace()
cs.add([
    CSH.UniformFloatHyperparameter("lr", 1e-6, 1e-1, log=True),
    CSH.UniformIntegerHyperparameter("n_estimators", 50, 500),
    CSH.CategoricalHyperparameter("criterion", ["gini", "entropy"])
])

for i in range(5):
    config = cs.sample_configuration()
    print(f"Sample {i+1}:", config)
```

Sampling is independent and uniform by default; however, `ConfigurationSpace` also exposes `sample_configuration(size, seed)` for reproducibility or batch draws and supports user-supplied *custom samplers*.

7.5.4 *Adding Conditions*

Real-world search spaces are rarely flat. Parameters such as `momentum` (only relevant for SGD) or `beta1/beta2` (only for Adam) must be *conditional* on higher-level choices. The example mirrors this classic scenario:

Listing 7.24 Conditional hyperparameters based on `optimizer`

```
import ConfigSpace as CS
import ConfigSpace.hyperparameters as CSH
from ConfigSpace.conditions import EqualsCondition

cs = CS.ConfigurationSpace()

optimizer = CSH.CategoricalHyperparameter("optimizer",
                                          choices=["sgd", "adam"])
cs.add(optimizer)

# momentum only when optimizer == "sgd"
momentum = CSH.UniformFloatHyperparameter("momentum", lower=0.0,
     upper=0.99)
cs.add(momentum)
cs.add(EqualsCondition(child=momentum, parent=optimizer, value="sgd"))

# beta1, beta2 only when optimizer == "adam"
beta1 = CSH.UniformFloatHyperparameter("beta1", lower=0.8, upper=0.999)
beta2 = CSH.UniformFloatHyperparameter("beta2", lower=0.8, upper=0.999)
cs.add([beta1, beta2])
cs.add(EqualsCondition(child=beta1, parent=optimizer, value="adam"))
cs.add(EqualsCondition(child=beta2, parent=optimizer, value="adam"))

print(cs)
```

Key Ideas Include

- *EqualsCondition* links a *child* hyperparameter to a *parent* being equal to a specific value.
- Multiple conditions (e.g., `InCondition`, `GreaterThan`) can be combined with logical *AND/OR* for intricate graphs.

7.5.5 *Adding Forbidden Clauses*

Sometimes a naive Cartesian product of domains produces invalid points (e.g., mutually exclusive flags, unsafe hardware voltages). Forbidden clauses *remove* such regions at sampling time, guaranteeing correctness without post-filters.

Listing 7.25 Prohibiting a == 0 *and* b == 0 simultaneously

```
import ConfigSpace as CS
import ConfigSpace.hyperparameters as CSH
from ConfigSpace.forbidden import (
    ForbiddenAndConjunction, ForbiddenEqualsClause
)

cs = CS.ConfigurationSpace()

a = CSH.UniformIntegerHyperparameter("a", lower=0, upper=5)
b = CSH.UniformIntegerHyperparameter("b", lower=0, upper=5)
cs.add([a, b])

f1 = ForbiddenAndConjunction(
    ForbiddenEqualsClause(a, 0),
    ForbiddenEqualsClause(b, 0)
)
cs.add(f1)

print("Hyperparameters:", list(cs.values()))
print("Forbidden clauses:", cs.forbidden_clauses)
```

Note Sampling respects `forbidden_clauses` natively; no runtime checks are needed when evaluating configurations.

7.5.6 A Complete Example

The final listing combines *all* previous concepts into a compact yet realistic deep learning search space:

Listing 7.26 Full configuration space with conditions and forbidden clauses

```
import ConfigSpace as CS
import ConfigSpace.hyperparameters as CSH
from ConfigSpace.conditions import EqualsCondition
from ConfigSpace.forbidden import (
    ForbiddenAndConjunction, ForbiddenEqualsClause
)

def build_search_space():
    cs = CS.ConfigurationSpace()

    # Basic hyperparameters
    cs.add([
        CSH.UniformFloatHyperparameter("lr", lower=1e-5, upper=1e-1,
            log=True),
        CSH.UniformIntegerHyperparameter("batch_size", lower=16,
            upper=128, log=True),
```

```
        CSH.CategoricalHyperparameter("activation", choices=["relu",
            "tanh", "sigmoid"]),
        CSH.Constant("seed", value=2025)
    ])

    # Conditional: dropout only if activation == "relu"
    dropout = CSH.UniformFloatHyperparameter("dropout", lower=0.0,
        upper=0.5)
    cs.add(dropout)
    cs.add(EqualsCondition(child=dropout, parent=cs["activation"],
        value="relu"))

    # Forbid batch_size == 16 AND lr == 0.01
    hs_bs = cs["batch_size"]
    hs_lr = cs["lr"]
    forbidden_combo = ForbiddenAndConjunction(
        ForbiddenEqualsClause(hs_bs, 16),
        ForbiddenEqualsClause(hs_lr, 0.01)
    )
    cs.add(forbidden_combo)

    return cs

if __name__ == "__main__":
    space = build_search_space()
    print("Final Configuration Space:")
    print(space)
    print("\nSample configuration:", space.sample_configuration())
```

What Next?

1. Pass `space.sample_configuration()` to `sklearn.model_selection.ParameterSampler`, Optuna's `UniformSampler`, or any black-box optimizer.
2. Serialize spaces with `ConfigSpace.write()`, enabling language-agnostic benchmarks or large-scale cluster jobs.
3. Combine ConfigSpace with *Optuna* (see Sect. 7.4) for pruning, multi-objective optimization, and distributed studies—ConfigSpace acts as the declarative layer, and Optuna as the execution engine.

With these building blocks, you can capture almost any configuration manifold—conditional, constrained, and ready for optimization, in just a dozen lines of code.

Chapter 8
Appendix B: Case Study—LLMs for EC Operators

Evolutionary computation relies on genetic operators such as mutation, crossover, and selection to explore solution spaces and drive populations toward fitter individuals. Traditional operators treat candidate solutions as opaque bit strings or numeric vectors, applying syntactic transformations (bit flips, arithmetic perturbations, segment exchanges) without regard for the *semantics* of the representation. This agnosticism is both a strength and a weakness. While it provides generality across problem domains, it becomes a liability when solutions encode structured artifacts such as programs, mathematical expressions, or natural language prompts. In these cases, random perturbations often produce invalid or nonsensical offspring, wasting fitness evaluations and slowing convergence.

Large language models offer a compelling alternative. Trained on vast corpora of code, mathematics, and prose, LLMs can *understand* what a candidate solution means and generate variations that are syntactically valid, semantically coherent, and informed by the evolutionary context, such as current fitness, population diversity, and the problem description. This section presents a complete, runnable case study that replaces classical mutation and crossover with LLM-powered operators, using the vLLM infrastructure introduced in Sect. 7.3.

8.1 Problem Setup—Symbolic Regression

Symbolic regression seeks a closed-form mathematical expression $f(x)$ that best fits a set of observed data points $\{(x_i, y_i)\}_{i=1}^N$. Unlike numeric regression, the goal is not merely to minimize error but to *discover* an interpretable formula, making it a classic benchmark for genetic programming.

H. Iba et al., *Large Language Models and Evolutionary Computation*,
Natural Computing Series, https://doi.org/10.1007/978-981-95-8597-7_8

8.1.1 Individual Representation

Each individual in our population is a short Python lambda string that evaluates to a callable function of one variable **x**. For example:

```
"lambda x: x**2 + 3*x - 5"
"lambda x: math.sin(x) * math.exp(-x/10)"
"lambda x: (x - 2) / (x + 1) if x != -1 else 0"
```

This representation is expressive, human-readable, and lies squarely within the competence of modern LLMs, which have been trained on millions of Python snippets.

8.1.2 Fitness Function

We measure fitness as the negative mean squared error over the target data, so that higher fitness is better:

$$\text{fitness}(f) = -\frac{1}{N}\sum_{i=1}^{N}\big(f(x_i) - y_i\big)^2. \tag{8.1}$$

Invalid individuals that raise syntax errors, runtime exceptions, or division by zero on any x_i receive a large penalty fitness of -10^9.

8.1.3 Target Function

For demonstration, we use a nontrivial target that traditional genetic programming often struggles with due to nested nonlinearities:

$$y = \sin(x) \cdot e^{-x/5} + 0.1\,x. \tag{8.2}$$

We sample $N = 50$ points uniformly in $[-5, 10]$.

8.2 LLM-Based Mutation

Classical genetic programming mutation selects a random subtree and replaces it with a randomly generated subtree of bounded depth. While syntactically valid given a grammar, the new subtree is semantically arbitrary and often moves the individual away from promising regions of the search space.

An LLM-based mutator, by contrast, can be prompted with the current individual, its fitness, and optionally its fitness trajectory, the problem description, and guidance on the desired mutation magnitude to balance exploration and exploitation. The model then proposes a *semantically meaningful* edit such as simplifying a subexpression, introducing a new term, adjusting a constant, or restructuring the formula, all while preserving syntactic validity.

8.2.1 Prompt Design

Below is the mutation prompt template used throughout this case study. Placeholders in curly braces are filled at runtime. Note the explicit output format instructions, which significantly improve the reliability of JSON parsing.

Listing 8.1 Mutation prompt template (blind variant)

```
MUTATION_PROMPT_BLIND = """You are an expert mathematician and Python programmer.

TASK: Mutate the following symbolic regression candidate to improve its fitness.

CURRENT INDIVIDUAL:
{expression}

CURRENT FITNESS (higher is better, 0 is perfect):
{fitness:.6f}

TARGET BEHAVIOUR:
The function should approximate a dataset where y depends on x through a
combination of polynomial, trigonometric, and exponential terms.

MUTATION GUIDELINES:
1. Make a SINGLE meaningful change: Adjust a constant, add/remove a term,
   change an operator, or restructure a subexpression.
2. Preserve syntactic validity (must be a valid Python lambda of x).
3. You may use: +, -, *, /, **, math.sin, math.cos, math.exp, math.log,
   math.sqrt, and numeric constants.
4. Keep the expression concise (under 80 characters if possible).

===== CRITICAL OUTPUT FORMAT =====
YOU MUST OUTPUT ONLY JSON. NO OTHER TEXT WHATSOEVER.
NO explanations before the JSON.
NO explanations after the JSON.
NO reasoning or thinking.
NO code blocks or markdown.
JUST THE RAW JSON OBJECT AND NOTHING ELSE.

Format: {{"mutated": "lambda x: ..."}}

NOW OUTPUT ONLY THE JSON OBJECT:"""
```

Design Rationale The phrase "You are an expert mathematician and Python programmer" primes the model for technical precision. Including the current fitness allows the model to gauge how aggressive the mutation should be, with lower fitness suggesting bolder changes. Listing allowed operators prevents the model from introducing unsupported functions such as numpy calls. The emphatic output format instructions are essential for reliable JSON extraction, as LLMs often add explanatory text before or after structured output.

We also provide an *informed* variant of the prompt that explicitly includes the target formula. This variant helps study how much domain knowledge improves convergence, though the target is unknown in practice.

Listing 8.2 Mutation prompt template (informed variant, excerpt)

```
MUTATION_PROMPT_INFORMED = """You are an expert mathematician and
    Python programmer.
...
TARGET FORMULA (the ground truth you're trying to approximate):
y = sin(x) * exp(-x/5) + 0.1*x

TARGET BEHAVIOUR:
The function should approximate the target formula above. Notice it has:
- A product of sine and exponential decay: sin(x) * exp(-x/5)
- A small linear term: 0.1*x
...
"""
```

8.2.2 Implementation

The following functions implement the core LLM mutation operator using asynchronous HTTP requests for parallelism. We use aiohttp to enable concurrent offspring generation, which dramatically reduces wall-clock time when the vLLM server can batch multiple requests.

Listing 8.3 Asynchronous LLM query function

```
import aiohttp
import json
import re
from typing import Optional

async def query_llm_async(session: aiohttp.ClientSession,
                          prompt: str,
                          server_url: str = "http://localhost:8000",
                          max_tokens: int = 256,
                          temperature: float = 0.7) -> str:
    """Send an async non-streaming completion request to vLLM."""
```

~~~python
    endpoint = f"{server_url}/v1/completions"
    payload = {
        "prompt": prompt,
        "max_tokens": max_tokens,
        "temperature": temperature,
        "stop": ["\n\n", "```", "END", "Note:"],
    }
    timeout = aiohttp.ClientTimeout(total=120)
    async with session.post(endpoint, json=payload, timeout=timeout) as
         response:
        response.raise_for_status()
        data = await response.json()
        return data["choices"][0]["text"].strip()
~~~

The JSON extraction function must handle messy LLM output robustly, as models sometimes add explanatory text despite explicit instructions.

Listing 8.4 Robust JSON extraction for mutation responses

~~~python
def extract_json_mutation(text: str) -> Optional[dict]:
    """Extract JSON object with 'mutated' key from LLM output."""
    text = text.strip()
    text = re.sub(r'```json\s*', '', text)
    text = re.sub(r'```\s*', '', text)

    try:
        parsed = json.loads(text.strip())
        if "mutated" in parsed:
            return parsed
    except json.JSONDecodeError:
        pass

    json_patterns = [
        r'\{\s*"mutated"\s*:\s*"([^"]+)"\s*\}',
        r'"mutated"\s*:\s*"([^"]+)"',
    ]
    for pattern in json_patterns:
        match = re.search(pattern, text, re.DOTALL)
        if match:
            try:
                if pattern.startswith(r'\{'):
                    return json.loads(match.group())
                else:
                    expr = match.group(1).strip()
                    if expr.startswith('lambda'):
                        return {"mutated": expr}
            except (json.JSONDecodeError, IndexError):
                continue

    lambda_match = re.search(r'lambda\s+x\s*:\s*[^"\n;]+', text)
    if lambda_match:
        expr = lambda_match.group().strip().rstrip('",;}')
~~~

```
        if expr.startswith('lambda x:') and len(expr) > 10:
            return {"mutated": expr}
    return None
```

The main mutation function combines querying with validation and retry logic.

Listing 8.5 Asynchronous LLM mutation operator

```
import math

def validate_expression(expr: str, x_samples: list[float]) -> bool:
    """Check that expr is a valid lambda and evaluates without error."""
    if not expr.startswith("lambda x:"):
        return False
    try:
        func = eval(expr, {"math": math, "__builtins__": {}})
        for x in x_samples:
            result = func(x)
            if not isinstance(result, (int, float)) or math.isnan(result):
                return False
    except Exception:
        return False
    return True

async def llm_mutate_async(session: aiohttp.ClientSession,
                           expression: str,
                           fitness: float,
                           x_samples: list[float],
                           server_url: str = "http://localhost:8000",
                           max_retries: int = 3,
                           temperature: float = 0.7,
                           informed: bool = False) -> tuple[str, bool]:
    """
    Mutate an expression using an LLM (async version).
    Returns (mutated_expression, was_valid).
    """
    prompt_template = MUTATION_PROMPT_INFORMED if informed else
        MUTATION_PROMPT_BLIND
    prompt = prompt_template.format(expression=expression,
        fitness=fitness)

    for attempt in range(max_retries):
        try:
            temp = temperature + 0.1 * attempt
            raw_response = await query_llm_async(
                session, prompt, server_url, temperature=min(temp, 1.0)
            )

            parsed = extract_json_mutation(raw_response)
            if parsed is None:
                continue

            mutated = parsed.get("mutated", "").strip()
```

```
            if not mutated:
                continue

            if validate_expression(mutated, x_samples):
                return mutated, True

        except aiohttp.ClientError:
            pass
        except Exception:
            pass

    return expression, False
```

Key Implementation Details We start with `temperature=0.7` for creative yet focused mutations. On retries, we increase the temperature to escape local minima in the model's output distribution. Before accepting a mutated expression, we compile it and evaluate it on a sample of x values, catching syntax errors, undefined names, and numeric pathologies such as NaN or division by zero. The function returns a tuple indicating whether the mutation produced a valid offspring, allowing the evolutionary loop to track the rate of invalid offspring.

8.3 LLM-Based Crossover

Classical subtree crossover swaps randomly selected subtrees between two parents. The resulting offspring often inherit incompatible fragments, leading to bloat (excessive tree growth) or degenerate fitness. An LLM crossover operator can intelligently *combine* the best features of both parents, much like a human mathematician who studies two candidate formulas and synthesizes a superior hybrid.

8.3.1 Prompt Design

Listing 8.6 Crossover prompt template (blind variant)

```
CROSSOVER_PROMPT_BLIND = """You are an expert mathematician and Python
    programmer.

TASK: Combine two symbolic regression candidates into a superior
    offspring.

PARENT 1:
{parent1}
Fitness: {fitness1:.6f}

PARENT 2:
{parent2}
```

```
Fitness: {fitness2:.6f}

TARGET BEHAVIOUR:
The function should approximate a dataset where y depends on x through a
combination of polynomial, trigonometric, and exponential terms.

CROSSOVER GUIDELINES:
1. Analyze the strengths of each parent (terms that likely contribute
   positively to fitness).
2. Combine complementary features: e.g., take the polynomial backbone
     from
   one parent and the periodic correction from another.
3. Simplify if possible---avoid redundant or canceling terms.
4. The offspring MUST be a valid Python lambda of x.
5. You may use: +, -, *, /, **, math.sin, math.cos, math.exp, math.log,
   math.sqrt, and numeric constants.

===== CRITICAL OUTPUT FORMAT =====
YOU MUST OUTPUT ONLY JSON. NO OTHER TEXT WHATSOEVER.

Format: {{"offspring": "lambda x: ..."}}

NOW OUTPUT ONLY THE JSON OBJECT:"""
```

8.3.2 Implementation

The crossover implementation follows the same pattern as mutation, with a separate JSON extraction function for the `offspring` key.

Listing 8.7 Asynchronous LLM crossover operator

~~~
def extract_json_crossover(text: str) -> Optional[dict]:
    """Extract JSON object with 'offspring' key from LLM output."""
    text = text.strip()
    text = re.sub(r'```json\s*', '', text)
    text = re.sub(r'```\s*', '', text)

    try:
        parsed = json.loads(text.strip())
        if "offspring" in parsed:
            return parsed
    except json.JSONDecodeError:
        pass

    match = re.search(r'\{\s*"offspring"\s*:\s*"([^"]+)"\s*\}', text)
    if match:
        try:
            return json.loads(match.group())
        except json.JSONDecodeError:
~~~

```
            pass

    lambda_match = re.search(r'lambda\s+x\s*:\s*[^"\n;]+', text)
    if lambda_match:
        expr = lambda_match.group().strip().rstrip('",;}')
        if expr.startswith('lambda x:'):
            return {"offspring": expr}

    return None

async def llm_crossover_async(session: aiohttp.ClientSession,
                              parent1: str, fitness1: float,
                              parent2: str, fitness2: float,
                              x_samples: list[float],
                              server_url: str = "http://localhost:8000",
                              max_retries: int = 3,
                              temperature: float = 0.5,
                              informed: bool = False) -> tuple[str, bool]:
    """
    Perform crossover between two parents using an LLM (async version).
    Returns (offspring, was_valid).
    """
    prompt_template = CROSSOVER_PROMPT_INFORMED if informed else
         CROSSOVER_PROMPT_BLIND
    prompt = prompt_template.format(
        parent1=parent1, fitness1=fitness1,
        parent2=parent2, fitness2=fitness2
    )
    for attempt in range(max_retries):
        try:
            temp = temperature + 0.1 * attempt
            raw_response = await query_llm_async(
                session, prompt, server_url, temperature=min(temp, 1.0)
            )
            parsed = extract_json_crossover(raw_response)
            if parsed is None:
                continue

            offspring = parsed.get("offspring", "").strip()
            if not offspring:
                continue

            if validate_expression(offspring, x_samples):
                return offspring, True

        except aiohttp.ClientError:
            pass
        except Exception:
            pass

    return (parent1 if fitness1 >= fitness2 else parent2), False
```

Crossover Versus Mutation Temperature We use a lower default temperature (0.5) for crossover than for mutation (0.7). Crossover should *recombine* existing genetic material rather than invent entirely new structures, and a cooler temperature encourages the model to stay close to the parents.

8.4 Traditional Baseline Operators

To provide a fair comparison, we implement traditional GP-style operators that operate at the syntactic level without semantic understanding.

Listing 8.8 Traditional mutation operator

```
import random

def traditional_mutate(expression: str,
                       x_samples: list[float]) -> tuple[str, bool]:
    """
    Traditional GP-style mutation: randomly modify constants or
        operators.
    Returns (mutated_expression, was_valid).
    """
    mutations = [
        lambda e: re.sub(r'(\d+\.?\d*)',
            lambda m: str(float(m.group()) * random.uniform(0.5, 2.0)),
                e, count=1),
        lambda e: re.sub(r'(\d+\.?\d*)',
            lambda m: str(float(m.group()) + random.uniform(-2, 2)), e,
                count=1),
        lambda e: e.replace('+', '-', 1) if random.random() > 0.5
            else e.replace('-', '+', 1),
        lambda e: e.replace('*', '/', 1) if random.random() > 0.5
            else e.replace('/', '*', 1),
        lambda e: e.replace('math.sin', 'math.cos', 1) if 'math.sin' in e
            else e.replace('math.cos', 'math.sin', 1),
        lambda e: e + " + " + str(round(random.uniform(-1, 1), 2))
            if len(e) < 60 else e,
    ]

    for _ in range(5):
        mutation_fn = random.choice(mutations)
        try:
            mutated = mutation_fn(expression)
            if mutated != expression and validate_expression(mutated,
                 x_samples):
                return mutated, True
        except Exception:
            continue

    return expression, False
```

Listing 8.9 Traditional crossover operator

```
def traditional_crossover(parent1: str, parent2: str,
                          x_samples: list[float]) -> tuple[str, bool]:
    """
    Traditional GP-style crossover: combine parts of two expressions.
    Returns (offspring, was_valid).
    """
    p1_body = parent1.replace("lambda x:", "").strip()
    p2_body = parent2.replace("lambda x:", "").strip()

    crossover_strategies = [
        lambda: f"lambda x: ({p1_body}) + ({p2_body})"
            if len(p1_body) + len(p2_body) < 50 else parent1,
        lambda: f"lambda x: ({p1_body}) * 0.5 + ({p2_body}) * 0.5",
        lambda: f"lambda x: ({p1_body}) * ({p2_body})"
            if len(p1_body) < 30 and len(p2_body) < 30 else parent1,
        lambda: parent1 if random.random() > 0.5 else parent2,
    ]

    for _ in range(5):
        strategy = random.choice(crossover_strategies)
        try:
            offspring = strategy()
            if validate_expression(offspring, x_samples):
                return offspring, True
        except Exception:
            continue

    return (parent1 if random.random() > 0.5 else parent2), False
```

We also include a random search baseline that generates random expressions from templates, providing a lower bound on expected performance.

Listing 8.10 Random expression generator for baseline

```
def generate_random_expression(x_samples: list[float],
                               max_attempts: int = 100) -> str:
    """Generate a random valid expression."""
    templates = [
        "lambda x: x",
        "lambda x: x**2",
        "lambda x: math.sin(x)",
        "lambda x: math.exp(-x)",
        "lambda x: x + {c}",
        "lambda x: math.sin(x) * {c}",
        "lambda x: math.sin(x) * math.exp(-x * {c})",
        "lambda x: math.sin(x) * math.exp(-x / {d}) + x * {c}",
        "lambda x: {c} * math.sin(x) + {d} * x",
    ]

    for _ in range(max_attempts):
        template = random.choice(templates)
```

```
        c = round(random.uniform(-2, 2), 2)
        d = round(random.uniform(1, 10), 1)
        expr = template.format(c=c, d=d)

        if validate_expression(expr, x_samples):
            return expr

    return "lambda x: x"
```

8.5 Putting It Together: A Parallelized Evolutionary Loop

The script below integrates all operators into a parallelized experimental framework. It supports four comparison methods: random search, traditional GP, LLM operators without target knowledge (blind), and LLM operators with target knowledge (informed). The use of `asyncio` enables concurrent generation of offspring, fully leveraging vLLM's batching capabilities.

Listing 8.11 Data structures for experiment tracking

```
from dataclasses import dataclass, field
from typing import Optional

@dataclass
class RunResult:
    method: str
    run_id: int
    seed: int
    best_fitness: float
    best_expression: str
    final_avg_fitness: float
    generations_to_best: int
    is_exact_match: bool
    expression_length: int
    invalid_offspring_count: int
    total_offspring_count: int
    fitness_history: list = field(default_factory=list)
    elapsed_time: float = 0.0

@dataclass
class ExperimentSummary:
    method: str
    num_runs: int
    best_fitness_mean: float
    best_fitness_std: float
    best_fitness_max: float
    exact_match_rate: float
    avg_expression_length: float
    avg_invalid_rate: float
    avg_time_per_run: float
```

Listing 8.12 Parallel offspring generation

```
async def generate_offspring_llm(session: aiohttp.ClientSession,
                                 population: list[str],
                                 fitnesses: list[float],
                                 xs: list[float],
                                 ys: list[float],
                                 x_samples: list[float],
                                 crossover_rate: float,
                                 mutation_rate: float,
                                 server_url: str,
                                 informed: bool = False) -> tuple[str, bool]:
    """Generate a single offspring using LLM operators (async)."""
    is_valid = True

    if random.random() < crossover_rate:
        p1 = tournament_select(population, fitnesses)
        p2 = tournament_select(population, fitnesses)
        f1 = evaluate_fitness(p1, xs, ys)
        f2 = evaluate_fitness(p2, xs, ys)

        child, valid = await llm_crossover_async(
            session, p1, f1, p2, f2, x_samples,
            server_url=server_url, informed=informed
        )
        if not valid:
            is_valid = False
    else:
        child = tournament_select(population, fitnesses)

    if random.random() < mutation_rate:
        child_fit = evaluate_fitness(child, xs, ys)
        child, valid = await llm_mutate_async(
            session, child, child_fit, x_samples,
            server_url=server_url, informed=informed
        )
        if not valid:
            is_valid = False

    return child, is_valid
```

The main evolutionary loop dispatches to the appropriate operator set based on the method parameter and collects detailed statistics for analysis.

Listing 8.13 Core evolutionary loop (abbreviated)

```
async def run_single_experiment_async(
        method: str,
        run_id: int,
        seed: int,
        generations: int = 30,
        pop_size: int = 10,
        mutation_rate: float = 0.8,
```

```
        crossover_rate: float = 0.5,
        elite_size: int = 2,
        server_url: str = "http://localhost:8000",
        informed: bool = False
) -> RunResult:
    """Run a single evolutionary experiment with specified method."""

    random.seed(seed)
    xs, ys = generate_dataset()
    x_samples = xs[::5]

    population = INITIAL_POPULATION[:pop_size].copy()
    random.shuffle(population)
    fitnesses = [evaluate_fitness(ind, xs, ys) for ind in population]

    best_expr, best_fit, best_gen = population[0], fitnesses[0], 0
    fitness_history = []
    invalid_count, total_offspring = 0, 0

    session = None
    if method in ["llm_blind", "llm_informed"]:
        session = aiohttp.ClientSession()

    try:
        for gen in range(1, generations + 1):
            # Track best individual
            gen_best_idx = max(range(len(fitnesses)), key=lambda i:
                 fitnesses[i])
            if fitnesses[gen_best_idx] > best_fit:
                best_fit = fitnesses[gen_best_idx]
                best_expr = population[gen_best_idx]
                best_gen = gen

            fitness_history.append({
                "generation": gen,
                "best_fitness": best_fit,
                "avg_fitness": sum(fitnesses) / len(fitnesses)
            })

            # Elitism
            sorted_indices = sorted(range(len(fitnesses)),
                                   key=lambda i: fitnesses[i], reverse=True)
            elites = [population[i] for i in sorted_indices[:elite_size]]

            # Generate offspring based on method
            if method in ["llm_blind", "llm_informed"]:
                num_needed = pop_size - elite_size
                total_offspring += num_needed

                tasks = [
                    generate_offspring_llm(
                        session, population, fitnesses, xs, ys, x_samples,
                        crossover_rate, mutation_rate, server_url,
                        informed=(method == "llm_informed")
```

```
                    )
                    for _ in range(num_needed)
                ]
                results = await asyncio.gather(*tasks)
                offspring = [child for child, _ in results]
                invalid_count += sum(1 for _, valid in results if not valid)

            elif method == "random_search":
                offspring = [generate_random_expression(x_samples)
                             for _ in range(pop_size - elite_size)]
                total_offspring += len(offspring)

            else: # traditional
                offspring = []
                while len(offspring) < pop_size - elite_size:
                    total_offspring += 1
                    # ... traditional operator logic ...
                    offspring.append(child)

            population = elites + offspring
            fitnesses = [evaluate_fitness(ind, xs, ys) for ind in population]

    finally:
        if session:
            await session.close()

    return RunResult(
        method=method, run_id=run_id, seed=seed,
        best_fitness=best_fit, best_expression=best_expr,
        # ... remaining fields ...
    )
```

Running the Experiments First, ensure the vLLM server is running as described in Sect. 7.3.2. The experiment script accepts command-line arguments to configure the number of runs, generations, population size, and which methods to evaluate.

```
pip install aiohttp matplotlib
python run_experiments.py --server_url http://<VLLM_HOST>:8000 --runs 5 --generations 30
```

The script outputs per-generation statistics to the console, generates optimization history plots, and saves complete results to a JSON file for further analysis.

8.6 Expected Experimental Results

We designed the experiment to compare four methods across five independent runs each, with 30 generations and a population of 10 individuals. All methods use identical initialization, selection pressure, and fitness evaluation; only the genetic operators differ.

8.6.1 Expected Results

Table 8.1 presents the expected outcomes based on the characteristics of each method.

Expected Observations Random search serves as a lower bound, occasionally stumbling upon reasonable approximations, but is unable to refine them systematically. A traditional GP should improve substantially over random search through iterative refinement, but syntactic operators struggle with the nested structure of the target function and often produce bloated expressions.

LLM operators in blind mode (without knowledge of the target formula) are expected to achieve roughly 20 times better final fitness than traditional GP. The model's semantic understanding allows it to make targeted improvements, such as introducing exponential decay when the residual pattern suggests it, or adjusting coefficients to reduce error. The exact match rate of around 40% reflects cases where the LLM successfully reconstructs the complete target structure.

LLM operators in informed mode (with the target formula provided in the prompt) represent an upper bound on performance. With explicit knowledge of the goal, the model can directly guide evolution toward the known solution, achieving exact matches in most runs. This variant is primarily helpful for validating the experimental setup and understanding the gap between blind and oracle-assisted search.

Table 8.1 Expected comparison of methods on the symbolic regression benchmark. Fitness is negative MSE (higher is better). The exact column indicates the expected rate at which methods discover expressions algebraically equivalent to the target

Method	Best fitness	Best (std)	Exact	Avg. length	Invalid
Random search	− 0.25	0.15	0%	28.0	0%
Traditional GP	− 0.03	0.02	0%	47.2	12%
LLM (blind)	− 0.001	0.002	40%	31.6	2%
LLM (informed)	− 0.0001	0.0003	80%	29.4	1%

[Optimization history plot would appear here] Expected patterns: Random Search: Flat line with occasional jumps Traditional GP: Gradual improvement with plateaus LLM (Blind): Rapid early improvement, then refinement LLM (Informed): Near-immediate convergence to optimum

Fig. 8.1 Expected optimization trajectories showing best fitness over generations for each method (mean ± std over five runs)

8.6.2 Expected Evolutionary Dynamics

Figure 8.1 illustrates the expected convergence behavior of each method.

Below is an expected evolutionary trace from the LLM (Blind) method, showing how the model progressively refines candidates:

Listing 8.14 Expected evolutionary trajectory for LLM (Blind)

```
Gen 1 | lambda x: math.sin(x) | Fitness: -0.287
Gen 5 | lambda x: math.sin(x) + 0.1*x | Fitness: -0.041
Gen 12 | lambda x: math.sin(x) * math.exp(-x/6) + 0.1*x | Fitness:
    -0.003
Gen 18 | lambda x: math.sin(x) * math.exp(-x/5) + 0.1*x | Fitness:
    -0.000
```

The LLM introduces the exponential decay term around generation 12 and then fine-tunes the constant from $-x/6$ to $-x/5$ by generation 18. This level of targeted refinement is challenging to achieve with random syntactic mutations.

8.7 Extensions and Best Practices

8.7.1 Prompt Engineering Tips

Including negative examples can significantly improve output quality. Showing the model a few "bad" mutations and explaining why they are undesirable help it avoid common pitfalls. For instance, one might add to the prompt examples like "adding a constant that cancels, such as lambda x: x + 5 - 5" or "trivial identity changes, such as lambda x: x * 1," and instruct the model to avoid such mutations.

In later generations, appending a summary of the population's best expression and fitness history provides the model with a sense of evolutionary progress and helps it avoid regressive mutations. If the target domain is known, such as physics or finance, priming the model with relevant terminology and functional forms can further improve results. Phrases like "common patterns include Gaussian decay, logistic growth, and harmonic oscillation" give the model practical prior knowledge.

The emphatic output format instructions demonstrated in our prompts (the "CRITICAL OUTPUT FORMAT" section) are essential for reliable JSON parsing. Without these instructions, models frequently add explanatory text that breaks automated extraction.

8.7.2 Handling LLM Failures Gracefully

LLMs are stochastic and may occasionally produce invalid or unhelpful output. As implemented above, retrying with a higher temperature often dislodges the model from degenerate completions. If LLM-based mutation fails after all retries, applying a lightweight traditional mutation such as perturbing a numeric constant by plus or minus 10% provides a useful fallback instead of returning the individual unchanged.

When generating many offspring in parallel, validating the entire batch and re-querying the LLM only for invalid entries amortize the cost of retries. Caching LLM responses keyed by expression, fitness, and operator type allows reuse when the same individual is mutated twice in a run, saving inference time.

8.7.3 Cost and Latency Considerations

LLM inference is orders of magnitude slower than executing a handful of Python instructions. Several mitigation strategies are available.

The parallelized implementation using `asyncio` demonstrated in this case study fully leverages vLLM's continuous batching. By submitting all offspring requests concurrently, we achieve much better GPU utilization than sequential requests would allow. Using a smaller 7B-parameter model in early generations for broad exploration, and then switching to a 32B or larger model for refinement in later generations, balances cost and quality.

Reserving LLM operators for "stuck" individuals whose fitness has remained unchanged for several generations, while applying cheap traditional operators otherwise, provides an adaptive approach. Structuring prompts so that the preamble, which contains the role, guidelines, and allowed operators, is identical across requests enables vLLM's prefix caching to reuse cached KV entries, reducing per-query latency.

8.7.4 Beyond Symbolic Regression

The techniques demonstrated generalize to any domain where solutions have a structure that LLMs can understand. In program synthesis, one can evolve Python functions to pass a test suite, using LLM-based mutation to fix bugs or refactor code. Prompt evolution applies these operators to evolve prompts for a downstream LLM task, such as classification, by using the LLM mutator to edit the prompt text to improve accuracy.

Hardware design presents another opportunity, evolving Verilog or VHDL modules where the LLM adjusts timing constraints or refactors logic. In molecule design, evolving SMILES strings with a chemistry-tuned LLM allows proposing substitutions that preserve drug likeness.

In each case, the key is to craft prompts that communicate the representation, the fitness landscape, and domain-specific constraints. This enables the LLM to act as a knowledgeable domain expert rather than a random bit flipper.

Chapter 9
Appendix C: Case Study—LLMs for AutoML

Traditional AutoML systems operate within rigidly defined search spaces where a human expert must enumerate which hyperparameters to tune, which architectures to consider, and which preprocessing steps to apply. This manual specification creates a fundamental bottleneck since the quality of the discovered solution is bounded by the creativity and foresight of the search space designer.

This case study introduces a paradigm shift called *LLM-driven AutoML*, where large language models serve as both the *designer* of the search space and the *generator* of executable machine learning programs. Rather than selecting from pre-implemented components, the LLM writes complete training scripts tailored to each configuration sampled by the optimizer. This approach transcends traditional hyperparameter tuning, enabling simultaneous optimization of hyperparameters (learning rates, batch sizes, weight decay, momentum coefficients), architectures (network depth, width, block types, attention mechanisms), data pipelines (augmentation strategies, normalization schemes, sampling policies), and training recipes (optimizer selection, scheduler configurations, regularization techniques).

We demonstrate this approach on ImageNet-100, a 100-class subset of the full ImageNet dataset that retains sufficient complexity while enabling tractable experimentation. The pipeline integrates vLLM (Sect. 7.3) for high-throughput inference, ConfigSpace (Sect. 7.5) for structured search space representation, and Optuna (Sect. 7.4) for sample-efficient black-box optimization.

9.1 System Architecture

Figure 9.1 illustrates the complete LLM-AutoML pipeline. The system operates in three phases.

H. Iba et al., *Large Language Models and Evolutionary Computation*,
Natural Computing Series, https://doi.org/10.1007/978-981-95-8597-7_9

```
+-------------------+      +-------------------+      +-------------------+
|  Task Description |      |  LLM (vLLM)       |      |  ConfigSpace      |
|  "Train a CNN on  | ---> |  Generates JSON   | ---> |  Search Space     |
|   ImageNet-100"   |      |  search space     |      |  Definition       |
+-------------------+      +-------------------+      +-------------------+
                                                              |
                                    +-------------------------+
                                    |
                                    v
                           +-------------------+
                           |  Optuna Study     |
                           |  (TPE/CMA-ES)     |
                           +-------------------+
                                    |
              +---------------------+---------------------+
              |                                           |
              v                                           v
     +-------------------+                       +-------------------+
     |  Sample Config    |                       |  Update Model     |
     |  from Space       |                       |  & Prune          |
     +-------------------+                       +-------------------+
              |                                           ^
              v                                           |
     +-------------------+      +-------------------+     |
     |  LLM (vLLM)       |      |  Sandboxed        |     |
     |  Generates        | ---> |  Execution        | ----+
     |  Training Script  |      |  & Evaluation     |
     +-------------------+      +-------------------+
```

Fig. 9.1 LLM-AutoML pipeline showing how the LLM designs the search space once, then generates executable training scripts for each Optuna trial

In the first phase (search space design), given a natural language description of the machine learning task, an LLM analyzes the requirements. It generates a structured JSON schema defining the hyperparameters, architectures, and training strategies to explore. This schema is then parsed into a ConfigSpace object.

In the second phase (program generation), for each configuration sampled by Optuna, the LLM receives the sampled values and generates a complete, executable Python training script. The script includes data loading, model definition, training loop, and evaluation logic.

In the third phase (evaluation and optimization), the generated script is executed in a sandboxed environment. Validation metrics are reported to Optuna, which updates its surrogate model and samples the following configuration. Pruning terminates unpromising trials early.

The key insight is that LLMs encode vast knowledge about effective ML practices, knowledge that would otherwise require months of manual experimentation to distil into a search space. By querying this knowledge programmatically, we bootstrap high-quality search spaces from natural language task descriptions.

9.2 Prerequisites and Setup

Before proceeding, ensure that vLLM, Optuna, and ConfigSpace are installed as described in Sects. 7.3.1, 7.4.1, and 7.5.1. Additionally, please install the following dependencies for the LLM-AutoML pipeline itself.

Listing 9.1 Core dependencies for LLM-AutoML

```
pip install torch==2.7.0 torchvision==0.22.0 --break-system-packages
pip install timm==1.0.15 --break-system-packages
pip install datasets==3.6.0 --break-system-packages
pip install requests --break-system-packages
```

Since the LLM will generate training scripts that use various deep learning libraries, it is essential to preinstall the standard packages that frequently appear in generated code. This prevents runtime failures due to missing imports.

Listing 9.2 Common libraries used in LLM-generated training scripts

```
pip install numpy scipy pillow --break-system-packages
pip install albumentations --break-system-packages
pip install tensorboard wandb --break-system-packages
pip install einops --break-system-packages
```

We assume a vLLM server is running with a capable reasoning model such as `Qwen/Qwen3-32B-AWQ` as described in Sect. 7.3.2.

```
./serve_vllm.sh -m Qwen/Qwen3-32B-AWQ -l 35488 -g 0
```

For ImageNet-100, we use the `imagenet-100` subset available via Hugging Face or prepare it manually from the full ImageNet dataset by selecting 100 classes.

9.3 Step 1: LLM-Driven Search Space Design

The first phase leverages the LLM's knowledge to design a comprehensive search space. Rather than manually specifying which hyperparameters to tune, we prompt the LLM with a task description and ask it to propose a structured search space.

9.3.1 Prompt Engineering for Search Space Generation

The prompt must be carefully designed to elicit structured, machine-parseable output. We request JSON in the JSON format with explicit type annotations compatible with ConfigSpace.

Listing 9.3 Prompt template for search space generation

```
SEARCH_SPACE_PROMPT = """You are an expert machine learning engineer.
    Given a task description, design a comprehensive hyperparameter
    search space for AutoML optimization.

TASK: {task_description}

Output a JSON object with the following structure:
{{
  "task_analysis": "Brief analysis of the task and key considerations",
  "hyperparameters": [
    {{
      "name": "parameter_name",
      "type": "float" | "int" | "categorical",
      "low": <number>,
      "high": <number>,
      "log": true | false,
      "choices": ["a", "b"],
      "default": <value>,
      "description": "Why this parameter matters"
    }}
  ],
  "conditionals": [
    {{
      "child": "child_param_name",
      "parent": "parent_param_name",
      "parent_value": "value_that_activates_child"
    }}
  ],
  "forbidden": [
    {{
      "clauses": [
        {{"param": "name1", "value": "val1"}},
        {{"param": "name2", "value": "val2"}}
      ],
      "reason": "Why this combination is forbidden"
    }}
  ]
}}

Requirements:
1. Include 10--20 hyperparameters covering architecture, optimization,
    regularization, and data augmentation.
2. Use a log scale for learning rates and weight decay.
```

```
3. Add conditionals for optimizer-specific parameters (e.g., momentum
   only for SGD).
4. Forbid nonsensical combinations (e.g., very deep networks with very
   high learning rates).
5. Consider the specific characteristics of the dataset and task.
6. Include modern architectures: ResNet, EfficientNet, ConvNeXt, vision
   transformer variants.
7. Include data augmentation options: MixUp, CutMix, RandAugment, and
   label smoothing.

Output ONLY valid JSON, no additional text or markdown formatting."""
```

9.3.2 *Querying vLLM for Search Space Generation*

The following code sends the prompt to the vLLM server and parses the response. The `VLLMClient` class supports both blocking and streaming queries, with streaming preferred for longer responses.

Listing 9.4 vLLM client for LLM queries

```python
import requests
import json
import re


class VLLMClient:
    """Client for interacting with vLLM server."""

    def __init__(self, server_url="http://localhost:8000"):
        self.server_url = server_url.rstrip("/")
        self.endpoint = f"{self.server_url}/v1/completions"

    def health_check(self):
        """Check if vLLM server is running."""
        try:
            response = requests.get(f"{self.server_url}/health",
                timeout=5)
            return response.status_code == 200
        except requests.RequestException:
            return False

    def query(self, prompt, max_tokens=4096, temperature=0.3,
        stream=False):
        """Send a prompt to vLLM and return the response."""
        payload = {
            "prompt": prompt,
            "max_tokens": max_tokens,
            "temperature": temperature,
            "stream": stream
```

```
        }

        if stream:
            return self._query_streaming(payload)
        else:
            return self._query_blocking(payload)

    def _query_blocking(self, payload):
        """Non-streaming query."""
        response = requests.post(
            self.endpoint,
            json=payload,
            headers={"Content-Type": "application/json"},
            timeout=300
        )

        if response.status_code == 200:
            result = response.json()
            return result["choices"][0]["text"].strip()
        else:
            raise Exception(f"vLLM error {response.status_code}: {response.text}")

    def _query_streaming(self, payload):
        """Streaming query for long responses."""
        payload["stream"] = True
        response = requests.post(
            self.endpoint,
            json=payload,
            headers={"Content-Type": "application/json"},
            stream=True,
            timeout=300
        )

        text = ""
        if response.status_code == 200:
            for line in response.iter_lines():
                if line:
                    try:
                        chunk = line.decode("utf-8").lstrip("data: ")
                        if chunk.strip() == "[DONE]":
                            break
                        data = json.loads(chunk)
                        if data.get("choices"):
                            text += data["choices"][0].get("text", "")
                    except (json.JSONDecodeError, KeyError):
                        continue
        else:
            raise Exception(f"vLLM error {response.status_code}: {response.text}")

        return text.strip()
```

The search space generation function extracts the JSON from the LLM response, handling various output formats, including markdown code fences.

Listing 9.5 Generating search space via LLM

````python
def extract_json(text):
    """Extract JSON object from LLM response, handling various formats."""
    text = re.sub(r"```json\s*\n?", "", text)
    text = re.sub(r"```\s*\n?", "", text)
    text = text.strip()

    start = text.find("{")
    if start == -1:
        raise ValueError("No JSON object found in response")

    depth = 0
    for i, char in enumerate(text[start:], start):
        if char == "{":
            depth += 1
        elif char == "}":
            depth -= 1
            if depth == 0:
                try:
                    return json.loads(text[start:i + 1])
                except json.JSONDecodeError as e:
                    raise ValueError(f"Invalid JSON: {e}")

    raise ValueError("Unbalanced braces in JSON")


def generate_search_space(task_description, client):
    """Generate a search space JSON from a task description using LLM."""
    prompt = SEARCH_SPACE_PROMPT.format(task_description=task_description)
    response = client.query(prompt, max_tokens=8192, temperature=0.3)
    return extract_json(response)
````

9.3.3 *Converting JSON to ConfigSpace*

The following utility converts the LLM-generated JSON into a ConfigSpace object, handling hyperparameters, conditionals, and forbidden clauses.

Listing 9.6 Parsing LLM output into ConfigSpace

```python
import ConfigSpace as CS
import ConfigSpace.hyperparameters as CSH
from ConfigSpace.conditions import EqualsCondition
```

```
from ConfigSpace.forbidden import ForbiddenAndConjunction,
    ForbiddenEqualsClause


def json_to_configspace(search_space_json):
    """Convert LLM-generated JSON to a ConfigSpace object."""
    cs = CS.ConfigurationSpace()
    hp_map = {}

    for hp in search_space_json.get("hyperparameters", []):
        name = hp["name"]
        hp_type = hp["type"]
        default = hp.get("default")

        try:
            if hp_type == "float":
                param = CSH.UniformFloatHyperparameter(
                    name=name,
                    lower=float(hp["low"]),
                    upper=float(hp["high"]),
                    default_value=float(default) if default is not None
                        else None,
                    log=hp.get("log", False)
                )
            elif hp_type == "int":
                param = CSH.UniformIntegerHyperparameter(
                    name=name,
                    lower=int(hp["low"]),
                    upper=int(hp["high"]),
                    default_value=int(default) if default is not None else
                        None,
                    log=hp.get("log", False)
                )
            elif hp_type == "categorical":
                choices = hp["choices"]
                param = CSH.CategoricalHyperparameter(
                    name=name,
                    choices=choices,
                    default_value=default if default in choices else None
                )
            else:
                continue

            cs.add(param)
            hp_map[name] = param

        except Exception as e:
            logging.warning(f"Failed to add hyperparameter {name}: {e}")

    for cond in search_space_json.get("conditionals", []):
        try:
            child_name = cond["child"]
            parent_name = cond["parent"]
            parent_value = cond["parent_value"]
```

```

            if child_name in hp_map and parent_name in hp_map:
                cs.add(EqualsCondition(
                    child=hp_map[child_name],
                    parent=hp_map[parent_name],
                    value=parent_value
                ))
        except Exception as e:
            logging.warning(f"Failed to add conditional: {e}")

    for forbidden in search_space_json.get("forbidden", []):
        try:
            clauses = []
            for clause in forbidden.get("clauses", []):
                param_name = clause["param"]
                value = clause["value"]
                if param_name in hp_map:
                    clauses.append(ForbiddenEqualsClause(hp_map[param_name],
                        value))

            if len(clauses) >= 2:
                cs.add(ForbiddenAndConjunction(*clauses))
        except Exception as e:
            logging.warning(f"Failed to add forbidden clause: {e}")

    return cs
```

This approach ensures that the LLM's domain knowledge about reasonable ranges, conditional dependencies, and invalid combinations is faithfully encoded in the optimizer's search space.

9.4 Step 2: LLM-Based Program Generation

Given a configuration sampled from the search space, the LLM generates a complete, executable training script. This is the key innovation: Rather than interpolating pre-written templates, the LLM writes bespoke code that implements the exact architecture, optimizer, and training recipe specified by the configuration.

9.4.1 Prompt Template for Code Generation

The prompt provides context about the task, the sampled configuration, and strict requirements for the output format.

Listing 9.7 Prompt template for training script generation

```
CODE_GENERATION_PROMPT = """You are an expert PyTorch engineer. Generate a complete, executable training script for image classification.

TASK: Image classification on ImageNet-100 (100 classes)
DATA LOCATION: {data_dir} with 'train' and 'val' subdirectories
TRAINING EPOCHS: {max_epochs}

HYPERPARAMETER CONFIGURATION:
{config_json}

CRITICAL REQUIREMENTS:
1. Output ONLY Python code---no explanations, no markdown, no comments before the code.
2. Start directly with ‘‘import’’ statements.
3. Use PyTorch and timm (PyTorch Image Models) library.
4. Implement the EXACT hyperparameters from the configuration above.
5. Use mixed precision training (torch.cuda.amp) for efficiency.
6. Print validation accuracy after each epoch as: print(f"EPOCH {{epoch}} ACCURACY: {{accuracy:.2f}}").
7. At the end print: print(f"BEST ACCURACY: {{best_accuracy:.2f}}").
8. Handle any missing optional parameters with sensible defaults.
9. Include proper error handling for data loading.
10. The script must be self-contained and complete.

Generate the complete Python script now:"""
```

9.4.2 Code Extraction and Validation

The code generation process includes robust extraction of Python code from LLM responses, which may consist of markdown formatting, explanatory text, or other artifacts.

Listing 9.8 Extracting Python code from LLM response

~~~
def extract_python_code(text):
    """Extract Python code from LLM response, handling various formats."""
    python_blocks = re.findall(r'```python\s*\n(.*?)```', text, re.DOTALL)
    if python_blocks:
        return max(python_blocks, key=len).strip()

    code_blocks = re.findall(r'```\s*\n(.*?)```', text, re.DOTALL)
    if code_blocks:
        python_like = [b for b in code_blocks if 'import ' in b or 'def ' in b]
~~~

```
        if python_like:
            return max(python_like, key=len).strip()

    lines = text.strip().split('\n')

    start_idx = 0
    for i, line in enumerate(lines):
        if line.strip().startswith(('import ', 'from ', '#!/', '#!',
            '"""', "'''")):
            start_idx = i
            break

    end_idx = len(lines)
    for i in range(len(lines) - 1, start_idx, -1):
        line = lines[i].strip()
        if line and not line.startswith('#'):
            if any(line.startswith(kw) for kw in ['import ', 'from ',
                'def ', 'class ',
                                                   'if ', 'for ', 'while ',
                                                       'with ',
                                                   'try:', 'except', 'return ',
                                                       'print(',
                                                   ' ', '\t', ')', ']', '}',
                                                       '"""', "'''"]):
                end_idx = i + 1
                break
            elif line.endswith((':', ')', ']', '}', ',', '"', "'")):
                end_idx = i + 1
                break

    code = '\n'.join(lines[start_idx:end_idx])
    return code.strip()
```

Comprehensive validation ensures the generated code meets all requirements before execution. The validation checks syntax, required imports, CUDA usage, the presence of a training function, and screens for dangerous operations.

Listing 9.9 Comprehensive code validation

```
import ast


def validate_code_comprehensive(code):
    """Comprehensive validation of generated code."""
    issues = []

    try:
        ast.parse(code)
    except SyntaxError as e:
        return False, f"Syntax error at line {e.lineno}: {e.msg}"

    required_imports = [
        (r"import\s+torch|from\s+torch", "torch"),
```

```
]
for pattern, name in required_imports:
    if not re.search(pattern, code):
        issues.append(f"Missing import: {name}")

cuda_patterns = [
    r"\.cuda\(\)",
    r"\.to\(['\"]cuda['\"]\)",
    r"\.to\(device\)",
    r"device\s*=\s*['\"]cuda['\"]",
    r"device\s*=\s*torch\.device\(['\"]cuda",
    r"torch\.device\(['\"]cuda",
]
has_cuda = any(re.search(p, code) for p in cuda_patterns)
if not has_cuda:
    issues.append("Missing CUDA usage")

if not re.search(r"def\s+(train|main)\s*\(", code):
    issues.append("Missing train() or main() function")

if not re.search(r"if\s+__name__\s*==\s*['\"]__main__['\"]", code):
    issues.append("Missing if __name__ == '__main__' guard")

if not re.search(r"EPOCH.*ACCURACY|accuracy.*epoch", code,
     re.IGNORECASE):
    issues.append("Missing epoch accuracy printing")

try:
    tree = ast.parse(code)

    class DangerousCallChecker(ast.NodeVisitor):
        def __init__(self):
            self.dangerous_calls = []

        def visit_Call(self, node):
            if isinstance(node.func, ast.Name):
                if node.func.id in ['eval', 'exec', '__import__']:
                    self.dangerous_calls.append((node.func.id,
                         node.lineno))
            elif isinstance(node.func, ast.Attribute):
                if node.func.attr == 'system' and
                     isinstance(node.func.value, ast.Name):
                    if node.func.value.id == 'os':
                        self.dangerous_calls.append(('os.system',
                             node.lineno))
            self.generic_visit(node)

    checker = DangerousCallChecker()
    checker.visit(tree)

    if checker.dangerous_calls:
        issues.append(f"Dangerous operations found")
except Exception:
    pass
```

```
    if issues:
        return False, "; ".join(issues)

    return True, "Validation passed"
```

9.4.3 Two-Phase Code Generation with Repair

The code generation process uses a two-phase approach. In the first phase, an initial generation is attempted with retries at increasing temperatures. If all attempts fail validation, the second phase uses LLM-based code repair, where the broken code and error messages are sent back to the LLM for correction.

Listing 9.10 Code repair prompt template

```
CODE_REPAIR_PROMPT = """You are an expert PyTorch engineer. The
    following Python training script has errors that need to be fixed.

ORIGINAL HYPERPARAMETER CONFIGURATION:
{config_json}

GENERATED CODE WITH ERRORS:
```python
{broken_code}
```

ERROR MESSAGE:
{error_message}

VALIDATION ISSUES:
{validation_issues}

Please provide a COMPLETE, CORRECTED Python script that:
1. Fixes ALL syntax errors.
2. Uses PyTorch with CUDA--MUST include .cuda() or .to(device) where
    device='cuda'.
3. Has all required imports at the top (torch, timm, etc.).
4. Is completely self-contained and runnable with: python train.py.
5. Prints ``EPOCH X ACCURACY: Y.YY'' after each epoch.
6. Prints ``BEST ACCURACY: Y.YY'' at the end.

Output ONLY the corrected Python code. Start with import statements. No
    explanations or markdown."""
```

Automatic fixes are applied for common issues such as missing CUDA setup, missing main guard, and syntax errors. These fixes reduce the need for expensive LLM repair calls.

Listing 9.11 Automatic code fixes

```
def apply_automatic_fixes(code, validation_msg):
    """Apply automatic fixes to common issues."""
    if "Missing CUDA usage" in validation_msg or "CUDA" in
         validation_msg:
        code = inject_cuda_support(code)

    if "__main__" in validation_msg:
        code = add_main_guard(code)

    code = fix_common_syntax_errors(code)

    if "accuracy" in validation_msg.lower():
        code = ensure_accuracy_printing(code)

    if "Dangerous operation" in validation_msg:
        code = remove_dangerous_operations(code)

    return code


def inject_cuda_support(code):
    """Inject CUDA device setup into the code."""
    if re.search(r"device\s*=\s*torch\.device\(['\"]cuda", code):
        return code

    lines = code.split('\n')
    inject_idx = 0

    for i, line in enumerate(lines):
        stripped = line.strip()
        if stripped.startswith(('import ', 'from ')):
            inject_idx = i + 1
        elif stripped.startswith(('def ', 'class ', '@')) and inject_idx
             > 0:
            break

    cuda_setup = '''
# Device setup
device = torch.device("cuda" if torch.cuda.is_available() else "cpu")
print(f"Using device: {device}")
'''

    lines.insert(inject_idx, cuda_setup)
    code = '\n'.join(lines)

    code = re.sub(
        r'(model\s*=\s*[^(\n]+\([^)]*\))(?!\.to)',
```

```
        r'\1.to(device)',
        code
    )

    return code
```

9.5 Step 3: The Complete Optimization Loop

With search space generation and code generation in place, we integrate everything into an Optuna optimization loop. The objective function samples a configuration, generates a training script, executes it, and reports the validation accuracy.

9.5.1 Optuna Objective Function

The `LLMAutoMLObjective` class encapsulates the entire trial logic, including configuration sampling, code generation, execution, and result tracking.

Listing 9.12 Optuna objective function for LLM-AutoML

```
from dataclasses import dataclass
from typing import Any, Dict, List, Optional
import optuna
from optuna.pruners import MedianPruner
from optuna.samplers import TPESampler


@dataclass
class TrialResult:
    """Result of a single optimization trial."""
    trial_number: int
    config: Dict[str, Any]
    accuracy: Optional[float]
    code: str
    output: str
    generation_time: float
    execution_time: float
    status: str


class LLMAutoMLObjective:
    """Optuna objective function using LLM for code generation."""

    def __init__(self, config_space, client, experiment_config):
        self.config_space = config_space
        self.client = client
        self.exp_config = experiment_config
```

```
        self.trial_results = []

    def sample_config_from_trial(self, trial):
        """Sample a configuration using Optuna's suggest methods."""
        config = {}
        cs_config = self.config_space.sample_configuration()

        for hp_name in cs_config:
            hp = self.config_space[hp_name]
            value = cs_config[hp_name]

            if hasattr(value, 'item'):
                value = value.item()

            if isinstance(hp, CSH.UniformFloatHyperparameter):
                config[hp_name] = trial.suggest_float(
                    hp_name, hp.lower, hp.upper, log=hp.log
                )
                config[hp_name] = float(value)
            elif isinstance(hp, CSH.UniformIntegerHyperparameter):
                config[hp_name] = trial.suggest_int(
                    hp_name, hp.lower, hp.upper, log=hp.log
                )
                config[hp_name] = int(value)
            elif isinstance(hp, CSH.CategoricalHyperparameter):
                config[hp_name] = trial.suggest_categorical(hp_name,
                     hp.choices)
                config[hp_name] = value

        return config

    def __call__(self, trial):
        """Execute a single optimization trial."""
        config = self.sample_config_from_trial(trial)

        gen_start = time.time()
        try:
            code = generate_training_script(
                config, self.client,
                self.exp_config.data_dir,
                self.exp_config.max_epochs
            )
            gen_time = time.time() - gen_start
        except Exception as e:
            gen_time = time.time() - gen_start
            self.trial_results.append(TrialResult(
                trial_number=trial.number,
                config=config,
                accuracy=None,
                code="",
                output=str(e),
                generation_time=gen_time,
                execution_time=0,
                status="failed_generation"
```

```
            ))
            raise optuna.TrialPruned()

        exec_start = time.time()
        try:
            accuracy, output = execute_script(
                code,
                timeout=self.exp_config.timeout_per_trial
            )
            exec_time = time.time() - exec_start

            if accuracy is None:
                self.trial_results.append(TrialResult(
                    trial_number=trial.number,
                    config=config,
                    accuracy=None,
                    code=code,
                    output=output,
                    generation_time=gen_time,
                    execution_time=exec_time,
                    status="failed_execution"
                ))
                raise optuna.TrialPruned()

            self.trial_results.append(TrialResult(
                trial_number=trial.number,
                config=config,
                accuracy=accuracy,
                code=code,
                output=output,
                generation_time=gen_time,
                execution_time=exec_time,
                status="success"
            ))

            return -accuracy

        except optuna.TrialPruned:
            raise
        except Exception as e:
            self.trial_results.append(TrialResult(
                trial_number=trial.number,
                config=config,
                accuracy=None,
                code=code,
                output=str(e),
                generation_time=gen_time,
                execution_time=time.time() - exec_start,
                status="failed_execution"
            ))
            raise optuna.TrialPruned()
```

9.5.2 Main Experiment Runner

The complete experiment runner orchestrates all three phases and produces a comprehensive results summary.

Listing 9.13 Main experiment runner

```
def run_experiment(config):
    """Run the complete LLM-AutoML experiment."""
    client = VLLMClient(config.server_url)

    if not config.mock_execution:
        if not client.health_check():
            raise ConnectionError(
                f"Cannot connect to vLLM server at {config.server_url}"
            )

    experiment_start = time.time()

    task_description = """
    Train an image classification model on ImageNet-100 (100-class subset).
    The model should achieve high accuracy while remaining trainable on a
    single GPU within 50 epochs. Consider modern architectures (ResNet,
    EfficientNet, ConvNeXt, Vision Transformer variants), data augmentation
    strategies (RandAugment, MixUp, CutMix), and optimization techniques
    (AdamW, SGD with momentum, cosine annealing, warmup).
    Target: Achieve >85% top-1 validation accuracy.
    """

    search_space_json = generate_search_space(task_description, client)
    config_space = json_to_configspace(search_space_json)

    sampler = TPESampler(seed=config.seed, n_startup_trials=5)
    pruner = MedianPruner(n_startup_trials=3, n_warmup_steps=10)

    study = optuna.create_study(
        direction="minimize",
        sampler=sampler,
        pruner=pruner,
        study_name="llm_automl_imagenet100"
    )

    objective = LLMAutoMLObjective(config_space, client, config)

    study.optimize(
        objective,
        n_trials=config.n_trials,
        catch=(Exception,),
        show_progress_bar=True
    )
```

```
    total_time = time.time() - experiment_start

    best_trial = None
    for trial in objective.trial_results:
        if trial.accuracy is not None:
            if best_trial is None or trial.accuracy > best_trial.accuracy:
                best_trial = trial

    return ExperimentResults(
        task_description=task_description.strip(),
        search_space_json=search_space_json,
        trial_results=objective.trial_results,
        best_config=best_trial.config if best_trial else None,
        best_accuracy=best_trial.accuracy if best_trial else None,
        best_code=best_trial.code if best_trial else None,
        total_time=total_time
    )
```

9.6 Experimental Results

We evaluated LLM-AutoML using the `Qwen/Qwen3-32B-AWQ` model (4-bit quantized) served via vLLM. The following subsections present our findings.

9.6.1 LLM-Generated Training Script

The following is a training script generated by the LLM for a specific configuration. This demonstrates the quality and completeness of the generated code.

Listing 9.14 LLM-generated training script using Qwen3-32B-AWQ

```
import torch
import torch.nn as nn
from torch.cuda.amp import GradScaler, autocast
from torch.utils.data import DataLoader
from torchvision import datasets, transforms
import timm
from timm.data.mixup import Mixup
from timm.loss import SoftTargetCrossEntropy
import os

CONFIG = {
    "architecture": "convnext_tiny",
    "learning_rate": 0.001,
    "optimizer": "adamw",
    "weight_decay": 0.05,
```

```
    "batch_size": 128,
    "use_mixup": True,
    "mixup_alpha": 0.2,
    "use_cutmix": True,
    "label_smoothing": 0.1,
    "drop_path_rate": 0.1,
    "lr_scheduler": "cosine",
    "warmup_epochs": 5,
}

EPOCHS = 50
NUM_CLASSES = 100
DATA_DIR = "/data/imagenet100"


def create_model():
    model = timm.create_model(
        CONFIG["architecture"],
        pretrained=False,
        num_classes=NUM_CLASSES,
        drop_path_rate=CONFIG["drop_path_rate"]
    )
    return model.cuda()


def create_dataloaders():
    train_transform = transforms.Compose([
        transforms.RandomResizedCrop(224),
        transforms.RandomHorizontalFlip(),
        transforms.AutoAugment(transforms.AutoAugmentPolicy.IMAGENET),
        transforms.ToTensor(),
        transforms.Normalize(mean=[0.485, 0.456, 0.406],
                             std=[0.229, 0.224, 0.225]),
    ])

    val_transform = transforms.Compose([
        transforms.Resize(256),
        transforms.CenterCrop(224),
        transforms.ToTensor(),
        transforms.Normalize(mean=[0.485, 0.456, 0.406],
                             std=[0.229, 0.224, 0.225]),
    ])

    train_dataset = datasets.ImageFolder(
        os.path.join(DATA_DIR, "train"), transform=train_transform
    )
    val_dataset = datasets.ImageFolder(
        os.path.join(DATA_DIR, "val"), transform=val_transform
    )

    train_loader = DataLoader(
        train_dataset, batch_size=CONFIG["batch_size"],
        shuffle=True, num_workers=4, pin_memory=True
    )
```

```
    val_loader = DataLoader(
        val_dataset, batch_size=CONFIG["batch_size"],
        shuffle=False, num_workers=4, pin_memory=True
    )

    return train_loader, val_loader


def create_mixup():
    if CONFIG["use_mixup"] or CONFIG["use_cutmix"]:
        return Mixup(
            mixup_alpha=CONFIG["mixup_alpha"] if CONFIG["use_mixup"] else 0,
            cutmix_alpha=1.0 if CONFIG["use_cutmix"] else 0,
            label_smoothing=CONFIG["label_smoothing"],
            num_classes=NUM_CLASSES
        )
    return None

def train():
    model = create_model()
    train_loader, val_loader = create_dataloaders()
    mixup_fn = create_mixup()

    if CONFIG["optimizer"] == "adamw":
        optimizer = torch.optim.AdamW(
            model.parameters(),
            lr=CONFIG["learning_rate"],
            weight_decay=CONFIG["weight_decay"],
            betas=(CONFIG.get("adamw_beta1", 0.9), 0.999)
        )
    else:
        optimizer = torch.optim.SGD(
            model.parameters(),
            lr=CONFIG["learning_rate"],
            momentum=CONFIG.get("sgd_momentum", 0.9),
            weight_decay=CONFIG["weight_decay"]
        )

    if CONFIG["lr_scheduler"] == "cosine":
        scheduler = torch.optim.lr_scheduler.CosineAnnealingLR(
            optimizer, T_max=EPOCHS - CONFIG["warmup_epochs"]
        )
    else:
        scheduler = torch.optim.lr_scheduler.StepLR(optimizer, step_size=30)

    warmup_scheduler = torch.optim.lr_scheduler.LinearLR(
        optimizer, start_factor=0.01, total_iters=CONFIG["warmup_epochs"]
    )

    if mixup_fn:
        criterion = SoftTargetCrossEntropy()
    else:
```

```
        criterion = nn.CrossEntropyLoss(
            label_smoothing=CONFIG["label_smoothing"]
        )

    scaler = GradScaler()
    best_acc = 0.0

    for epoch in range(EPOCHS):
        model.train()
        for images, targets in train_loader:
            images, targets = images.cuda(), targets.cuda()

            if mixup_fn:
                images, targets = mixup_fn(images, targets)

            optimizer.zero_grad()
            with autocast():
                outputs = model(images)
                loss = criterion(outputs, targets)

            scaler.scale(loss).backward()
            scaler.step(optimizer)
            scaler.update()

        if epoch < CONFIG["warmup_epochs"]:
            warmup_scheduler.step()
        else:
            scheduler.step()

        model.eval()
        correct, total = 0, 0
        with torch.no_grad():
            for images, targets in val_loader:
                images, targets = images.cuda(), targets.cuda()
                outputs = model(images)
                _, predicted = outputs.max(1)
                total += targets.size(0)
                correct += predicted.eq(targets).sum().item()

        acc = 100.0 * correct / total
        print(f"EPOCH {epoch+1} ACCURACY: {acc:.2f}")

        if acc > best_acc:
            best_acc = acc
            torch.save(model.state_dict(), "best_model.pth")

    print(f"BEST ACCURACY: {best_acc:.2f}")
    return best_acc


if __name__ == "__main__":
    train()
```

This generated script demonstrates several noteworthy characteristics. The LLM correctly implements mixed precision training using PyTorch's automatic mixed precision (AMP) with `GradScaler` and `autocast`. It properly configures MixUp and CutMix augmentation using the timm library's `Mixup` class. The code includes a learning rate warm-up phase followed by cosine annealing. All hyperparameters from the configuration are correctly integrated into the training loop.

9.6.2 Expected Performance Characteristics

Based on the pipeline design and the quality of LLM-generated code demonstrated above, practitioners can expect the following characteristics when running the complete optimization loop.

The LLM-generated search space typically contains 14 to 18 hyperparameters covering architecture selection, optimization parameters, regularization, and data augmentation. The search space includes three to five conditional relationships for optimizer-specific parameters and one to three forbidden clauses for memory-exceeding combinations.

Code generation reliability depends on the LLM model used and the quality of the prompt engineering. With proper validation and automatic fixes, the majority of generated scripts should be syntactically correct and executable. Standard failure modes include incorrect import statements, missing augmentation implementations, and GPU memory overflow when using large batch sizes and deep models.

The TPE sampler in Optuna typically finds good configurations within the first 10 to 15 trials, demonstrating sample-efficient exploration of the LLM-designed search space. Modern architectures like ConvNeXt and EfficientNet variants tend to perform well on ImageNet-100 when combined with AdamW optimization and appropriate augmentation strategies.

9.7 Discussion and Extensions

9.7.1 Cost Analysis

LLM-AutoML introduces inference costs alongside GPU training costs. Search space generation requires approximately 2000 tokens as a one-time cost. Code generation per trial requires approximately 3000 to 5000 tokens. For a 30-trial experiment, the total token usage is approximately 120K tokens.

With efficient vLLM serving, the inference overhead is negligible compared to training time (minutes versus hours per trial). The quantized Qwen3-32B-AWQ model provides good quality at reduced memory requirements.

9.7.2 Scaling Considerations

For larger-scale studies, several strategies can improve throughput. Multiple vLLM instances can be run behind a load balancer to generate code in parallel while training jobs queue on GPUs. Configuration and code pairs can be cached to avoid redundant LLM calls when configurations are retried. A hierarchical search approach can first optimize architecture choice with short training runs and then refine hyperparameters for top architectures.

9.7.3 Multi-Objective Extension

Optuna supports multi-objective optimization natively. LLM-AutoML can be extended to jointly optimize accuracy and training efficiency.

Listing 9.15 Multi-objective LLM-AutoML extension

```
def multi_objective(trial):
    config = sample_config(trial)
    code = generate_training_script(config)

    start = time.time()
    accuracy, _ = execute_script(code)
    training_time = time.time() - start

    return -accuracy, training_time

study = optuna.create_study(
    directions=["minimize", "minimize"],
    sampler=optuna.samplers.NSGAIISampler()
)
```

9.7.4 Limitations and Mitigations

Generated code may contain subtle bugs or suboptimal implementations. Mitigations include using a lower temperature for code generation, adding unit tests in the execution sandbox, and prompting for code with inline comments explaining key decisions.

The LLM's training data may bias the search space toward popular but not necessarily optimal configurations. This can be partially addressed by prompting for novel or experimental approaches.

Complete ImageNet training remains expensive. For rapid prototyping, consider proxy tasks such as ImageNet-100 or CIFAR-100, or use early stopping based on epoch-10 accuracy.

Future work may explore using LLM self-reflection to iteratively refine generated code based on training failures, incorporating retrieval-augmented generation with recent ML papers to leverage state-of-the-art techniques, and extending to other domains, such as NLP, reinforcement learning, and scientific computing.

Name Index

H. Iba et al., *Large Language Models and Evolutionary Computation*,
Natural Computing Series, https://doi.org/10.1007/978-981-95-8597-7

Symbol index

H. Iba et al., *Large Language Models and Evolutionary Computation*,
Natural Computing Series, https://doi.org/10.1007/978-981-95-8597-7

Index

H. Iba et al., *Large Language Models and Evolutionary Computation*,
Natural Computing Series, https://doi.org/10.1007/978-981-95-8597-7

MIX
Papier aus verantwortungsvollen Quellen
Paper from responsible sources
FSC® C105338
www.fsc.org

If you have any concerns about our products,
you can contact us on
ProductSafety@springernature.com

In case Publisher is established outside the EU,
the EU authorized representative is:
Springer Nature Customer Service Center GmbH
Europaplatz 3, 69115 Heidelberg, Germany

Printed by Libri Plureos GmbH
in Hamburg, Germany